Turning Houses into Homes

1950s home

Turning Houses into Homes

A History of the Retailing and Consumption of Domestic Furnishings

CLIVE EDWARDS
Loughborough University, UK

ASHGATE

Published by
Ashgate Publishing Limited
Gower House
Croft Road
Aldershot
Hants GU11 3HR
England

Ashgate Publishing Company
Suite 420
101 Cherry Street
Burlington
VT 05401-4405
USA

Ashgate website: http://www.ashgate.com

British Library Cataloguing in Publication Data
Edwards, Clive, 1947–
    Turning houses into homes : a history of the retailing and consumption of domestic
    furnishings. – (The history of retailing and consumption)
    1.House furnishings industry and trade – History – 18th century 2.House furnishings
    – History – 18th century 3.Dwellings – History – 18th century 4.House furnishings
    industry and trade – History – 19th century 5.House furnishings – History – 19th
    century 6.Dwellings – History – 19th century 7.House furnishings industry and trade
    – History – 20th century 8.House furnishings – History – 20th century 9.Dwellings –
    History – 20th century 10.Consumption (Economics) – History
    I. Title
    381.4'5645'09

Library of Congress Cataloging-in-Publication Data
Edwards, Clive, 1947–
    Turning houses into homes : a history of the retailing and consumption of domestic
    furnishings / Clive Edwards.
        p. cm. — (The history of retailing and consumption)
    Includes bibliographical references.
    ISBN 0-7546-0906-5 (alk. paper)
        1. House furnishings industry and trade—History. I. Title. II. Series.

    HD9773.A2E38 2004
    338.4'7684'009—dc22

2003056903

ISBN 0 7546 0906 5

Typeset by IML Typographers, Birkenhead, Merseyside
Printed and bound in Great Britain by MPG Books Ltd, Bodmin, Cornwall

Contents

The History of Retailing and Consumption: General Editor's preface

It is increasingly recognized that retail systems and changes in the patterns of consumption play crucial roles in the development and societal structure of economies. Such recognition has led to renewed interest in the changing nature of retail distribution and the rise of consumer society from a wide range of academic disciplines. The aim of this multidisciplinary series is to provide a forum of publications that explore the history of retailing and consumption.

Gareth Shaw
University of Exeter

List of figures and tables

Tables

Preface and acknowledgements

This book has brought together two particular interests of mine: the history of the retailing of home furnishings, and their subsequent consumption. Having been engaged in the commercial side of these activities before an academic career, it has been particularly stimulating to put practice into a historical and contextual narrative. Although my own experience has been limited to the second half of the twentieth century, the book's time span is much wider. I have deliberately tried to locate the retailing and consumption of home furnishings in a longer continuum, to show that the roots of both retail and consumption practices have a long history. Arguably, the trade only becomes an industry in the eighteenth century, but this does not negate the contribution and practices established by retailers and consumers prior to that time.

Turning Houses into Homes draws upon historical texts, academic works, newspaper and trade press material, catalogues and trade literature. The assistance of librarians both in the United Kingdom and the USA is gratefully acknowledged. Papers presented at CHORD Conferences that have stimulated thoughts on the subject have also inspired me. The Bibliography indicates the growing interest in the history of both retailing and consumption. I am indebted to the scholars who are, and have been, working in the fields of retailing and consumer studies. I trust that this work successfully synthesizes and builds on their work, in relation to my specific topic and approach.

I thank the Director of Loughborough University School of Art and Design for sponsoring the period of study leave that has made the production of the book possible in a reasonable time without the demands of teaching. My thanks also go to Huw Jones, who has ably copy-edited my script. Finally I would like to thank my wife Lynne for her sterling work, not only as a proof-reader, but also as a companion on the field trips, especially those which involved 'going to the shops'.

Chapter 1

Introduction

Home is emphatically the sweetest word in the English language, the object of our choicest care and the most enduring recollections. (J. H. and Jas. Parker, *Our English Home*, 1861)

There is currently a growing interest in the histories of consumption, interiors , the home and retailing. This work attempts to make connections between them to illuminate each one and show something of their relationship. The debates around consumption that are based on considering goods as markers of self, as a spur to economic growth, and as a way of making constructed meanings, have opened up discussions to allow investigation of, for example, the study of identity, women's role in consuming, and an emphasis on distribution and use, as opposed to production. The general aim of this work is to use these and other debates to create a history that looks closely at the relationships between methods of sales and purchase of goods for the home, and their subsequent consumption. The book also has two aims that are more specific. One is to map the history, changes, development and structures of the retail home furnishing industry and to consider its role in the home-making process. It will particularly look at the economics and geographies of the business and its relationships with its markets – the homemakers. The other aim is to analyse and explore the nature, growth and transformation of the markets, and consider the activities of the industry's customers, the consumers of home furnishings. In this way, issues of consumption are considered in relation to the broader set of intentions, therefore the book will survey a wide historical period to demonstrate both the continuities and changes that are the basis of developments in the manufacture, purchase, consumption and use of furnishing goods. The geographical spread extends from being mainly British-based or influenced in the early part of the work, to a wider Western point of view by the twentieth century, in order to explain the transfer of ideas about economics and consuming practices, as well as examining the growing internationalism and transculturation of both retailing and consumption.

The history and analysis of the practice of creating a domestic interior is a fascinating arena since it encompasses a number of considerations which, when brought together, contribute to a closer understanding of the natures and processes of retailing, homemaking and consuming. It also allows discussion of some of the major historical changes that affected developments in consumption practices. John Benson has defined the societies that allowed these changes to occur as those 'in which choice and credit are readily available, in which social value is defined in terms of purchasing power and material possessions, and in which there is a desire, above all, for that which is new, modern, exciting and fashionable'.[1]

In the sixteenth and seventeenth centuries, these included the growth of a new 'world of goods' that expanded through the diffusion of consumer products into the lives of more social groups. In the eighteenth century, while goods were used as part of a social performance for some social groups, there was concern that excessive or luxury consumption by the lower classes was an unstabilizing influence against social order. On the other hand, the expansion of individual consumption was considered intrinsic to the health and wealth of the nation. The development of a market economy and the growth of consumer desires indicate that people started to care about things that money could buy, over and above their use value, and they developed strategies and infrastructures to achieve this. The idea that qualitative and quantitative changes occurred somewhere in the early-modern period is now generally accepted, but scholars have moved away from the idea that the changes were all based on the desire and ability to emulate.[2] However, a truly consumerist society 'involves large numbers of people staking a real portion of the personal identities and their quest for meaning – even their emotional satisfaction – on the search for and acquisition of goods'.[3]

In the nineteenth century, the issue of domesticity made consuming reputable through ideas of comfort and respectability as a middle way between the extremes of necessities and luxuries. Finally, in the twentieth century modernity and personality became the central issues of consumption whereby individuals are always choosing an identity, which consumption may assist or hinder. During the twentieth century, the domestic was all but expunged from modernist culture but it actually flourished at a popular level of consumption. [4] The conventions of modernism, established on formal, approved, correct, impersonal, prescribed, universal and alien ideals were received with ambivalence in many countries during the period 1930–1970. More recently, the home has been recognized as a central site for post-modern culture, which embraces geniality, cosiness, the familiar, the informal, the intimate, the unpretentious. The search for individual identity was assisted by changing cultural values and hindered by restricted purchasing power and the creation of anxiety over choices[5]. Hence, the 'authenticity of self' may be made or broken by goods and their modes of consumption.

---

[1]   Benson, J. (1984), *The Rise of Consumer Society in Britain 1880–1980*, p. 4.

[2]   See Campbell, C. (1992), 'The desire for the new', in Silverstone, R. and Hirsch, E. (eds), *Consuming Technologies: Media and Information in Domestic Spaces*. See also Stearns, P. (1997), *'Stages of Consumerism: Recent Work on the Issues of Periodization'*, *The Journal of Modern History*, 69, March, pp. 102–117.

[3]   Stearns, P. (1997), *'Stages of consumerism: Recent work on the issues of periodization'*, *The Journal of Modern History*, 69, March, p. 105.

[4]   See Reed, C. (1996), *Not at Home: The Suppression of Domesticity in Modern Art and Architecture*.

[5]   Slater, D. (1997), *Consumer Culture and Modernity*, pp. 52–4.

A good deal of work has been published on specific aspects of the home, especially in material culture journals and social science studies, which has considered many aspects of the home, and the issues that they raise.[6] These include notions of consumption; the role of gender and education; the purchase of status and symbolism as identity; matters of taste and style, and questions of choice. In addition, the less prosaic, but none the less essential, physical aspects such as the acquisition processes, which include marketing, retailing and distribution, have begun to be considered seriously. This work is an attempt to draw these together.

Parts of the methodology are based on the mapping of other disciplines upon the topic to demonstrate that an understanding of the retail/consumption interface can best be interpreted through a range of disciplines, which incorporate economics, history and sociology, as well as more specific design and business history. A synthesis of these approaches within my framework will demonstrate the developing relationships between the retailing and the consuming of the domestic environment. The methodology also includes economic and cultural geographies that have allowed for a re-evaluation of both domestic and retail sites, spaces, and their relations with culture, which will further help to explain the changes.

The anthropological position will explore what homes people make, why 'things' are important to them, and how they use or consume them, as well as the roles of ritual and cultural behaviour. The links between the past and present in various aspects of the home are also of interest to this position, since it is the choice of objects that will tell us about the home, and by extension the culture that produced, sold and consumed them. This material culture approach to the home is valuable as the interior is a prime example of the inter-connectedness of 'things'. The choice and meaning of objects in the household can reflect general significances, but close analysis of the processes of acquisition and use also allows for the avoidance of the grand narrative, and the illumination of micro-histories that give close-ups of the 'history of the everyday'.[7] Through this multidisciplinary approach it is hoped to 'close the loop' between the retailing and consumption of home furnishings.

Debates relating to consumption are often rooted in the methodologies of the social sciences, so issues such as choice, lifestyle, alienation and identity are explored as they relate to the home and its furnishings. Some social scientists consider the idea that humans are rational and follow calculated ways of acquiring goods to fulfil particular functions in their lives. Economists and other social scientists suggest that on the other hand consumers are irrational and seek goods to provide pleasure and sensation.[8] Why otherwise do people

---

[6] See Bibliography.

[7] For example, see Perrot, M. (1990), *A History of Private Life*, and Roche, D. (2000), *A History of Everyday Things*.

[8] For example, see Colin Campbell's work.

continually aspire to acquiring goods, why is fashion so powerful, and why do we dream of acquisitions that are only fulfilling until the next time?

A particular issue that this book aims to explore is that there has been a continuously developing set of connections between the retailer and the consumer. The important, but often contradictory, role of the retailer as both a supplier and adviser is considered in relation to the needs and aspirations of consumers who wish to turn their houses into homes. This is not only in terms of goods and services where the retailer is a facilitator, but also of advice on issues of suitability, taste and style, which have often meant a special cultural relationship with consumers that is much more than simply an economic one.

Roche has neatly summed up how the three major aspects of this study can be interrelated: 'Three forms of knowledge converge-that of objects and styles [home], that of production and commercial circuits [retailing], through which the hierarchy of reception is formed, and that of consumption where we find, as ever, stability confronted with change.'[9] The following sections provide an overview of these three main areas – the home, retailing and consumption – that form the basis of this work.

The home

The home is both an idea and a reality.[10] As an idea, it is the concept of bourgeois comfort and is a mentally fixed point in life. As a reality, it is the result of the interplay between necessity, availability and aspirations, which are represented in terms of goods and services and through the choices of the people that live in it. The idea of home is further rooted in a number of different aspects, including privacy, security, family, intimacy, comfort and control, as well as personal input, the nature of relationships, the surroundings, and the wider material, social and cultural aspects. More specifically, most agree that home is a symbolic environment, representing one's identity through the things therein. Woodward sums it up:

> The semiotic value of domestic material culture varies according to the needs of the situation; objects sometimes have a public role in the home as a signifier of status, style or taste, and other times do very private psychological work for the viewer, which revolves around the object serving as a focus for managing self-identity, family relations or self-esteem.[11]

'Being at home' is culturally determined and usually reflects socio-economic status. When homes have doubled up as workplaces, this status has often been

---

[9] Roche (2000), *A History of Everyday Things*, p. 170.

[10] For a useful discussion of the meaning of the word 'home' see Hollander, J. (1991), 'It all depends', *Social Research* (58)1, Spring, pp. 31–49.

[11] Woodward, I. (2001), 'Domestic objects and the taste epiphany', *Journal of Material Culture*, 6(2), pp. 120–21.

very limited. As economic organization changed through the seventeenth and eigheenth centuries, the connection between home and commerce gradually became defined. Hareven suggests that the 'emergence of the home as a specialized retreat for the family was a part of the process of industrialization as well as urbanization'.[12] These processes led to the separation of work and home and the removal of other functions to special places. A dichotomy eventually became apparent when people saw homes as an escape from commerce and industry, although ironically, it was through the products of commerce that a home of status could be achieved.

What were the differences between domicile and 'home'? Initially, the domestic spaces were centres of activity including work, welfare, learning and worship. The nature of the individuals living in the space was not always a family group. The idea of home was firsly based partly on changes in sociability. Once internal space started to be divided up and privacy became more important, the nature of 'home' gradually changed during the period 1500–1800. Certainly, by the nineteenth century bourgeois families in Europe and the urban middle classes in North America had recast the home as a completely private affair. The characterization of these spaces therefore became very important.

It seems likely that the notions of physical comfort, alongside the more elusive psychological comforts that accrue from a self- selected room layout, appropriate types of furnishings and decent levels of physical well-being, were part of this same process of the gradual emergence of the home as a retreat.

The changing nature of domestic life and the concomitant development of the role of women and their status within society have, particularly in the twentieth century, incurred alterations in the traditional tasks of furnishing, housework and meal preparation.[13] The demise of domestic servants and the impact that this had on middle-class families, and indeed the decline of the family as a middle-class institution, are part of this cultural change. Homemaking tasks have also included inputs from males, which have implications for issues of roles, gender and the meaning of home.[14]

For most of the period I am looking at, it seems clear that not only do a person's surroundings reflect the culture of a particular period but they are often also indicators of how the majority of people use things to represent themselves to each other. So what mechanisms are brought into play when the home is seen as an entity expressing relationships between people and social

---

[12] Hareven, T. K. (1991), 'The home and family in historical perspective', *Social Research*, 58(1), p. 264.

[13] See Sarti, R. (2002) *Europe at Home: Family and Material Culture 1500–1800*.

[14] See for example, Davidoff, L. and Hall, C. (1987), *Family Fortunes: Men and Women of the English Middle Class 1780–1850*, and Tosh, J. (1999), *A Man's Place: Masculinity and the Middle Class Home in Victorian England*.

structures?[15] The short answer, developed in later sections, is language. However, the use of furnishings as an acquired language and one that is implemented to create homes is a double-edged sword. There is a contrast between the ideal, established views of 'language' conventions (taste) versus the real or individual self-expression. Much advice about home creation has sent confused messages that suggest that being individual is the goal, but following the established taste or customs is part of that process.

Household furnishings are paradigmatic consumer goods that enter the home as the result of negotiations between producers and buyers, most often with the retailer acting as intermediary. Although the goods have an initial status or symbolism, the retailer adds value to them, the buyer constructs additional meanings when they are 'at home', and even when the goods are later discarded, another set of connotations may accrue.

The retailer's role, in conjunction with his customer, is therefore pivotal in the process of turning houses into homes.

Retailing

The interaction and interdependence between producers, retailers, wholesalers and consumers creates a distributive system. The character of such a retail system is very much a result of its environment.[16] The environment, which varies constantly, affects the level and extent of demand, which is the energizer of the system. The factors that might affect this include consumer needs and preferences; the size of the population and its demographics; the money supply and income of a region; the technology of the supply chain; the level and quality of management skills, and the role of fashion and the professional tastemakers. The home, mediated through these factors, acts as a locus of consumption for those within it.

It is clear from the above that there is considerable interaction between retailers, producers and consumers. From around 1500, there was a discernable upward trend in the English economy, which gradually provided disposable income for increasing numbers of the growing middle class, and this stimulated a growth in the retail market and the provision of goods and services. This was

---

[15] Lawrence, R. (1987), 'What makes a house a home?', *Environment and Behaviour*, 19(2), March, pp. 154–68. Lawrence suggests that there are cultural dimensions based on shared values, rituals, lifestyles, layouts of houses that create relationships between some or all groups. Secondly, he identifies the socio-demographic aspects based on understanding of meanings mediated by gender, age, demography social life religion and so on, and thirdly, he identifies psychological aspects based on the communication of information such as self-esteem, values, life stages and so on. See also Hayward, G. 'Home as an environmental and psychological concept', *Landscape*, 20, pp. 2–9.

[16] Bucklin, L. P. (1972), *Metamorphosis in Retailing*, in Benson, J. and Shaw, G. (1999), *The Retailing Industry*, Vol. 1, p. 84.

through the agency of markets, fairs, itinerants and shops. Commentators from the late sixteenth century onward were fully aware of the changed climate of goods and their purchase. Initially, restrictions of custom, practice and law related to fair prices, and open markets had an effect on the control of buying and selling, but pressure grew, and by the mid-seventeenth century something like a retail system was fully functional. This included, for example, the development of the fixed shop, the growth of a network of suppliers and services, the provision of credit, the application of book-keeping, and the development of a transport infrastructure. Restrictions were far less stringent, so shopkeepers could be innovative in their approach to their dealings with customers. This was combined with the decline of political arguments against luxury, which meant that the incentive to purchase goods was unleashed.

By the eighteenth century, the retail system was fully established and the role of tastemaker had been conferred on many branches of retailing. Even in the seventeenth century, it seems clear that retailers were more than simply providers of goods. Their services in terms of homemaking, including design ideas, fitting up goods and customizing, were evident. However, the shopkeepers' attitudes to either embracing or refusing change both presented risks, and therefore failures in retail business were commonplace. Despite the threat of bankruptcy and loss of income, it was clear that the retail trade played an important role in the national economy.

In the nineteenth century the growth in incomes, the expanding market and the rise of an acknowledgement of the role of goods in life fuelled the development of retailing. There always had been gradations of outlets to meet differing classes of trade. In the nineteenth century, this led to a hierarchy of shops including department stores, specialist stores, general stores, complete house furnishers, and vertically integrated businesses that both made and sold furnishings. The rise of 'mass consumerism' towards the end of the century meant that goods intended for the lower end of the social scale were sold through an aggressive retail system which included shops, but also encompassed mail order agents, second-hand stores and so on.[17]

During the twentieth century, furniture retailing developed further on the lines established in the nineteenth. As stated previously, this included specialist stores and department stores but in addition, the century witnessed the growth of the multiple-branch operation, the retail warehouse, and expansions of mail order systems. In business terms there were changes in the infrastructure. The sole trader declined in relative importance in the face of these structural changes, which particularly featured a rise in multiple-branch operations. The trend towards agglomeration and amalgamation was a feature of the last few decades of the twentieth century, as was the growing internationalism of retailing.

---

[17] See Fraser, W. H. (1981), *The Coming of the Mass Market, 1850–1914.*

Structural changes in retailing are based on a number of factors. Savit points to the need for historians to map changes in distribution systems, as not only the story of famous names or locations, but also as a series of interactions between social, economic, and geographic factors.[18] A history of retailing will weave the individuals, events, trends and themes together to create patterns: some that have survived, some that have come and gone, and others that are nascent. This work is an attempt at a contribution to this process of mapping.

Consumption

Retailing cannot be understood fully without some analysis of the consumption practices that feed it. Consumption is an economic act, but is also part of the process of an individual's attempts at both differentiation and definition. Consumption creates an expressive social demeanour. Individuals and their motives make up the act of consuming. Their particular consumption practices are themselves based on custom, and therefore on stability, but also on novelty and mobility. One of the major developments in consumer behaviour was the change from being 'users of things' to 'consumers of commodities'.

This change in the nature of consumption is reflected in the emphasis given to the change from modernist to post-modernist forms of consumer activity. Whereas consumption was originally seen as the object of production in early twentieth-century Fordist considerations of the relationship between the two, in more recent years a range of other factors (such as marketing and identity) have been suggested as being more influential, and point to consumption as being as much (if not more) a cultural phenomenon as an economic one. As consumer society becomes more culturally based, as social life becomes less structured and regulated, as the use value of goods is subsumed in a series of signs, and as distinctions become blurred, an understanding and knowledge of goods, their meaning and 'value' becomes an increasingly important part of post-modern culture. Consumption then has an increasing cultural importance in post-Fordist societies.

The analysis of consumption therefore includes consideration of issues such as identity, lifestyle, liberation and alienation, and choice.[19] Commodities convey information about class and gender, freedom and constraint and an individual's knowledge of goods. A person's pre-history, education and social position also inform individual consumption. Goods also carry culturally defined meanings, which other consumers recognize, and therefore form part of an information system that is part of social life. For a long while society made a

---

[18] Savitt, R. (1989), 'Looking back to see ahead: writing the history of American retailing', *Journal of Retailing*, 65,(3), pp. 326–55.

[19] See Featherstone, M. (1991), *Consumer Culture and Postmodernism*, for a useful survey of theories associated with consumption.

direct link between correct habits of consumption and character formation; therefore, any inappropriate objects sent the wrong messages about one. We will see that one role of the retailer was to be a mediator in this process.

Many scholars have applied themselves to the issues of consumption and consumerism. At the end of the nineteenth century, Thorstein Veblen considered that consumption had cultural as well as economic aspects, although his simplistic argument around 'conspicuous consumption' was limited as it was based only on pecuniary emulation.[20] However, consumption has always been an index of social status and differentiation, as Bill Lancaster sums it up: the 'tension between hedonism and self-restraint is usually expressed in condemnatory remarks by elite observers on the consuming patterns of lower or newer social groups.[21]

The Marxist approach which equates consumerism as a tool to create profit and maintain social control is mirrored in the idea that retailers do not produce anything and are therefore of little real value. However, retailers could be said to be at the nexus of Marx's ideas of use – value (function) and exchange – value commodity or sign. By offering advice and the opportunity for selection, they can satisfy both the use values needs and exchange value wants.

For the Frankfurt school, consumers are created and manipulated, consumers are regarded as passive, and all consumption is predicated on capitalism. For them, consumption is control as opposed to authentic existence. Consumption is in fact very varied and differentiated, since every commodity has an identity value that may or may not be related to particular individuals and is influenced by choice decisions.

More productive is the emphasis that social anthropologists, most famously, Mary Douglas, give to the idea that goods are a part of a system of symbols through which meaning is created. The symbolic purpose of goods is therefore 'to make visible and stable the categories of culture'.[22] If we take Bourdieu's idea of these categories as being based on 'cultural capital' – that is, social background and education – it can be argued that these factors provide distinctions within society. These categories are defined as 'habitus' where they are based on similar economic and cultural resources within a social group but with contextual nuances.[23] His concept of 'habitus' expresses social difference so as to differentiate social groups and their lifestyles that are constructed through goods. However, individuals have to choose for themselves, so the final meanings are not group-specific ones. For Bourdieu, cultural capital as well as economic capital affects these consumer decisions.

---

[20] Veblen, T. (1899), *The Theory of the Leisure Class: An Economic Study in the Evolution of Institutions*.

[21] Lancaster, B. (1995), *The Department Store: A Social History*, p. 162.

[22] Douglas, M. and Isherwood, B. (1979), *The World of Goods: Towards an Anthropology of Consumption*, p. 62.

[23] Bourdieu, P. (1984), *Distinction: A Social Critique of the Judgement of Taste*, p. 77.

Income is not completely relevant, though education is. Distinctions between people are based on codes to identify positions, and the codes have to be learnt. Cultural consumption (or taste) is therefore a pattern of social behaviour that legitimizes forms of power and control, based on distinction. Taste is therefore ideologically based on class as quality and category. The ideas of these 'shared attitudes' became the idea of the 'lifestyle' that is recognizable today. Again, the retailer has a major role to play in the creation and dissemination of these ideas as appropriate to their place in the market.

Contrary to these ideas of social groups that have fixed codes of their own are those of Weber and Campbell, who consider that consumers do not conform to a single plan of class-based behaviour but operate within a character type, using expressive goods for themselves. Just as important as possessing these goods is the imagination of possessing them through dreaming, so that the hedonistic and 'romantic' consumer is never satisfied.[24] Campbell's influential 'Romantic ethic' theory suggests that pleasure in consuming is seeing or indeed imagining each act of consumption as a new experience. For him it is the 'desiring' rather than the 'having' that is the key to understanding contemporary consumption. New products, or at least the imagined pleasures accruing from new products, keep feeding the cycle of anticipation and subsequent disillusionment.[25]

It seems that individuals do differentiate themselves, but this often occurs within particular social groups. In other words, there is a place between an individual's consciousness and the (theoretical) abstract systems of an external world. As Glennie and Thrift put it, 'This is the space of everyday social life, a flow of responsive and relational activities that are structured, practical-moral and joint in character'.[26] Paradoxically, the stable categories of culture are often maintained, in part at least, by changes in consumption: 'Consumption as a strategy for establishing stability and survival does not lead away from its transformative, subversive potential; the maintenance of the status quo is not achieved through stasis.'[27]

The individual versus the prescribed was and is a major issue. In either case, the process of an individual's consuming negates generalities and the alienation this causes, so that people can use the goods provided to help to create an image of themselves. We are free to apply our own skills and ideas to the assemblage of goods and to develop our surroundings as we wish.

---

[24] Campbell (1993), 'Understanding traditional and modern patterns of consumption in eighteenth century England: a character action approach.'

[25] Campbell, C. (1987), *The Romantic Ethic and the Spirit of Modern Consumerism*. See also Bachelard, G. (1994), *The Poetics of Space*.

[26] Glennie, P. and Thrift, N. (1996), 'Consumer identities and consumption space in early-modern England', *Environment and Planning* A, 28, p. 40.

[27] Pennell, S. (1999), 'Consumption and consumerism in early modern England', *The Historical Journal*, 42(2), p. 563.

However, this process is hindered by a number of factors, including a lack of control over the product choice and availability (retailer as tastemaker), the cluttered and confused messages from personal history, our location in society, and on occasion by biological and/or locational factors.

The concept of lifestyle, although probably overworked as a marketing term, can assist in this analysis. The idea that the consumer is a problem-solver with needs to be satisfied is one approach to the issue of self-expression. These needs (which range from pure necessity to pure hedonism) are part of a lifestyle to be developed, maintained, and probably changed at times. This lifestyle is based on a set of variables including culture, values, demographics, social status, reference groups, the household itself and the individual. Social status reveals the structure and ranking of individuals based on observable characteristics that are culturally defined. Specific cultural indicators based on age, race, gender, finance, credit ratings, living arrangements and so on assist in this structure. Reference groups reinforce the roles of a range of aspects of behaviour as well as the nature of opinion leaders in them. These roles may change in specific groups. Finally, the individual's own perception, learning and memory, in tandem with personal characteristics such as motives, personality and emotions, will have a bearing on lifestyles.

To close the loop, it is useful to consider the interaction of consuming and retailing that is found at the point of a consumer's disposition to buy goods. This disposition when latent expresses a want, although the action is passive: in other words, it is desiring but not engaging. The second stage is where the disposition can be habitual or intuitive, meaning that the customer will buy goods based on habit to include simple, regular or known purchases. The third disposition is consciously to decide to make a purchase based on choice. This is often the case with regard to home furnishings, as these purchases are usually based on a set of choice criteria. The criteria vary, but can include the technical, usually related to performance; the economic, which ranks goods and the effort needed to acquire them, and the cost involved; the psychological, based on image of self, status and fashion, and finally the choice of retail outlet, based on its reputation, stock, advice and assistance.

Consumption is often more constrained than is imagined. These constraints are reinforced by family and friends, socio-economic status, position in the life cycle, education, sexual orientation, and the ruling taste of pre-established conventions and ideas of appropriateness. It is part of the retailer's job to recognize these dispositions and constraints, and therefore to act as a conduit for change. By offering consumers the idea that particular goods will improve their lives, and that to leave things unchanged may pose a risk to their self-identity, they achieve modifications to lifestyles. This role is significant as it is constructed socially, politically and economically, and is then often perceived to be a natural condition. If the natural condition keeps changing, then it would appear that the purchase of new goods and the disposal of older ones is part of this cultural turnover, and is the real nexus between the consumer, the retailer and the home.

Chapter 2

The development of a consuming culture

Rich house fully equipped with furniture. Praise is due to your inventor, for he bestowed a great benefit on mankind. (Giles Corrozet, *The Blazon of the House*, 1539)

In the medieval period, furnishings were acquired and used in relation to function and need, and only occasionally for self-indulgent purposes. Indeed Carson has suggested that rich and poor lived similarly – the better off simply having more and superior goods of the same types.[1] In this situation, social standing or distinction was not judged so much by goods as by social precedence. Nevertheless, the codes of precedence, controlled by sumptuary laws in some cases, were gradually eroded as changes in society took effect based on developments in commerce, education and culture. By the end of the period, the concept of gentility had taken the place of precedence. Gentility was expressed through goods, and goods were acquired through the market place. The retailer's role as an arbiter of taste was nascent. The rise of gentility was also expressed through the withdrawal of elites from communal living into a more private lifestyle that marked one of the significant changes from the Middle Ages to the early-modern period.[2] In addition to this new privacy, there was a considerable growth in urban society. All these changes affected the furnishings of homes.

The urban freemen and their families, as distinct from the feudal lords and the Church, were acutely aware of the need to respond to changing social conditions, and of the developing importance of the home. Whilst the nobility were often peripatetic in their behaviour (which had an impact on the nature of their furnishings and possessions), the bourgeois town dwellers kept a fixed abode. In addition, the slow process of distinction between the social groups began as changing lifestyles and rising prices helped some groups, such as commodity dealers, to move upward socially whilst hindering any similar movement for labour-based workers. The divergences continued as the influences of a growing gentility, education and culture took effect as self-fulfilling markers of distinction. Consumer goods, including home furnishings, were developing into a considerable and growing part of these markers.

---

[1] Carson, C., Hoffman, R. and Albert, P. (Eds) (1994), *Of Consuming Interests: The Style of Life in the Eighteenth Century*, p. 523.

[2] For these changes, and details of household regulations, see Girouard, M. (1978), *Life in the English Country House*.

The idea that there were little decorative furnishings in some medieval and early-modern homes was questioned as long ago as 1951, when R. W. Symonds wrote about domestic comfort in the medieval home and dispelled a long-held illusion.[3] In fact, the consumption of textiles, in the form of cushions, wall cloths, door and bed curtains, was impressive and indicated a continuing and growing interest in the nature of people's immediate surroundings. This was, of course, subject to regional variations and the nature of the social groups that used them, but it certainly shows the beginnings of a developing pattern.

Although there was a lack of awareness of the concept of comfort, as we understand it, there still existed a clear combination of both refined and primitive behaviour that affected house decoration, and this was based mainly on textiles. Textiles, easily portable and often exotic in colour and pattern, could relatively simply create a furnished effect. In any event, when funds allowed, the priority for household spending was on furnishing textiles, especially beds and bedding, and this not only provided softness, warmth, privacy and decoration, but also status.

Alexander Neckham's twelfth-century description of how a bedroom should be furnished confirms the early use of textile furnishings in the Middle Ages. It is also an early example of the purveying of advice on room design and planning:

> In the bedchamber let a curtain go around the walls decently, or a scenic canopy, for the avoiding of flies and spiders ... A tapestry should hang appropriately. Near the bed let there be placed a chair to which a stool, may be added and a bench nearby the bed. On the bed itself should be placed a feather mattress to which a bolster is attached. A quilted pad of striped cloth should cover this on which a cushion for the head can be placed. Then sheets of muslin, ordinary cotton, or at least pure linen, should be laid, Next a coverlet of green cloth or of coarse wool, of which the fur lining is badger, cat, beaver or sable, should he put all this if there is lacking purple or down ...[4]

In this piece of guidance, the emphasis on function and appropriateness is evident but there is clearly a conscious effort to achieve some small degree of physical comfort. By the thirteenth century, the taste for textile furnishings had not diminished. In the tax assessment of the urban merchant Simon de Leverington of Kings Lynn, taken between 1285 and 1290, the emphasis on 'comfort' in the sense of warmth and repose is clear.

---

[3] Symonds, R. W. (1951), 'Domestic comfort in the medieval home: An illusion dispelled', *Connoisseur*, Antique Dealers' Fair number. The argument may be more easily substantiated in the case of furniture, which was often immobile.

[4] Holmes Jr., U. T. (1952), *Daily Living in the Twelfth Century, Based on the Observations of Alexander Neckam*, pp. 82–3, cited in Hassall, W. O. (1962), *How They Lived: An Anthology of Original Accounts Written Before 1485*.

Silk Quilt	10s.0d.
Bedspreads (16)	
Sheets (20)	£3.1s.2d.
Featherbeds (8)	
Cloths (6) and Towels (8)	14s.0d.
4 Chests	06s.0d.

Even in the case of a craftsman, Richard le Barbur of Kings Lynn, assessed at the same time as Leverington, there is slight evidence of an interest in domestic comforts:

Bedspreads (2)	2s.0d
Cloth (1) and towel	2s 0d
1 Chest	2s 0d
Boards and Chequer	1s.0d[5]

One hundred years later, the bed, or rather its furnishings remained the main attraction. Arnold Monteney's inventory of 1386 had:

> one great chamber [amongst others] striped in white and red of worsted, that is to say 1 coverlet, 1 tester, 1 bed-ceiling, 3 curtains, 6 hangings of 5 yards in length, and 2 and a half in width, 2 tapestries for forms, each of four yards in length and 6 cushions ...[6]

However, chambers were not the only spaces to benefit from the use of textile furnishings. The inventory of the furnishings of the hall in the home of Richard Toky, a London grocer, made in October 1391, demonstrates this well:

> One dorser, [wall cloth at the back of a bench] 2 costiers, [window or bed curtain] 4 quysshyns [cushions] of red and blod [blue] worsted, 8 bankers [cloth covering a chair or bench and its cushion] lined with canvass, 10s; one painted table for cups, 5s; a wash bowl and stand of lead, 2s 6d; 3 basins and washbowls of denaunt work, 11s 4d; one large bowl, 5s; one table with trestles, 2s 6d; another painted table, 8d; 7 quysshyns of tapestry work, 20d; one pair of table of sprews, 2s; 3 quysshyns of red tapestry work, 12d; one braunch of iron, 4d; one pees of a washbowl, 2d; 3 forms, 12d; one pair of andirons,14d; an iron candlestick, 6d; one lance with a shield, 2s; polaxes, 3s; one arblast with the takell, 2s; 2 dorsers, 2 bankers 6 quysshyns, 3s 4d; 2 chairs, 20d; 2 dorsers and 2 bankers of blod and black, 20d; one pair of andirons 20d. Total £3.0s 2d.[7]

For most of the Middle Ages, the particular use of rooms was not specifically set, and they were used in a variety of ways, dependent upon circumstances. The selection of goods in the hall of Richard Toky's house (in the above example) demonstrates the potential of the space for a variety of uses. In addition,

---

[5] Owen, D. M. (Ed.) (1984), *The Making of King's Lynn*, pp. 235–6 and 246–7, cited in Dyer, C. (1989), *Standards of Living in the Later Middle Ages*, p. 206.

[6] Steer, F. W. (1958), 'Smaller houses and their furnishings in the seventeenth and eighteenth centuries', *Journal of the British Archaeological Association*, 3rd Series, Vol. 20–21, p. 155.

[7] Cited by Symonds (1951), 'Domestic comfort in the medieval home. An illusion dispelled', p. 42.

it is also clear that many rooms were not permanently furnished: rather they were dressed as the occasion arose.[8] Penelope Eames has argued persuasively that great medieval households had to be organized to allow furnishings to be moved daily, as within a stage set which used portable props as required to suit the action.[9] This then seems to connect well with John Lukacs's idea that the medieval people were more interested in an 'external world' than a private, internal, or individual one. Lukacs suggests that self-consciousness was not well developed in the medieval period. He sees this lack of self-interest reflected in their interiors.[10] Although there is evidence of some consumer activity in the pre-modern period beyond basic subsistence and needs, with some aristocrats and certain urban groups having an interest in fashion and acquisition, it was only really from the sixteenth century that anything resembling a self-conscious and personal attitude to domestic furnishings could be discerned on a wider scale. Even then, we must take note of Carol Shammas's warning when she reminds us that 'it might be going too far to suggest that the average household in the sixteenth or even seventeenth century showed many of the signs of the affective or sociable side of domesticity'.[11] Nevertheless the construction of permanent housing, developments in retail and transport infrastructure, and an increasing range of goods, encouraged a commodity culture.

As has probably always been the case, the decisions about objects, and the actual acquisition of them is determined by an individual's age, location, financial position and point in their life cycle. It has already been established that possession of furnishings of any quality or meaningful value was not only a representation of wealth but also of position or rank.[12] A comparison between the two inventories below highlights this point. The 1397 inventory of two of the properties and possessions of Thomas Woodstock, Duke of Gloucester read:

	Pleshey Castle		London house	
Arras tapestries and hangings	£381	(20%)	£16	(6%)
Beds	£295	(16%)	£68	(25%)
Furniture	£2	(0%)	£7	(2%)
Silver plate	£192	(10%)	£124	(45%)
...				
Total	£1910		£276[13]	

---

[8] For more on this, see Eames, P. (1971), 'Documentary evidence concerning the character and use of domestic furnishings in England in the fourteenth and fifteenth centuries', *Furniture History*, 7, pp. 41–60.

[9] Ibid. p. 47.

[10] Lukacs, J. (1970), 'The bourgeois interior', *American Scholar*, 339(4), p. 623.

[11] Shammas, C. (1980), 'The domestic environment in early modern England and America', *Journal of Social History*, 14, p. 9.

[12] See for example Avery, T. (1997), 'The furnishings of Tattershall Castle c. 1450-1500. A display of wealth and power', *Apollo*, 145, April, pp. 37–9.

[13] Cited in Dyer (1989), *Standards of Living in the Later Middle Ages*, p. 77.

Contrast this with the inventory of Robert Oldman, reeve of Cuxham Oxfordshire, taken 1349–52:

Canvas Cloth	9d.
Tapet [figure cloth]	3d.
Tapet with sheet	3s 4d.
Tapet, 2 sheets 4 blankets	5s 4d.
Table cloth	1s 6d.
Towel	6d.
2 cloths	8d.
1 coffer	1s 0d.
2 stools	8d.
1 form	1½d.[14]

These two examples demonstrate *in extremis* Carson's point about ownership of goods reflecting quality and quantity. One hundred years later, the lot of the peasant had changed little. Richard Sclatter, a smallholder of Elmley Castle, Worcestershire, was inventoried in 1457 as possessing:

3 badly worn coverlets	2s.
2 worn canvasses	4d.
1 sheet	4d.
1 mattress	2d.
4 pillows	4d.
3 boards for a bed	4d.
2 boards with two trestles	6d.
1 table board	3d.
1 chair	3d.
1 form	2d.
1 chest (with various necessaries in the same)	2s.2d.
1 chest	6d.
1 other chest	6d.[15]

Although still sparse, there is evidence in this inventory of a bed and table, a chair and some bedding which, although sometimes 'worn' and poorly valued, represented some improvement in the lifestyle of the peasant.

The growth of supply and demand

The sixteenth century witnessed the beginnings of a commercial revolution that changed the basis on which lifestyles were developed from those based on a

---

[14] Harvey, P. D. A. (1976), *Manorial Records of Cuxham, Oxon 1200–1359*, Oxford Record Office, pp. 153–9, cited in Dyer, (1989), *Standards of Building in the Later Middle Ages*, p. 170.

[15] Hereford and Worcester RO, 899.95 BA 989/2/28, cited in Dyer (1989), p. 170.

fixed hierarchy, sumptuary laws and precedent to those based on freedom of choice aided by a tendency to consume using money and exchange. This resulted in the development of infrastructure and methods of business to service the various demands.

Cary Carson has posited that 'ordinary people in England and northern Europe enjoyed a rising standard of living in the hundred years or so before the end of the seventeenth century. These were necessary improvements affecting dress, diet, shelter and furnishings. The growing level of 'comforts' in a home can best be seen in contemporary inventories. For example, the range of furniture in the inventory dated October 1566 of Christopher Yarworthe, of Easthorpe, near Southwell, Nottingham, showed some limited distinction between rooms and their uses as well as specific furniture forms:

> In the hall an aumbre, a bord, a paire of trestles, 2 forms, 2 chairs and other implements, 10s.0d.
> In the parlour 2 mattresses, 2 coverlettes, 2 bolsters, two pillows, 3 pairs of sheets and 2 towels, 10s.0d.
> In the said parlour 2 chests and three bedsteads 5s 0d.
> Total £15.2s.2d [16]

These changes in comfort through goods also represent an infrastructure that made and supplied them to customers. For the majority of consumers at this time, reliance on fairs, markets, and in the case of furniture, craftsmen-retailers, remained the basis of trade. However, in the case of textiles, it was often the mercer who supplied the soft furnishings of a home.

The conventions of consumption in the early-modern period stressed the importance of textiles and, in particular, the bed, just as the medieval example of Neckham illustrated. The bed had been an important investment, often bequeathed upon death to the next-of-kin.[17] It is clear, though, that the bed and its accoutrements took pride of place in the home. According to Carole Shammas, between 20 and 25 per cent of total household investment went into bedding over the period 1550–1774.[18] Contemporary sources certainly reflect this engagement with the bed. In 1688, Randall Holme specified a very comprehensive listing of 'things useful about a bed and bed chamber':

> Bed stocks, as Bedposts, sides, ends head and tester.
> Mat or sackcloth bottom.
> Cord, bed staves, and stay or the feet.
> Curtain rods and hookes, and rings, either brass or horn.
> Beds of chaffe, wool or flocks, feathers, and down in ticks or bed tick
> Bolsters, pillows.
> Blankets, Ruggs, quilts, Counterpane, caddows [rough woollen covers].
> Curtains, Valens, Tester Head cloth; all either fringed, laced or plaine alike.
> Inner curtains, and valens, which are generally white silk or linen.

[16] *Nottinghamshire Household Inventories*, Thoroton Society (1962), Vol. XXII, p. 108.

[17] See examples in Wright, L. (1962), *Warm and Snug*, p. 54.

[18] Shammas (1980), 'The domestic environment in early modern England and America', p. 10.

Tester bobs of wood gilt, or covered suitable to the curtains.
Tester top either flat, or raised, or canopy like, or half testered.
Basis or the lower valens at the seat of the bed, which reacheth the ground, and fringes for state as the upper valens, either with inch fringe, caul fringe, tufted fringe, snailing fringe, gimpe fringe with tufts and buttons, vellum fringe, &c.[19]

Apart from this exhaustive list of the components of a bed, other sources give an idea of the nature and role of textiles for use in decorating an interior. In the inventory of Henry Lord Peircie (Percy), dated 6 December 1632, an interesting range of textile furnishings is recorded:

In the press at the side of the wardrobe; Item three long black velvet, laced with silver lace; two large window curtains of green baysel; one old green cloth carpet with silk fringe; two pairs of fustian blankets, one pair of them olde; three of the best sort of woollen blankets; one large crimson rug, old and stayned belonging to the yellow printed saye bed: two olde green rugs; one piece of the finest sort of hangings, herbagrie; one old piece of herbagrie with half-moons; one piece suitable to the hangings in the new buildings: two piece of forest work; five pieces of hangings bought of Sir Joecelyn Peircie; eighteen pieces of verders; five old pieces of old hangings, ymagery upon a table near to the press of diverse suites (£88.1.5.0).[20]

This listing includes curtains, carpets, bedding and hangings and the descriptions suggest a comprehensive mix of old and worn, new and second-hand textile goods.

A growing and increasingly sophisticated retail trade that is exemplified by the chapbook entitled *The Plain Dealing Linnen Draper* published in 1696 supported the acquisition of these textile goods. This work is useful, not only for its detail about the various cloths and their prices, but also for what we can glean from it concerning consumption patterns and matters of comfort. The very fact that a publication was produced giving information on calicoes and linens for window and bed curtains, for sheeting, napkins, wall hangings and towels indicated a demand: indeed a demand from the country (rather than just the town) that was partly satisfied by the draper through the chapmen.[21]

During the sixteenth and seventeenth centuries, Britain saw itself change into a powerful European state. This change was built upon important developments in agriculture; internal and external trade and commerce; by a doubling of the population, and by other factors such as greater religious tolerance, a growing international presence and a gradual change in the nature of governance. All these factors encouraged economic growth. In addition, the

---

[19] Holme, Randall (1688), *The Academy of Armoury*, cited in Wills, G. (1971), *English Furniture 1550–1760*, p. 72.

[20] 6 December 1632 Inventory of Henry Lord Peircie (Percy) in Denvir, B. (1988), *From the Middle Ages to the Stuarts: Art, Design and Society*, pp. 197–99.

[21] Spufford, M. (1984), *The Great Reclothing of Rural England*, p. 107.

importance of a growing freedom from famine and chronic food shortages, and from cycles of boom and bust, also helped tradesmen move markets towards a wider populace base, so that the more 'ordinary' people were not only able but also willing to become consumers at a range of differing levels. More people began acquiring goods, using services, and engaging in social, recreational and educational activities that went far beyond meeting or improving basic physical needs.

These changes reflected a revised societal structure through the change from the external considerations of basic subsistence to the more conscious purchasing decisions based more upon an awareness of self-identity. Perhaps for the first time in Western history, a considerable number of ordinary people deliberately assumed a personal appearance and demeanour, established attractive and comfortable abodes, and conducted themselves in ways that were more class-bound than culture-bound.[22] The use of goods to mark the increasingly nuanced strata of society is clear. In any particular locality, there was often originally a generally shared material culture, but by the seventeenth century, some people might have possessed more cultural and material affinity with families many miles away, rather than with their own neighbours. This may be expressed in design terms as the distinction between vernacular and local design types that are identified geographically, and high-style design types that are located socially.

For some, these socially defined lifestyles began forming an accepted understanding that a class of people have a cohesiveness found in a common style of dress, furnishings and, more generally, behaviour that would confirm their similarities, and, just as important, their distinction from other groups. In addition, the idea of self-improvement within the social group was gradually considered to be quite natural. This meant that the acquisition of goods was seen as an imperative – an indication of social worth and standing. William Harrison, writing in 1577, explained the new attitude:

> The farmer … [will] think his gains very small towards the end of his term
> if he has not six or seven years rent lying by him, therewith to purchase a
> new lease, besides a fair garnish of pewter on his cupboard… three or four
> feather beds, so many coverlets and carpets of tapestry, a silver salt, a
> bowle for wine, and a dozen spoons to furnish up the sute …[23]

Although these changes were important and demonstrated cultural shifts, it is probable that the depth of the market was not as great as some suggest, but that it did penetrate below the social and economic elites and created the beginnings of a middle market. Lorna Weatherill's analysis of inventories seems to

---

[22] Carson, C. Hoffman, R. and Albert, P. (Eds) (1994), *Of Consuming Interests: The Style of Life in the Eighteenth Century*, p. 513. It is of some relevance that around the period 1500-1550, the word 'home' begins to take on connotations of personal space and identity as opposed to an original and broader meaning of place of origin.

[23] Harrison, William (1587), *The Description of England 1577*, p. 197.

confirm the idea that a middle-range market existed but did not extend below the small farmer.[24] This middle group was characterized as a class of persons (yeomen) who benefited from fixed expenses and rising selling prices, thus creating net profits that provided surpluses to spend as discretionary income.

By the mid-sixteenth century, there was also an understanding that goods represented status and power as well as often having intrinsic value. William Harrison, although prone to exaggeration, gives an insight into the changes of the time.

> In noblemen's houses it is not rare to see abundance of arras, rich hangings of tapestry, silver vessel, and so much other plate as may furnish sundry cupboards to the sum oft times of 1,000l or 2,000l ... Likewise in the houses of knights, gentlemen, merchantmen, and some other wealthy citizens, it is not geason [uncommon] to behold generally their great provision of tapestry, Turkey work, pewter, brass, fine linen, and thereto costly cupboards of plate worth 500l or 600l or 1,000l to be deemed by estimation. But as herein all these sorts do far exceed their elders and predecessors, and in neatness and curiosity the merchant all other, so in time past the costly furniture stayed there, whereas now is descended yet lower, even unto the inferior artificers and many farmers, who, by virtue of their old and not of their new leases, have for the most part learned also to garnish their cupboards with plate, their joint beds with tapestry and silk hangings, and their tables with carpets and fine napery, whereby the wealth of our country does infinitely appear.[25]

This well-known extract indicates the change in the adoption of fine furnishings that reflected an increase in personal wealth and a propensity to consume, as well as in opportunities to purchase goods, so that more social groups were able to engage in the consumption of goods, once the sole preserve of noblemen. The changes in consumption patterns, due in part to changes in social competition and status, encouraged the purchase of novel goods, and hastened the search for separation (privacy) and personal 'comfort'. The development of privacy and comfort as concepts, as well as the notions of 'suitability' and appropriateness, are evident when, *circa* 1610, Lady Compton stated:

> I will have all my houses furnished and all my lodging chambers to be suited with all such furniture *as is fit* [emphasis added]; as beds, stools, chairs, suitable cushions, carpets, silver warming pans, cupboards of plate, fair hangings and such like. So for my drawing chambers in all houses I will have them delicately furnished both with couch, canopy, glass, carpet, chairs, cushions, and all things thereto belonging.[26]

The issue of the 'appropriateness' of domestic decoration and building was an important one, and it remained a theme in house furnishing well into the

---

[24] Weatherill, L. (1988), *Consumer Behaviour and Material Culture in Britain 1660–1760.*

[25] Harrison (1587), *The Description of England 1577*, p. 197.

[26] Goodman, G. (1839), *The Court of King James*, cited by Jourdain, M. (1924), *English Decoration and Furniture of the Early Renaissance.*

twentieth century.[27] The individual's status was directly reflected in the home, and this reflection had to be seen to be suitable and in accord with their social position. Sir Henry Wootton in his *Elements of Architecture* of 1624 recognized this need:

> Every man's proper mansion house and home, being the theatre of his hospitality, the seat of self fruition, the comfortablest part of his own life, the noblest of his son's inheritance, as kind of private princedom; nay to the possessor thereof, an epitome of the whole world: may well deserve by these attributes, according to the degree of the master, to be decently and delightfully adorned.[28]

The issue of appropriateness of position is noted in reference to 'the degree of the master' mentioned above, which seems to reflect precedence in another form.

The changes identified by Harrison and Wootton can also be measured by Shammas's work on the quantity and quality of linen in households. Between 1660 and 1700, Shropshire inventories show a steady rise in the number of pairs of sheets owned: three sheets to a bed in the 1660s and 1670s. By the period 1690–1710, this had increased to five sheets per bed. An equivalent group from Suffolk inventories found that in the 1580s the median value of their linen was 7s., whereas in the 1680s it was £1.6s.0d. On another measure, their personal wealth overall rose in value by 85 per cent, but the value of their linen rose by 271 per cent.[29] Shammas encapsulates this process: 'The Tudor practice of devoting over one half of consumer goods investment to bedding, linen, and brass/pewter followed a medieval pattern that had been established by the richer elements in society and had filtered down to the plebs by the sixteenth century.'[30]

This leads to a consideration of changes in consumption as attempting to create difference. Contemporary authors were aware of the distinctions offered by 'old money' and 'new money'. Gervase Markham in his *Book of Humour* (1625) made the important observation that 'Gentry or gentilitie is taken two ways, that is to say either by acquisition or descent.'[31] This points out that by using the prescribed conventions, goods and services, people with the money and the aspirations to an improved position in society could often make their mark. On the other hand, there was a cachet around property and goods that were acquired by descent that created a visual narrative of the family history.[32]

---

[27] This theme will be returned to in later sections.

[28] Wootton, Sir Henry (1624), *Elements of Architecture*, p. 82, cited in P. Tristram (1989), *Living Space in Fact and Fiction*, pp. 35–6.

[29] Spufford, M. (1984), *The Great Reclothing of Rural England*, pp. 115–17.

[30] Shammas (1980), 'The domestic environment in early Modern England and America', p. 10.

[31] Markham, G. (1625), *The Book of Humour*, p. 58, cited in Carson, Hoffman and Albert (Eds) (1994), *Of Consuming Interests*, p. 556.

[32] See McCracken's idea of patina below.

In the former case, the main driving force of this form of consumption was the growth of towns and urban communities.

Urbanization

The rise of London and, to a lesser extent, other cities, brought with it an increase in population and a concomitant desire to spend upon the development of urban spaces, including homes. This had a very favourable effect on the trades and businesses associated with house building and furnishing, obviously as a response to a rise in demand for goods themselves, but also partly as a result of people choosing particular goods as signs of wealth and position. The selection of goods in this hot-house atmosphere was also to meet the challenges of others in the same social group, through imitation (following an example) and emulation (equalling or excelling). In 1606, Giovanni Botero commented in his *A Treatise Concerning the Cause of the Magnificence and Greatness of Cities* on the emulatory process that encouraged this development of building and associated trades:

> Experience teacheth that the residence of noblemen in cities makes them to be more glorious and more populous, not only by cause they bring their people, and their families unto it, but also more by cause a nobleman dispenseth much more largely through the access of friends unto him and through the emulation of others in a Citie where he is abiding and visited continually by honorable personages than he spendeth in the country where he liveth ...[33]

This recognition of accessibility to the taste of others and attempts at emulating them helped to develop the market for the ever-growing range of goods and services that consumers demanded.

The so-called 'Great Rebuilding' emphasized the medieval impermanence of dwellings, and the beginning of a growth of vernacular permanent building in the fifteenth century. This escalation of construction work was enhanced by extensions and rebuilding from the late sixteenth to the early eighteenth century.[34] Shammas's analysis of improvements in possessions is also reflected in buildings. She has quantified improvements, in terms of room spaces in provincial homes. In her analysis of inventories she found that in the 1590s, 'poor and average' Oxfordshire households had a mean of 3.6 rooms, whilst one hundred years later, in 1690 the same wealth groups in Worcestershire had

---

[33] Botero, G. (1606), *A Treatise Concerning the Cause of the Magnificence and Greatness of Cities*, trans. Pearson R., Chapter X, cited in Fisher, F. J (1948), 'The development of London as a centre of conspicuous consumption in the sixteenth and seventeenth centuries', *Transactions of the Royal Historical Society*, 30, p. 198.

[34] For the 'Great Rebuilding' see Hoskins, W. G. (1953), 'The rebuilding of rural England, 1570–1640', *Past and present*, 4, pp. 44–59, and Machin, R. (1977), 'The Great Rebuilding: A reassessment', *Past and Present*, 77, pp. 33–56.

a mean of 4.6 rooms.[35] Evitt has also pointed out that low-status farm labourers' inventories from 1560–1600 show that 56 per cent had three or more rooms and by 1630–40, 79 per cent had three or more, often classified as hall, chamber and parlour.[36]

In 1685 Nicolas Barbon, himself an entrepreneur and builder of new parts of London, commented upon the beneficial economic effects of the 'Great Rebuilding' particularly in the capital. He noted how the building of great works provided employment for 'all those trades that belong to the furnishing of a house … as upholsterers, chair makers, etc.'[37] Barbon was also a perceptive commentator on the acquisitive nature of people and the impact this had on trade and business. In his *A Discourse on Trade*, he pointed out that: 'if strictly examined, nothing is absolutely necessary to support life but food: for a great part of mankind go naked, and lye in huts and caves'. However, he went on to say: 'The wants of the mind are infinite, man naturally aspires, and as his mind is elevated, his senses grow more refined and more capable of delight.'[38] In fact, he argued that as demand for strict necessities used up a very small proportion of peoples' resources, most wants will be 'of the mind', which, by definition, makes them luxuries. He further observed that 'Fashion or the alteration of dress is a great promoter of trade, because it occasions the expense of cloaths before the old ones are worn out: it is the spirit and life of trade: it makes a circulation and gives value, by turns to all sorts of commodities: keeps the great body of trade in motion.'[39] It is these ideas that are directly reflected when the furnishing of interiors is undertaken with a view to representing something of oneself, rather than simply attending to functional needs.

Another contemporary writer, Bernard Mandeville, in his *Fable of the Bees*, asked the question: 'why distinguish between luxuries, necessaries and decencies and conveniences when considering goods?' He suggested that they are all mutable and variable and therefore do not need to be classified in a hierarchical way. In fact, the acquisition of material goods, particularly those associated with homemaking was, in his view, like Barbon, of positive benefit to society:

> The greatest excesses of luxury are shown in buildings, furniture, equipage, and cloaths; clean linen weakens a man no more than flannel; tapestry, fine painting or good wainscot are no more unwholesome than bare walls; and a rich couch or a gilt chariot are no more enervating than the cold floor or a country cart.[40]

---

[35] Shammas, C. (1980), 'The Domestic environment in early modern England and America', *Journal of Social History*, 14, p.7.

[36] Evitt, A. (1967), in Finsberg, H. (ed.), *Agrarian History of England*, IV, Table 10, p. 443.

[37] Barbon, N. (1685), *An Apology for the Builder*, p. 32.

[38] Cited by Crowley, J. E. (2000), *The Invention of Comfort*, p.150.

[39] Barbon, N. (1690), A *Discourse on Trade*, cited in Saumarez-Smith, C. (1993), *Eighteenth Century Decoration: Design and the Domestic Interior in England*, p. 53.

[40] Mandeville. B. (1970), *Fable of the Bees*, p. 144.

In addition, what he considered to be more important and crucially different was the distinction between people who had the ability to buy, and those with both the ability and the willingness to pay. Although these ideas were not universally held, and the consumption of imported goods, especially textiles, exotic timbers and other 'luxuries' were seen as potentially disastrous for the economy of the nation, the need to satisfy the palpable demand was obvious to retailers.

Retail shops and business types

To satisfy this growing and disparate demand, a range of business types and systems was steadily established and operated. Of course, markets and fairs were widely used to distribute goods including house furnishings of various sorts, but fixed shops operating in urban spaces were also part of the infrastructure from early on. These shops might be showrooms of merchants dealing in imported or ready-made goods, or they might be the retail outlet of a direct producer. In other cases, the retailer will have worked on bought-in materials to change their identity and fabricate a new product, either for special order or for stock. This was most likely the case with regard to items for the home, especially where textiles were involved. It is also evident that the shop and home of the maker and/or seller was often the same, and that 'the shop' was not necessarily an autonomous selling space. In many cases, it remained part of the household economic unit well into the eighteenth century. Other means of distribution included itinerants who would sell to the more rural populations, and at the other extreme, the makers and suppliers of specialized products who created 'special orders' in exclusive workshops.

By the thirteenth century, in London at least, the development of retailing and the establishment of shops as trading outlets were well established.[41] The medieval shops were diverse in type and style, appearing to have been greater in number and smaller in size than their later counterparts in the sixteenth century and onward, and they ranged from purely retail selling premises to multi-use premises for production, storage, living and selling purposes. Salzman has published building contracts that give some indication of the format of shops in medieval England.[42] Included are London examples from 1310 for a contract to build three shops with two storeys above; a contract from 1369 to build twenty shops, each gabled, having windows on the street front, all of one design, and another contract of 1497 from Canterbury where the contract was for four houses, each to have a shop on the ground floor.[43]

---

[41] Keene, D. (1990), 'Shops and shopping in medieval London', in Grant, L. (Ed.), *Medieval Art, Architecture and Archaeology in London*, British Archaeological Association Conference Transactions 1984, pp. 29–46.

[42] Salzman, L. F. (1967), *Building in England Down to 1540*, p. 418.

[43] Ibid., Appendix B, p. 418, 441 and 554.

Although none of these can be identified as premises for specific merchandise, it seems likely that suppliers of domestic furnishings operated from such premises. Indeed, an early example of a shop selling goods for the home is found in an inventory of 1333, which shows the contents of the store of Richard de Elsyng, a merchant with three shops in Soper Lane, London. In one of his shops were '2 chests, three stalls and a room above'. The total value of the inventory of 1750 items was £284. Amongst these were fabrics including woollens, worsteds, fustian, taffeta and silks, as well as finished goods including bedcovers, chasubles, cushions and a piece of arras.[44]

In view of the importance of textiles, it is not surprising that mercers and drapers were amongst the earliest suppliers of home furnishings. They probably extended stocked lines in relation to demands and established a trend whereby mercers and drapers developed their businesses into the supply of home furnishings and furniture, and even later into full-scale department stores.[45] However, in these early stages, it is clear that the retailers of domestic furnishings and equipment were by the very nature of the demand, many and varied. Mercers supplied silks; drapers supplied woollen cloths; upholsterers made the textiles into hangings and curtains, whilst carpenters, joiners and turners produced and sold an increasing range of wooden artefacts and furniture.

In addition, there were distinctions between those who made and sold goods, those who sold ready-made goods only, and those who imported goods. Importantly, evidence from later retail businesses shows that these three categories were never mutually exclusive enterprises. Having said that, it is clear that the development of specializations in retailing, especially outside London, was a slow process.[46] For example, a mercer in Leicester in the fifteenth century was described as follows: '[He] was at the same time draper, haberdasher, jeweller, grocer, ironmonger, saddler, and dealer in timber, furniture and hardware.'[47] Although some architects had operated as overseers of the building and furnishings of some houses, it seems that it was not really until the eighteenth century that a comprehensive furnishing service was offered 'under one roof' in the form of the complete house furnisher and decorator.

In the business of making and supplying furniture and furnishings, there were no clearly defined ways of selling. Since market stalls or open shops were used for the sale of foodstuffs, cloth and so on, it was probably also the case with textiles and sundry furnishing articles. Whilst the craft-based production of furniture, initiated through the carpenter and then the joiner, was the basis of

---

[44] Keene (1990), 'Shops and shopping in medieval London', p. 38. PRO E/154/1/18A.

[45] See further below. Also see Berger, R. (1993), *The Most Necessary Luxuries* ... .

[46] See Berger, R. M. (1980), 'The development of retail trade in provincial England ca. 1550–1700', *Journal of Economic History*, (XL) 1, March, pp. 123–8.

[47] Power and Poston, *English Trade in the 15th Century*, cited in Davis, D. (1966), *A History of Shopping*, p. 18.

much of the trade, the artisan's workshop was probably the centre of business dealings. Nevertheless, the idea of some form of showroom in the early stages of retail development is probably apparent in the premises of Richard de Elsyng (see above). It is also likely that a craftsman-maker invited customers into his house to see work in progress and to view samples of merchandise. In many cases, the role of the various furniture and furnishings retailers was still combined with that of maker.[48] This notion of buying from the maker not only offered the opportunity to deal direct with the master, but also to influence the production and to have some guarantees on goods seen as work in progress.[49]

One of the most significant of the trades to develop in this period was that of the 'upholder' or upholsterer who supplied and fitted all the textile furnishings of a home. The *tapissier* and the *fourrier* originally carried out the fitting up of domestic textiles in large households. Their work included the supply of canopies, wall tapestries, table carpets and other soft furnishings for interior decoration. The upholsterer subsumed these posts during the sixteenth and seventeenth centuries. Originally, the upholsterers were dealers in old clothes, old beds, old armour and other diverse sorts of materials that conveyed an unsavoury image of their trade. An inventory of an upholsterer's stock taken in 1356 listed an odd mix of goods including armour, pickaxes, sledgehammers and feather beds.[50] The upholsterers' shabby and unattractive image took some time to eliminate. In Stow's *Survey of London* of 1598, he observed that Birchin Lane in the City of London 'had for the most part dwelling Fripperers or Upholders that sold olde apparel and householde stuffe'.[51] Their reputation remained suspect into the seventeenth century. At various times they were accused of handling stolen property, and selling contrary to the established customs of the City of London and the guild.

As with other crafts, the upholders' guild was established in part to protect and in part to control the activities of their members. The bye-laws they created to do this can give useful insights into their retail trading practices. The 1679 Ordinances of the Upholders' Company include a provision that the Company could enter the 'House, shop or booth of offending members and carry away goods'.[52] The reference to the locations is valuable as it indicates three potential sites of retail business and a diversity of outlets. The house is the dwelling (and place of business), the shop may be a showroom but could also be a workshop that doubled as a site of selling, and the booth indicates a temporary trading place. A little later, in 1686, a charter was granted to the

---

[48] Carrier, J. G. (1994), 'Alienating objects: The emergence of alienation in retail trade', *Journal of the Royal Anthropological Institute*, 29, pp. 359–80.

[49] This idea of 'guarantee' was still potent in the nineteenth and twentieth centuries, with goods having retailers' labels affixed to them.

[50] Houston, J. H. (1993), *Featherbedds and Flockbedds*, p. 3.

[51] Stow (1598), *Survey of London*, Everyman Edition, 1980.

[52] Houston, (1993), *Featherbedds and Flockbedds*, p. 30.

Company of Upholders by James II, giving them powers of search in 'the City of London, and the suburbs thereof and within seven miles in circuit of the same city and in all and every or any [of] the fairs and markets within this realm of England.'[53] So again, there is an expectation that the products of the upholsterers will be on sale, not only in the city but also in fairs and markets right across the country.

Some further idea of retail selling practices can be found in the upholders' bye-laws. They declared that there should be no direct selling other than through channels recognized by the Company:

> No person ... do at any time go about the streets or any other places proffering any wares belonging to the said art or mystery of an Upholder or which are usually made or sold by Upholderers to sell from shop to shop, house to house, or in any Inn or place other than in open shop, fair or market ...'[54]

In addition to this restrictive practice, clearly intended to protect *bona fide* tradesmen, the bye-laws noted that if a maker had no shop premises, the only place from which the Company would allow him to sell his goods was his own abode:

> No person or persons using the Art or Mystery of an Upholder within the City of London ... and not keeping an open sale shop shall make or cause to be made any ware belonging to the trade of an upholder to be put on sale by him in any other place than his chamber or other such convenient place of aboad [sic] as he or they shall make known unto the said Master ...[55]

By the very early seventeenth century, inventory evidence suggests that the living quarters, the selling space (shop) and the workshops were often in the same premises, especially in provincial towns.[56] For example, in 1605 the upholsterer Nicholas Webster of Southampton was recorded as having a back and fore chamber, hall, kitchen, stables, loft and a shop that held his stock of beds, cloth, valances, blankets and pillows. The probate value of his stock was more than twice as much as the contents of the private chambers, being £24.19s.7d., as opposed to £11.14s.4d.[57] In 1626, John Stretton, an upholsterer of Oxford, is recorded as having a shop and 'chamber over the shop' which was well stocked with textiles, leather, tickings, and necessities for running a simple upholstery business. Thirdly, the 1638 inventory of James King of

---

[53] Ibid., p. 31.

[54] Ibid., p. 58. This method of selling has remained an issue for *bona fide* retailers with premises ever since.

[55] Ibid., p. 59. These issues were addressed in terms of all internal trade in *The Trade of England Reviewed*, published in 1681, which complained about the disadvantages brought to shopkeepers by hawkers who sold direct. The issue was still alive in the latter part of the twentieth century.

[56] For London shops, see Brown, F. E. (1986), 'Continuity and change in the urban house: Developments in domestic space organisation in seventeenth century London', *Comparative Studies in Society and History*, 28(3), p. 578.

[57] Beard, G. (1997), *Upholsterers and Interior Furnishing in England, 1550–1840*, p. 11.

Odiham also included 'a chamber over the shop' where a not inconsiderable stock valued at £56.15s.0d. included bedsteads, cupboards, tables, stools, textile furnishings.[58] The 1670 inventory of London upholsterer William Ridges shows a very different picture in terms of scale, though the principle remains the same. Ridges operated a business with five rooms devoted to the display of merchandise and a further six rooms for production operations. The success of this enterprise, situated in Cornhill, a prime retail location for upholsterers at the time, is evident from the total inventory value of £17 567.0s.0d. [59]

By the early seventeenth century, wealthy clients were beginning to require consciously co-ordinated interiors in line with newly fashionable tastes. As the upholsterer had already undertaken part of this role, it was natural that he would begin to assume full responsibility for all furnishing supplies. This role was eventually to develop into the business of the complete house furnisher or the profession of interior decorator. Upholsterers were becoming arbiters of taste, not only through access to important homes and the circles of the wealthy but also through their skills in introducing new styles and being in a position to influence public taste. In addition, and unlike many other retailers, they had to be skilled in running a complex enterprise, employing a range of suppliers and craftspeople, and to be able to offer an individual service to each customer that often included working in their homes.

The upholsterer could only operate successfully with the assistance of the silk mercer, the passementier, the embroiderer, the cabinet-makers and a whole range of other sub-contractors including feather dressers, linen drapers, glass merchants, blacksmiths, carvers, gilders and the whole spectrum of building crafts. It was the upholsterer who was responsible for the overall works, and it was he who often took a profit on these other suppliers' efforts. Indeed, at the time (1615), it was noted that the upholstery business potentially provided a very profitable living, even so, it had its critics:

> The trade of an upholsterer doth not require any art or skill for the exercising of it, inasmuch as he hath all things made to his hand, and it is only to dispose them in order after such time as they are brought to him … and so he is like to Aesop's bird, which borroweth of every bird a feather, his art resting merely in the overseeing and disposition of such things which other men work, and in the putting feathers into a tick, and sewing them up when he hath done, the which one that hath been an apprentice unto it but seven days is able to perform.[60]

---

[58] Ibid., p. 11–12.

[59] Ibid., p. 12.

[60] Tolley's Case, 1615, cited in Lipson E. (1948), *Economic History of England*, pp. 281–2. The issue arose from an interpretation of the Statute of Apprentices 1563, which finally agreed that an upholsterer was not a trade within the definition of that statute. This is important in as much as it recognized that the upholsterer was an entrepreneur and co-ordinator within a retail environment, more than a crafsman-maker.

Location

In London, the retailing of furniture and furnishings through fixed shops was certainly established in the Middle Ages. One of the earliest references is found in 1333, when the shop of Richard de Elsyng (see above) was located in Soper Lane, London. As with other crafts and trades, retailers specializing in particular merchandise established their businesses in the same areas of a town. The close relationship between a retailer and his suppliers and ancillary artisans (as well as his customers in many cases) demanded proximity of location. Therefore, the positioning of upholsterers next to mercers for example, is no coincidence. For instance, Cornhill in the City of London had been a prime retail site for furniture-related businesses:

> This [Birchin] lane and the high street near adjoining [Cornhill] have been inhabited for the most part with wealthy drapers; from [Birchin] lane on that side of the street to the stocks in the reign of Henry VI [1422–1461] had ye for the most part dwelling fripperers and upholders that sold old apparel and household stuff.[61]

Random examples of merchants in the Cornhill area include William Ridges (mentioned above), Edward Phillips, who traded as an upholsterer in 1584, and Peter Jackson, who ran an upholstery business in Cornhill in the 1640s.[62] In 1663, Pepys famously mentions a visit to Cornhill to buy chintz.[63] This location remained important for upholsterers well into the eighteenth century.

The retail trade often follows the movement of its customers, so it is not surprising to find that as the locus of society gravitated towards Westminster, the luxury trade businesses moved that way as well. By the mid-seventeenth century, the fashionable furniture trade once established close to St Paul's Churchyard migrated from there down Fleet Street and into the Strand. By the end of the century, a further relocation occurred towards Long Acre and Covent Garden. Importantly, there is some evidence of a trend towards establishing showrooms in fashionable areas and leaving workshops in other locations where rents were cheaper.[64]

Pricing

Although the issue of the general reaction to retailers in the early-modern period is beyond the scope of this chapter, it is clear that the matters of pricing

---

[61] Stow (1598), *Survey of London*, p. 178.

[62] Heal, A. (1953), *The London Furniture Makers, from the Restoration to the Victorian era 1660–1840*.

[63] Pepys, S. (1970) *The Diary of Samuel Pepys: A New and Complete Transcription*, Latham and Matthews, W. (Eds).

[64] See Heal and trade card collections.

and credit were two of the main areas of dispute by those opposed to shopkeepers.[65] The idea of a fair price, which was acceptable to both buyer and seller, was recognized early on in retail trading. A just price can be set based on negotiation between buyer and seller, rather than imposition.[66] The original medieval open market and stall arrangements were part of this process of appearing open and straightforward in trading methods.[67] As business developed and the nature of transactions became more sophisticated, then the old arrangements of open market stall or window in a house, as well as the conduct of business in high streets or market places, was to change. As shops became interiorized, as products became more difficult for the purchaser to know the value of, and as the retailer became more often an intermediary than a maker, it followed that the knowledge required to set prices and service standards became based more upon mercantile considerations than on virtuous ones.[68] For the retailer, the need for guidelines to codify behaviour away from ideals of morality to those based on economic relationships grew, and precipitated a demand for commercial advice books.[69] As retailing became more sophisticated, so did the required infrastructure.

Customer service

With the growth of a 'consumer society' by the seventeenth century, a range of new commercial activities were developed which the retailer used to win clientele. Amongst these were the provision of services such as delivery, credit, special orders and personal advice. Some of these functions are demonstrated by entries in Samuel Pepys's diary. For example, in June 1660 he recorded that 'Mr. Morrice the upholsterer came himself today to take notice [of] what furniture we lack in our lodgings in Whitehall.'[70] This highlights a feature of the furnisher's trade whereby much of his time was allocated to visiting customers to assist in the selection of goods. In December 1664, Pepys evidently purchased a mirror from a specialist supplier who had to come to fit it up: 'Then came the looking glass man to set up the looking glass I bought yesterday, in my dining room.'[71] The visit of the upholsterer to his house has already been mentioned, but a further example of the bespoke business can be seen in March 1667, when Pepys records how he went to 'Mr. Povey's house

---

[65] For this, see Cox, N. (2000), *The Complete Tradesman: A Study of Retailing 1550–1820*, Chapter 2, and Benson, J. and Ugolini, L. (2003), *A Nation of Shopkeepers: Five Centuries of British Retailing*, pp. 36–42.

[66] Auctions are an example of socially determined prices and values for goods.

[67] Cox (2000), *The Complete Tradesman*, p.84.

[68] Carrier (1994), 'Alienating objects', pp. 359–80.

[69] Thanks to Elizabeth Rothenburg for pointing this out (CHORD September 2002).

[70] Pepys Diary, 22 June 1660.

[71] Pepys Diary, 16/17 December 1664.

... and he was now at work with a cabinet-maker, making of a new inlaid table.'[72] Although these few references are limited, they do reflect a growth in service-based retailing.

A growing internal trade inevitably had to rely on a transport system to support it. The *Carrier's Cosmographie*, published in 1637, indicates that a carrying business of sorts was part of the trading infrastructure. When newspaper advertising grew in the latter part of the seventeenth century, the carting system developed accordingly. The need to transport goods, either by road or by sea, was a result not only of delivering raw materials to centres of production, but also of consumers buying merchandise away from their immediate locality. A pattern of buying that used local suppliers and itinerants for 'everyday goods' and used urban retailers for less regular purchases had developed. Nancy Cox gives a number of examples of provincial customers who purchased not only from the local market town but also from other centres relatively distant from the home, by means of the network of carriers, or if more local, via their own servants.[73]

Credit was another service offered to customers.[74] It had already become part of the accepted way of doing business, but it was still a difficult issue to manage successfully, especially without proper accounting systems. In 1609 an Act was passed to avoid double payment of debts that took account of the practice of maintaining a 'shop book' of debts owing.[75] Although this was intended to benefit the customers by limiting the shop book as evidence of debt to one year, it did bring into general acceptance the idea of a book debt. The problem for the shopkeeper was not only the servicing of the extended credit but also and more often an inadequate knowledge of book-keeping – an issue that commentators in the eighteenth century often referred to.[76] This brief look at retail services can best be illustrated by considering contemporary examples that illuminate the process, and bring us back to the furnishing of the home.

How did people acquire furniture?

The range of methods consumers used to acquire furniture and furnishings for the home was inevitably varied: from shops and booths to market stalls; from auctions or second-hand dealers; from gifts and bequests, to the employment of local or well-known craftspeople. Although not all these methods are noted, the

---

[72] Pepys Diary, 25 March 1667.

[73] Cox (2000), *The Complete Tradesman*, p. 123.

[74] See Muldrew, C. (1993), 'Interpreting the market: The ethics of credit and community relations in early modern England', *Social History* (18)2, May, pp. 163–81. See also Chapter 5 in Cox (2000) ibid., *The Complete Tradesman*.

[75] Act to avoid the double payment of debts, 7 JAC1 c. 12, cited in Cox (2000), *The Complete Tradesman*. See also Chapter 5.

[76] Cox (2000), *The Complete Tradesman*, p. 147.

description of the day-to-day nature of purchases for the home is part of the rich pickings to be found in Samuel Pepys's diary. The particular entries relating to the purchase of domestic goods cast light on a number of aspects of the business of buying goods for the home. For example, on 2 October 1660 Pepys recorded that he went 'home again, where my dear wife tells me what she hath bought today: viz. a bed and furniture for her chamber with which very well pleased'.[77] Although one example is insufficient to generalize, the entry does indicate that some women were acting as purchasers of furnishing goods for their own consumption at least.[78] Two years later, on 18 November 1662, Pepys complained about the costs his wife was incurring in her purchases, even though they were apparently for the household: 'My wife came home having been abroad today, laying out above 12L in linen and copper and a pot and bedstead and other householde stuff, which troubles me also.'[79]

Samuel Pepys's diary also exemplifies the varied reasons why people buy goods. On 11 August 1663, Pepys's wife was returning to London after an absence, so he had to 'buy a bedstead, because my brother John is here and I have now no more beds than are used'.[80] This shopping to meet an immediate functional need is still common. Pepys was also fully aware of the nature of fashion in the home, as well as in matters of dress. On 23 January 1667 in St James's, Pepys saw 'counterfeit windows in the form of doors with looking glasses instead of windows which makes the room seem both bigger and lighter I think; and I have some thoughts to have the like in one of my rooms'.[81] Although he did not record a purchase, this emulation was clearly an incentive. On another occasion, on 19 October 1668, Pepys recorded how he went out after dinner 'by coach with wife, Deb, and Mr. Harman the upholsterer and carried him to take measure of Mr. Wren's bed at St. James's: I being resolved to have just such another made for me'.[82] Not only is the blatant imitation interesting, but also the manner of planning the work is also fascinating. It was clearly a family occasion and the upholsterer was no doubt there in an advisory capacity, rather than as just an order-taker. The next month a similar outing occurred but involved more shopping:

> I took my wife and boy to Hercules Pillars, and there dined, and thence to our upholsterer's, about some things more to buy, and so to see our coach, and so to the looking-glass man's, by the New Exchange, and so to buy a picture for our blue chamber chimney, and so home.[83]

---

[77] Pepys Diary, 2 October 1660.

[78] See also Glennie and Thrift (1996), 'Consumers' identities and consumption spaces in early modern England', p. 30. Weatherill, L. (1986), 'A possession of one's own: women and consumer behaviour in England 1660–1740', *Journal of British Studies*, 25, April, pp. 131–56.

[79] Pepys Diary, 18 November 1662.

[80] Pepys Diary, 11 August 1663.

[81] Pepys Diary, 23 January 1667.

[82] Pepys Diary, 19 October 1668.

[83] Pepys Diary, 23 November 1668.

The saga of the work done for his wife's bed hangings is interesting as it shows how the upholsterer worked closely with the customer, and how a considerable amount of her own work went into the decorative scheme. The work started on 10 January 1666 when Pepys 'found my wife busy about making her hangings for her chamber with the Upholsterer'.[84] Two days later he recorded that he went 'home to my poor wife, who works all day at home like a horse at the making of her hangings for our chamber and the bed'.[85] After another eleven days' work, on the 21 January 1666 he noted that the 'new bedchamber [has been] completed by wife'. It is of passing interest to note that the old red hangings from her room were re-hung in Pepys's dressing room. Two years later, the issue of recycling of materials arose again when Pepys recorded how 'My wife is upon hanging the long chamber, where the girl lies, with the sad stuff that was in the best chamber, in order to the hanging [of] that, with tapestry.'[86]

Pepys again gives us a very personal insight into the time and effort involved in making furnishing choices. On 5 September 1663, he recorded that 'Creed, my wife and I to Cornhill and after many trials bought my wife a chinke; that is a painted Indian calico for to line her new study, which is very pretty.'[87] Cornhill was a fashionable shopping street with many mercers' businesses, so the 'trials' may indicate a number of visits to various shops. This idea of 'shopping around' before making a purchase is seen again when, in 1664, Pepys wanted to buy a new table. He wrote that he went 'calling among the Joyners in Wood street [off Cheapside, London] to buy a table; and bade in many places but did not buy till I came home to see the place where it is to stand to judge how big it must be'.[88] A third example from October 1668 explained the pleasures of shopping: 'After dinner [taken at noon] my wife and I and Deb out by coach to the Upholsterers in Long Lane, Alderman Reeves, and then to Alderman Crow's to see a variety of hangings and were mightily pleased therewith and spent the whole afternoon thereupon.'[89] One of the last notes he makes is an entry for 1 January 1669. Pepys recorded that he was 'up and with W. Hewer to the New Exchange and there he and I to the cabinet shop to look out and did agree for a cabinet to give my wife for a New Year's gift and I did buy one, cost me 11L which is very pretty, of walnut tree and will come home tomorrow.'[90]

Finally, Pepys also gives a view into one of the perennial pitfalls of purchasing goods, which incidentally also casts light on the purchase process.

---

84 Pepys Diary, 10 January 1666.
85 Pepys Diary, 12 January 1666.
86 Pepys Diary, 24 July 1668.
87 Pepys Diary, 5 September 1663.
88 Pepys Diary, 24 August 1664.
89 Pepys Diary, 15 October 1668. Alderman Crow is mentioned ten times in Pepys's diary.
90 Pepys Diary, 1 January 1669.

In this case, he bought cloth from a mercer, but employed an upholsterer to fix it. Pepys went 'to Lumberd Street to choose stuff to hang my new intended closet and have chosen purple'.[91] The following day he went to confirm the order with 'my Mercers in Lumberd Street and there agreed for our purple serge for my closet'.[92] The day after that, he noted the full realization of his colour choice: 'My closet is doing by upholsterer, which I am pleased with, but fear purple will be too sad for that melancholy room'.[93] This is a fine example of the exciting anticipation of purchasing something new, tinged with anxiety over its suitability once it was at home.

The entries in Pepys's diary confirm that patterns of retailing (and of consumption) were already very varied and complex. Although his examples are London-based, consumer goods were available throughout the country with certain provisos, and it is clear that by the late seventeenth century, urban developments had grown sufficiently to support shopping areas, designed to provide for the general needs of the particular locality.[94] In the case of furniture and furnishings, acquisition procedures varied, often depending upon the location of the consumer.

The example of the itinerant trader, who was often seen as the shadowy figure in the retail trade, clearly met the needs of some customers, but was also seen as a thorn in the side of fixed shopkeepers.[95] Near the end of the reign of Elizabeth I, the upholsterer's company complained that there had 'of late risen up a great company of idle and wandering persons or petit chapmen, commonly called hawksters who pass with upholstery wares from town to town by pack horse whereby petitioners are much impoverished'.[96] Various attempts were made by official action to licence traders but the system was not successful. In any event, they seemed to have met a need. In one example from 1656, an itinerant upholsterer supplied the Reverend Giles Moore of Horsted Keynes in Kent with assorted furnishing requisites. Moore's diary recorded that:

> I bought of Wm. Clowson, upholsterer itinerant living over against the crosse at Winchester, but who comes about the country with his packs on horseback,
>
> | | |
> |---|---|
> | A large fine coverlet with birds and bucks | £2.10.0 |
> | A sett of striped curtaines and valance | £1.8.0 |
> | A coarse 8qr. Coverlet | £1.2.0 |

---

[91] Pepys Diary, 20 August 1666.

[92] Pepys Diary, 21 August 1666.

[93] Pepys Diary, 22 August 1666.

[94] Cox (2000), *The Complete Tradesman*, p. 75. See also Walsh, C. (2003), 'Social meaning and social spaces in the shopping galleries of early modern London', in Benson and Ugolini (2003), *A Nation of Shopkeepers*, pp. 52–80.

[95] Cox (2000), *The Complete Tradesman*, pp. 32–3.

[96] Historic Manuscripts Commission, Salisbury, xiii, 609–10, cited in Lipson, E. (1948), *Economic History of England*, II, p. 92.

| 2 middle blankets | £1.13.6 |
| One beasil or Holland tyke or bolster | £1.4.0 [97] |

A year later, Moore was buying further goods from the same dealer. He recorded how: 'I payd to William Clowson, itinerant upholsterer, for 6 yds, and 3 qrs. of Bristol carpeting at 3s. a yd., £1.'[98]

The opposite extreme of a customer calling on the maker and ordering bespoke goods is found in the example of Sir Richard Legh of Lyme Hall, Cheshire. In a letter written to his wife from London *circa* 1675, he wrote:

> Went to see the famous pendulum maker Knibb, and have agreed for one [clock] ... I have agreed for one finer than my father's and it is to be better finished ... I would have had it in olive wood (the case I mean), but gold does not agree with that colour, so took their advice to have it black ebony, which suits your cabinet better than walnut tree wood, of which they are mostly made. Let me have thy advice herein by the next.[99]

The reply was positive, but the letter reveals far more than an agreement between husband and wife. The concern with having a 'finer' object than his father's indicates the buyer's desire to advance himself, and the acceptance of the maker's advice regarding colouring, which is then justified by Legh's remarks about existing furniture, shows something of the complexity of making a purchase at this level.

Setting up home was not only a matter of shop purchases or buying from an itinerant salesman. Possessions could be acquired in other ways. The purchase of second-hand goods was common, as the role of the upholsterer as an appraiser and second-hand furniture dealer confirms. This purchase of second-hand goods also reveals the nature of the market that could be made from discarded, probably less fashionable, goods that were replaced or even part-exchanged by customers for new. These sorts of goods could also be bought direct from an executor's sale. The evidence of an inventory dated 25 February 1565, of the yeoman Thomas Sudbury of South Muskam, shows that the executors sold livestock, kitchen equipment and the following used furniture:

> To John Pele, who bought a truss bed, a featherbed, a mattress and a bolster, a pillow and 2 blankets and one coverlet for £1.13.4d.
> To William Wallys, an aumbre for 4s.
> To Christopher Simpson, a mattress and a painted cloth 5s.
> To Margaret Maple, a chair for 7d.[100]

---

[97] Diary of the Revd Giles Moore, *Sussex Archaeological Society Transactions*, 1 (1848), pp. 65–127, cited by Davis, D. (1966), *A History of Shopping*, p. 143.

[98] Dictionary of Traded Goods Project, Wolverhampton, Ref. Moore 16/04/1657 SY0141MREG.

[99] Cited in Scott, A. F. (1974), *Every One a Witness: The Stuart Age*, p. 84.

[100] Kennedy, P. A, (1963), *Nottinghamshire Household Inventories*, Thoroton Society, 22, pp. 85–9.

In other cases, valuable textiles and furniture items, for example, would be inherited upon death or purchased from an executor's sale.[101] A third instance is by gift. Mrs Elizabeth Freake noted in her diary for 16 July 1698 that:

> My dear sister Norton sent me towards furnishing my bare walls. A large fine tortoiseshell cabinet, which now stands in my best chamber, valued at near a hundred pounds ... My dear sister Austin sent me towards my house furniture, five great china jars for my best chamber (now in my closet carefully laid up by Eliz. Freake). And a new long cane squab-now stands in the great parlour.[102]

Elizabeth also made purchases on her own volition: 'About the same time I bought myself a new green damask bed, and all my tapestry hangings for the parlour and two chambers and the dining room; with two great glasses.'[103]

For much of the populace, the purchase of goods for the home was primarily a functional necessity, but there was clearly a growing sense that goods, for the middle ranks at least, could easily become the site of new kinds of meanings, particularly cultural meanings, which were applied over the old moral imperatives of the Renaissance. Furniture, for example, might be seen as a valuable possession to be handed down to later generations, an expression of fashionable taste, or a reflection of a person's self-image rather than simply a functional object. It could also be said that the idea of comfort and 'homeliness' were beginning to be identified, as was the suggestion that the character of the owner might be expressed through their possession of particular goods and their disposition within the home. The growth in house building and urban living, developments in retail and transport infrastructures, and an increasing range of goods to engage with, indicate that trade and commerce were the catalysts for change, which gave people the opportunity to make themselves through their possessions. The house was one of the most important sites for this process. It was in the eighteenth century that these ideas developed further and more rapidly than ever.

---

[101] See Campbell, T. (1990), 'Cardinal Wolsey's tapestry collection', *Antiquaries Journal*, 76.

[102] Freake, Mrs E. (1698), *Diary 1671–1714*, entry for 16 July 1698, cited in Scott (1974), *Every One a Witness: The Stuart Age*.

[103] Ibid.

Chapter 3

The rise of the retail tastemaker: eighteenth-century furniture and furnishing retailing and distribution

> The finest shops are scattered up and down the courts and passages. The grand company which they draw together, the elegant arrangement and parade made by the shops, whether in stuffs exposed to sell, fine furniture, and things of taste, or the girls belonging to them, would be motive sufficient to determine those that walk, to make their way in preference to any other. (Msr Grosley, *Tour*, 1765)

By the early eighteenth century furniture distribution had developed an infrastructure that was fully able to meet the demands of its customers. However, these demands grew rapidly over the century, and the industry had to adapt to the changes. Christina Fowler even suggests that 'by the late 1700s the nation had seen an almost complete reversal in selling methods from those observed as the century dawned'.[1] This does not mean, for example, that fixed shop retailing suddenly appeared and hawking and itinerant selling disappeared, just that the relative significance of these changed considerably over the century and continued to do so within the next. The steady growth of urban centres and the relative decline in agricultural employment meant that urban populations became increasingly reliant on retail outlets for goods, especially foodstuffs. In addition, the expanding population, the changes in standards of living, and improvements in transport infrastructures had an impact on retailing. In the case of the furniture and furnishing trades, the growth of shops, the separation of workshops from showrooms and the role of the retailer as a specialist adviser meant that the structure of the trade changed, as well as the nature of purchasing. In addition, the continuing development of support services such as import-export merchants, transport facilities, finance, advertising and promotion meant that retailing and distribution took on an increasingly important role in the economic life of the country. Shops reshaped and responded to the changing circumstances in both number and size. By mid-century, Shop Tax information gathered in 1759 showed around 140 000 retail premises, of which one sixth were in London. The later Shop Tax of 1786 focused on specialist retail outlets, and excluded artisans selling their own

---

[1] Fowler, C. (1999), 'Changes in provincial retailing during the eighteenth century, with particular reference to central-southern England', in Alexander, N. and Akehurst, G. (Eds), *The Emergence of Modern Retailing, 1750-1950*, p. 40.

products.[2] Estimates are that the majority of rural parishes over most of England had shops, earlier in occurrence in the south and later in the north.[3] Although it is impossible to know the number and location of furniture and furnishing shops it seems that they were concentrated in urban areas as that was where the customer base was located or drawn to. In one calculation, it has been estimated that by the 1750s the ratio of shops to population in London was not to be exceeded until the end of the nineteenth century.[4] Without doubt, the eighteenth century saw the growth and consolidation of a retail sector that was distinct from manufacturing and making.

As we have seen in the example of Pepys, apart from any purely commercial aspects, shops proved to be important arenas for experiencing goods and developing consumption practices, both for men and women. It is clear that 'selling was a very active process of sustained social interaction between seller and prospective buyer and [it is evident] that women played important roles in both capacities'.[5]

On the evidence of expansion, it might be assumed that it was relatively easy to establish a business, but to operate profitably over a lengthy period was quite another matter. The skills associated with successful retailing had to be quickly assimilated, often alongside the production and development of the products that were being sold. The selection of an appropriate site, the choice and training of staff, the shrewd purchase of stock, the promotion of the business, the setting of levels of service, the management of credit and accounts, and the importance of client satisfaction were all of utmost consequence in maintaining a viable business. In addition to these practical aspects, there needed to be a demand for the goods offered, and an ability to satisfy that demand: only then could a successful business in furniture distribution operate. This chapter examines some of these aspects.

The role of retailer

The furniture retailer (amongst many others) had a dual relationship with his customers. On the one hand, he was responsible for undertaking and responding to the orders of his clients in this service-oriented business where advertisements often requested consumers to favour the particular supplier with their 'commands'. On the other hand, the furniture retailer was also an arbiter of taste, one who could advise, guide and instruct the customers on

---

[2] See Cox, N. (2000), *The Complete Tradesman*, p. 34–5.

[3] See Chapter 2 in Cox (2000), *The Complete Tradesman*.

[4] Mui, H. C. and Mui, L. H. (1989), *Shops and Shopping in Eighteenth Century England*, pp. 44–5.

[5] Glennie P. and Thrift, N. (1996), 'Consumers identities and consumption spaces in early modern England', *Environment and Planning* A, 28, p. 34.

matters of elegant furnishings. The furniture retailer then had a dual role as a consultant and as a servant. This developing relationship was not only one-way. By inviting customers to be attended to in his particular shop, the merchant was offering goods that were supposed to express a dignity and gentility (only found there), so the act of buying them actually conferred these aspects onto the purchaser. The customers were initiated into the culture of shopping in all its manifestations, so that in the best circumstances the retailer was the conduit for the purchase of good taste, comfort and gentility that the consumers would then display as their own.

On the other hand, the pleasures of shopping and the purchase of goods were tempered by the consumer's growing need to be aware of changing fashions, the value of goods and the levels of service on offer by competing retailers. In many cases the buyer had to have a relationship with the seller that was, to a degree, quite personal, and which not only encompassed the supply of goods but also other services, of which credit was probably the most important. The personal relationship was important, as Carrier has identified, as the goods were often seen as possessions acquired from one by another, rather than impersonal 'traded' commodities.[6] Furniture falls into this categorization, especially where the seller was also the maker, and there are often mentions by diarists and letter-writers referring to 'my upholsterer' or 'my mercer'. By the early nineteenth century, these patterns began to be modified as production methods changed, and retailing altered as a result. The whole process became more impersonal, especially in the lower ends of the trade. Nevertheless, in the more exclusive furniture and house furnishing businesses, something like the personal service image of the 'family solicitor' still remained.[7]

Location

Although the eighteenth century saw some major changes in retail operations, there was also much continuity with the past. For example, at one level of trade, the shop was still often located at the home of the seller. The family worked in the business, apprentices lived with the family and the tasks of running a home and a shop were intertwined. On another level of trade, the establishment of showrooms separate from workshops became an increasing feature, whilst rural communities might still purchase from local craftsmen, itinerants or by a form of 'mail order'.

Therefore, the location of eighteenth-century furniture businesses seems to have been brought about by a mix of tradition, convenience and planning.

---

[6] Carrier, J. G. (1994), 'Alienating objects: the emergence of alienation in retail trade', *Journal of the Royal Anthropological Institute*, 29, pp. 363–5.

[7] Ibid., p. 367–9. This idea of a professional rather than a tradesman is further developed in the nineteenth century.

Traditionally, most trades had tended to locate themselves within a particular quarter of a town, although this location changed according to trading patterns. Convenience was a factor, as from a practical point of view it was advisable to establish workshops close to suppliers and showrooms close to the customer base. Planning was based on careful noting of the movement of populations and their tastes, the location of raw material sources, and the changing characteristics of a neighbourhood.

The prime location for a furnishing business in England had to be London. Defoe, in his preface to *The Complete English Tradesman*, commented upon the importance of the capital as a market.[8] He noted that all the counties of England relied upon the city of London for the consumption of their products and employment of their peoples. It was not only the pre-eminent centre for furniture-making, but also the main port for raw materials' importation, as well as for the export of finished goods, in addition to being its own largest market. The example of London can also help to explain the locational factors mentioned.

While the trade relied on bespoke orders and remained in a handicraft stage, it was essential for the maker to be close to his customers and his fellow suppliers. As the centre of gravity of society moved westward from the old City of London that had supported centres such as Cheapside and Cornhill, the area around St Paul's Cathedral developed a close concentration of furniture-makers who had moved there from other areas of the City. After the Great Fire of 1666, the fashionable centre of London again moved westward towards the newly developed areas of Bloomsbury Square, St James' Square and Red Lion Square. In the first three quarters of the eighteenth century, in the alleys and courts around Covent Garden and St Martins Lane, the most fashionable cabinet-makers and upholsterers worked to service this trade. Examples of these furniture businesses include famous names such as William Vile and John Cobb, John Bradburn, Thomas Chippendale, William France and Samuel Beckwith, and William Hallett.[9] Incidentally, this was the same area as Wedgwood chose to establish his second London showroom, as Pall Mall was considered 'too accessible to the common folk ... for as you know that my present sett of customers will not mix with the rest of the world'.[10]

By the 1750s there was another wave of development in the fashionable parts of London. Building activity in areas such as Hanover Square, New Bond Street, Grosvenor Square and Berkeley Square, naturally encouraged cabinet businesses to move towards Soho, Bond Street and Golden Square. The carver and gilder Samuel Norman moved to Soho Square after a fire at his Covent

---

[8] Defoe, D. (1826), *The Complete English Tradesman*, Preface.

[9] For more details of these and other makers mentioned, see Beard, G. and Gilbert, C. (Eds) (1986), *Dictionary of English Furniture Makers*.

[10] Wedgwood letter to his partner; Wedgwood Museum MSS E. 18149–25, cited by Adburgham, A. (1979), *Shopping in Style*, p. 64.

Garden premises, while cabinet-makers William Ince and John Mayhew had premises in Broad Street, Golden Square, Marshal Street and Carnaby Market.

In view of this trend, it is not surprising to find that businesses moved quite often. For example, the cabinet-making partnership of John Gordon and John Tait was initially situated in King Street, near Golden Square, for two years from 1772, then moved to Little Argyle Street for a further period of five years. In 1779 the business moved again to Swallow Street, and then finally to Oxford Street.[11]

By the fourth quarter of the century, there was a further expansion of the London population, this time northward. The area round Oxford Street and Tottenham Court Road was developed to service the new building of Portman Square and the Bedford Square areas. To support this trade, there were over twenty-four firms listed as subscribers to Sheraton's *Cabinet Dictionary*, published in 1803. These included the well-established firm of Gillow and Co. in Oxford Street, whilst Mathias Lock (1752) Pierre Langlois (1763) and John McLean (1803) were all found in the nearby Tottenham Court Road.

Another area of eighteenth-century London that witnessed an influx of retail furnishing businesses was Mayfair. According to Hughes, from 1730 to 1790 at least fifty house furnishers had established themselves in Bond Street alone[12] and there were many others in the surrounding streets. However, certain of the 'older' areas remained with enough suppliers to continue to maintain a presence. Broker's Row in Moorfields in the City for example, had at least seven businesses during the 1780s–90s that supplied the export trade as well as the home markets, and in 1803 there were ten businesses listed as Sheraton subscribers.[13] In fact, the Soho area remained an important centre, and even the very old established area of St Paul's Churchyard still supported a few businesses.

From another point of view, the high reputation of London-based businesses was used by craftsmen, who relocated to the provinces, to demonstrate that they had the latest knowledge of fashionable practice and design. At the beginning of the century an example was published in Edinburgh. The *Edinburgh Courant* (29 December 1708) noted that 'there is lately come from London to this place, an Upholsterer who mounts all kinds of Beds after the Newest Fashions.'[14] At the other end of the century an advertisement in the *Derby Mercury* of 1795 made known that a Joseph Cooper 'has now begun the

---

[11] There may be other reasons, but business location based on customer catchment areas was and remains important.

[12] Hughes, G. (1964), 'Furnishers of Georgian Mayfair', *Country Life*, 19 November, pp. 1328–9.

[13] Fleming, E. (1997), 'Staples for genteel living: The importation of London household furnishings into Charleston during the 1780s', *American Furniture*, pp. 344–5.

[14] Pryke, S. (1989), 'A Study of the Edinburgh furnishing trade taken from contemporary press notices 1708-1790', *Regional Furniture*, 3, p. 53.

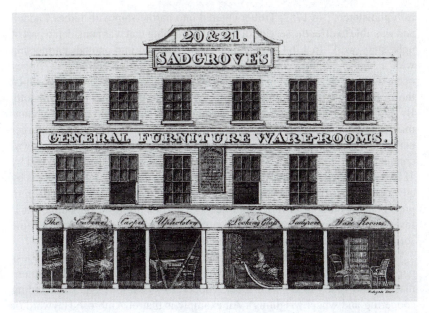

Figure 3.1 Sadgrove, Broker's Row, Moorfields, warehouse trade card

upholstery trade, for which purpose he has engaged a person from London, duly qualified to execute that business in all its branches in the best and most complete manner.'[15] A variation was offered in an advertisement in the *Newcastle Courant* (19 May 1792), where John Dobson pointed out that not only was he a master of the fashionable French and Turkish modes of furnishing, but that through his London contacts he 'assures his friends, the least change of fashions cannot take place, but he will have it sent down immediately'.[16]

These examples demonstrate that the development of a flourishing and status-conscious furnishing business was not limited to the capital. The expansion of other urban centres based on local industries and amenities, meant that cities such as York, Norwich, Bristol, Liverpool and Edinburgh had a range of important and successful retail furnishing outlets.[17] The example of the firm of Trotter in Edinburgh particularly demonstrates the growth of the entrepreneur furniture maker and supplier.[18] The earliest mention of the firm was in 1747, when the business of Robert Young and Tom Trotter was described

---

[15] Symonds, R. W. (1955), *Furniture-making in 17th and 18th Century England*, pp. 130–31.

[16] Stabler, J. (1991), 'English newspaper advertisements as a source of furniture history', *Regional Furniture*, 5, p. 96.

[17] See, for example, Gilbert, C. (1976), 'Wright and Elwick of Wakefield 1748–1824', and 'George Reynoldson, Upholsterer of York', *Furniture History*, 12, pp 34–50.

[18] Pryke, S. (1992), 'At the sign of the Pelican', *Regional Furniture*, 6, pp. 10–21.

as 'upholsterers'. In 1752, Trotter entered into partnership with James Caddell and was able to offer the service of funeral furnishing that was considered part of upholstery work. In 1764 Young and Trotter entered into another partnership with a 'cheap oriental carpet maker' to make Scotch carpets. In 1772 they opened a new 'Wareroom' in Princes Street specifically for cabinetwork, whilst the Upholstery warehouse remained in the original premises in Luckenbooth. By 1773 the business was formally designated as 'Upholsterers and Cabinet-makers', although they had been supplying cabinetwork since 1754. A merger between Young and Trotter and the rival business of William Hamilton was completed in 1790, and in 1797 Trotter's son William joined the firm, so that by 1805 it was called William Trotter. In 1797 the firm demonstrated its success by advertising that 'the extensive stocks they employ in the trade enables them to prevent being outdone in variety or price'.[19] This practice is not uncommon, and reveals how a business could grow organically and in some cases become something of an institution in a community.

In terms of service, the role of the furniture maker who was located in less populous areas was more general and wide-ranging. At its basic level, furniture making had much to do with local woodcrafts of various types (excluding coopering and wheel wrighting). An example is that of Ambrose Hayward of Selling in Kent, a general woodworker, who is recorded as making furniture including bed-settles, chairs and dressers.[20] On the other hand, some rural firms were able to offer a full service comparable to large cities. The details of the firm of William Bastard of Blandford, Dorset, are also instructive.[21] Not only were they offering full building, joinery and cabinet-making services, but also had facilities and materials for japanning, silvering of mirrors, the supply of glass and the finishing of furniture. One intriguing aspect of the inventory that Polly Legg has published is the reference to stocks in 'the shop next the street'.[22] Legg suggests that this was part showroom and part store, based on the wide range of objects (which include raw materials, finished products, tools and accessories) and the quantities mentioned. What seems clear, though, is that the business had a shop frontage on the street.

Showrooms

The separation of the 'shop' from meaning the maker's work and sales place to being a place of display of goods only was important. The 'interiorization' of the shopping process was central to the changing relationship between the buyer

---

[19] *Edinburgh Evening Courant*, 2 December 1797, cited in Pryke (1992), 'At the sign of the pelican', p. 19.

[20] Gilbert, C. (1991), *English Vernacular Furniture*, p. 17.

[21] Legg, P. (1994), 'The Bastards of Blandford', *Furniture History*, 30, pp. 15–42.

[22] Ibid., p. 27.

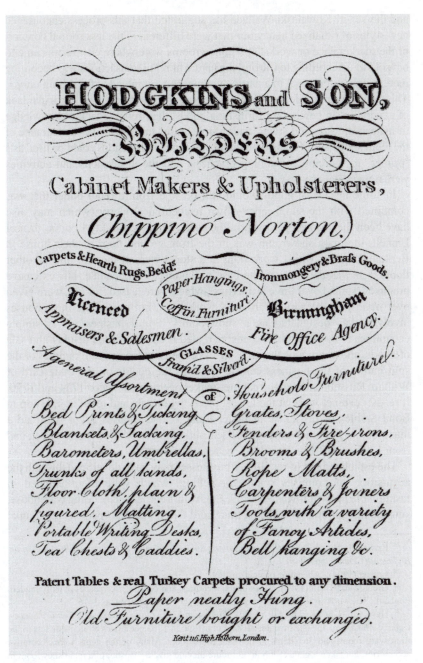

Figure 3.2 Hodgkins and Son trade card

and the seller. Kowaleski-Wallace has suggested that this process encouraged new styles of ritualized behaviour that were different to the less formal contacts of the marketplace or workshop.[23] Showrooms were where customers came to be 'sold to'. According to Carrier, the nature of retail transactions was becoming increasingly impersonal in a particular environment intended for selling only.[24] This trend towards 'alienation' was often aided by the customers' particular lack of experience in purchasing furnishing goods, their relative lack of knowledge of materials, tastes and styles, and in some cases the 'exclusive' appearance of the retail shop itself. On the other hand, it is evident that shops could be used as a 'primer' in sourcing consuming practices, and the discussions and activities were not always one-way.[25]

In some instances, goods would still be sold from a retail outlet that was combined with the shopkeeper's own residential property (which may also have been the workshop). Even in the case of the top-quality London firm of Linnell, the main showroom was in the front ground floor of their house in Berkeley Square, whilst workshops and stores were at the rear and on other floors.[26] It was the same in the case of Thomas Chippendale. His extensive premises (spread over three properties), which were leased in 1753, were given over mainly to the various artisans' workshops, but one of the three houses involved was designated as a showroom.[27] For a business, it is simple economics to use the more expensive rented premises for the display and sale of goods, and to produce the items in less expensive locations. Examples of the split nature of the business can be found in the details on the trade card of William Russell, a turner and cabinet-maker operating between 1754 and 1770. It reads: 'cabinet work at the lowest prices wholesale and retail at his shop in Bond Stables or his house in Fetter Lane',[28] and Charles Pryor who had a manufactory in Paradise Row, Chelsea, and a shop at 96 New Bond Street, and from 1790, at 472 The Strand.

The establishment of retail-only businesses may have developed through the acquisition of premises solely for selling, which were often situated in fashionable parts of towns. In 1759, Caldwall's carpet and bedding warehouse, situated at Holborn, published a trade card that noted that 'persons residing at

---

[23] Kowaleski-Wallace, E. (1997), *Consuming Subjects: Women Shopping and Business in the Eighteenth Century*, pp. 79–81.

[24] Carrier (1994), 'Alienating objects', p. 369.

[25] Glennie and Thrift (1996), 'Consumers, identities, and consumption spaces in early modern England', The whole article has informed this section, but see especially pp. 34–6.

[26] Hayward, H. and Kirkham, P. (1980), *William and John Linnell, Eighteenth Century London Cabinet-Makers*, p. 45. The inventory listing drawn up in 1763 comprises 88 items or sets in the front ware room, and 367 items in the back ware room. Many of the items were decorative accessories, but taken together with the furniture they do give a snapshot of a retail showroom in the mid-eighteenth century.

[27] Gilbert, C. (1978), *The Life and Work of Thomas Chippendale*, p. 22.

[28] Heal, A. (1953), *The London Furniture Makers*, p. 154.

the court end of town may likewise be served at his warehouse in Piccadilly'.[29] Variations occurred in the arrangement of businesses. In 1799 George Oakley, had a stock of goods 'for supplying the wholesale houses and their customers in the City' at 35 St Paul's Churchyard, and at 67 New Bond Street he operated an 'elegant printed furniture warehouse'.[30] This shop had a high reputation. In 1805 the London correspondent of the Weimar publication *Journal de Luxus und der Moden* wrote: 'all people with taste buy their furniture at Oakeleys [*sic*] the most tasteful of the London cabinet-makers'.[31]

The eighteenth-century use of the term 'warehouse' often corresponded with a retail display. For example, the business of Warren and Co., which in 1763 was listed in directories as a 'warehouse for all sorts of elegant furniture, pictures, china etc.' in Vine Street, Piccadilly, was clearly operating as a retailer.[32] By the middle of the eighteenth century, these kinds of 'wareroom shops' grew in numbers and in the splendour in which they were fitted out. Writing at mid-century, one anonymous author described cabinet-makers' showrooms in the following manner:

> Many of their shops are so richly set out that they look more like palaces and their stocks are of exceeding great value. But this business seems to consist, as do many others, of two branches, the maker and the vendor; for the shopkeeper does not always make every sort of goods that he deals in, though he bears away the title.[33]

'Bearing away the title' is an important indicator that shopkeepers not only sold other makers' goods but that they had instigated a form of 'own-label' branding to identify the goods they sold. Therefore, it is probable that some trade labels found on items of eighteenth-century furniture refer to the retailer rather than to the actual maker. In any event, it seems clear that the 'label' was an agent of trade that was mostly used for advertising and far less to identify furniture.[34] There would be no real need to apply such labels for immediate local consumption, which seems to suggest a wider network of supply. In advertising terms, these agents of trade are a reminder that would bring a customer back to the particular shop for another item, or they might act as a recommendation to another customer.[35]

---

[29] Ibid. p. 33.

[30] Edwards, R. (1964), *The Shorter Dictionary of English Furniture from the Middle Ages to the Late Georgian Period*.

[31] Cited in Edwards (1964), *The Shorter Dictionary of English Furniture*, entry for Oakley.

[32] Warren and Company was a long-lasting business: By 1795, it was trading in Coventry Street, in Bond Street by 1808, and in Air Street, Piccadilly, from 1811 to 1819.

[33] *General Description of All Trades* (1747), quoted in Joy, E. T. (1968), *The Connoisseur's Complete Period Guides*, p. 544.

[34] See Introduction to Gilbert, C. (1996), *Pictorial Dictionary of Marked London Furniture, 1700–1840*.

[35] Lovell, M. (1991), 'Such furniture as will be profitable: The business of cabinet-making in eighteenth century Newport', *Winterthur Portfolio*, 26(1), p. 44.

Whatever the case, many tradesmen who were designated as cabinet-makers and/or upholsterers were operating as entrepreneurs involved in buying and selling, rather than being primarily engaged in producing furniture. Indeed, the issues of the introduction of novelties (designing), management, and accounting often took them away from the bench. Writing in 1767, Justus Moser observed that:

> The trading craftsman in England first learns his trade, then he studies commerce, The journeyman of a trading cabinet maker must be as qualified an accountant as any merchant … [The master] will keep in touch with people of taste and visits artists who might be of assistance to him.[36]

A further distinction between the functions of wholesaling and retailing was also often blurred. The trade cards of furnishing businesses frequently stated specifically that the business was wholesale or retail, or a combination of both. For example, Stephen Wood, a London cabinet-maker, noted on his trade card, *circa* 1725, that 'Gentlemen, Merchants, and Country Chapmen may have the best of goods, wholesale or retail at the lowest prices.'[37] The reference to Chapmen perhaps indicates a truly wholesale function as a supplier to itinerant traders, and reminds us that the role of the itinerant vendor was still of some commercial importance. In a similar manner, the cabinet-maker and upholder: Thomas Draper of Lower Moorfields noted on his trade card 'Merchants, country shopkeepers and dealers may be supplied wholesale upon the very best of terms and on the shortest notice.'[38]

Contrary to these general suppliers of all sorts of furniture, there were specialist retailers who established businesses to meet a particular branch of house furnishing: niche marketing, as a business system was well understood in the eighteenth century. The business of chair supply is a good example. A contemporary commentator wrote in 1747, identifying four separate dealers in chairs.

> Though this sort of household goods [chairs] is generally sold at the shops of cabinet-makers for all the better kinds and at the turners for the more common, yet there are particular makers for each. The cane chair makers not only make this sort (now almost out of use) but the better sorts of matted , leather bottomed and wooden chairs, of which there is a great variety in goodness, workmanship and price; and some of the makers who are also shopkeepers are very considerable dealers from £3000 to upwards of £5000 in Trade. The white wooden, wickers and ordinary matted sort, commonly called kitchen-chairs and sold by the turners are made by different hands but are all inferior employs. Those covered with stuffs, silks etc., are made and sold by the Upholsterers.[39]

---

[36] Cited in Huth, H. (1974), *Roentgen Furniture*, p. 58.

[37] Heal (1953), *The London Furniture Makers*, p. 49.

[38] *Connoisseur Year Book* (1960), p. 21.

[39] Anon., (1747), *A General Description of All Trades*.

The decision to specialize in the retailing of a particular type of merchandise and become known as a specialist in that area was often the route to a successful business. For example, there was the business of supplying goods to meet the taste for Indian and Chinese furnishings that began in the later seventeenth century and continued on and off during the eighteenth century. This taste was met by the likes of Mrs Ann Wraughton (1694), who specialized in the sale of japanned and Indian cabinets in her Covent Garden shop, and Mrs Savage, who ran an 'East India Warehouse over the New Change' (1732).[40]

Another group of specialist retailers dealt in mirrors. Examples of these enterprises were John Minshall's Looking Glass Store of Hanover Square, Luke Young's Looking Glass Manufactory in Covent Garden (with a warehouse in Watling Street to supply merchants, sea-captains and chapmen) and Gumley's looking-glass shop that was established in the gallery over the New Exchange.[41] In the latter case, it is clear that the store was more than just a mirror business, as a contemporary description by Richard Steele of Gumley's shop interior shows: 'In the midst of the walk are set in order a long row of rich tables, on many of which lie cabinets, inlaid or wholly of corals, ambers, in the like parts.'[42] Steele also used Gumley's showroom as the backdrop to his satirical piece:

> I shall now give an account of my passing yesterday morning, an hour before dinner, in a place where people may go and be very well entertained, whether they have, or have not, good taste. They will certainly be well pleased, for they will have unavoidable opportunities of seeing what they most like, in the most various and agreeable shapes and positions, I mean their dear selves. The place I am going to mention is Mr. Gumley's Glass-gallery over the New Exchange … No imagination can work up a more pleasing assemblage of beautiful things, to set off each other, than are here actually laid together.[43]

Niche marketing was often about novelty. Another example shows how retailers searched for 'something different' for their stocks. Richard Wright, writing to John Grimstone on 16 January 1772, mentioned to this client that, he was restocking, revealing that 'I have got a friend that is gon [sic] to China to pick up anything curious.'[44]

---

[40] Heal, A. (1953), *The London Furniture Makers*, pp. 160 and 209.

[41] The New Exchange was built in 1608–9 and was described by Daniel Defoe in his *Tour Through England and Wales* (1724–6): 'The trade for millenary goods, fine lace etc., which was so great above stairs for many years, being since scattered and removed, and the shops, many of them left empty: but those shops of which there were eight double rows above and the shops and offices round it below, with the vaults under the whole, did at first yield a very great sum.' The New Exchange had clearly lost its way, as it was demolished in 1734. See further Walsh, C. (2003), 'Social meaning and social space in the shopping galleries of early modern London', in Benson and Ugolini (Eds), *A Nation of Shopkeepers*.

[42] Steele, R., *The Lover*, 13 May 1715, quoted in Edwards, R. and Jourdain, M. (1955), *Georgian Cabinet Makers*, p. 41.

[43] Ibid.

[44] Gilbert, C. (1976), 'Wright and Elwick of Wakefield 1748–1824', *Furniture History*, 12, p. 45.

Whatever the goods, whether they reflected seasonal changes and novelty or referred more to ideas of stability and hierarchy, they had to be promoted and sold.

Sales and selling

Merchandise was sold in a variety of ways, dependant upon need and circumstance. We have seen from Pepys that some customers at least wanted instant gratification by taking possession of their purchase(s) as soon as possible. The advertising, often on trade cards, that indicated availability from stock was surely an incentive to purchase from that particular dealer. One example will suffice. During the period 1727–44, 'At Hodson's looking glass and cabinet warehouse in Frith Street, Soho, is ready made a great variety of all sorts of furniture in the neatest and most fashionable manner by choice and experienced workmen employed in his own house.'[45] The importance of ready-made and available goods was clear. In 1779 the German traveller J. W. Archenholtz recorded with evident satisfaction that:

> There is for instance a sort of people in London called cabinet-makers, who have always a warehouse filled with every kind of new furniture ready to use … This custom is exceedingly convenient for strangers who come to London with the intention to settle. In a few hours a house may be hired and in a day or two completely furnished.[46]

Selling from stock clearly went on, particularly for the lower to middle markets, but often the case must have been that a customer required something

Figure 3.3   Hodsons warehouse, *c.* 1730–40

[45] Heal (1953), *The London Furniture Makers*, Hodson's Trade Card, p. 80. Whether the reference to house is to be taken literally or not, it is of interest to note that in the retail furnishing trade, businesses were still referred to as 'houses' by members of the trade until quite recently.

[46] Archenholtz, J. W. (1779), *A Picture of England*, pp. 221–2, cited in Lubbock, J. (1995), *The Tyranny of Taste*, p. 170.

slightly different, or in the instance of upholstery, with a cover differing from that in stock, or indeed the goods may have been made to measure. In these cases, the bespoke special order was taken and was probably the prerogative of a different sort of retail outlet.[47]

It seems clear that the range of sales could be from a simple ready-money cash sale right through to a full-scale furnishing of a home. Some retailers appear to have been able to meet any demand. For example, the *circa* 1790 trade card of Robert Mulligan of Mint Street, Southwark, demonstrates the range of services commonly offered by many eighteenth-century furniture retailers. Although he was primarily a sworn appraiser, bedstead maker and undertaker, he also:

> buys and sells all sort of household goods both new and second-hand. Makes cabinet and upholstery work in general and furnishes houses on easy terms, sells by auction household goods estates and merchandise of every kind by commission or otherways and lends money on household furniture.

Although the trade card evidence may be skewed by marketing considerations (they were, after all, a form of advertising), it does reflect the range of businesses that 'furniture retailers' undertook, notably including a range of financial services.

The growth of some businesses was quite impressive. As Pat Kirkham has pointed out, 'the increases in demand for high quality goods was not met by expanding petty production but by increasing the size of firms and the scope of their production'.[48] The progress of a major commission for furnishing a substantial house was quite complicated, and therefore needed a considerable degree of managing. The first task would be to arrange a site visit to measure up rooms and furniture, and to discuss requirements. This would be followed by the preparation of small sketches and estimates. Once the order was placed, the goods would be produced or acquired from suppliers, and subsequently delivered. After dispatch of the finished goods, they would be assembled, set up and fixed. On completion, the bill could be presented.[49]

For the selection of bespoke items or special orders, much use must have been made of pattern books, both of textiles and of furniture designs. The use of pattern books and sketches formed part of the service offered by a competent house-furnishing retailer. In May 1754 James Cullen & Co. advertised in a lengthy text that they had 'useful and ornamental furniture, never executed in this place before, whereof sketches, elegantly drawn may be seen'.[50] The published

---

[47] The Gillow records include numerous examples of special orders with details of the customer, the materials used and so on.

[48] Kirkham (1988) *The London Furniture Trade*, p. 57.

[49] A sophisticated infrastructure was needed to support these businesses. The records of Gillow and Co. give some idea of the documentation and accounting required.

[50] Pryke, S. (1989), 'A study of the Edinburgh furniture trade taken from contemporary press notices 1708–1790', *Regional Furniture*, 3, p. 56.

pattern books of designers and architects were also valuable sales aids. For example, Gillows wrote to a customer in 1765 referring to an enquiry for a bookcase: 'if any of Chippindales [*sic*] designs be more agreeable, I have his book and can execute them and adapt them to the places they are for'.[51] To further assist customer choice, the selection process could have included the inspection of samples of finished work or even models made up for the purpose.[52]

Although advertisements for specific brands or even individual items of furniture are rare in the eighteenth century, the advertising that was carried out usually publicized a retail outlet and its range of products, or a specific sale of stock. The role of advertising was particularly important in explaining what was on offer, not only in terms of goods but also of services. For example, the business of Thomas Fidoe, of the Three Golden Chairs in Cheapside, which operated between 1711 and 1731, stocked 'beds, ready-made … made full fashionable and as well as if bespoke, from nine to thirteen feet high, more or less if required'. [53] The anxieties of provincial customers looking to furnish fashionably their more public rooms were also addressed by similar techniques. In 1755 Mr Pope of London encouraged his customers to buy his new and stylish paper-hangings by offering them 'made according to the plan given, & every breadth match'd & numbered, so that they are put up with the greatest ease by any country upholsterer'.[54] Other promotional tools and marketing methods included visiting clients in their home. In 1774, William Armitage of Leeds offered to wait upon 'any Lady or Gentleman … in any part of the country … not exceeding one day's journey'.[55] If this practice was not convenient, the shopkeeper made himself accessible at all hours, if the example of Thomas Trotter of Edinburgh is anything to go by. In 1781 he wrote that he was available either at his shop in the Luckenbooths from 10 a.m. till 8 p.m., and after that at his house in Gosford's Close.[56]

Pricing and finance

Whatever the size of enterprise, capital expenditure, material costs, overheads and labour charges, all had to be covered in addition to the creation of a profit margin. There was no resale price maintenance in the eighteenth century, and it was common practice for buyers to both haggle about the final price and to delay payment as a matter of course. This often meant that enormous mark-ups were put onto base costs to compensate for these problems that were endemic

[51] Snodin, M. and Styles, J. (2001), *Design and the Decorative Arts Britain 1500–1900*, p. 226.

[52] See Pryke, S. (1994), 'Pattern furniture and estate wrights in eighteenth century Scotland', *Furniture History*, 30, pp. 100–105.

[53] Trade card in Beard and Gilbert (1986), *Dictionary of English Furniture Makers*.

[54] *Public Advertiser*, 15 May1755, cited in Cox (2000), *The Complete Tradesman*, p. 215.

[55] *Leeds Mercury*, 28 July 1774, cited in Mui and Mui (1989), *Shops and Shop Keeping*.

[56] Pryke, S. (1992), 'At the sign of the Pelican', *Regional Furniture*, 6, p. 17.

in the eighteenth century. The ideal of a fair price and open-market dealing, discussed above, was disappearing as the trade developed, and this often caused dispute. One example involved a highly regarded furnishing firm – John Linnell – and their customer, Mr Drake of Shardeloes, Buckinghamshire. He was concerned about the charges made by Linnell for supplying furnishings to his home. Drake consulted another cabinet-maker, a J. Wicksted, for a price appraisal. Wicksted was rather circumspect, and not a little duplicitous in his reply. His letter of 15 September 1768 stated that:

> I think in most of the articles of your bill you are charged rather too much. I never charge more for morine, lace, line fringe &c. than what I have set down … I would good Sir do anything in my power to serve you, but should be very sorry to have my name mentioned upon this occasion, as it is done privately, for I would not do any tradesman a prejudice …[57]

Fine words, but the point was made, if you shop with an important and smart firm such as Linnell, you have to pay the price.

Another well-known and fashionable craftsman, Samuel Norman, also suffered from the indignity of having his prices looked into on more than one occasion. A bill submitted in 1760 by Norman to the Duke of Bedford was queried, and Charles Smith and Robert Hyde then valued the goods. On this occasion, they found the goods 'to be charged the same prices that are general when of equal goodness', but the Duke was determined to reduce the bill by £20.[58] In fact, Norman's financial management appears to have been disastrous, as by 1767 he was declared bankrupt.

The erratic nature of payments and the demand for continual stylistic changes also put great pressure on the cash flow of businesses. Hence, there are many examples of furniture makers entering into business contracts with partners able to supply working capital. The example of Chippendale's business relationships with Rannie and Haig are documented,[59] and despite the pitfalls, the potential profits from furnishing businesses must have encouraged many partnerships on this basis.[60]

A sound financial underpinning for business, often based on credit, was essential when liquidity problems caused by delays in payment were often combined with a chronic bad debt situation. It would appear that many firms suffered at one time or another, and bankruptcy appears to have been a

---

[57] Eland, G. (Ed.) (1947), *Shardeloes Papers of the Seventeenth and Eighteenth Century*, p. 19.

[58] Kirkham, P. (1969), 'Samuel Norman, a study of an eighteenth century craftsman', *Burlington*, August, p. 505.

[59] Gilbert (1978), *The Life and Work of Thomas Chippendale*, pp. 11–15.

[60] See Kirkham, P. (1974), 'The partnership of William Ince and John Mayhew 1759–1804', *Furniture History*, 10, pp. 56–67. The partnership of Ince and Mayhew lasted over forty-five years and had a considerable trade: for example, £17 000 in 1768 and £20 000 in 1796. The partners owned property including a country house and the London business and dwelling. It is of note that they charged the highest premiums for apprentices, which would reflect not only their craft status but also their skills in management and retailing.

common form of demise for these sorts of businesses. Chippendale, in correspondence relating to his firm's commission for Nostell Priory during 1770, sardonically says: 'I have been obliged to do business for ready money only, in order to support myself in the best manner I could and that but very poorly.'[61] Nevertheless, credit had become one of the major tools of business. For relatively expensive items such as furniture, it was a good selling tool, as it was offered not just for delayed payments, but also for the immediate sale of goods, and later payment for them by instalments. In 1707 Christopher Thornton of Southwark noted that 'you may also be furnished with chests of drawers, or looking glasses at any price paying for them weekly as we shall agree'.[62] Indeed, 'easy terms' began to feature in many retailers' literature. Robert Mulligan of Mint Street, Southwark, noted that he 'buys and sells all sorts of household goods both new and second-hand, makes cabinet and upholstery work in general, furnishes houses on easy terms, sells by auction household goods … and lends money on household furniture …'.[63]

The relations with a small number of highly influential and exclusive customers who only settled their accounts annually (or less frequently) could have the effect of putting traders in a vulnerable position. That was less likely to occur in the case of those who dealt only in cash sales with the middling sort. One example of a furniture retailer who faced this challenge directly was George Oakley of 8 Old Bond Street. Not only did he operate on a cash-only basis, but also he appears to haved displayed prices on the goods in his shop. His trade card (*circa* 1809–14) stated that:

> The number of artists and mechanics as well as the large capital necessarily employed in this concern, together with the extensive stock kept for ye accommodation of the public are obvious reasons, which render it impossible to conduct it by giving credit. The lowest price is therefore annex'd to every article for ready money or good bills …'[64]

Whilst many cabinet-making firms suffered cash-flow problems through wealthy patrons delaying payments of their accounts, in other circumstances profit margins were squeezed by demands for discounts. The correspondence of Bristol businessman John Pinney illustrates this. In 1791 he wrote to one cabinet-maker:

> As I am desirous of paying ready money for every article I purchase for family use, I request you will furnish me with your Account charging the lowest Cash prices, or allow me a discount, if charged at the credit price, which ever you please.[65]

---

[61] Gilbert (1978), *The Life and Work of Thomas Chippendale*, p. 33.

[62] British Museum, Heal Collection.

[63] Heal (1953), *London Furniture Makers*, p. 116.

[64] British Museum Banks Collection, DE 627.

[65] Walton, K. M. (1976), 'Eighteenth century cabinet-making in Bristol', *Furniture History*, 12, pp. 59–63.

At the other extreme, the issue of credit caused many problems. James Brown, an upholsterer in London, had to claim payment from his customer the Revd Daniel Williams in the ultimate manner. The Reverend's goods were auctioned off in 1791 to pay Brown's bill, originally submitted seven years earlier in 1784.[66] In 1792 the accounts of another upholsterer, Thomas Devenish, showed that he had book debts outstanding for over ten years. His executors recorded his list of debtors in 1802, and noted them as either (a) good, easy to collect, (b) repayable by instalments, (c) bad or irretrievable, or (d) exceeded the Statute of Limitations.[67] These various examples indicate a market place that was supported by a variety of financial mechanisms, which, whilst widely recognized, had to be kept under control. These mechanisms were another demonstration of the beginning of a mature and established trade.[68]

Retail shops and business types

During the eighteenth century, manufacturing and distribution of furniture had developed into a reasonably complex set of interconnected business types that were organized on a number of levels. These included (a) working masters or journeymen making furniture in their own workshops for wholesalers or retailers, (b) the integrated manufacturing firms operating from extensive premises (including showrooms), combining a variety of skilled workmen, which sold direct to clients, (c) craftsmen-shopkeepers working from their own premises both making and selling, and (d) furniture retailers with showrooms that sold bought-in goods. The latter three types sometimes operated appraising, auctioneering and second-hand departments as well.

The working masters were described in 1747 as 'those masters who keep no shops nor stocks but principally follow making and dispose of their goods as fast as they are finished'.[69] They were essentially producers, but in some instances they sold goods to the public. The same description continues with reference to cabinet-makers, and says that: 'if a person is only a working master, £100.00 besides his tools will do tolerably, [to set up a business] but if he keeps stock for sale, it may increase accordingly to two or three thousand'. These working masters were established in many towns. An indication of the organization of some Parisian examples probably reflects a general situation. In the 1737 inventory of Jean Boucault, there was a shop and a small storage room, but merchandise was listed in the basement and the bedroom, where, in addition to his own furniture, were 24 armchairs, 6 frames and 6 other chairs. In

---

[66] PRO c107.109.

[67] City of Westminster Archives, Devenish Letter Book.

[68] For a discussion of retail credit generally in the eighteenth century, see Cox (2000), *The Complete Tradesman*, Chapter 5.

[69] Anon. (1747), *A General Description of All Trades*.

another example in the same city, two chambers on the first floor of a master cabinet-maker's house held 36 tables, 8 pedestal tables, 24 armchairs, 12 chairs, 9 stools, a bed and 8 bedsteads.[70]

The second category, an integrated manufacturing firm,[71] was able to deal with any furnishing requirement, from a window blind to a complete house-furnishing scheme. This business type was the mainstay of the quality trade until the late nineteenth century. Well-known eighteenth-century examples include the businesses of Gillow and Co., Vile and Cobb, Linnell, Chippendale, and Seddon. These firms' surviving documents have been analysed and published in a variety of forms.[72]

A first-hand account of this sort of business is found in the 1786 journal of Sophie von La Roche, a visitor to London. She described her visit to Seddon's premises and recorded that 400 apprentices were employed on 'any work connected with the making of household furniture- joiners, carvers, gilders, mirror workers, upholsterers, girdlers-who mould the bronze into graceful patterns-and locksmiths'.[73] This workforce was:

> housed in a building with six wings. In the basement, mirrors are cast and cut. Some other departments contain nothing but chairs, sofas and stools of every description, some quite simple other exquisitely carved and made of all varieties of wood and one large room is full up with all the finished articles in this line.[74]

Having discussed the manufacturing part of the business Sophie also recorded the showroom:

> One large room is absolutely filled up with finished articles in this line [carved woods] while more rooms are occupied by writing-tables, cupboards, chests of drawers, charmingly fashioned desks, large and small chests, work cum toilet tables made of every possible kind of wood and in every possible form, from the simplest and cheapest to the most elaborate and expensive.[75]

The comprehensiveness of the firm is indicated by Sophie's comment: 'The entire story of the wood as used for both inexpensive and costly furniture and the method of treating it can be traced in this establishment.' The firm's growing commercial success can be followed through the value of their fire

---

[70] Paradailhé-Galabrun, A. (1991), *The Birth of Intimacy, Privacy, and Domestic Life in Early Modern Paris*, pp. 113–4.

[71] Pat Kirkham identifies this group as 'the comprehensive manufacturing firm'.

[72] For Gillow, see Gillow & Co. Archives, Westminster Public Library and Archives; for Linnell, see Hayward, H. and Kirkham, P. (1980), *William and John Linnell, Eighteenth Century London Furniture Makers*, and for Chippendale see Gilbert, C. (1978), *The Life and Work of Thomas Chippendale*.

[73] Williams, C. (Trans.) (1933), *Sophie in London*, 1786, pp. 173–5.

[74] Ibid., p. 174.

[75] Gilbert, C. and Wood, L. (1997), 'Sophie von la Roche at Seddons', *Furniture History*, 33, p. 31.

insurance cover. In 1756, Seddon's was covered for £500; by 1770 the amount was £7700, and by 1787, it had risen to £17 500.[76]

Descriptions of the London-based business of Linnell, made in 1763, are also exceptionally revealing of a major complete furnishing company. In this case, the premises included a cabinet shop, a glass room, a chair room, an upholsterer's shop, a carver's shop, a gilder's shop, storerooms, counting house, the joiner's shop and a sawpit and showrooms.[77] Again, here is an example of virtually complete vertical control over all the processes of furniture making and selling from primary timber conversion through finishing processes, to the fitting up in the customer's house. This control ensured that important commissions could be properly attended to, and that customers received personal service.

There was also a trend towards the co-ordination of the distribution function under an upholsterer or cabinet-maker. These were often based on the amalgamation of trades: for example a cabinet-making business might grow to include chair-making and glass dealing, a carver might include gilding in his repertoire, and chair-makers might become upholsterers. Partnerships of cabinet-makers and upholsterers often developed into highly successful businesses. The example of Ince and Mayhew, whose business lastedforty-five years, testifies to this.[78] Over all these (and other) possible changes, the major development was the rise of the upholsterer to become the controlling force in the supply of furnishings and decorations.[79]

It was clearly most profitable, as well as being practical for the customer, for one firm to provide all the needs of a client's furnishings, even if they were not all made by the same supplier. Indeed, the coordinator could take a profit on any sub-contracted work; therefore, the more comprehensive the range of trades that were under one controlling management, the more successful the business might be. The entrepreneurs who developed these comprehensive firms were mainly based in their own workshops, though they employed other craftsmen to supplement their own skills. This enabled them to work at their own specialisms whilst acting as co-ordinators of others' products.[80] A useful example of this is the 1792–5 report of an upholsterer who had trade accounts with smiths, turners, stonemasons, bricklayers, painters, plasterers, plumbers, glaziers, paperhangers, tin men and suppliers of ceramic requisites.[81] This

[76] Hughes, G. (1957), 'George Seddon of London House', *Apollo*, 65, pp. 177–81.

[77] Kirkham, P. (1967), 'The careers of William and John Linnell', *Furniture History*, 3, p. 31.

[78] Kirkham, P. (1974), 'The Partnership of William Ince and John Mayhew 1759–1804', *Furniture History*, 10, pp. 56–9.

[79] For a discussion about the practice of the upholsterer, see Fowler, J. and Cornforth, J. (1984), *English Decoration in the Eighteenth Century*, Chapter 4, and Edwards, C. (2001), 'Organisation of the trade of the eighteenth century upholsterer', in Mertens, W. (Ed.), *Interior Textiles in Western Europe 1600–1900*.

[80] This section acknowledges the work of Pat Kirkham, and her definitions of the comprehensive manufacturing firm.

[81] Unknown cause, PRO C 114/181.

same upholsterer, from his London shop, supplied goods to a range of customers in towns as different as Beamish, Dublin and Southampton. Also of interest is his client list, which included both ends of the social scale and an absolutely extraordinary range of sales. At one end were the Margrave of Ansbach and the Earle of Ormonde, the latter being billed with an account of £5746.13s.3d. At the other end of the social spectrum, the upholsterer charged a Mr F. Ford, the amount of 4s.6d. for taking down a bed, and he also charged a Mr L. Burton, 2s.2d. for supplying 6 yards of chintz.

The third group, the craftsmen-shopkeepers who made and/or sold furnishings, were distinguished from working masters by Collyer as follows:

> Those who work only for shops [working masters], and keep no goods by them, take ten pounds with an apprentice who when out of his time may commence such another master with only a chest of tools of value eight to ten guineas and a little wood; but they who keep shops and vend their own goods to the consumer, or for exportation, have more with a lad, who will require a few hundreds if he sets up in the same manner.[82]

One example of this type of craftsman-shopkeeper is Abner Scholes of Chester, whose inventory was drawn up in 1736. He sold goods to both private customers and other retailers. He also purchased from other cabinet-makers and chair-makers, as well as suppliers of soft furnishings.[83] At the other end of the century, a valuable example of the same sort of trading is the business of James Eykyn of Wolverhampton. His clientele included other tradesmen, manufacturers, and the landed elite of the Black Country and parts of Shropshire. Although he clearly produced furniture and furnishings in his own workshop (attached to his premises), he was also a retailer of the many ancillary items required for the home.[84]

The distinctions between craftsmen and retailer are demonstrated by the example of the business of turners. Turners were clearly divided between 'real mechanics' and a 'set of shopkeepers, many of them in a very large way [who] engross as to the buying and selling part, all the produce of the real turners and many trades beside'.[85] As the turners were split between makers and sellers, so it was with another important craft. The upholsterers who were often the leaders amongst the furnishing businesses of the mid-eighteenth century not only made all sorts of soft furnishings but also 'keep large shops in which they

---

[82] Collyer, J. (1761), *Parents and Guardians Directory and the Youth's guide in the choice of a Profession or Trade*, p. 86.

[83] Chester RO Inventory of Abner Scholes 1736 (WS series), cited by Mitchell, I. (1974), 'Urban markets and retail distribution 1730–1815', D Phil.

[84] Collins, D. (1993), 'Primitive or not? Fixed shop retailing before the industrial revolution', *Journal of Regional and Local Studies*, 13(1), p. 29.

[85] Anon. (1747), *General Description of all Trades*. The term 'engrossing' would indicate some kind of wholesale function as well as a retail one.

sell beds, blankets, quilts, counterpanes and some of them deal in all kinds of furniture which they buy of the cabinet-makers, chair makers etc.'.[86]

Mortimer's *Universal Director* (1763) carefully pointed out the distinction between working masters and the fourth group – the retailers. Mortimer only listed those:

> such as either work themselves or employ workmen under their direction; and that not one of those numerous warehouses which sell ready-made furniture bought of the real artist is to be met with in this work, the plan of which is to direct the private gentleman to the fountain-head in every department.[87]

This distinction between custom work and ready-made was important, as it recognized the changes occurring in furniture retailing and was able to guide customers as to the shop type appropriate to them. By 1788, retail-only outlets appeared to be seriously challenging the existing workshop selling arrangements. *The Cabinet-makers' London Book of Prices* complained that:

> The goods manufactured for the use of sale shops is a grievance which it would be pointless to point out to you [the masters] – every man of the smallest consideration must see from what cause that evil arises, and wherein lies the remedy to prevent impositions on the public, and to secure to the fair trader that approbation he so justly merits.[88]

Although the categories used above are helpful in considering the eighteenth-century furnishing trade, there were clearly many overlaps and variations. The distinctions are also blurred due to the wide range of other outlets, including the sale of second-hand, imported or other goods produced by specialists and retailed by various shopkeepers. As was seen in the examples from Pepys's diary, customers would frequent a varied range of shop types, dependant on the particular purchase needs. What is clear is that a true retail function of buying and selling was developing in the furniture business, often without any involvement in the production of the goods sold.

To gauge the growth of the retail furnishing trade in the eighteenth century is not easy, but we can use the results of the historians Mui and Mui, who have tabulated the major trades in London, Bristol, Norwich and Manchester at two points: 1783 and 1822–3. In their household-furnishing category, they show that in London, the percentage of businesses rose from 7.5 per cent to 10 per cent and the number of shops rose from 217 to 1145. In Bristol, the percentage rise was from 6.9 per cent to 10.1 per cent with shop numbers rising from 20 to 113, whilst in Norwich the percentage rise was 12.5 per cent to 14.3 per cent and shop numbers rose from 31 to 67. In Manchester, there was a rise from 4.4 per cent to 8.1 per cent with shop numbers growing from 7 to 77.[89] Although

---

[86] Collyer (1761), *Parents and Guardians Directory*, p. 286.

[87] *Mortimer's Universal Directory*, (1763), p. 11.

[88] Dedication to the First Edition of *The London Cabinet-makers' Book of Prices* (1788).

[89] Mui and Mui, (1989), *Shops and Shopkeeping in Eighteenth Century England*, Table 7, p. 68.

these figures are not accurate, they do give a sense of the upward trend. Mui and Mui have also analysed the profitability of a cross-section of independent businesses in York by investigating the income and expenditure of those businesses upon which taxes were assessed. Although the furniture examples are limited, one instance cited from 1797 shows that the average income of cabinet-makers was £163 (within a range of £100–£200), whilst their expenditure averaged £120 (within a range of £80–200). These average results clearly show a healthy annual surplus of income over expenditure.[90] Despite this, the balance of debits and credits was often fragile. The results of failure were severe for any business, but for others these collapses were sometimes another source of saleable merchandise.[91]

Other outlets

Auctions were a common way of disposing of stock or possessions, particularly in the event of a death or bankruptcy. In some cases the auctions would be carried out at the home of the deceased, in other cases on the premises of the business. A famous example of the latter was conducted on the 17 March 1766, when the *Public Advertiser* published details of an auction sale planned to realize the assets of the partnership of Chippendale and Rannie. Amongst the items in the advertisement were:

> A great variety of fine mahogany and tulip wood cabinets, desks, and bookcases, cloaths presses, double chests of drawers, commodes, buroes, fine library, writing, card, dining and other tables ... fine pattern chairs and sundry other pieces of curious cabinet work ...[92]

Although these items were perhaps aimed at other retailers and the public, the sale of other parts of the business stock, including quantities of timber board, veneer and feathers, were clearly more attractive to trade buyers. In a similar vein were sales of cabinet-makers' stocks-in-trade. The details of these sales can give a picture of the quantities of objects in stock at a furniture making establishment, and an example is worth quoting in full. The advertisement for the sale of Francis Croxford's stock-in-trade in 1733:

> To be sold ... several fine walnut-tree, mahogany, mehone, and other desks and bookcases with glass doors, and several fine mahogany clothes chests ornamented with brass, mahogany, walnut-tree and pigeon-wood quadrille tables, fine mahogany dining tables of all sizes, and dressing glasses and dressing tables of several sorts, walnut-tree, mahogany and

---

[90] Ibid., pp. 62–3.

[91] Sales of 'stock-in-trade' as a result of either bankruptcy or business closure were common. See below.

[92] Quoted in Wills, G. (1969), *English Furniture 1760–1900*, p. 14.

other desks, fine walnut-tree chests upon chests and about one hundred dozen of chairs of several sorts.[93]

The large quantities may give rise to a suspicion about the genuine nature of the sale. Merchants sometimes encouraged sales by offering time-limited inducements. Indeed, the case of the repetition of advertisements (119 times) for the sale of cabinet-maker James Faucon's long list of household goods and works, from 16 February 1731 to 26 September 1732, is unexplained, but may have been simply a marketing tactic. Indeed, it appears that, in America at least, there was a trade in goods made specifically for sale by auction. S. and J. Rawson Jr of Providence, Rhode Island, had labels printed for their furniture which stated: 'Knowing the deception in work made for auction, we trust that if people would examine for themselves, and compare the work and pieces, that businesses, so destructive to all good work and deceptive to the public, would have an end.'[94] Certainly, the 'legitimate' trade elsewhere also took exception to auctions. One correspondent to the *Edinburgh Evening Courant* wrote in March 1788:

> tradesmen and shopkeepers complain much at this time of dullness in business and want of employment ... [a reason for this is] their customers going to sales and roups [auctions] with the ready money they ought to pay their debts with. It is notorious that at some late sales of furniture, higher prices were given than the articles cost a dozen years ago.[95]

Other outlets for goods included lotteries and raffles. These were sometimes organized by individuals, other times by businesses. Pepys explained the process at the lottery of Sir Arthur Slingsby, where:

> good sport it was to see how most that did give their ten pounds did go away with a pair of gloves only for their lot...and one I stayed to see drew a suit of hangings valued at 430L; and they say they are well worth the money.[96]

The goods in this lottery included a coach, plate jewels and a variety of furnishing tapestries, gilt leather hangings, chairs, cabinets and marble tables. Slightly less prestigious but on the same principle was the raffle organized in 1699, by John Renshaw, a London cabinet-maker who offered an 'exceedingly fine desk and bookcase of fine mahogany with embellishments of tortoiseshell and brass'. By buying a raffle ticket for 2s.6d., one had a single chance to acquire the article.[97] The practice continued in the eighteenth century. In 1770,

---

[93] *Daily Post*, 12 July 1733, quoted in Edwards, R. and Jourdain, M. (1955), *Georgian Cabinet Makers*, p. 33.

[94] Monahon, E. B. (1980), 'The Rawson family of Providence Rhode Island', *Magazine Antiques*, July 1980, p. 243.

[95] Pryke (1989) 'A study of the Edinburgh furnishing trade taken from contemporary press notices 1708–1790', pp. 55.

[96] Pepys's Diary, 20 July 1664. Lotteries were granted as favours to private individuals, and were limited in number to eight a year at this time.

[97] Gilbert, C. and Murdoch, T. (1993), *John Channon and Brass Inlaid Furniture 1730–1760*, p. 18.

lottery tickets were sold by the furnishing firm of Wright and Elwick in Wakefield, Yorkshire, where they produced tickets to dispose of 'fine India goods, which we have upon hand'. They sent out letters with a catalogue of the lots with terms, and a batch of tickets for sale to the party addressed and their friends.[98] This was probably a successful sale since soon afterwards Wright was sending to China for re-stocking.[99] The practices of eighteenth century furniture retailers, including limited-time sales, part exchanges, special sales purchases, deferred or weekly payments and so on, became part of the expected ways of doing business and continued in the following centuries.

Despite the establishment of a complex retail system based on shops, the older markets and fairs still played a role in the distributive system, albeit one that was in some decline, in terms of furnishings at least. On 4 June 1763, John Lawson, a cabinet-maker and upholsterer of Cambridge, informed the public through the pages of the *Cambridge Chronicle* that 'he had taken a shop next door to the Black-bean in Bridge Street'. In the same year, he advertised that he would have a 'booth with a very great choice of goods' at the annual Sturbridge Fair, situated just outside Cambridge. Less than a year later, on 7 April 1764, he had moved to Shoemaker Row in Cambridge, and on the 7 June 1766 there was an auction of all the shop's goods, 'as he was leaving off all branches of business except bespoke goods'.[100] This is an interesting example of the various ways a tradesman might operate to maximize his business. In this case, it may not have been enough to survive.

The publication of Owens's *Book of Fairs* in the mid-eighteenth century and its subsequent reprints into the nineteenth century indicate the continuing value of fairs to a range of constituents. The 1756 edition of Owen tells of one fair held at Portsmouth in July with products on sale from cutlers, cabinet-makers, linen and woollen drapers, along with ready-made apparel and bed furniture produced by others.[101] In 1770 Richard Matheson, a cabinet-maker of Southwark, London, advertised in the *Cambridge Chronicle* that 'he sold his goods at the annual Stirbitch (Sturbridge) Fair' which was held in September outside Cambridge.[102] The fairs met the needs of the rural population, but also provided an opportunity for local businesses and the itinerant tradesmen to stock up with goods, so the wholesale function was important until manufacturers began to sell by samples and representatives.

The itinerant salespersons, including chapmen, hawkers, peddlers and Scotchmen, continued to perform an important role in the distribution system. City-based makers and sellers advertised that they supplied chapmen with

---

[98] Gilbert, C (1976), 'Wright and Elwick of Wakefield, 1748–1824', *Furniture History*, 12, pp. 39–650.

[99] See note 44 above.

[100] Beard and Gilbert (Eds), G. *Dictionary of English Furniture Makers*, p. 532.

[101] Cited in Cox (2000), *The Complete Tradesman*, p. 195.

[102] *Cambridge Chronicle*, June 1770.

goods at 'wholesale'.[103] Having purchased stock, the chapmen would travel around selling door-to-door. One recorded example of such a purchase relates to Nicholas Blundell of Liverpool, who in 1723 bought at his door some 'Indian Chink Callico' from a visiting peddler.[104] Although itinerants seemed to provide a useful service to the customers they served, the established retail businesses were often condemning them. The Upholsters' Company had already expressed concerns about the hawking of their wares.[105] Hawking was often considered unfair trading. Mitchell cites the example of the chapman Samuel Reddish, who dealt in upholstery goods. In 1738 he hired a room in the Angel Inn, Macclesfield, and sold carpets and covers, having circulated handbills advertising his arrival. He repeated this process in 1739, and again in 1740. The local authorities eventually wanted to charge him stallage, as he was a hawker.[106] Even more frustrating for established shop-based businesses were the itinerant salespeople who came into a town and set up to sell furniture for a limited period. One example temptingly offered the public 'a large assortment of new furniture to be sold at the lowest prices in the large Assembly Room' in Kirkgate, Leeds, in 1781.[107] Retailers would have objected to this interference with their trade, but the itinerant sellers probably wooed customers by the lure of special 'sales'.

Trading

The buying and selling of furnishing goods beyond the national boundaries had been a part of the trade for centuries. By the eighteenth century the popularity of foreign goods reached massive proportions as the demand for novelty and luxury increased. The demand for Oriental textiles or French *objets d'art* and furniture was high, therefore their importation and sale in shops were profitable. Joshua Gee, in his *The Trade and Navigation of Great Britain Considered*, noted this taste for foreign goods, especially those of France:

> England takes from France, Wine, Brandy, Linen, Fine Lace, Fine Cambricks, and Cambrick Lawns to prodigious Value, Brocades Velvets and many other rich silk Manufactures, which are either run in upon us, or come by way of Holland; the Humour of some of our Nobility and Gentry being such that although we have those Manufacturers made as good, if not better than the French, yet they are forced to be called by the name of French, to make them sell.[108]

---

[103] See note 37 above.

[104] Cited in Cox (2000), *The Complete Tradesman*, p. 122.

[105] See page 28.

[106] Mitchell, I. (1984), 'The development of urban retailing 1700–1815', in Clark, P. (Ed.), *The Transformation of English Provincial Towns 1600–1800*.

[107] Mui and Mui (1989), *Shops and Shopkeeping in Eighteenth Century England*, p. 244.

[108] Gee, J. (1729), *The Trade and Navigation of Great Britain Considered*, p. 13, cited in Saumarez-Smith, C. (1993), *Eighteenth Century Decoration*, p. 138.

The cachet of the French name or label was clearly a selling point. The French had established themselves as the tastemakers and leaders of the luxury goods market since the seventeenth century. This fact was not lost on retailers, who were aware of the important role of fashion in marketing, especially in high-margin products such as luxury furniture and textiles. Therefore, the importation and sale of such goods was common. In the case of French furniture, for example, the importation of finished and semi-finished items was a regular occurrence. One fashionable London-based furnishing partnership was in this business. It temptingly advertised that 'Mayhew and Ince respectfully announce that they have an assortment of French furniture, consigned from Paris, for immediate sale, very much under the original cost, which may be seen at their Warehouse, Broad Street, Soho.'[109]

There were many examples of personal involvement in the direct importing of furniture. According to the Duke of Marlborough, he thought that his waning popularity meant that he might be picked upon by customs officers. Writing from Tournai to the Duchess in 1710, he said:

> I should be glad if you are in London, that you would give Mr Manwaring [cabinet-maker] the trouble of speaking to some at the Custom House. I have sent by Captain Sanders one picture and some looking glasses. They are not of any value; but I find among other marks of declining favour, that I must meet with trouble at the Customhouse. The best way will be to send nothing more from hence; for everything may be had in England perhaps a little dearer.[110]

A less illustrious 'problem case' was recorded in February 1723, when Nicholas Blundell noted how he:

> went to Leverpoole and pay'd Patrick Kelley for a dozen Chears he brought me out of Ireland, but I could not get them out of the Custom-house.
>
> | Irish Chears one Dozen | 02 00 00 |
> | Gratuity to the Sailors | 00 01 00 |
> | Duty for the 12 Chears | 00 10 05½[111] |

To satisfy the demand for products and to avoid excise duty at the same time, the smuggling of furniture (amongst other commodities) became big business. By the mid-eighteenth century the smuggling of furniture into England to avoid duty was clearly a lively trade. The two main methods used were either to declare the items to customs for a lower value as lumber, or to use the services of a diplomat who brought furniture into the country through the 'diplomatic bag' and thus avoid duty entirely.[112]

---

[109] Cited in Wills, G. (1969), *English Furniture 1760–1900*, p. 68.

[110] Cited in McQuoid, P. (1905), *Age of Walnut*, p. 234.

[111] DTG Project: Blundell 11/02/1723 NY0282BLNN.

[112] Wills, G. (1965), 'Furniture smuggling in eighteenth century London', *Apollo*, 82, pp. 112–17.

The avoidance of duty by declaring a lesser value did not mean that the trick always worked. In 1761 the cabinet-maker Thomas Chippendale tried to avoid duty on some particular imports by declaring them below their true value. He was challenged, and on this occasion the customs officers took advantage of the regulations, seized the goods, and only paid the declared worth to Chippendale. This was, of course, much less than their true cost, so Chippendale incurred a large loss, whilst the excise department disposed of the goods at the true market value and made a profit.[113]

The other method, which used the diplomatic bag, was made public in 1772 by a petition of Masters and Journeymen Cabinet-makers of London and Westminster, who complained that the system was allegedly disrupting the employment and livelihood of English cabinet-makers. This plea was not successful and in 1773, there was another attempt to involve Parliament in the problem. This time it was considered, and a committee was appointed to report on the matter.[114] Its report showed that goods that were not for personal use were often imported in the diplomatic bag. The case of Baron Berlindis, the Venetian Resident, proved the point.[115] Goods imported under his name were found in three different cabinet-makers' shops,[116] the most famous being John Cobb, of the Vile and Cobb partnership. These few examples have identified three of the most well-known eighteenth century furnishing businesses involving themselves in dubious practices in order to gain a trading advantage.

Although the degree of interference in trading was meant to be limited, there were, in fact, a number of examples of government actions that were taken, either to encourage exports, or discourage imports of luxury goods, including furnishings. In 1701, for instance, an Act was passed which imposed duties on imported manufactured cabinetwork from the East Indies.[117] This was in response to a petition from London cabinet-makers, joiners and japanners who had complained that this trade was not only hurting home business, but was also hurting their own export trade:

> The large quantities of japan'd goods expected shortly to be brought from the Indies, will not only tend to the ruin of the japan-trade here in England, but will also obstruct the transportation of our English lacquer to all Europe, which is a considerable advancement to His Majesties Customs, whereas the Indian lacquer being exported from hence draws back the custom.[118]

---

[113] Joy, E. (1951), 'Chippendale in trouble at the customs', *Country Life*, 110, 24 August, p. 569.

[114] *Journals of the House of Commons,* Vol. 34, p. 297; Report and Appendix, pp. 349–55.

[115] The items brought in under his name included 76 chair fronts, 24 marble slabs, 18 arm'd chairs, 19 cabriole chairs and many other assorted chair parts.

[116] The three involved were Wall and Riley of Gerrard Street, Cullen of Greek Street, and Cobb of St Martins Lane. Further details can be found in Wills (1965), 'Furniture smuggling in eighteenth century London'.

[117] 12 and 13, Will, c.41.

[118] *Tracts on Trade*, 13(1). The Case of the Japanners of England, 1710.

Attempts to direct parts of the trade and by implication to protect English furniture businesses are nowhere better seen than in the English attitude to the North American colonies. The Commissioners of Trade were informed in 1732 that:

> The people of New England being obliged to apply themselves to manufactures more than other of the Plantations, who have the benefit of a better soil and warmer climate, such improvements have been lately made there in all sorts of mechanic arts, that not only scrutore, chairs, and other wooden manufactures ... are now exported from thence to the other plantations, which if not prevented, may be of ill consequence to the trade and manufacture of this Kingdom.[119]

By using improvements in the mechanic arts, the colonists were not only supplying their own needs but also establishing an export trade to other parts of the Americas. No doubt, the plentiful supply of materials and ease of transport offset the high labour costs that were in themselves commuted by the mechanization of parts of the process.

It also seems that some colonists, probably influenced by religious convictions, were not anxious to own imported goods of the latest London taste. This prudent attitude is evident in contemporary records: 'this man lives well; but though rich, he has nothing in or about his house but what is necessary. He hath good beds in his house but no curtains; and instead of cane chairs, he hath stools made of wood.'[120] Nevertheless, for many of the middle classes of the American trading cities there remained a taste for fashionable imported English goods.

How did people acquire furniture?

As has been shown above, the range or sources for acquiring furniture was quite wide and most of the categories well known to modern readers were available in the eighteenth century. Shops, of course, the craftsmen-makers, agents, auctions, single sales, markets, fairs, lotteries and even smuggling were common. For the purchaser, the process of shopping itself was clearly part of the pleasure of the consumption process. A poem from 1735 demonstrates this well:

> [Lady's taking] their wonted range
> Through India shops to Motteux's or the Change
> Where the tall jars erects its stately pride
> With antic shapes in China's azure dy'd;
> Their careless lies a rich brocade unroll'd
> Here shines a cabinet with burnished gold.[121]

---

[119] Symonds, R. W. (1955), *Furniture-making in 17th and 18th Century England*, p. 71.

[120] Ibid., p. 154.

[121] Dodsley, 'The Toyshop' (1735), cited in Sydney, W. C. (1891), *England and the English in the Eighteenth Century*, Vol. 1, p. 51.

As looking and longing were part of the shopping process, it is not surprising that some shopkeepers spent large amounts of money on the fitting out and decorating of their premises. The German diarist and bluestocking Sophie von La Roche commented upon this phenomenon:

> [she] was struck by the excellent arrangement and system which the love of gain and the national good taste have combined in producing, particularly in the elegant dressing of large shop windows, not merely to ornament the streets and lure purchasers, but to make known thousands of inventions and ideas and spread good taste about.[122]

Sophie saw that shops were more important than simply being an economic conduit. Their role as arbiters of taste was also important. In many cases, they also had an air of exclusivity. G. F. Wendeborn wrote in 1791 of the luxury shops that 'it is not the chance-customer that drops in who supports [these] shops that betray such opulence'.[123] If some were content to visit the fashionable streets and simply indulge in window-shopping, others took the business very seriously.

The question of who undertook the purchasing of home furnishings in the eighteenth century is a problem. Generally, production was characterized as male, and consumption as female. Evidence sends mixed messages that reflect the need for further research. Sarti has usefully pointed out that even if women had a more intense relationship with goods and possessions, that did not mean that they had a 'greater propensity to consume than men did'.[124] Indeed, evidence can be found to support the idea that the retailers regarded men as the prime portion of the market. Nevertheless, women were clearly involved in decisions to do with the home and purchases for it.

Lady Shelborne records a 'shopping trip' in her diary (in the manner of Pepys):

> Called my Lord with whom we first went to Zucchi's, where we saw some ornaments for the ceiling ... from there to Mayhew and Ince where is come beautiful cabinet work, and two pretty glass cases for one of the rooms in my apartment and which though they are only deal and to be painted white, he charges £50.00 for. From there to Cipriani's ... from there to Zuccarelli's ... and from there home it being half past four.[125]

In the above case, it seems evident that Lady Shelborne was a decisive force in the purchasing process, and this may not have been exceptional.

Amanda Vickery has considered aspects of the gender divisions of domestic purchases. She suggests that while women were involved in most minor purchasing decisions, in the case of capital goods, such as furniture, the men

---

[122] Williams, C. (Trans.) (1933), *Sophie in London* [1786], p. 237.

[123] Wendeborn, G. (1791), *A View of England Towards the Close of the Eighteenth Century*, (2 vols), Vol 1, p. 191.

[124] Sarti, R. (2002), 'Women as Consumers', *Europe at Home: Family and Material Culture 1500–1800*, pp. 214–21.

[125] Lady Shelburne, cited in Edwards (1964), *Dictionary of Furniture*, entry on Ince and Mayhew.

had an 'ultimate sanction' over the purchases.[126] She gives two furniture examples recorded by Elizabeth Shackleton in the 1770s. Although Elizabeth ordered small items of common furniture, it was John Shackleton who went to Gillows in Lancaster to make important purchases, and it is his name that appears in their ledgers; when her newlywed son departed to Lancaster for his furniture, she noted: 'Tom going from Newton to Lancaster to buy new mahogany furniture.'[127] In conjunction, Charles Saumarez-Smith suggests that after around 1760, individual women developed a special interest in interiors and their furnishings. This, he argues, was often related to both the establishment of social gatherings and the actual planning of interiors, which created 'a sphere of influence independent of men'.[128]

Another example of a woman conducting business is the case of Mrs Purefoy of Shalstone Manor, Bucks. On 14 July 1736 she wrote to a Mr King, a chair-maker of Bicester:

> As I understand you make chairs of walnut tree frames with four legs without barrs for Mr. Vaux of Caversfield, if you do such I desire you will come over here in a weeks time any morning but Wednesday, I shall want about 20 chairs.[129]

This business transaction was relatively local, but she also dealt with London firms, by mail. On 11 January 1735, she wrote to Antony Baxter in Covent Garden, London, requesting patterns of bed quiltings: 'I desire you will send me by Webster the Buckinghamshire carrier ... some patterns of quilting you mention, together with the lowest prices of each pattern.' After receiving the samples, her son wrote back with their choice from the selection, saying that they wanted to ensure that the goods supplied matched the sample. A week later, he wrote to the suppliers again, saying:

> Since you warrant the quilting as good as the pattern and if it so proves my Mother will have five and forty yards of it at ten shillings and sixpence a yard. But if it is not so good you must expect to have it returned for she would not have any of the others [patterns] if she might have it for nothing.

By the 10 March the material had been made and delivered. The Purefoys wrote in acknowledgement: 'Have received the quilting ... [it] was very bare measure'.[130] A few years later, on 8 February 1743, Mrs Purefoy wrote to Mr Belchier, a cabinet-maker of St Paul's Churchyard, as follows:

---

[126] For an analysis of men's consumption, see Finn, M. (2000), 'Men's things: Masculine possessions in the consumer revolution', *Social History* 5(2) pp. 133–55. See also the section on second-hand purchases below.

[127] Vickerey, A. (1993), 'Women and the world of goods: A Lancashire consumer and her possessions, 1751–81', in Brewer and Porter (Eds), *Consumption and the World of Goods*, p. 281.

[128] Saumarez-Smith (1993), *Eighteenth Century Decoration*, pp. 233–4.

[129] Eland, G. (Ed.) (1931), *Purefoy Letters,* Vol. 1, p. 165.

[130] *Purefoy Letters*, cited in Clabburn, P. (1988), *National Trust Book of Furnishing Textiles*, p. 109.

> This desires Mr. Belchier to send me a round neat light mahogany folding table with four legs, two of them to draw out to hold up ye ffolds. It must be four feet two inches wide. Send it (with the prices thereof) by Mr. Zachary Meads, the Bucks [a carrier] who sets out of London on Monday nights and Friday nights.[131]

Other instances show that furnishing a home was often a joint exercise. The acquisition of furnishings has often been a social activity, with husband and wife or two friends making joint decisions When Benjamin Franklin purchased curtain cloth in London, he was advised by his wife Deborah that he might use his own taste or make a purchase based on what 'we talked about before you went away'.[132] The idea of a private network of contacts, issues of appropriateness and regional matters of taste, and the relative infrequency of purchases meant that advice on purchases was always welcome. Although the rise of home advice stylists was only to develop fully in the nineteenth century, there were clear manifestations of similar processes operating between families and friends in the eighteenth century. For example, the Duchess of Marlborough, in a letter to Mrs Jennens, the wife of her solicitor, wrote about furnishing purchases:

> I have looked upon this damask by daylight, the pattern is not so large as he stated; but he has kept it so ill that it looks full as old as what I have, which is better than if it were a fine fresh damask. But I think it is a good argument to him to sell it cheap, for tho' I like it very much for this use; I would not buy it for any other. But don't part with it, for I would have the whole piece on any terms that you can get it. I shall want a vast number of feather beds and quilts I wish you would take this opportunity to know prices of all such things as will be wanted in that wild unmerciful House, [Blenheim] for the man you go to is famous for low prices ...[133]

In America, a similar pattern of enquiries, this time for furniture as well, can be found when Esther Edwards Burr wrote to her friend in Boston in 1753:

> Eve – I am going to trouble you about business now – I want to know how a body may have some sorts of Household stuff – what is the price of a mehogane case of drawers ... in Boston and also a Bulow table and tea table and plain chairs with leather bottoms and a couch covered with stamped camblet or china all of that wood.[134]

Esther continued

> I should be glad to know what is most fashionable-weather to have looking glasses or sconces for a paylor [parlour] and what for a chamber. Please to send me word by the first opportunity for 'tis time I was looking out, for 'tis but about 10 months and we move [sic].

---

131 Cited in Clabburn (1988), *National Trust Book of Furnishing Textiles*, pp. 107–8.

132 Garrett, E. (1990), 'Furnishing the early American home', *Antiques*, September, p. 547.

133 McQuoid (1905), *Age of Walnut*, p. 235.

134 Karlsen, C. F and Crumpacker, C. (Eds) (1984), *The Journal of Esther Edwards Burr 1754–57*, p. 170, cited in Garrett (1990), *At Home*, p. 45.

Advice was even more important for those purchasing from overseas. Henry Hill of Philadelphia wrote to his sister, Mary Hill Lamar, in London with a plan of his new house. He asked her to acquire some mirrors. She gave the plan to an upholsterer, who made her some drawings, 'when I shall strive to fix on something that is handsome and as cheap as possible'.[135] In some cases, the overseas purchaser's arrangements were quite professional and they employed agents to buy for them. William Franklin of Burlington, NJ, wrote to his London agent in 1765 ordering yellow silk and worsted damask curtains, and he particularly specified that Mrs Franklin:

> desires you will employ Mr. Timothy Golding upholsterer in Brewer Street near Golden Square, as she is acquainted with him and thinks he will do it in the best and most reasonable manner when he knows it is for her.[136]

For North Americans who wanted to keep up with London fashions, the employment of an agent seems a common practice. Virginian planters used these agents for a wide range of goods, including furniture, wallpaper, mantels and other more mundane accessories. This created problems for customers, not only with buying goods, sight unseen, but also in terms of having any influence over delivery and quality control. In correspondence with John Norton and Sons, merchants of London and Virginia, Peter Lyons wrote: 'I know they [the London tradesmen] think anything good enough for Virginia but they should be informed better, and be made to know that the people of Virginia have a good taste and know when they are imposed upon.'[137]

The importance of London in this American trade is evident. However, even though the styles were set in London, there continued to be concerns with material goods and the values they represented, although these seem to be outweighed by the kudos of imported goods. The citizens of Charleston, for example, bought either direct from London or through merchants based in Charleston. The case of purchasing London-supplied goods was a clear example of the search for self-identity over function. In 1783, Joseph Lewis, a London cabinet-maker and upholsterer, supplied Charlestonian Thomas Hutchinson with the following furniture: two pier glasses with gold and varnished japan borders, two girandoles with dolphins, twelve carved mahogany oval-backed chairs, two inlaid card tables, an inlaid Pembroke table, a satinwood liquor case, a ladies dressing-table of mahogany, and a six-foot wainscot double-screwed bedstead with satinwood posts, fitted with fine, white

---

[135] Smith, J. J. (Ed.) (1854), *Letters of Doctor Richard Hill and his Children*, cited in Garrett (1990), *At Home*, p. 46.

[136] Letters from William Franklin to William Strahan, *Pennsylvania Magazine of History and Biography* 35, 4 (1911), p. 432, cited in Garrett (1990), *At Home*, p. 267.

[137] Correspondence cited in Gilliam, J. K. (1998), 'The evolution of the house in Early Virginia', in Thompson, E. (Ed.), (1998), *The American Home*, p. 190.

fringed-lace petticoats, valance and bases.[138] A local retailer could have supplied similar merchandise to all of these items, but the perceived value of London-made goods to the consumer outweighed any financial advantage that may have accrued from working with a local maker. Incidentally, Lewis had to sue the estate of his customer for non-payment. Even as late as 1794, Henry Wansey's description of William Bingham's house in Philadelphia clearly shows that the fashionable taste was still being dictated and furnished from London. The mention of the retail supplier's name is of interest:

> I found a magnificent house and gardens in the best English style, with elegant even superb furniture. The chairs of the drawing room were from Seddon's in London, of the newest taste; the back in the form of a lyre, adorned with festoons of crimson and yellow silk.[139]

All this activity in the acquisition of new and fashionable goods ensured that the English manufacturing and distributive trades were seen as beneficial to the country as well as to the individuals concerned. A contemporary commentator, F. A. Wendeborn, wrote in 1791:

> Those frequent changes in fashion, in regard to dress and furniture, are a great support of British manufacturers; they promote trade, and keep all sorts of tradesmen employed; they increase the pride the wants and the cares of families, and procure employment for others; they are beneficial to government by impost and taxes ...'[140]

When the fashionable goods became *démodé* or began to show signs of wear, they might enter another market and be sold in the second-hand shops or auctions.

Second-hand purchases

As with clothes, there was a flourishing trade in second-hand and used furniture in the eighteenth century. The easy disposal of second-hand and unwanted goods had a twofold influence on the market. Firstly, it made space for new and fashionable goods in the homes of those who could afford them, and secondly, for those who could not afford new, it gave them access to furniture which when it was new they could only aspire towards. This eventually gave them an opportunity to participate on the fringes of style and quality. Second-hand furnishing goods were usually sold either by auction, through furniture stores

---

[138] Fleming, E. (1997), 'Staples for genteel living: The importation of London household furnishings into Charleston during the 1780s', *American Furniture*, pp. 336–7.

[139] Wansey, Henry, *Excursion to the United States of North America in the summer of 1794* (2nd Edn), p. 123. Quoted in Montgomery, C. (1966), *American Furniture: The Federal Period*, p. 42.

[140] Wendeborn, F. A. (1791), *View of England Towards the Close of the Eighteenth Century*, cited in Saumarez-Smith (1993), *Eighteenth Century Decoration*, p. 311.

or through specialist brokers. These sales were not just for those who could not afford to buy new. There is some evidence of the collecting of old things for their own sake. John Hervey's *Book of Expenses* showed that in 1690 he bought 'a parcel of old china for my dear wife, and a pair of china rowlwaggons (tall cylinder vases). In 1692, he paid £1.17s.6d. for a chest of drawers bought at Stow Green Fair. This was the same John Hervey who, in 1696, paid fashionable London cabinet-maker Gerrit Jensen £70 for a set of pier glasses, table and stands.[141]

On occasion goods would be bought at house sales or auctions. Nicholas Blundell, a resident of Liverpool, recorded his visit to a sale in June 1718.

> 'I went to the Sail of Goods at Croxtath ... [held after the death of Lord Molyneux] [and purchased the following]:

Press for hanging in my Wife's Cloths	01 10 00
Plod for Window Curtons	00 06 06
A Sedar Chest of Drawers	01 10 00
Ovell Table	00 01 06
Under Quilt	00 03 00
Frame for warming plates	00 02 06
Pictures three	00 04 06[142]

Blundell also recorded some details of his visit to another sale in March 1726:

> I went to the Houses of Antony Fleetwood & Richard Buckley deceas'd to see if there was any thing proper for me to buy, when the Sale was, I found Thomas & John Melling & Robert Bootle at Buckleys they had been [ap]praising goods there, I stay'd & smoked a Pipe at Buckleys.[143]

Parson Woodforde of Norfolk also recorded a number of furnishing purchases over a period in the late eighteenth century, which shows a range of methods. On 12 January 1788 he discussed the delivery of a sofa from 'my upholsterer, Mr Horth'. On 13 November 1789 Woodforde recorded that he 'bought this day of William Hart, cabinet-makers on Hog Hill, Norwich, 2 large second-hand double flapped mohogany [*sic*] tables also one second-hand mohogany dressing table with drawers also one new mohogany wash stand for all which paid 4.14.6 ...'. On 2 April 1793 Woodforde attended the sale of goods of Mrs Michelthwaite where he bid for 'a very handsome mahogany sideboard, a very good and large Wilton carpet, and a mahogany cellaret', the first two of which he successfully purchased. The next day he noted that 'we brought home the carpet that I bought, and gave orders to Sudbury my upholsterer to send home my sideboard by 2 men'. Six months later he again employed Sudbury the upholsterer to supply new tables. The upholsterers 'took my two large tables

---

[141] Wills, G. (1971), *English Furniture 1550–1760*, p. 104.

[142] *Dictionary of Traded Goods*, Blundell 17/06/1718 NY0230BLNN.

[143] Ibid., Blundell, 07/03/1726 NY0315BLNN.

and smaller one in part of exchange for the others and he is to allow me for the three, only £2.18.0.'[144] These purchases then included new furniture direct from the maker, second-hand furniture from a dealer and from an auction, as well as part exchange. It would not have been surprising if Woodforde purchased furnishings from newspaper advertisements as well, since they were a major source of information on sales.

For example, in 1704 an announcement in *The Postman* appeared which offered for sale the following second-hand hangings: 'three suites of Hangings, one of forest tapestry, one clouded camlet, and one of blue printed linsey; the first two very good, scarce the worse for wearing, to be sold very reasonable'.[145]

Stana Nenadic suggests that the reasons for this abundance of second-hand goods was built on 'business failure, death, and high levels of middle rank movement between towns and cities [which] all ensured a vast supply of high value second-hand household good, particularly in urban areas'.[146] She goes further, to argue that second-hand purchases were not only a pragmatic decision but were also based on supply problems. In terms of furniture, Nenadic suggests that, particularly in non-London sites, timber shortages, the high cost of new materials, and small production facilities all encouraged 'recycling in the middle ranks'. This probably reflects a situation where demand outstripped supply for a while. Nenadic also argues that in the eighteenth century, well-made furniture from selected timbers was an asset that could be realized into cash and represent a form of saving.[147] This explains the propensity of many retailers and cabinet-makers to offer appraising services that valued the goods either for their own purchase and subsequent sale or as a guide to others. Retail trade cards confirm this: for example, the business of Wilkinson and Sons in Cheapside *circa* 1779 advertised: 'Estates, stock in trade, and all sorts of household furniture appraised, bought and sold by commission'.[148]

The measure of the usefulness of second-hand goods was found in their function, quality and patina rather than necessarily in their style. The example of Parson Woodforde demonstrates the happy mix of old and new furniture. Pragmatic decisions were the order of the day. Sara Pennell makes reference to Edward Belson, a journeyman distiller, who in 1710 furnished the bedroom for

---

[144] Beresford, J. (Ed.) (1929), *The Diary of a Country Parson* (J. Woodforde), pp. 2–3 and 148–51.

[145] See McQuoid (1905), *Age of Walnut*, p. 158.

[146] Nenadic (1994), 'Middle rank consumers and domestic culture in Edinburgh and Glasgow 1720–1840', p. 130, The evidence she uses are the confirmation (probate) and sequestration inventories that were much more plentiful in Scotland than in England in the later eighteenth and nineteenth centuries.

[147] Ibid., p. 135.

[148] Trade Card, Guildhall Museum and Library Collection, London.

his new wife with the latest printed-paper hangings and fashionable fabrics for the bed hangings, but Pennell then notes that the bedstead and bed were purchased second-hand.[149] The logic probably being that whilst the hangings of the bed were on view, the bed and bedsteads were hidden behind the fabric façade.

The amazing diversity of the retail infrastructure of eighteenth-century furnishing trades was clearly a response to the equally varied needs and demands of the consumers they served. The next chapter will consider these requirements.

---

[149] Pennell, S. (1999), 'Consumption and consumerism in early modern England', *The Historical Journal*, 42(2), p. 560.

Chapter 4

From being to well-being: the growing demand for comfort and convenience in the eighteenth-century home

> Convenient houses, handsome furniture, pleasant gardens in summer, neat clothes, and enough money to bring up their children … These I have named are the necessary comforts of life, which the most modest are not asham'd to claim, and which they are very uneasy without.
> (B. Mandeville, *Fable of the Bees*)

That there was growth in the production and consumption of goods in the eighteenth century is not generally disputed. What is in question is the rate of change, the constitution of the market, and the nature of consumption.[1] There is general agreement that the English were already comparatively wealthy at the beginning of the eighteenth century, and aggregate real incomes rose during the century.[2] This economic process was sufficient to support an expansion of demand, which seemed natural at the time. Sir Joshua Reynolds expressed this idea of progress in terms of ownership of goods: 'The regular progress of cultivated life is from Necessaries to Accommodations, from Accommodations to Ornaments.'[3] In other words, it was seen as natural that there was a progression from necessities to decencies to luxuries.

The growth in the consumption of goods was not simply an eighteenth-century phenomenon. Evidence shows that consumption patterns had begun to increase in the latter part of the seventeenth century.[4] There is no reason to suspect that the picture provided by inventories up to 1730s – the growth of ownership of material possessions – did not continue for the rest of the century, particularly as the economically active middle levels of society were at the forefront of the expansion.[5] As has already been remarked, contemporary commentators from various disciplines had noted the changes in consumption patterns. Perhaps the extreme comment was in 1776, when the economist

---

[1] For an introduction to these discussions, see Brewer, J. and Porter, R. (Eds) (1993) *Consumption and the World of Goods*. Also see Fine, B. and Leopold, E. (1990), 'Consumerism and the industrial revolution', *Social History*, 15(2), pp. 151–79.

[2] Styles, J. 'Manufacturing, consumption and design', in Brewer and Porter (1993), *Consumption and the World of Goods*, p. 537.

[3] Reynolds, Sir J. (1778), Dedication to the King, in *Discourses on Art*.

[4] Weatherill, L. (1988), *Consumer Behaviour and Material Culture in Britain 1660–1760*.

[5] Although inventory analysis after the 1730s is difficult due to the relaxation of the inventory requirement upon death, sporadic inventory examples, and other evidence can be used. See Shammas, C. (1990), *The Pre-industrial Consumer in England and America*.

Adam Smith wrote that 'consumption is the sole end and purpose of all production'.[6] Assuming that consumption was the *raison d'être* of productivity, it had to be nurtured to maintain or increase production levels. Smith said further that 'the business of commerce is to produce the greatest quantities of the necessaries of life for the consumption of the nation'.[7] This growth was to be sustained by advances that were both incremental and induced.

The incremental advances were based on the growth of trade, population growth, urbanization, transport improvements, development of shops, and increased disposable incomes. The growth of urban centres in general, and the importance of London in particular, have become major factors in any analysis of consumption patterns in the eighteenth century.[8] This is not surprising, bearing in mind that London accounted for 10 per cent of the English population. It also had more shops and therefore more opportunities to see new items; it handled 80 per cent of the imports and had a monopoly of the Far East trade, and as well as playing a central role in inland trade, it was a centre of manufacturing in its own right. To support this expansion, urban improvements such as lighting, paving and cleaning became part of a developing system that was, in part fuelled by the needs of distributors and consumers.[9] Naturally enough, other regional areas that had trading contact with London were likely to follow the patterns of urbanization and consumption that were set there, in addition to their own ideas. These factors clearly applied to other cities as well. In fact, although London remained the largest city, the growth of provincial cities was faster than London throughout the Georgian period. The consequence of the growth in urban settings therefore not only made the status of the home an important issue, but also offered the retail locations from which it could be created.

The induced advances are more difficult to assess, but would appear to have been made by encouraging consumer spending through shops and displays, advertising, pattern books, visual models and changing fashions. Together, these created a culture of consumption that was fed and promoted vigorously.[10] Interestingly, Smith considered necessaries as 'not only the commodities which are indisputably necessary for the support of life, but whatever the custom of the country renders it indecent for creditable people, even of the lower order, to be without'.[11] If the retailers controlled the supply of the

---

[6] Smith, A. (1776), *Wealth of Nations*, cited in Berg, M. and Clifford, H. (Eds) (1999), *Consumers and Luxury, Consumer Culture in Europe 1650–1850*, p. 20.

[7] Berg, M. and Clifford, H. (1999), *Consumers and Luxury*, p. 23.

[8] In 1750 the population of London was 675 000, and by 1800 it had risen to 950 000. Cited in Sarti, R. (2002), *Europe at Home: Family and Material Culture 1500–1800*, p. 109.

[9] Stobart, J. (1998), 'Shopping streets as social space: leisure, consumerism and improvement in an eighteenth century town', *Urban History*, 25(1), pp. 3–21.

[10] Jones, E. C. (1973), 'The fashion manipulators: Consumer tastes and British industries 1660–1800', in Cain, L. and Uselding, P., *Business Enterprise and Economic Change: Essays in Honour of H. F. Williamson*.

[11] Cited in Berg and Clifford (1999), *Consumers and Luxury*, p. 20.

commodities required to support the 'customs of the country', even in part, their role clearly becomes increasingly important.

In previous centuries, much of the production and consumption of furniture had been of a limited nature, with local businesses supplying the requirements of most consuming groups. By the early part of the eighteenth century, the geographical separation of furniture production from the sites of consumption was sufficiently important to be commented upon. It is clear that the division was not a new phenomenon in other trades, but in furniture, it appears to have been the case. Daniel Defoe commented:

> Come next to the furniture of a country grocer's house; it is scarce credible to how many counties of England, and how remote, the furniture of but a mean house must send them; and how many people are everywhere employed about it; nay and the meaner the furniture, the more people and places employed.[12]

However, later in the same work, his *Complete English Tradesmen*, Defoe discussed the needs of the same grocer, and the example seems to confirm the pre-eminence of London as a furnishings supplier:

> The hangings, suppose them to be ordinary Linsey-Woolsey, are made at Kidderminster, dy'd in the country, and painted or watered at London. The chairs, if of cane, are made at London; the ordinary matted chairs, perhaps made in the place where they live. Tables, chest of drawers etc. made at London; as also the looking glass.[13]

It seems clear that the satisfaction of the demand for furniture and furnishings was undertaken on a variety of levels. The first was the best London makers, who were quite able to supply all that was required to furnish a new home wherever it was situated. Secondly, in the middle to lower levels many items did not need to be made in a bespoke way, so that manufacture in batches to a general specification (often supplied by pattern books) meant that even local makers could make some economies. To maintain levels of trade and choice, the various models needed only to be altered in detail. However, in either case, the existence of an accepted and customary design or visual language was a necessary part of the whole process. In conjunction with this was the development of a near-universal language of appropriateness that meant that the consumers' progress, from necessities to accommodations, and then onto ornaments or luxuries, was often a matter of taking advice as to the correct models to be purchased through the retailer.

The eighteenth century therefore saw important changes in the domestic environments of the British and those areas influenced by them. Changing lifestyles that were based partly on urban development and rebuilding, partly on the greater acquisition of possessions (both financed by an increase of

---

[12] Defoe, D. (1727), *The Complete English Tradesman*, Vol. 1, pp. 263 and 266.
[13] Ibid., p. 333.

incomes), and partly on the growth of an idea of polite society, became a major feature of the century. As many of these changes were fuelled by commercial prosperity, as long as these changes were reflected in appropriate behaviour as well as appropriate standards of living, many critics were satisfied. This meant that people would often be judged by what they owned, and how they conducted themselves. The idea that society would be upset by the increase in the consumption of luxury goods emphasized the importance of the notion of taste or appropriateness (see the discussion of morality below).

The distinctions between social levels can also be seen in the differences between 'old' and 'new' wealth. In the case of old wealth (gentry and nobility), McCracken has posited the idea of 'patina' as a representation of status prior to and after the eighteenth century. He goes on to suggest that during the eighteenth century the fashion system took over, and status, at least for 'new money', was to be found in novel things rather than old.[14] However, Pennell suggests that in addition to the purchasing of new products, older goods or heirlooms offer people some fixed points in their image of self, and help to consolidate the familial ties.[15] These distinctions were acknowledged indirectly at the time. G. Lichtenberg, whilst on a visit to the papier-mâché maker Baskerville, ironically commented upon the differences between inherited and self-made wealth: 'The rooms are furnished in the fine taste of those people who, instead of inheriting their wealth, have earned it on their own.'[16]

In addition, the public display of goods, the establishment of social codes and manners and the development of 'polite society' through the exercise of taste were crucial to the maintenance of virtues in the face of the apparent 'vice' of luxury consumption. These features also played a role in continuing the progress of urbanization and the development of trade. In many cities, the opportunities for the *nouveau riche* to demonstrate their newly acquired possessions were plentiful, but the domestic interior remained one of the most potent arenas for these demonstrative gestures. As Carson has pointed out, gentility needed props and settings, as it was ultimately theatre.[17] However, they had to be appropriate to make the correct impression.

Towards the end of the century, the drawing room or saloon was arguably the most important room in the house.[18] It was the main reception room, and like other rooms, was to be furnished in accordance with the demands of social politeness, manner and appropriate taste. This meant using the 'correct'

---

[14] McCracken, G. (1988), *Culture and Consumption*, pp. 37–43.

[15] Pennell (1999), 'Consumption and consumerism in early modern England', p. 559.

[16] Quoted in Huth, H. (1971), *Lacquer of the West*, p. 117.

[17] Carson, C., Hoffman, R. and Albert, P. (Eds) (1994), *Of Consuming Interests: The Style of Life in the Eighteenth Century*, p. 521.

[18] In larger houses the saloon would have been the main reception room, whilst the drawing room was a more relaxed family room.

furnishings. Sheraton gave an example of this when he warned against introducing books pictures, and globes into the drawing room, as these would interfere with conversation. On the other hand, 'The grandeur then introduced into the drawing room is not to be considered as the ostentatious parade of its proprietor, but the respect he pays to the rank of his visitants.'[19]

The Earl of Shaftesbury summed up the effort required: 'the inward ornaments of houses, apartments, furniture, the ranging, order, and disposition of these matters. What pains! What study! Judgement! Science!'[20] For many people the study and judgement required did not come easily, so they increasingly relied on the retail tradesman for advice and direction. Pattern books established the appropriate models for particular styles, and in conjunction with pattern books on architecture, provided a full repertoire of designs. The retailer often made the connections on behalf of his customers.

For all social groups, the understanding of 'what was on offer' in the high street was, according to Glennie and Thrift, based on 'complex understandings of goods and identities, in which much understanding was embodied in habituated ways of being and doing, rather than drawing on intellectual representations of commodities and behaviours'.[21] This indicates that there are systems of knowledge that form and inform everyday life which are practical, contextually specific, and are learned and carried by people and objects. These schemes of understanding link people and objects into the appropriate consumption practices. In the case of home furnishings, these practices were probably calculated more carefully than purchases that were more pedestrian. Pattern books might be consulted. Shop displays would be considered and compared. Other people's homes could be looked at,[22] and decisions would be made, according to a number of criteria. These decisions were intellectualized to a degree, for instance in terms of a form of cost-benefit analysis (function versus prestige). This can be expressed by thinking of objects and the particular features that differentiate them from each other. For example, why purchase a new chair rather than a new suit? Why new as opposed to second-hand? Even within the genre chosen, comparative analysis may be undertaken by 'shopping around'. Which shop was likely to have an understanding of the 'systems of knowledge'? Which would best guide the prospective purchaser? What were the features of this shop's products over another? Why were they important to the consumer? What advantages or benefits did they bestow? The latter may be

---

[19] Sheraton, T. (1803), *The Cabinet Dictionary*, p. 218.

[20] Earl of Shaftesbury (1711), *Characteristics of Men, Manners, Opinions, and Times*, cited in Saumarez-Smith (1993), p. 52.

[21] Glennie, P. and Thrift, N. (1996), 'Consumers, identities and consumption spaces in early-modern England', *Environment and Planning* A, Vol. 28, p. 37.

[22] The practice of visiting houses, not just as a guest, was commonplace in the eighteenth century. See Tinniswood, A. (1989), *A History of Country House Visiting*, Oxford. The large quantity of travel and topographical publications in the eighteenth century with descriptions of homes and their furnishings was another source of information.

at any one time functional, emotional, and expressive, and so on. It was therefore a very important part of the retailer's role to suggest answers to these questions. In fact, that was the nature of selling and sales promotion. However, this is not to say that individuals were completely in the hands of the retailers.

The issue of the location of any object in someone's life and its subsequent attribution of meaning and consumption continues from first thoughts of acquisition, to purchase, through use, onto final disposal, during which time the meanings attached to the goods may vary considerably. Consumption clearly goes beyond the point of purchase and the process develops with ownership. Goods become part of a search for stability and security, and therefore consolidate status and custom as much as providing evidence of their (initial) newness and the owner's taste. However, apart from the construction of a public image, there should be room to consider the individual motives that may be far removed from the physical properties of the goods. Sara Pennell, in her analysis of consumer motivation, suggests that 'the achievement of dignity and security within oneself, one's household, one's community' might be some of the imagined values invested in the acquisition of an object. These imaginative dimensions are demonstrated in her examples of a person's ownership of a tablecloth without its apparently contextualizing paraphernalia (for example, a table).[23]

Clearly, consumers did not necessarily follow their ideas and ideals in a regular or planned way. Goods acquisition was not based on a one-off purchase of all requirements, rather the opposite, as the acquiring of home furnishings, in particular, was (and is) based on accretion and accumulation from a variety of sources, as well as disposal of a wide range of goods. How were goods characterized before purchase and consumption? How did consumers make the choices necessary to deal with the wide range of goods (the nature of which changes rapidly) and the maintenance of a lifestyle, house and family? How were goods characterized after purchase – that is, what changes in meanings were invested in an object over time? Ann Smart Martin has proposed a useful model that posits three prerequisites (the lack of any one halting the process) before a good can become a possession. Firstly, is it affordable? Secondly, is it available? And thirdly, is it desirable?[24] The affordability question is straightforward at one level, but raises issues of how value is determined and how the object compares to others in a hierarchy of needs and wants. It also highlights the role of credit as an enabling service for some at least. The availability question focuses on the production, marketing and distribution system, but may also relate to gifts, inheritances and second-hand objects. The desirability issue is based on both functional and emotional considerations that

---

[23] Pennell (1999), 'Consumption and consumerism in early modern England', pp. 560–61.

[24] Martin, A. S. (1993), 'Makers, buyers, and users: Consumerism as a Material Culture Framework', *Winterthur Portfolio*, 28(2/3), p. 156.

may vary at times and places in a customer's life. All these points were recognized by Postlethwayt in 1757:

> The mechanics wife will not buy damask of fifteen shillings a yard: but will have one of eight or nine. She does not trouble herself much about the equality of the silk; but is satisfied with making as fine a show as a person of higher rank or fortune.[25]

Fashion and taste

Although it seems that forms of self-consciousness (in the sense that individuals were knowingly able to express themselves) were well established by the eighteenth century, there were also 'standardized' systems of social communications. So ordinary people adopted, and then adapted to their own various special needs, a system of courtly behaviour borrowed ultimately from a protocol developed in France and disseminated through Amsterdam and London to provincial England and the colonies. Standardized architectural spaces equipped with fashionable furnishings became universally recognized settings for social performances that were governed by internationally accepted rules of etiquette.[26] The mechanic's wife mentioned above knew damask was fashionable. Although she had to settle for an inferior quality, she was still able to join in the 'system.'

For many social groups, the importance of entertainment and the social round and the subsequent display of oneself and one's home meant that fashion had a major role to play in the maintenance of self-image. Although the fashion system was particularly influential in matters of personal dress and adornment, furniture was also affected by the changes fashion demanded.[27] Defoe, the astute observer of his times, wrote in 1727 that 'the fashions alter now in the more durable kind of things, such as Furniture of houses, Equipages, Coaches, nay even of Houses themselves'. This meant that:

> This must needs give a new turn to the trade, and that of course gives new methods and new measures to the Manufacturers, obliges them to a continual study of novelty, and to rack their inventions for new fashions, introduces new customs, and even gives a turn to Trade it self.[28]

In terms of the home, the example of the chintz craze showed how the 'novel' goods were purchased as much for the 'sign-value' as for the 'use-value' – a

---

[25] Postlethwayt, M. (1757), *Britain's Commercial Interest Explained and Improved*, Vol. 2, p. 395, cited in Berg and Clifford (1999), *Consumers and Luxury*, p. 7.

[26] Carson, Hoffman and Albert (Eds) (1994), *Of Consuming Interests*, p. 523.

[27] Adam Smith noted that clothes were out of date in a year, and furniture fashions were superseded every five or six years. *Theory of Moral Sentiments* (1759), p. 195, cited in Berg and Clifford (1999), *Consumers and Luxury*, p. 10.

[28] Defoe (1727), *The Complete English Tradesman*, Part 2, p. 6.

fact that retailers were very well aware of. Defoe had noticed this particular demand early in the century. In 1708 he wrote:

> ... [chintz] crept into our houses, our closets and bedchambers, curtains, cushions chairs, and at last beds themselves, were nothing but calicoes and Indian stuffs, and in short everything that used to be made of wool or silk relating to the dress of the women or the furniture of our house, was supplied by the Indian trade.[29]

One hundred years later, in its advice to new entrants to the furniture trade, a guide published in 1829 expressed the same sentiments: 'In a business where change and caprice rule with unbounded sway – in that the fashion of today may become obsolete tomorrow – an inventive genius and discriminating judgment are certainly essential qualifications.'[30]

The need to change, to be seen to be fashionable and to reject the taste of the previous generation was to become noticeable even in rural districts. James Spershott, a joiner of Chichester, Sussex, commented upon these transitions in his memoirs. They included this passage, which referred to his youth in the early eighteenth century:

> I observ'd in those days the household furniture ... was almost all of English oak ... but with younger people it was now in fashion to have deal dressers with shelves over for pewter, etc. Their tables and chests of drawers of Norway oak called wainscot. With the higher sort, walnuttree veneering was most in vogue and esteem'd for its beauty above anything else ... The best chairs were turn'd ash, dyed or stuffed, with Turkey or other rich covers.[31]

Even if rural areas were being affected by fashions, the urban middling classes were disproportionately responsible for the surge in demand for fashionable goods. Writing in a similar vein to Spershott, but this time referring to urban homes in Bath, John Wood saw a change from the 1720s, when furnishings were mean, slight and of little value. As new building advanced, new objects were brought in:

> Walnut tree chairs, some with leather and some with damask or worked bottoms supplied the place of such as were seated with cane or rushes; the oak tables and chests of drawers were exchanged; the former for such as were made of mahogany, the latter for such as were made either of the same wood or with walnut tree; handsome glasses were added to the dressing tables nor did the proper chimneys or peers of any of the rooms long remain without well framed mirrors of no inconsiderable size.'[32]

---

[29] *A Review of the State of the British Nation*, 29 January 1708, p. 602, cited in Saumarez-Smith (1993), *Eighteenth Century Decoration*, p. 48.

[30] Stokes, J. (1829), *The Complete Cabinet Maker and Upholsterer's Guide*, p. 4.

[31] Quoted in Knell, D. (1992), *English Country Furniture*, p. 76.

[32] Wood, J. (1765), *A Description of Bath*, pp, 3–5, cited in Ayres, J. (1981), *The Shell Book of the Home in Britain*, p. 25.

The issue of enhancement was then commented upon:

> Beds, window curtains and other chamber furniture, as well as woollens
> and linen were, from time to time, renewed with such as was more fit for
> gentlemen's capital seats than houses appropriated for common lodgings;
> and the linnen for the table and bed grew better and better til it became
> suitable even for people of the highest rank.[33]

This passage reflects Defoe's earlier comments of 1713, when he wrote of a
London house: 'Here I saw out of a shopkeeper's house, velvet hangings,
embroidered chairs, damask curtains ... in short furniture equal to what
formerly sufficed the greatest of our nobility.'[34]

In contrast, a 1768 inventory of a cottage in New Brentford, Middlesex,
shows the range of household effects that an artisan-labourer possessed.
Although not so elegant as the examples above, it shows an interesting (and
probably typical) mix of the old and new, combined with some thought for
comfort. The bedroom furniture included a four-poster bedstead, and a half
tester turn-up bedstead, both with textile furnishings. The home boasted
five tables, two of which were described as wainscot dining tables. There
were four cane and five rush-bottomed chairs, as well as a leather-covered
elbow chair. For storage, they had a deal clothes chest, a wainscot chest
with drawers veneered in front, and a mahogany tea chest. Other items included
eight prints and two small looking-glasses.[35] These changes seem to reflect
Sir Joshua Reynolds' observations about progression from necessities to
luxuries.

Demand for particular goods was also derived from other changes in
furnishings. One such change was the development in polite social habits, such
as tea drinking, social entertaining, reading and writing, which meant that
practical, functional furniture forms were required, and this will be discussed
further below. Another demand came from people who desired objects for their
own intrinsic worth: the polished surfaces with dramatically coloured and
grained veneers, rare timbers from the Indies, and contrasting inlays of wood
and metals all excited the visual appetite, as well as satisfying other egotistical
demands. When goods were desired but were financially out of reach, it was
often possible to purchase substitutes or simulations.[36] These ideas reflect the

---

[33] Ibid.

[34] *Review*, 1713, cited in Saumarez-Smith (1993), *Eighteenth Century Decoration*, p. 50.

[35] Middlesex Sessions Books 1229, 1768 (Middlesex Guildhall), quoted in Joy, E. T. (1968),
The Connoisseur's Complete Period Guides, p. 592. The preparation of inventories during the
eighteenth century declined dramatically after the first quarter of the century. There are some
useful examples in Spufford, M. (1984), *The Great Reclothing of Rural England*. For the later part
of the century, auction records may prove useful in determining the range of furnishings owned in a
household.

[36] Berg, M. (1999) 'New commodities, luxuries and their consumers in eighteenth century
England', in Berg and Clifford (1999), *Consumers and Luxury*. See also Benhamou, R. (1991),
'Imitation in the decorative arts of the eighteenth century', *Journal of Design History*, 4, pp. 1–14.

analysis of the economist, Adam Smith, who pointed out that desirability in goods was based on four factors: colour, form, variety or rarity, and imitation.[37] The goods in furniture shops could meet all these desires for all aspects of the interior.

The development of polite society had ramifications for furniture as much as other decorative arts. This meant that commodities placing one in society were often more than signifiers of position and taste. For example, the proper provision of comfort and pleasure for visitors and guests was clearly important. Sophie von la Roche indicated as much when she wrote of a visit to Lord Harcourt in the 1780s. She describes the reception room and its contents:

> Chests in the finest workmanship, holding the necessaries for all kinds of games, and lined on top with books of all varieties and languages; a piano, music, violin … numerous sofas and all kinds of arm and easy chairs; ladies work tables besides, so as all the guests may do exactly as they please.[38]

The ability to create a room or space in which all the objects and equipment were co-ordinated in a manner that reflected Adam Smith's desirability factors was a major aim of tasteful eighteenth-century furnishing practice. Starting with the architectural shell, the selected style could be applied in all of the aspects of decoration and furnishings. This ideal result, which may be manifested by toning curtain and bed drapes, colour-co-ordinated carpets and matching sets of chairs for example, was easily obtained, subject to financial restraints, by purchasing the ensemble complete. It is no coincidence that the rise of the complete house furnisher, who was able to create and sell these schemes, occurred in the early eighteenth century.[39]

Self-consciousness and difference

The growth of eighteenth-century consumption has sometimes been explained by contemporary commentators in terms of emulation. Again, the observant Daniel Defoe thought that 'the poorest citizens strive to live like the rich, the rich like the gentry, the gentry like the nobility and the nobility striving to outshine one another, [it was] no wonder that all the sumptuary trades encrease'.[40] Another contemporary writer, N. Forster, was also aware of the change in demand, seemingly brought about by fashionable emulation:

> In England, the several ranks of men slide into each other almost imperceptibly, and a spirit of equality runs through every part of their

---

[37] Smith, A. (1762–3), *Lectures on Jurisprudence*, cited in Berg and Clifford (1999), *Consumers and Luxury*, p. 8.

[38] Williams (trans.) (1933), (trans.), *Sophie in London* [1786], p. 275.

[39] See Chapter 3.

[40] Defoe (1727), *The Complete English Tradesman*, Vol. 2, Part II, p. 167.

constitution. Hence arises a strong emulation in all the several stations and conditions to vie with each other ... In such a state as this, fashion must have uncontrolled sway. And a fashionable luxury must spread through it like a contagion.[41]

Lady Kildare demonstrated the point well in a letter to her husband in 1757, when she said: 'I shall wish to have our house look sprucish. Every mortal's house here [in London] is so pretty and smart, and well furnished, that I do long to have ours so too a little.'[42] The process even spanned continents. John Drayton wrote of residents of the American city, Charleston, in 1802: 'Charlestonians sought in every way to emulate the life of London society.'[43]

In spite of these comments, our analyses of the reasons for consumption are now much less clear-cut than these contemporary writers. Stana Nenadic argues that although emulation clearly played a part in many areas of consumer behaviour, this was only one of a number of motivations, all of which were variable and complex.[44] Consumption processes might in fact indicate a number of differing messages. These could include the desire to establish a status difference, the desire to establish a particular community distinction, or the desire to establish an individual identity.[45] The latter was particularly so in towns, where spending on furnishings was part of the process of establishing one's family, particularly if others in the town had little knowledge of your background. Contrary to this, the well-established rural family often had little need to demonstrate their position in a hierarchy. As the concept of status already existed and was acknowledged, conspicuous consumption of fashions and furnishings may well have been tempered by this awareness.[46] In the case of poorer homes, it is often an internal status that is declared through goods which is not in itself comparative or emulative. Consumption of objects is as much about maintaining and consolidating status and standing as it is about embracing novelty.[47] Therefore, the goods that people either bought or ignored, according to their preferences and finances, helped in the process of defining or redefining a group identity. As these identities were different, the

---

[41] Forster, N. (1767), *An Enquiry into the Present High Price of Provisions*, quoted in McKendrick, N., Brewer, J. and Plumb, J. H. (1982), *The Birth of Consumer Society*, p. 11.

[42] *The Correspondence of Emily Duchess of Leinster*, Vol. 1, p. 59, quoted in Fowler, J. and Cornforth, J. (1986), *English Decoration in the Eighteenth Century*, p. 65.

[43] Fleming, E. (1997), 'Staples for genteel living: The importation of London household furnishings into Charleston during the 1780s', *American Furniture*, p. 335.

[44] Nenadic, S. (1994), 'Middle rank consumers and domestic culture in Edinburgh and Glasgow 1720–1840', *Past and Present*, 145, p. 124.

[45] For work in this area see Bourdieu, P. (1984), *Distinction: A Social Critique of the Judgement of Taste*; Douglas, M. and Isherwood B., (1980), *The World of Goods: Towards an Anthropology of Consumption*, Miller, D. (1987), *Material Culture and Mass Production*.

[46] See Sleep, J. (1994) 'Consumer behaviour across an urban hierarchy 1650–1725', *Regional Furniture Society Newsletter*, 21, Winter, pp. 12–13.

[47] Pennell (1999), 'Consumption and Consumerism in Early Modern England', *The Historical Journal*, p. 559.

trickle-down theory or emulation does not particularly help, as the incompatible lifestyles made certain objects more appropriate than others.

Colin Campbell has suggested that the theory of emulation, which simply uses purchasing power to attain status, should be questioned. In addition, the trickle-down phenomenon does not necessarily indicate a motive of emulation: the facility to copy does not mean that this is the reason; perhaps there is an actual desire for goods for their own sake.[48] Clearly, then, there can co-exist examples of consumption as imitation or copying, emulation which is trying to equal or even excel, as well as attempts at personal or group distinction. Glennie has usefully pointed out that many consumers were adapters not mere adopters, 'to be counted among the creators of consensual cultures'.[49]

Another slant on consumption patterns that is not based on emulation has been suggested by Stana Nenadic, who has pointed to the value of the extensive market in second-hand goods (which by definition were unfashionable), in the eighteenth century, especially in Scotland.[50] The twin attractions of second-hand goods appear to be that they often represented quality and usefulness and retained some resale value as well as the more pragmatic issue of simply being available and affordable. This apparent willingness to include second-hand goods in an interior may appear to negate the argument about goods 'going together', but it is likely that second-hand goods were used in non-public rooms or in homes that were not aspirational. Indeed, as Nenadic points out, the second-hand purchases were often acquired because of their functional value rather than their status value.[51]

Despite the practical purchasing decisions identified above, what were the other purchasing motives or intentions of the consumer? When consequences are recognized as objects, the analysis of intention can be useful. In other words, we can try to use furniture objects (amongst others) to assist in interpreting eighteenth-century consumer ambitions. Campbell suggests that the key to this understanding is recognition of particular personal characters; the individuals' desires to express ideals in themselves.[52] In the case of furniture and interiors, the selection of particular merchandise directly relates to this. Not only do interiors and their furnishings tell others about the occupants, but they also remind the owners of themselves and their position.[53]

---

[48] Campbell, C. (1993), 'Understanding traditional and modern patterns of consumption in eighteenth century England: a character action approach', in Brewer and Porter (Eds), *Consumption and the World of Goods*, pp. 40–57.

[49] Glennie, P. (1995), 'Consumption within historical studies', in Miller, D. (Ed.) *Acknowledging Consumption*, p. 169.

[50] Nenadic, S. (1994), 'Middle rank consumers and domestic culture in Edinburgh and Glasgow 1720–1840', *Past and Present*, 145, p. 129.

[51] Ibid., p. 132.

[52] Campbell (1993), 'Understanding traditional and modern patterns of consumption in eighteenth century England: a character action approach', pp. 40–57.

[53] This particular role for the interior reached it peak in the mid-nineteenth century.

Whilst this remains the case, the home will inevitably be bound up with individual self-concepts.

The accepted symbolic meanings of objects as 'codes' were intended to establish both differentiation from others and integration within a particular strata of society.[54] The former was aimed at separating the owner and emphasizing his/her individuality and thus creating distinction, whilst in the latter, the object symbolically expressed the integration of the owner into a context that was both narrow (the building) and broad (the social stratum).[55] Therefore, one of the most valuable symbolic functions of goods, and especially of furnishings, was 'making visible and stable the categories of culture'.[56] This process was not lost on contemporaries. Thomas Sheraton clearly demonstrated this when giving advice to upholsterers (retailers) upon their role: 'When any gentleman is so vain and ambitious as to order the furnishings of his house in a style superior to his fortune and rank, it will be prudent in an upholsterer, by some gentle hints to direct his choice to a more moderate plan.'[57] In addition, Sheraton noted that even 'in furnishing a good house for a person of rank, it requires some taste and judgment, that each apartment may have such pieces as is most agreeable to the *appropriate* use of the room'. [my emphasis].[58] So not only did the retailer have to make sure that the standard of furnishing was congruous with a social level, but also that the particular schemes were suitable for specific room types.

As Sheraton was well aware, the bourgeois preoccupation with good taste meant that consumers often had to employ upholsterers to assist with the choice of tasteful furnishings. A German journalist reported how:

> [the upholsterer] tells one immediately what colours go together, how much each article costs, what one must choose in order to guard against the style becoming old-fashioned after some years, what changes must be made in a house, what sort of carpet to go in the dining room ... and so on and so on.[59]

This reliance upon the retailer is not surprising as many people had little or no experience of purchasing stylish house furnishings on a regular basis. This service was to be one of the reasons for the upholsterer, later the retail furnisher, to be considered as a professional arbiter of domestic taste during the century and the one that followed. Sheraton again spelt it out:

---

[54] Douglas, M. (1992), 'Why do people want goods?' in Heap, S. and Ross, A. (Eds), *Understanding the Enterprise Culture: Themes in the Work of Mary Douglas*.

[55] Csikszentmihalyi, M. and Rochberg Halton, E. (1981), *The Meaning of Things, Domestic Symbols and the Self*, pp. 38–9.

[56] Douglas, M. and Isherwood, B. (1980), *The World of Goods*, p. 59.

[57] Sheraton, T. (1803), *The Cabinet Dictionary*, p. 215.

[58] Ibid.

[59] *London und Paris*, 1800, pp. 186–7, quoted in Kirkham, P. (1988), *The London Furniture Trade, 1700–1870*, p. 67.

There is certainly something of sentiment expressed in the manner of furnishing a house as well as in personal dress and equipage; particularly so in the appearance of some apartments. And it is the business of an upholsterer not to recommend anything that would offend the known sentiments of his employer, when virtue and morality are not the question, but mere indifferent opinion.[60]

Thus far, this discussion of fashion and taste has focused on the urban consumer. The rural inhabitants were also part of the system albeit often on a different scale. The shifts in ownership and spending patterns of eighteenth century consumers can be developed using Lorna Weatherill's conclusions. The ownership patterns she has recognized include the idea that often the minor gentry were less likely to own particular goods than commercial and professional levels, despite the former's higher social standing.[61] She cites the example of window curtains which, from the data used, shows the following ownership range: 28 per cent of dealing trades, 26 per cent of gentry, 13 per cent of craft trades, and 5 per cent of yeomen. Other spending pattern examples illustrate the distinction between the urban and rural distribution of goods. The possession of looking-glasses in London was 77 per cent, in major towns, 58 per cent, in other towns 50 per cent, and in rural or village areas 21 per cent, thus confirming the preponderance of these status objects in cities.

The differences between the urban and the rural, as well as between status groups, were also reflected in the total interior effect. *The Book of Trades* (1804) commented on the distinctions:

What a difference is there between the necessary articles of furniture to be found in a cottage and the elegantly furnished house of a merchant or peer. In the former, there is nothing but what is plain, useful, and almost essential to the convenience of life: in the latter, immense sums are sacrificed to magnificence and show.[62]

These apparent differences fuelled the morality argument.

Morality

Although many contemporary writers extolled the benefits of consumption,[63] there were some voices raised against it. Particular contemporary commentators denounced consumption as a 'vice', and by extension, also condemned the retailers. Defoe wrote a chapter discussing tradesmen who 'by the necessary consequences of their business are obliged to be accessories to the propagation

---

[60] Sheraton (1803), *The Cabinet Dictionary*, p. 216.

[61] Weatherill (1988), *Consumer Behaviour and Material Culture in Britain 1660–1760*, p. 191, Table 8:2.

[62] *The Book of Trades* (1804), Part lll, pp. 123–5.

[63] See 'The Consumer Revolution' in McKendrick, Brewer, and Plumb (1982), *Birth of a Consumer Society*, pp. 9–34, especially the references to Mandeville's *Fable of the Bees*.

of vice, [the buying of unnecessary goods] and the encrease of wickedness of the times ...'.[64] The sorts of merchants that Defoe complained about were the tailors and mercers whom he saw as tempters and manipulators of vanity. According to Defoe, the same problems occurred with the sellers of house furnishings:

> The Upholder does the like in furniture, till he draws the gay ladies to such excesses of folly that they must have their houses new furnished every year; everything that has been longer than a year in use must be called old, and to have their fine lodgings seen by persons of any figure above twice over, looks ordinary and mean.[65]

To overcome this trend and to stop 'all excesses in cloathing, furniture and the like' would have required sumptuary laws, and this idea was anathema in the generally non-interventionist climate of the eighteenth century. Conversely, the idea of sensibility as a branch of morality was seen as important. Sensibility represented a feeling of goodness, emotion and a response to beauty, of which any lapses were considered to breed bad taste. Therefore, 'taste' became an important part of an individual's moral character. This clearly gave support to the opposite 'vice' of being 'in the fashion'. Indeed, a lack of virtue could be expressed by failing to show the correct judgement in matters of taste; therefore, objects that demonstrated good taste also indicated respectability. Not to be in fashion was perhaps seen to imply a dubious moral standing, therefore a consciousness of matters of taste was not necessarily seen as the seeking of status but more as a protector of one's own good name.[66]

In the case of furniture, cabinet-makers Ince and Mayhew point out that even if large amounts of money were spent on furnishings, this should be balanced with decorum and grace to obtain a tasteful effect. They wrote that: 'in furnishing all should be with Propriety-Elegance should always be joined with a peculiar neatness through the whole house, or otherwise an immense expense may be thrown away to no purpose either in use or appearance.'[67]

The dichotomy between the vice of supplying attractive and fashionable goods and the morality of clients who were trying to show a degree of sensibility and taste, was no doubt of little consequence in the actual marketplace. Bernard Mandeville explored this idea in his famous *Fable of the Bees*, published in 1714. He considered that the 'vice' of fashionable goods was not a moral issue, as although:

> the greatest excesses of luxury are shewn in buildings, furniture, equipage and cloaths: clean linen weakens a man no more than flannel; tapestry, fine paintings or good wainscot are no more unwholesome than bare walls; and

---

[64] Defoe (1727), *The Complete English Tradesman*, Vol. 2, Part 2, p. 149.

[65] Ibid.

[66] See Tristram, P. (1989), *Living Space in Fact and Fiction*, for details of similar approaches in eighteenth- and nineteenth-century literature, p. 162. Also Appleby, J. (1993), 'Consumption in early modern social thought', in Brewer and Porter (1993), *Consumption and the World of Goods*.

[67] Ince and Mayhew (1762), *Universal System of Household Furniture*, Preface.

a rich couch, or a gilt chariot are no more enervating than the cold floor or
a country cart.[68]

In other words, goods in themselves cannot corrupt or debilitate. Ironically, it
was a Frenchman who later denounced the excess of luxury as affectation.
Louis-Sébastien Mercier said of the setting up of a home: 'the furnishings are
given an over-abundant and unsuitable magnificence. A superb bed that
resembles a throne, a carved dining room, andirons fashioned like jewels, a
toilette in gold and lace, are surely signs of puerile ostentation.'[69] Alongside
(and in contrast to) the demand for luxury, style and fashionable living, there
was a growing tendency towards informality and comfort.

Invention of comfort and the idea of home

The changes in the internal layouts of the new urban brick-built town houses
were piecemeal and long-winded, but they were the backbone and framework
for the new aspirations that in turn encouraged the demand for comfort. The
development of the specialization of living spaces (to provide privacy), the
increasing importance of the hearth and fireplace (to avoid smoky fires), and
the impact of glazing (to combat draughts) were all part of the developing
comfort infrastructure which was well-established during the seventeenth
century. Apart from these improvements in the physical facilities, the idea of
control over one's surroundings and a concern for politeness, respectability
and cleanliness are also related to the issues of comfort, and could be seen as
part of the psychological motivations in the growth of comfort as an idea and an
ideal.

In his work on the invention of comfort, John Crowley makes two
assumptions about this subject, both crucial.[70] One is that people can get used
to anything, and the other that at any one time, people think that the way they
live is the right way to live. It is only when there is a comparative situation
that desire and fashion encourages entry into consumption patterns that are
ultimately derived from an apparent dissatisfaction or 'discomfort' with
existing lifestyles. This comparative element in society is an aspect of the idea
of an apparently natural development or hierarchy of distinction that climbs
from necessities to luxuries that Barbon, Mandeville and Reynolds have
referred to. During the eighteenth century a growing proportion of society were
moving from being 'users of things' to being 'consumers of commodities'. If
commodities equate to comfort in a broad sense, this can be seen as one of the

---

[68] Mandeville, B. (1714), *Fable of the Bees*, cited in Saumarez-Smith (1993), *Eighteenth Century Decorations*, p. 144.

[69] *Le Tableau de Paris*, 1781–8, Vol. 1, p. 166, cited in Paradaihlé-Galabrun, A. (1991), *The Birth of Intimacy: Privacy, and Domestic Life in Early Modern Paris*, p. 146.

[70] Crowley, J. E. (2000), *The Invention of Comfort*, p. 290.

key issues of the eighteenth century, in the same way that the issue of luxury has been identified.[71]

The way in which this new idea of comfort began to exercise the minds of the eighteenth century is confirmed by Crowley when he points out that it was 'Anglo-American political economists, moral philosophers, scientists, humanitarian reformers, even novelists ... [who] sought to evaluate the relations of body, material culture, and environment in the name of physical comfort'.[72] Taxing the mind was not the only consideration. The fiscal benefits of taxing people's 'comforts' soon became apparent, the hearth and window taxes being the best-known. In 1798 the American, Alexander Hamilton recommended that taxes should be levied not only on the house type, size and number of rooms, but also on chimneys, staircases, papered walls, cornices and stucco ceilings. Congressional debates on the 1798 direct tax assessments noted that 'houses are articles of expense, and produce nothing. They are merely instrumental (and when they do not exceed the measure of convenience they are necessary) to our enjoying other comforts.'[73] The progressive nature of the tax meant that luxury and comfort came at a price.

These considerations of comfort were apparently less troubling in the hinterlands. Dr Johnson, commenting on the lack of window glass in Scotland, noted that 'the greater part of our time passes in compliance with necessities, in the performance of daily duties, in the removal of small inconveniences, in the procurement of petty pleasures ... The true state of every nation is the state of common life.'[74] Matters of comfort are clearly relative.

There seemed to be confusion between comfort and the issue of status in eighteenth-century culture. Initially, social status was often expressed through prestige goods and the idea of gentility, rather than comfort in the physical sense. However, part of the agenda of political economy in the eighteenth century was to legitimize material consumption, whether of products related to gentility or those associated with the comforts of life. There was soon a consensus that levels of consumption could demonstrate both gentility and well-being (in the sense of physical comfort and prosperity).

Malthus's work on population, published at the end of the century, considered that 'a good meal, a warm house, and a comfortable fireside in the evening' were desirable and that this aspiration:

> put in motion the greatest part of that activity from which spring the multiplied improvements and advantages of civilised life; and ... the pursuit of these objects and the gratification of these desires, form the principle happiness of the larger half of mankind, civilised or uncivilised,

---

[71] See, for example, Berg and Clifford (Eds) (1999), *Consumers and Luxury*.

[72] Crowley (2000), *The Invention of Comfort*, p. 142. Purchase tax was levied from 1799, and revenues had been gathered on imported goods, windows and so on for some while prior to that.

[73] Ibid., p. 105.

[74] Ibid., p. 174.

and are indispensably necessary to the more refined enjoyments of the other half.[75]

This reflected not so much a concern with 'how the other half lived', but that there was enough to go round, and that all could share some of the pleasures of comfort. By the end of the eighteenth century, it is clear that there was some idea of a general understanding of the notion of comfort, in England and North America in particular.

The fact that the home comforts had improved for a wide swathe of the population impressed Josiah Tucker. He wrote in the last quarter of the eighteenth century that: 'were an inventory to be taken of household goods and furniture of a peasant, or mechanic in France, and of a peasant or mechanic in England the latter would be found on average to exceed the former in value by at least three to one'.[76] He went on to say that the English had:

> better conveniences in their houses, and affect to have more in quantity of clean, neat furniture, and a greater variety (such as carpets, screens, window curtains, chamber bells, polished brass locks, fenders etc. Things hardly known abroad among persons of such a rank) than are to be found in any other country in Europe, Holland excepted.[77]

Even allowing for a degree of patriotic exaggeration, there had clearly been great strides in the material well-being of large groups of English peoples.

Another comparative example may demonstrate the nature of these improvements. The furniture in the living room of one farmer in 1676 simply comprised 'one longe table, 6 joyned stooles, one cuppbord, 3 chairs and one little table'. Things had improved considerably by the 1750s. A typical farmhouse in the Yorkshire Dales was furnished with 'a dresser, a table, a clock, chairs, and a long settle in the Fore house'. In the parlour and closets were 'beds and bedding, chests of drawers, a little table, chairs and a corner cupboard'. In the bedrooms were 'two chaff beds, a chest, two tables, four chairs, and accessories'.[78] By comparison, the craftsman potter was even better off in the 1740s:

> In the Hall a clock and case, a looking glass, a writing desk and table and stand, a dozen Sedge [matted] chairs. In the parlour a corner cupboard and

[75] Malthus, T. (1798), *Essay on the Principle of population*, cited in Crowley (2000), *The Invention of Comfort*, p. 168.

[76] Tucker (1931), *A Selection from His Economic and Political Writings*, Schuyler, R. L. (Ed.), quoted in McKendrick, Brewer and Plumb,(1982), *The Birth of a Consumer Society*, p. 26.

[77] Ibid.

[78] Gilbert, C. (1991), *English Vernacular Furniture 1750–1900*, p. 32. The inventory of Mathew Heslop of Langton upon Swale of 1751 shows the total value of his furniture and furnishings was £21. Compare this with the value of his livestock and crops at £88. See also de Vries J. 'Between purchasing power and the world of goods, understanding the household economy in early modern Europe', in Brewer and Porter (Eds), *Consumption and the World of Goods*, pp. 100 and 104, where he argues that growing numbers of possessions did not increase the value of estates, rather their relative value fell.

china and a tea table, an oval table, a tea table, a card table a dressing table
and hand board, twelve cane chairs.[79]

These contrasting examples help to confirm both Malthus's and Tucker's
observations about the home comforts of the English people. In all of these
cases, the visual results of home-making may reflect a desire to show, but also
may reflect a desire for domestic stability and security that comes from the
acquiring and use of goods and the establishment of 'home'. The inventories do
not distinguish between dates of purchase or sites of acquisition, but we can
consider that furnishing was an evolving process that changed as people's
status moved. In fact, the quest for comfort was probably much more to do with
perceived needs than with competition in the wider world.

Two features link comfort and consumption patterns in the period. The first
was the growing distinction between the public and private apartments of a
large house, and the gradual separation of work from the home in the labouring
classes, both of which brought about an increase in demand for private
furniture designed for relaxation. The second was the idea that since luxury
was potentially a 'vice' and bare necessity was to be avoided, comfort
represented a middle way that was appropriate to a wide spectrum of society,
even if it was manifested in different ways.

In 1756 the English poet Thomas Gray, writing to a friend about another
acquaintance, made the point about the distinction between ease and comfort
compared with luxury:

> Whenever any occasion calls you this way, his other great chair holds open
> its arms to receive you, if not with all the grace, yet with as much good-
> will as any Duchesses quilted péché-mortel, [couch] or sofa with a triple
> gold fringe.[80]

This example of a comfortable home does not represent the full range of
domestic situations. Those who were not living in their own homes often had
less in the way of furnishing comforts. This description of a rented room from
1767 illustrates the point:

> A half-tester bedstead with brown linsey-woolsey furniture, a bed and a
> bolster ... a small wainscot table, two old chairs with cane bottoms, a
> small looking glass six inches by four in a deal frame painted red and
> black, a red linsey-woolsey curtain.[81]

There were many who were far more wretched than this.

---

[79] Weatherill (1988), *Consumer Behaviour and Material Culture in Britain, 1660–1760*,
pp. 33–4.

[80] Cited in Gloag, J. (1956), *Georgian Grace*, p. 202.

[81] Consideration on the Expediency of Raising ... the Wages of servants that are not domestic,
particularly Clerks in Public Offices (BMT152/4, 1767), quoted in Joy (1968), *The Connoisseur's
Complete Period Guides*, p. 834.

Physical changes in the home

Although the idea that a home was, for some, a reflection of self and status as well as a conscious planning exercise, it was apparently not particularly part of the early eighteenth-century psyche. Some elites were purchasing objects based on conscious choice to display in architect-designed and planned houses, but at other levels goods were acquired locally and were based on need and use. Indeed, for many the purchase of second-hand furniture was common and the hiring of furniture pieces as required, was a normal transaction.

Later in the century some of these attitudes had changed. The elites had recognized that goods and their arrangement in a building demonstrated their particular choices and tastes, which could reflect on them and their choice of style and architect. It is clear that the middle classes were also aware of these stylistic messages, but were as concerned with the self-conscious expressions of style and taste as with matters of comfort, albeit within particular stylistic parameters. This comfort would include an understanding of room differentiation and use, even if some rooms were still used for business or work. This concern would also recognize the changing roles of objects. For example, the importance of the grand bed declined, whilst that of the dining set rose. In addition, specific objects were introduced to assist in the co-ordination of social practices, for example the taking of tea.

These new attitudes did not go unobserved. In 1783 a German visitor to England noted that 'in regard to the arrangement and decoration of the rooms, English women rival those of every other nation. The commonest handicraftsman has in addition to his workroom at least one room in which he receives strangers and in which nothing is to be seen that suggest his trade.'[82]

It has already been suggested that the theatre is a metaphor for the home. The home puts on a show of personality and the accumulation of possessions. Therefore, the home acts as a stage, with its props, its front stage, back stage and private 'wings'. Each area of the home, then, had a particular part to play in the presentation of self. The stage metaphor also reflects the distinctions made by Erving Goffman in terms of the representation of the self as being based on a 'front' and a 'back'. By presenting one's public face as stylish and refined did not necessarily imply that that was the case in private. These thoughts were already recognized by contemporary commentators.[83] When visiting England in 1784, La Rochfoucauld noted that:

> at first I was quite astonished at all this [cleanliness] and did all that I could
> to make sure whether this cleanliness was natural to the English and so

---

[82] German visitor cited in Kelly, J. A. (1921), *England and the Englishman in German Literature of the Eighteenth Century*, p. 69 cited in Saumarez-Smith (1993), *Eighteenth Century Decoration*, p. 311.

[83] Goffman, E. (1971) *The presentation of Self in Everyday Life*.

pervaded all their activities, or whether it was a superficial refinement. I was led to see quite clearly that it was only external: everything that you are supposed to see partakes of this most desirable quality, but the English contrive to neglect it in what you are not supposed to see.[84]

Room use

The role of the hall as an introductory statement of what might be found in the rest of the house often meant that the decoration and furnishings would need either to act as a foil to the main interior, or sometimes to be a dramatic statement in their own right. In 1768 Isaac Ware pointed out his distinction between the front and back in the example of halls in town and country dwellings. He suggested that in the town houses, halls did not need to be as elegant, as the area was a place for servants, whereas in the country it ought to be large and noble, as it could serve for a variety of functions.[85] These functions included 'serving as a summer room for dining; as an anti chamber in which people of business or of second rank wait and amuse themselves; and it is a good apartment for the reception of large companies at public feasts'.[86]

For much of the century the main items to be found in the hall were chairs or benches specifically designed for that situation. Furniture suppliers were aware that these represented another self-positioning possibility: '[the chairs] are such as are placed in halls, for the use of servants or strangers waiting on business – they are generally made of all mahogany with turned seats and the crest or arms of the family painted on the centre of the back'.[87] The basic form of these chairs was standardized, but there were variations dependent upon the price paid. Both Chippendale, and Ince and Mayhew illustrate hall chairs in their pattern books, and interestingly, both suggest a painted finish if mahogany should prove too expensive. Whatever finish was used, the hall 'ought always to be expressive of the dignity of its possessor'.[88] This idea of dignity was carried into the dining room.

The dining room, although established in the seventeenth century, was an ambiguous space. The architect Robert Adam noted in his *Works* that 'dining rooms were considered as the apartments of conversation, in which we have to pass a great deal of our time. This renders it desirable to have them fitted up with elegance and splendour, but in a style different from that of the

---

[84] De la Rochfoucauld, F. (1784), *A Frenchman in England*, p. 4, cited in Saumarez-Smith (1993), E*ighteenth Century Decoration*, p. 308.

[85] Fowler, J. and Cornforth, J. (1984), *English Decoration in the Eighteenth Century*, p. 66.

[86] Ibid.

[87] Sheraton (1803), *The Cabinet Dictionary*, p. 250.

[88] Ibid., p. 217.

apartments. Instead of being hung with damasks, tapestry etc. they are always finished with stucco and adorned with statues and paintings that they may not retain the smell of victuals.'[89]

After sitting through a long dinner, François de la Rochefoucauld described how when the tablecloth was removed, 'the most beautiful table that it is possible to see' was revealed. He went on to say it:

> was most remarkable that the English are so much given to the use of mahogany; not only are their tables generally made of it, but also their doors and seats and the handrails of their staircases. Yet it is just as dear in England as in France ... At all events, their tables are made of most beautiful wood and always have a brilliant polish like that of the finest glass.[90]

Stana Nenadic has also commented upon the rise of the dining 'set' between 1760 and 1810 in middle-rank Scottish households. She suggests that as the bed had once been the major piece of furniture in late seventeenth century households, so it was that the dining set became most important in the later eighteenth century. Changes in fashion from small folding tables and various placements within the room to larger, more formal tables changed the character of the dining room.

Nenadic also cites a passage which closely reflects the comments of Rochefoucauld, recalling early nineteenth-century life in Edinburgh New Town, which discusses the care and attention lavished on the dining table: 'The furniture was nearly all rosewood or old Spanish mahogany, especially the many leaved dining table ... which were always in a condition of the highest polish.'[91]

This emphasis on mahogany represents an example of the search for novelty. A contemporary commented on this taste for exotic timbers in place of the more traditional walnut:

> My Lords contemptuous of his Country's Groves,
> As foreign Fashions foreign Trees too loves:
> Odious! upon a Walnut-plank to dine!
> No – the red-veined Mohoggony be mine!
> Each Chest and Chair around my Room that stands
> Was Ship'd thro' dangerous Seas from distant Lands.[92]

The continual use of mahogany alongside other woods that moved in and out of popularity is revealing. It is an example of the establishment of particular

---

[89] Adam, R. (1773), *Works*, Vol. I, Plate V, cited in Fowler and Cornforth (1984), *English Decoration in the Eighteenth Century*, p. 67.

[90] De la Rochefoucauld, F. (1784), *A Frenchman in England* (1933), p. 152.

[91] Nenadic (1994), 'Middle rank consumers and domestic culture in Edinburgh and Glasgow 1720–1840', *Past and Present*, p. 142.

[92] Wharton, T. (1748), *Poems on Several Occasions*.

timber types that were recognized as being appropriate to a particular item, room or use. In the case of mahogany, it was, as has been shown, especially destined for the dining room. Other items of furniture were designed and sold for particular roles in the etiquette of dining. The sideboard table was used 'for a dining equipage, on which the silver plate is placed',[93] whilst the sideboard itself was introduced in the last quarter of the eighteenth century, designed to hold all the necessaries for serving and dining. By the end of the century, the gendered role of rooms was apparently understood. Thomas Sheraton used adjectives such as 'handsome', 'large' and 'substantial' to evoke an idea of the required furniture style for a dining room, thus giving a hint of the sort of impression that was to be projected.[94]

Depending on the scale of the room and the collection of books, prints and drawings, there would be a whole range of furniture accessories deemed necessary for the library. There could be specially designed reading and writing chairs, which remained popular throughout the century. Although made in a variety of fashionable styles, they were all contrived so that they could be sat upon astride, having the book set upon an adjustable shelf on the back rail. [95]

Reading tables and stands were also introduced to support books at various slants. These were either freestanding upon a pedestal, or designed to sit on a table. They feature in Ince and Mayhew's *Universal System of Household Furniture* and also in the 1797 edition of *The Prices of Cabinet Work*.[96] More sophisticated were the combined writing and reading tables variously known as artists', architects' or Cobb tables. These combined rising tops with drawer space and accessories. The reason they were called Cobb tables was explained in Smith's 1828 description of them. He said that John Cobb 'was the person who brought that very convenient table into fashion that draws out in front, with upper and inwards rising desks, so healthy for those who stand to write, read or draw'.[97] The use of the word 'convenient' clearly relates to the design of a whole range of furniture that was planned to make the use of the library as efficient and as pleasant as possible.

In most libraries, furniture items intended to assist access would also have been indispensable, as books were often shelved to the cornice. These items took a wide variety of forms, usually as steps or ladders, including telescopic poles, miniature staircases, as well as convertible tables or chairs that had built-in steps. Sometimes they were architectural in conception and resembled a flight of stairs, whilst in other cases they were hidden away until required. These metamorphic models were often based upon the 1774 patent of Robert

---

[93] Sheraton (1803), *The Cabinet Dictionary*, p. 304.

[94] Ibid., p. 218.

[95] Ibid., p. 17 and Plate 5.

[96] *The Prices of Cabinet Work*, Plates 26 and Plate 11 respectively.

[97] Smith, J. T. (1828), *Nollekens and His Times*, Vol. II, pp. 243–4.

Campbell.[98] In a similar vein was the metamorphic library chair that could be deftly turned from an elbow chair into a set of steps.[99]

Inevitably, the most important items of the library, especially if the architect had not supplied built-in storage, were the bookcases. Although the well-known example of the Pepys' bookcases (often considered to be the first, and now in Magdalene College) dates from 1666, bookcases were only to grow in popularity during the eighteenth century. The freestanding press or library case, often based on architectural forms, was the mainstay of library rooms, and this continued to be the case into the nineteenth century. In smaller or more private rooms, book storage was often integrated to form a composite piece called a bureau bookcase.[100]

According to some scholars, the library lost much of its 'all-male' connotations towards the end of the century.[101] These connotations were implied rather than obvious, as Sheraton only recommended these rooms be furnished 'in imitation of the antiques'.[102] The influence of the female and the change of role for the library from a studious space to a more family-orientated room meant that a wider range of activities was included, which called for more specialized furniture. Examples might include writing tables for both men and women, screen tables designed to shield one from the heat of a fire,[103] and specially designed chairs for convenient and comfortable sitting at these table types.[104]

By the early nineteenth century, the architect and garden-planner Humphrey Repton wrote: 'the most recent modern custom is to use the library as the general living-room; and that sort of state room formerly called the best parlour, and of late years the drawing room, is now generally found a melancholy apartment, when entirely shut up and opened to give the visitors a formal cold reception'.[105] Certainly, by 1820 Maria Edgeworth could write that 'the library drawing room

---

[98] Robert Campbell, Pat. No. 1086, 11 November 1774. This patent referred to making library steps in writing, library, dining, card, breakfast, dressing or other tables. The continuing success of the design may be gauged by the fact that Morgan and Sanders were making library steps based on Campbell's principle in the early nineteenth century; see, Austen, B., 'Morgan and Sanders and the patent furniture makers of Catherine Street', *Connoisseur* (November 1974). They are illustrated in Sheraton, T., *Drawing Book*, Plates 5 and 22. Although Campbell patented the design in 1774, Sheraton, writing in *circa* 1793 pointed out that if makers did not want to bother with altering the model to avoid the patent, the steps were available from Robert Campbell and Son Marylebone Street, London, 'with a sufficient allowance for selling them again.' (Appendix, p. 43).

[99] For library steps, see further, Pinto, E. H. (1963), 'Georgian library steps', *Antiques*, January, pp. 102–4.

[100] This term was not contemporary. It was coined in the nineteenth century. At the time the piece was known as a desk and bookcase.

[101] Thornton, P. (1984), *Authentic Decor*, p. 150.

[102] Sheraton (1803), *The Cabinet Dictionary*. p. 216.

[103] For example, see *The Price of Cabinet Work* (1797). Plate 6.

[104] Sheraton (1793), *Drawing Book*, Appendix, Plate 10.

[105] Repton, H. (1816), *Fragments on the Theory and Practice of Landscape Gardening*, cited in Fowler and Cornforth (1984), *English Decoration in the eighteenth century*, p. 75.

with low sofa, plenty of moveable tables, open bookcases, and all that speaks the habits and affords the means of agreeable occupation'.[106]

The ascending order of importance of a suite of rooms as described by Isaac Ware in 1756, indicates a changing role for particular apartments.[107] The progression from the saloon via antechamber, drawing room, bed chamber and finally to the dressing room represents a move towards making the closet and dressing room the focal points of the house. The opportunity for personal display in dressing rooms was therefore too good to miss, thus explaining why much dressing furniture is often of fine quality and high style. Mrs Boscawen, writing in 1748, recorded proudly that: 'This afternoon I saw company in my dressing room for the first time since it being finished.'[108] For women's dressing rooms, a range of special tables, boxes and stools, mirrors and chests of drawers were developed; whilst for men, shaving stands, dressing glasses and storage items were introduced. These new storage items also reflect the desire to organize and categorize possessions according to function and use.

Dressing tables were known and used in the seventeenth century, but during the eighteenth they became much more elaborate. They incorporated a wide variety of toilet requisites, and could be very complex and costly objects. An interesting example of an extreme design is the Rudd or reflecting dressing table. This was a four-legged table with pullout drawers, some fitted with mirrors that lifted up at various angles. First illustrated in Hepplewhite's *Guide* (1788), it was also shown in a simplified form in the *Cabinet Maker's London Book of Prices*. The model was published again in 1797, but by 1803 Sheraton could claim that it was 'not much in present use'.[109] Perhaps this indicates the relatively short span of popularity of a novel item.

Dressing tables were not exclusively for women. Sheraton designed one to 'accommodate a gentleman or lady with conveniences for dressing',[110] although men tended to use dressing units, variously known as dressing stands, commodes or chests. There were differences between these items, the chest usually being a chest of drawers with the top drawer fitted out for convenience. The dressing commode seems hardly different except that the chest might be fitted with a hinged top having a mirror on the underside, whereas the commode would frequently have had a freestanding toilet mirror stood upon it.[111] The dressing chest fits into the taste for multi-purpose furniture in that it

---

[106] *Letters from England* p. 229 cited in Fowler J. and Cornforth, J. (1984), *English Decoration in the eighteenth century* p.75.

[107] Ware, Sir Isaac (1756), *A Complete Body of Architecture*, Book III, p. 328, quoted in Tristram, P. (1989), *Living Space in Fact and Fiction*, p. 250.

[108] Fowler and Cornforth (1976), *English Decoration in the Eighteenth century*, p. 81.

[109] Sheraton (1803), *The Cabinet Dictionary*.

[110] Ibid., p. 202. Also see Plate no. 214 in Thornton (1984), *Authentic Decor*.

[111] Even with this distinction, there appear to be examples of both versions.

was compact and was fitted with a variety of drawers: one for a night stool, one for a square bidet, one for a basin and two cups, and one for a water bottle. In addition, a glass frame was usually hinged under the top.[112]

Apart from these, other special-use items included shaving tables and stands, the distinction generally being that the stands did not have basins. Night tables, introduced in the mid-century, are illustrated in Ince and Mayhew's *Universal System*, with one example conveniently offering a rising top for reading. Night tables, bidets, and the like were often disguised to look like another furniture type or were hidden within other units for the sake of decorum.

In addition to the physical need for space-saving furniture, there was also a demand for dual-purpose items, and this was often, though by no means always, related to the size of the family. The example of press beds is instructive. The idea of beds in cupboards had for a long time been in use in vernacular homes, but in polite society, sensibility and social pressure suggested that a bed in a dining or living room was not *de rigeur*. This idea may also have been related to concerns about health. As early as 1691, Thomas Tryon was complaining that press bedsteads did not allow proper air circulation,[113] and over one hundred years later Loudon warned that press bedsteads were 'objectionable, as harbouring vermin and being apt to soon get out of order when in daily use'.[114]

Regardless of these warnings, press beds were to become popular throughout the century. Ideal for garret bedrooms and servants, they were also made for grander clients. Imposing examples might well have followed the 1772 patent of Thomas Gale, who invented a mechanism for a wardrobe/bedstead that raised the false doors to make a tester for the bed, which then unfolded from the inside. When closed, the whole object resembled a bookcase or wardrobe.[115] The models made for David Garrick and Sir Edward Knatchbull are of a high quality, whilst the records of the Gillow firm show them producing a range of models for most tastes.[116]

The press bedstead was an interesting example of a basic product type that was available in a number of varieties, each of which indicated a different status. At the top of the range was the library press bed, which incorporated shelving for books on either side of a middle section covered by double doors. According to Richard Gillow, these were intended 'to stand in a Dining Room as a

---

[112] *The Price of Cabinet Work* (1797).

[113] Tryon, T. (1691), *The Way to Health, Long Life and Happiness*, p. 440.

[114] Loudon, J. C. (1839), *An Encyclopedia of Cottage, Farm and Villa Architecture and Furniture*, revised edn, pp. 331–2.

[115] T. Gale, Patent No. 1002, 1 February 1772.

[116] Garrick's press bed/wardrobe is in the Victoria and Albert Museum. For the Knatchbull commission, see Gilbert, C. (1978), *The Life and Works of Thomas Chippendale*, p. 231. A number of examples are shown in the Gillow ES (estimate sketch books) held at Westminster Central Library, London.

handsome piece of furniture to make an additional bedroom occasionally'.[117] A letter written in 1770 explains about the purchase of a 'cloaths' chest bed' 'which is a very handsome piece of furniture and much in fashion amongst young gentlemen even those who have rooms of their own'.[118] A little less imposing was the wardrobe press bed. This was a wardrobe shape that combined a pullout bed hidden behind wood or mirror doors. At the bottom of the selection were bureaus and table beds, where the beds unfolded from behind or from underneath.[119] Eighteenth-century bedroom and dressing furniture was clearly intended to provide the maximum in convenience and personal comfort. This requirement was also found in the saloons and drawing rooms.

Sheraton is very clear as to the purpose of a drawing room: it is 'to concentrate the elegance of the whole house, and is the highest display of richness of furniture'.[120] He goes on to say: 'The grandeur then introduced into the drawing room is not to be considered, as the ostentatious parade of its proprietor, but the respect he pays to the rank of his visitants.' Parson Woodforde noted in his diary for August 1783 how: 'Mr and Mrs Townsend behaved very genteel to us. The drawing room in which we drank tea &c. was hung with silk. The chairs of the same kind of silk and all the woodwork of them gilded, as were the settees. The looking glass, which was the finest and largest I ever saw, cost at second hand £150.0.0 …'.[121] The reference to the second-hand nature of the mirror appears to have no hint of derogatory meaning.

The idea of performance has already been touched upon as a metaphor, but Mimi Hellmann has pointed out that performance in interiors can also be seen in a very real sense. The ability to operate complex pieces of furniture reflected or denied an appearance of grace and ease with such objects. In a way, the operating of these sorts of pieces was an accomplishment by the individual for the viewers in the assembled company. Furniture had taken on a 'performative role' in elite social life.[122] If attempts at social exclusion were being eroded by the greater availability of furniture and equipment, then as Hellmann suggests, even if the material signs were easy to purchase, it was important that they were not easy to perform. The furniture and its role had to be learnt.[123]

---

[117] Richard Gillow letter to Matthew Wilson, November 1778. See Gillows Letter Book, 1778–81, 344/169, Gillow Archive.

[118] Letter from William Grant to Mrs Ross, cited in Bamford, (1983), *A Dictionary of Edinburgh Wrights and Furniture Makers 1660–1840*, pp. 17–18.

[119] For press beds, see Edwards, C. (1990), 'Press Beds', *Furniture History*, XXVI, pp. 42–8, and Jones, D. (1988), 'The press bed in Scotland', *Scottish Society for Art History Yearbook*, pp. 28–35.

[120] Sheraton, T. (1803), *The Cabinet Dictionary*, p. 218.

[121] Woodforde, Parson, *Diary*, 28 August 1783. Beresford, J. (Ed.) (1929), *The Diary of a Country Parson*.

[122] Hellmann, M. (1999), 'Furniture, sociability, and the work of leisure in eighteenth century France', *Eighteenth Century Studies*, 32(4). p. 425.

[123] Ibid., p. 437.

These items that have modes of combining complex functions within one piece of furniture were often multi-purpose as well. This no doubt added to the convenience as well as to the amusement value of a model. These pieces, sometimes called *meubles à surprises*, were well known in France and became of interest in England in the later part of the eighteenth century.[124] By the end of the century, there was a great demand for this sort of furniture. Sheraton's designs included ladies' writing tables which had spring-loaded pen and ink drawers, and a spring-weighted screen operated by lead weights and pulleys;[125] a lady's dressing table with rising back mirror and side mirrors',[126] and the Harlequin table, so called because it used complicated mechanisms that were similarly employed in the *commedia dell'arte*.

The example of the 'ingenious mechanick' John Joseph Merlin, who established a specialist museum/shop selling metamorphic or combined-function furniture and other mechanical devices, demonstrates a sense of marketing as well as invention. The sorts of objects that could be found in Merlin's premises included:

> neat little writing-reading- or working-tables, combined with charming soft toned pianos … Others with pianos concealed, and clever desks with lights attached for quartettes set up in less than three minutes, which if not required for music might be converted into a nice piece of furniture for playing chess.[127]

Amongst other pieces of furniture that Merlin designed was the Quartetto music cabinet, which 'contains flutes, violins and music books; and by touching a spring key, it will rise to a proper height and form music desks for four performers'. [128] Perhaps the best example of Merlin's attempts to amuse and interest the public's demand for metamorphic furniture was the 'curious new invented tea table by which any lady can fill twelve cups of tea and shift them round by the pressure of the foot, without the assistance of her hands'.[129] The operation of this item was probably no mean accomplishment, and would have certainly been an amusing performance.

Apart from the rather special case of Merlin, it is significant that specialist retailers had established themselves by the end of the century to meet this demand for so-called metamorphic furniture.[130] The niche market, which had

---

[124] For metamorphic furniture, see, for example, de Plas, S. (1975), *Les Meubles à Transformation et à Secret*, Paris.

[125] Sheraton (1793), *Drawing Book*, p. 388.

[126] Ibid., p. 397.

[127] Von la Roche (1786), *Sophie in London*, p. 140.

[128] Merlin Museum catalogue, cited in Wright, M. (1985), 'John Joseph Merlin: The ingenious mechanic', exhibition catalogue, London, Kenwood, p. 76.

[129] Von La Roche (1786), *Sophie in London*, p. 140.

[130] For example, Morgan and Sanders, who traded in Catherine Street, Strand, London, from 1803 to 1817. They took out a number of patents for metamorphic furniture and retailed other designs. Ackermann published their shop interior in the *Repository of Arts* (1809).

originated as specialist suppliers of invalid furniture, grew into the business of manufacturing and retailing folding, and campaign furniture and developed further into a wide range of adjustable, folding, and transforming furniture.[131] Although much of this furniture was not particularly required for space-saving, there was a notion of decorum, in which the alternative use of a piece of furniture is hidden, that was part of a wider feeling that the specialized use of space, rational systems of storage and the careful planning of limited resources were both practical and morally superior. This was to be developed further in the nineteenth century.

---

[131] See Brawer, N. (2001), *British Campaign Furniture: Elegance under Canvas 1790–1914.* This work has a useful gazetteer of the manufacturers and retailers of these products.

Chapter 5

The retail revolution: the response to the demands from the nineteenth-century consumer

The *upholsterer's* eye, in fine frenzy rolling,
Glances from ceiling to floor, from floor to ceiling;
And, as imagination bodies forth,
The form of things unknown, the upholsterer's pencil
Turns them into shape, and gives to airy nothing
A local habitation and a NAME.
(Maria Edgeworth, 1812, *The Absentee.*)

One of the themes of this book is that retailing is a mix of responses based on a continuity of practice combined with changes made in reaction to circumstances. The home furnishing retailers in the nineteenth century were able to continue a tradition that had been fully established in the eighteenth century, which required them to supply goods, and more especially services and advice, to a growing population. This same customer base, which was able to indulge in the benefits of increased spending power and a need for differentiation in tastes, also encouraged the development of new retailing methods, products and services, but also responded to established policies already set by retailers.

The 'retail revolution' was a process that operated at different speeds and intensities within varied trades. There was not a homogenous transformation of the whole of the retail trade. In some cases, such as grocery, there were major changes that went right through the distribution system, whereas in the retailing of furniture and furnishings, the scope and rate of change was less uniform. Nevertheless, there were important changes that will be examined in this chapter. They include the growth of the department store and its connections with 'the home' in a wide sense; the growth of a range of specialist retail furnishers who offered various levels of service and quality, and the continuing separation of the making process from the sales procedures. Despite these changes, there remained a continuing need for advice that was still met by the retailer. This raises a fourth theme in this chapter, which considers the conflict between critics and the retailers over their apparent role as arbiters of styles and tastes.

As has been shown in the previous chapter, the upholsterer was considered an arbiter of taste and a guide to fashionable living. His knowledge of fashion, like the mercer, could apparently benefit from a French accent and the playing of a performance for the customer. One such was the fictional upholsterer Mr Soho, who was overheard in discussions with Lady Clonbrony about her apartment that was to be fitted up for a gala. No one could be more sensible than Mr Soho of the sales value of a French name:

> Your la'ship sees – this is merely a scratch of my pencil. Your la'ship's sensible – just to give you an idea of the shape, the form of the thing. You fill up your angles here with *encoinieres* – round your walls with the Turkish tent drapery – a fancy of my own – in apricot cloth, or crimson velvet, suppose, or *en flute*, in crimson satin draperies, fanned and riched with gold fringes *ensuite* ...[1]

The performing characteristics of the upholsterer are also nicely caught in this passage:

> Mr. Soho was speaking in a conceited dictatorial tone asserting that there was no 'colour in nature for that room equal to the belly of the fawn', which belly of the fawn he so pronounced, that Lady Clonbrony understood it to be la belle uniform, and under this mistake repeated and assented to the assertion, till it was set to rights with condescending superiority by the upholsterer. This first architectural upholsterer of the age, as he styles himself, and was universally admitted to be by all the world of fashion, then, with full powers given to him spoke *en maître*. The whole face of things must be changed, There must be new hangings, new draperies, new cornices, new candelabras, new everything![2]

Despite this amusing mockery of the fashionable furnisher from the early part of the century, it was clear that they continued to play a leading role in establishing tastes. This was not universally accepted as a good thing. In 1853, *Fraser's Magazine* published an article noting that:

> the whole domain of decorative art and of furniture [had fallen under the control of] a parcel of dealers, who make their market out of the foolish vanity of that large section of the public which is stimulated to extravagance.[3]

The role of retailers and their responsibilities were issues that dominated much of the nineteenth-century debates about design. The critic Charles Eastlake was also aware of one of the perennial problems that design reformers seemed to grapple with. This was the apparently powerful role of the retailer: 'At the furniture warehouse they [the public] are in the upholsterer's hands; at the china shop they are as easily taken over by the obsequious vendor of wine glasses and dinner plates. The carpet merchant leads them by the nose ...'.[4] But

---

[1] Edgeworth, M. (1812), *The Absentee*, pp.12–13.

[2] Ibid.

[3] *Fraser's Magazine* (1853), article entitled 'Furniture books'.

[4] Eastlake, C. (1872), *Hints on Household Taste*, p. 3. It is interesting to see that the sculptor Eric Gill was making similar points some eighty years later in *Art and Business* (1940): 'so people are dependent upon the salesman and the salesman is only concerned with what will sell. Saleability is his only criterion – if a thing sells it is good and if it won't sell it is bad – or at any rate not worth making.'.

Eastlake was fully aware that consumer aspirations meant that 'in the eyes of Materfamilias there is no upholstery which could possibly surpass that which the most fashionable upholsterer supplies'.[5]

Eastlake was directly concerned with the matter of encouraging shops to stock what he considered 'well-designed furniture' and the reasons why retailers appeared to refuse to do so:

> The upholsterers declared themselves willing to give more attention to the subject of design as soon as the nature of public taste became defined. The public on the other hand, complained that they could only choose from what they saw in the shops. It is not improbable that there was a little apathy on both sides, but it was necessary that one should take the lead and it is certain that at the present time when well-designed and artistic furniture is offered for sale at a reasonable price, and under proper management, there is no difficulty in finding purchasers.[6]

Even worse, British consumers could be compared badly with European ones. Rather confirming Eastlake's comment about apathy, Hungerford Pollen wrote in his *British Manufacturing Industries* that:

> [the] advantage that the French have is in the superior intelligence of their patrons and buyers. There are enormous fortunes in England, and the owners and makers of them spend money liberally in furnishing their homes…On the whole, however, they are more in the hands and under the direction of dealers and makers than the French.[7]

An example of this issue of control by the retailer over the public taste is illustrated by a certain arrogance in the response by John Maple of Maple and Co. to the Select Committee on the Sweating System, when asked how he did business. He replied with an example: 'I had an order given me the other day for doing the Hotel Victoria; my order was £45 000 … My bill was sent in for furnishing the hotel and I supplied what I like, and what I thought was right and proper.'[8] Even the building trade press noticed these changes in purchasing methods. In December 1900, *The Illustrated Carpenter and Builder* wrote: 'Until recently when a man wanted to furnish he would visit all the dealers and selected piece by piece of furniture … Today he sends for a dealer in art furnishings and fittings who surveys all the rooms in the house and he brings his artistic mind to bear on the subject.'[9] These two examples appear to support Eastlake's claim that there was a degree of apathy, and by inference, consumers were abrogating their responsibilities for home furnishings to the retailer.

John Ruskin suggested the most radical of reforms. In 1867 he recommended that, as all retail commerce was only interested in profit, he would:

---

[5] Eastlake (1872), *Hints on Household Taste*, p. 3.

[6] Ibid., p. 62. The situation had changed little one hundred years later.

[7] Pollen, J. H. (1876), *British Manufacturing Industries*, pp. 161–2.

[8] *Select Committee on the Sweating System* (1888), p. 630.

[9] *The Illustrated Carpenter and Builder*, December 7 1900, Supplement, p. 2.

put an end to this source of baseness by making all retail dealers merely
salaried officers in the employ of trade guild; the stewards that is to say of
the saleable properties of those guilds and purveyors of such and such
articles to a given number of families.[10]

Despite these criticisms, there was still an aura of professionalism at some
levels of the trade. The magazine *House Furnisher*, writing in 1873, considered
that 'your true upholsterer is a man of the most varied and important
qualifications, and is often as necessary and as trusted an agent in many homes
as are the family lawyer and doctor'.[11] If taken seriously, this role as an arbiter
of taste carried a degree of responsibility to match their clients' needs with
appropriate goods. The *Cabinet and Upholsterer's Advertiser*'s advice to its
trade readers in 1877 continued a theme, which already had a long history. It
considered that the supplier should ensure that: 'the furniture [sold] should
correspond with the dimensions of the house to be occupied and both should be
in a proper relation to [the customers] real position in life'.[12] Thomas Sheraton
had expressed opinions on this issue of appropriateness seventy-five years
earlier.

Location

The ancient arrangement of trades operating in a particular street or quarter
continued and even grew in the nineteenth century. The eighteenth-century
trend of a slow process of separation of manufacturing from retailing
continued, although this was by no means universal. In 1820 the traditional
area of St Paul's Churchyard was still a popular location for furniture
businesses as were the areas of St Martin's Lane and Covent Garden. Even in a
predominantly retail area such as Oxford Street or Tottenham Court Road in
London, small workshops that supplied the retailers were established in the
streets behind the thoroughfares. As in previous centuries, the location of retail
shops was influenced by the proximity of or ease of access to both suppliers and
potential customers, but during the nineteenth century, the sources of supply
became more widespread, as did the customer base. As the centre of retail trade
again moved westward in London, so did the traders. London's Oxford Street
already had a reputation as a furnishing street in the eighteenth century, and this
continued into the nineteenth. By the early nineteenth century, Tottenham
Court Road, a well-known 'furniture street', also exemplifies this process of

---

[10] Ruskin, J. (1867), *Time and Tide in Weare and Tyne*, Letter XXI, p. 62.

[11] *House Furnisher* (1873). It is of interest that this metaphor was also used by R. and A. Garrett
in their work *Suggestions for Huge Decoration in Painting, Woodwork and Furniture*, published in
1876, where they said that: 'Decorators may be compared to doctors. It is useless to put yourself
under their direction unless you mean to carry out their regime' (pp. 9–10).

[12] *Cabinet and Upholsterer's Advertiser*, 7 July 1877, p. 7.

development. From around 1800, furnishers began to establish themselves in the locality, having often removed from the areas of Soho and St Martin's Lane. In 1818 Tottenham Court Road was equipped with street lighting, which must have had a beneficial effect on business. Other locational factors influenced its development. The Regents Canal passed nearby, so this was useful for timber deliveries and so on. By the mid-century, the transport infrastructure included buses that used the street as a thoroughfare, and useful rail links had been established. The Euston terminus and the Metropolitan line stations were close by. The growth of the area is reflected in Tallis's comments when he wrote in 1839 that Tottenham Court Road was twenty-five years previously (in 1813) 'almost the least busiest thoroughfare – and now there is as much and more trade done in it than in any other street in the metropolis'.[13] It is no coincidence that four of the most well-known English furnishing stores were established in this street within ten years of each other: Hewetsons by 1838, Heals in 1839, Maples in 1842 and Oetzmann in 1848. The businesses of Catesby, and Wolfe and Hollander followed these. Nevertheless, the reputation of the street had still not reached its peak. In 1873 the *House Furnisher* remarked upon the entry of Shoolbred and Co. into the furniture trade.[14] It noted that: 'there is room, ample and to spare, for all fair and honest traders; and although it may be long before the Tottenham Court Road rivals New Bond and Oxford Street, we may hope yet to see the locality redeemed from being a by-word among streets'.[15]

Selling methods and displays

The apparent obsession of customers with the latest thing, the fashionable and the stylish was ridiculed by reformers and commentators alike in the nineteenth century, but was harnessed by the retailers to make business. In 1812 Maria Edgeworth's fictional upholsterer, Mr Soho, used all his selling skills whilst at the home of Lady Clonbrony. He particularly stressed the fact that his customer was being privileged to see certain goods before other clients had seen them:

> And let me reflect. For the next apartment, it strikes me – as you la'ship don't value expense – the Alhambra hangings – my own thought entirely – Now before I unroll them, Lady Clonbrony, I must beg you'll not mention I've shown them. I give you my sacred honour, not a soul has set eyes upon the Alhambra hangings except Mrs Dareville, who stole a peep; I refused absolutely refused the Duchess of Torcaster – but I can't refuse your la'ship – so you see ma'am (unrolling them) scagliola, porphyry columns supporting the grand dome – entablature, silvered and decorated

---

[13] Tallis, J. (1839), *London Street Views*, reprint 1969.

[14] The business of James Shoolbred was first established in 1820, and grew to become one of the more important department furnishing stores.

[15] *House Furnisher*, 10 June 1873.

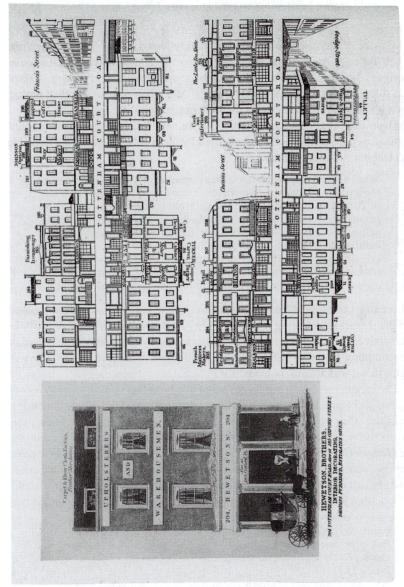

Figure 5.1 Hewetson Brothers, Furnishers, Tottenham Court Road, 1841

with imitative bronze ornaments: under the entablature, a *valence in pelmets,* of puffed scarlet silk, would have an unparalleled grand effect, seen through the arches – with the TREBISOND TRELLICE PAPER, would make *à tout ensemble,* novel beyond example. On that trebisond trellice paper, I confess ladies, I do pique myself.[16]

The evident fascination with the fashionable, and more importantly the avoidance of the unfashionable, was again reflected by the fictional Mr Soho when he told his customer in response to her appreciation of a particular design: 'There's only objection which is one sees it everywhere – quite antediluvian – gone to the hotels even.'[17] What could be worse than having your home looking like a commercial interior.

Over fifty years later, Charles Eastlake still talked about the 'counter' influences to a sensible selection of goods by the purchaser, and again ridiculed the language of the shopman:

> When Materfamilias enters an ordinary upholsterer's warehouse, how can she possibly decide on the pattern of her new carpets, when bale after bale of Brussels is unrolled by the indefatigable youth, who is equal in his praises of every piece in turn? Shall it be the 'House of Lords' diaper, of a yellow spot upon a blue ground; or the 'imitation Turkey,' with its multifarious colours; or the beautiful new moiré design; or yonder exquisite invention of green fern leaves tied up with knots of white satin ribbon? The shopman remarks of one piece of goods that it is 'elegant'; of another that it is 'striking'; of a third that it is 'unique'; and so forth.[18]

This extract continues to describe total confusion, until a choice is made based on the shop man declaring it 'fashionable.' At the end of the section, Eastlake perceptively comments on the carpet choice, and by implication, the nature of consumption patterns: 'while new, it is admired; when old, everybody will agree that it was always 'hideous'.[19]

The location and nature of the layout of goods and services offered by a store immediately gave the consumer an image that they could judge, and decide if it reflected their own self-image.[20] Most successful retailers knew this instinctively, but the trade press explicitly examined the issue. In the *Journal de Menuiserie* (1863) the authors pointed out that there was a 'need to impress buyers [which] has given birth to artificially arranged displays ... One could also say that in principle the store should be for the objects found there, what a case is for a jewel or a rich binding for a book'.[21] A very revealing article was

---

[16] Edgeworth (1812), *The Absentee,* pp. 12–13.

[17] Ibid., p. 13.

[18] Eastlake (1872), *Hints on Household Taste,* pp. 11–12.

[19] Ibid., p. 12.

[20] For a useful discussion of aspects of American window and shop display see Leach, W. (1989), 'Strategists of display and the production of desire', in Bronner, S. J. (Ed.), (1989), *Consuming Visions: Accumulation and Display in Goods 1880–1920.*

[21] Cited in Auslander (1996), *Taste and Power,* p. 323.

published in the *Furniture Gazette* in October 1875. It explained how the displays of shops could be ranked in terms of status. It is worth quoting in full, as it not only discusses display but also gives a valuable indication of the hierarchy of the nineteenth century London furnishing trades:

> First we have the high class houses, represented by such firms as those of Gillows, Morant, Dowbiggin &c., whose reputation is such for the superiority of their productions that it is not necessary for them to make any display whatsoever. Secondly there are firms famous for the production of articles of high artistic order, of whom Jackson and Graham are a fair representative house. Their windows are never crowded with goods, but exhibit frequently one article only, rarely more than two or three, but these are always distinguished for some rare excellence of design or colouring. A third and distinct class deal only in old furniture which realises high prices leaving a goodly residuum of profit … their windows look as if they had migrated thither from the South Kensington Museum. A fourth class represented by such firms as Shoolbred and Co. Marshall and Snelgrove and Maple, make magnificent displays, in their large well-arranged windows of resplendent carpets, rich curtains fabrics, and inlaid cabinet work. A fifth class makes good displays of useful ordinary goods judiciously ticketed with a view of attracting by price more than by pattern or texture. The houses of Meeking, Tarn, Oetzmann, Whiteley and Venebales are representative of this class. Then there is the sixth and very numerous class who depend solely upon ticketing and startling announcements [where the goods are] 'shovelled in piles' into the windows.[22]

The hierarchy of display, recognizable today as it was in 1875, reflects the image that the store wanted to project and the sort of customer base it was trying to build up. At the peak of the ranking were the exclusive stores situated in the best areas of town, supplying an elite and exclusive 'carriage trade'. The second level reflects an 'artistic approach' to display that Eastlake would have appreciated. This created an effect of the shop being a gallery with exclusive and expensive products. The third group, who can be called antique dealers, had a varied press. Eastlake cautioned against the 'pseudo-Gothic joinery which is manufactured in the back-shops of Soho', going on to say: 'no doubt good examples of medieval furniture and cabinet-work are occasionally to be met with in the curiosity shops of Wardour Street', but his general tone was critical.[23] The fourth shop group mentioned aimed their displays at the upper middle classes and the professions, where all the trappings of an arriviste could be had and homes could be furnished in the most palatial manner. These stores had affinities with the department store. The fifth group met the demands of the lower middle class and the artisans, who were guided mainly by price and good value. The final group emphasized price, credit terms and availability as paramount, which generally appealed to the working class, who were often limited to this sort of shop.

---

[22] *Furniture Gazette*, 2 October 1875, p. 193.
[23] Eastlake (1878), *Hints on Household Taste*, p. 64.

The internal displays also reflected the tone of the store. For the lower-graded shops, selling displays were basic: 'It is simply this-taking the central corridor as a starting point, the furniture is made to radiate up to the walls, or to speak more plainly the goods are placed according to size commencing with the smallest.'[24] For higher-grade stores, one of the most inventive and enduring selling and display methods was model rooms. Unlike fashions, where merchandise could be tried on and experienced, furniture and furnishings needed to be seen together in a setting so customers could visualize how the goods 'went together'. Model rooms were therefore important as guides to prospective householders. It is certain that by 1876, the display of furnishings in room settings or 'vignettes' was being used as a promotional tool. At the Centennial Exhibition in Philadelphia in 1876, they were particularly commented upon:

> An interesting feature of the Exhibition is the method that the upholsterers, decorators, and furniture dealers have chosen to display their goods to the best advantage. This method consists in dividing the section allotted to them into rooms, which are afterwards fitted up as a parlour, library, boudoir, dining room or any special apartment.'[25]

The ideas spread rapidly from then on into retail stores, and were reproduced as images in the catalogues they produced. For example, in Shoolbred's catalogue published in 1889, it was stated that 'the arrangement of a complete suite of rooms, furnished in various styles ... will be found of great assistance in the selection of furniture, carpets, and decoration etc., the cost of each article in the room complete being marked in plain figures'.[26]

The department stores were among the leaders of practices that linked display techniques intended to sell goods to other areas. This connection between department store layouts of a range of comparative goods and the displays in museums and international exhibitions is evident. In another example, the exotic might be infered by displays that reflected the bazaar. In Zola's novel *Au Bonheur des Dames*, a passage describes the owner of a department store who:

> had recently been the first to buy in the Levant, at very reasonable terms, a collection of antique and modern carpets, or rare carpets such as had only been sold by antique dealers at very high prices; and he was going to flood the market with them, he was letting them go at almost cost prices, was simply using them as a splendid setting which would attract art connoisseurs to his shop.[27]

[24] *The Cabinet Maker*, November 1880.

[25] Smith, Walter (1876), *Masterpieces of the Centennial Exhibition*, cited in Grier, K. (1988), *Culture and Comfort: People, Parlours and Upholstery, 1850–1930*, p. 49.

[26] Shoolbred and Co., London, catalogue, 1889.

[27] Cited in Bayley, S. (Ed.) (1989), *Commerce and Culture from Pre-industrial Art to Post-industrial Value*.

Figure 5.2   Atkinson and Co. showroom, Westminster, 1890

Pricing and credit

For retailers, competitive pricing and the granting of credit were two of the
keystones to the success or failure of a business. The establishment of books of
prices in the eighteenth century was mainly as a guide for payments to
journeymen, but probably gave a basis for the costing out of goods and the
subsequent setting of a retail price, especially when the maker was also the
vendor. As the industry grew, a range of methods of pricing and credit
developed, but old ways were slow to disappear completely. During the early
nineteenth century, in rural areas in America it was still possible to use the old
barter system. Thomas Ogden of West Chester, Pennsylvania, often advertised
his willingness to barter his products. In 1819 he announced that 'Boards, Bedstead stuff and other materials used in his business, will be received in
payment.' In an 1824 announcement he stated that: 'The subscriber wishes to
exchange furniture for 1000 bushels or a less quantity of good lime to be
delivered in April.'[28] As late as 1849, Maria Silliman Church purchased a
bedstead and a bureau from a New York cabinetmaker named Woodruff, and
settled the account 'for lumber.'[29]

---

[28] Schiffer, M. B. (1978), *Furniture of Chester County*, p. 273.

[29] Silliman Church papers, NYPL, cited in Garrett (1990), *At Home*.

Figure 5.3   Saunders and Wooley shop front design, 1840

However, in retail shops in urban centres, the idea of an exhibited retail price for cash sales developed rapidly, supported by window display, ticketing and advertising. One example of a furniture retailer who embraced these approaches was George Oakley of 8 Old Bond Street. Not only did he operate on a cash-only basis, but also he displayed prices on the goods in his shop. His trade card (*circa* 1809–14) stated that:

> The number of artists and mechanics as well as the large capital necessarily employed in this concern, together with the extensive stock kept for ye accommodation of the public are obvious reasons, which render it impossible to conduct it by giving credit. The lowest price is therefore annex'd to every article for ready money or good bills ...[30]

Although Oakley's was a respected and select business, the changes in retail selling methods that occurred were not without critics. In 1819 it was suggested that 'cheap shops are a great evil and a much greater eye-sore to the regular traders ... because cheap selling is usually a mere pretence ...'. These shops could be identified 'by the vehemency and number of their placards, signs and tickets', but the public should understand that 'manufactured goods of near every description have standard prices, at which they are retailed in the

[30] British Museum Banks Collection, DE 627.

market'.[31] The changes in retailing generally were also commented upon. In 1833 a question from the Select Committee on Manufactures, Commerce and Shipping asked one witness: 'Does not the increase of that practice [fixed price ticketing] arise from an entire change in the mode of carrying on the retail business, that is, that it has now become more casual and less dependant upon regular constant customers to particular shops than it used to be formerly?' The witness replied in the affirmative, and suggested that it had only occurred in the last ten to fifteen years.[32] This seems to indicate a change from businesses relying on a few regular customers to serving a wider range of passing customers.

It seems clear that one of the major distinctions to develop in the century was between retail outlets that provided credit and those that traded for cash only. Although the old problems of debt collection that plagued the eighteenth-century furniture dealers were still evident in the nineteenth century, the nature of much of the house furnishing business meant that the extension of credit was a necessary part of trading. The letter books of the retail furnisher Miles and Edwards's from the late 1830s demonstrate some of the burdensome issues arising out of the granting credit. One instance showed the Duke of Sussex, who owed £1200 and was only prepared to pay in instalments, whilst the Duke of Newcastle who owed £59.16s.4d. for three years, only paid up when the partners eventually charged interest on the outstanding balance; and in another case the partners settled for a payment of 2s.6d. in the pound to clear a debt.[33] Some customers clearly took advantage of the retailers' goodwill. Miles and Edwards had to write to Lord Molyneaux to chase monies owing for a specially made desk:

> Sixteen months [after the goods were made] we apply for our money, but no sooner is this done than we receive a torrent of abuse stating our charges to be exorbitant &c &c &c ... We offer to take it back and return the money but even this does not appear to satisfy your Lordship, as we not only have the piece of furniture returned to us, having evidently seen some service since it left our warehouse (if we judge from the number of ink marks upon it) but what is still more distressing, your Lordship evidently loses your temper.[34]

Although credit was to remain important for the retail furniture business, there were moves to emphasize the benefits of cash transactions. In October 1831 Jolly and Sons of Bath advertised their new shop in the *Bath Chronicle*, and emphasized that:

---

[31] Several Tradesmen, *The London Tradesmen*, pp. 120 and 118, cited in Alexander, D. (1970), *Retailing in England During the Industrial Revolution*, p. 163.

[32] *Select Committee on Manufactures, Commerce and Shipping*, BPP, 1833, VI, qq, 1418–21 and 1437–42, cited in Benson, J. and Shaw, G. (1992), *The Evolution of Retail Systems, c. 1800–1914*, p. 32.

[33] Mallett, F. (1970), 'Miles and Edwards of London', *Furniture History*, 6, p. 75.

[34] Ibid., p. 76, citing Letter Book November 1836.

[Economy] can only be obtained by an exclusive Ready Money System, no article being delivered unless upon prompt payment. The advantages of this system are great. By it the tradesman is enabled to purchase on the very best terms and from the quickness of his return, and his not incurring any risk of loss from bad debts a very small profit will remunerate him: the benefit thus arising to the consumer can only be judged by comparison.[35]

Gareth Shaw has pointed out these new methods of cash selling accounted in part for the growth of innovative developments in retail practice during the century. He cites the changing attitude to credit, in the drapery business especially, which was cited in evidence to the Select Committee on Manufactures in 1833 as a reason for business growth achieved through the freeing up of working capital: 'the limitation of credit given by the retail trade [was] one part of the improved system of business'.[36] From this followed an emphasis on cash payment, ticketing and fixed prices, which in turn attracted 'lower to middling classes of people'.

Fifty years later, for Oetzmann and Co., cash payment before or on delivery was considered more favourable than credit. The firm warned that 'any other method of payment, however short may be the credit given, entails an expensive system of book-keeping, a staff of clerks, collectors, inquiry agents and unfortunately too often the expense of solicitors and a loss by bad debts'. The cash system avoided these costs.[37]

Nevertheless, credit was popular and remained an important part of many retailers' business strategies, whether for working-class or middle-class consumers. For the working classes, the use of mail order, scotch drapers, and itinerants, most of which offered the opportunity for weekly payments, was still important. In addition to these traditional methods, a new version of the weekly system was introduced. This development was check trading. The Provident Clothing and Supply Company was established in 1881, and soon developed links with furniture retailers. The customer used 'checks' to pay the retailer the normal price of the goods, and then paid back to the check company weekly amounts that included interest. The retailer was happy with this arrangement, as the responsibility for the debt was removed. This led to other sources of finance, which the customer would buy into, thus allowing the retailer to avoid involvement in the granting of credit. Indeed one of the first specialist finance houses to fund credit sales was the Civil Service Mutual Furnishings Association, established in 1877.[38] In 1890, John Robinson and James Syme set up the Robinson-Syme Ballot and Sale Furnishing Society for a similar market. The Rules noted that the 'society has been formed to provide

---

[35] Moss, M. and Turton, A. (1989), *A Legend of Retailing: House of Fraser*, p. 19.

[36] BPP 1833, Q. 1389, cited in Benson and Shaw (1992), *The Evolution of Retail Systems, c. 1800–1914*, p. 137.

[37] Oetzmann and Co. *c.* 1871, *Hints on House Furnishing and Decoration*, p. 294.

[38] BPP 1907–1, cited in Benson and Shaw, *The Evolution of Retail Systems, c. 1800–1914*, p. 32.

members of building societies and others, with the ordinary requisites for furnishing houses or apartments, and on such easy terms as cannot fail to make this undertaking ... a great success'. By using manufacturers and wholesalers or other firms on a published trading list, the customer could order goods and the supplier would be paid by the society, the member then paying back as agreed.[39]

Apart from 'simple' credit, there was a move towards other systems, including hire purchase. Although it was available in the eighteenth century, it was to be organized on a systematic basis in the later nineteenth century. In 1899, John Rawlings, a Surrey furniture trader, explained his improved system of credit. He offered a rental arrangement that could be converted to a later purchase with an allowance for any rent paid. This appears to have been an early form of true 'hire purchase', whereby the goods were not the property of the owner until the instalments had been completely paid. It was suggested that the system first operated in the pianoforte trade, and because of 'the beneficial system, today (1899) there is scarcely a home without its piano'. [40] Rawlings noted that one of the valuable features of the system was that it 'renders the furniture on approval during the hiring, and is the best guarantee that can be offered for soundness and efficiency of goods'.[41]

Although the home was often seen as an area where a woman could be responsible for its decoration and functions, the granting of credit to women was problematic, as the responsibility for her debts was unclear in law.[42] The case of *Jolly* v. *Rees* (1864) decided that husbands were not liable for debts if the goods his wife had purchased were not 'necessary' and he had forbidden her to pledge his credit. This remained the basis of common law for some time. The Married Woman's Property Act of 1882 did little to improve the situation for women, and it was not until 1935 that married women had full contractual rights and liabilities.

Branding and own-label policy

Part of the promotion of home furnishings, as well as of the stores that sold them, referred back to a time when customers bought goods directly from the maker. This was the practice of labelling items of furniture with the makers' details, a process that was very common in the eighteenth century. The procedure altered somewhat in the nineteenth century, as retailers often either

---

[39] *Rules of the first Robinson-Syme Ballot and Sale Furnishing Company*, 1890. BL.

[40] Rawlings, J. (1899), 'Improved System of Credit', unpublished pamphlet, British Library, BL 08228. ff.11.(6), p. 14.

[41] Ibid., p. 6.

[42] See also Rappaport, E. (1996), 'A husband and his wife's dresses': Consumer credit and the debtor family in England 1864-1914', in De Grazia, V. (Ed.), (1996) *The Sex of Things*.

removed any trace of the maker's details or, replaced them with their own fixed label on an item. The manufacturers criticized these practices. The American trade journal *Cabinetmaker* raised an important question in its issue of April 1871:

> Why does every furniture dealer in the country advertise himself as a manufacturer ...? For wholesale dealers and jobbers who ... do not even own a cent's worth of interest in a manufactory it is simply a fraud. If there is any advantage in manufacturing, the firms who invest their money in buildings, stock, machinery, and labour, are entitled to that advantage, if there is no such advantage, why claim such an empty honour by advertising yourselves as manufacturers, when you are simply wholesale dealers.[43]

In 1875 an Edinburgh cabinetmaker wrote a letter to the trade press raising the same points:

> ... These houses [West End businesses] will disapprove of your giving designs from the real manufacturers, as they assert that all the goods they sell are either made by themselves or to their order. This, as is known to anyone acquainted with the trade, is not the case; with very few exceptions that are all supplied from the East End of London, which they affect so much to despise, although their conveyances are daily seen in the neighbourhood taking away goods, to say nothing of the visits of buyers for the purpose of purchasing.[44]

Another trade journal aired the same issue two years later. Here the author noted the reality of the purchasing process and pointed out how London shops decried their own sources of supply: 'In the West End it is of everyday occurrence that salesmen and furniture dealers run down East End furniture while they themselves actually go down to Curtain Road to replenish their stocks.'[45] Nevertheless, both parties were aware of this method of business, and wholesalers' catalogues printed without manufacturing or supplier's details allowed for later overprinting by the retailer. This had the advantage of personalizing a wholesale range, and ensured that customers were unable to make price comparisons of branded goods. By applying the specialist furniture retailer's name onto these anonymous products, they gave the image of expertise, as opposed to the department stores that often had totally unnamed goods.

The issue of labelling and the apparent misinformation that might be given was raised in Parliament in a wider investigation about 'sweated labour'. In 1888 John Blundell Maple explained his firm's policy about labelling when questioned by the Select Committee on the Sweating System. Maple explained

---

[43] *Cabinetmaker* (US), 29 April 1871, cited in Harrison, S. G. (1997), 'The nineteenth century furniture trade in New Orleans', *Antiques* 151, May, p. 756.

[44] *Furniture Gazette*, October 1875.

[45] *Cabinet and Upholstery Advertiser*, October 1877.

that if the goods stated 'Maple and Co.' they were of their own manufacture. If the label said 'From Maple and Co.', the goods were from their premises, and if it stated 'Manufactured by Maple and Co.', they were manufactured specially for them.[46] The subtle differences would have been lost on most customers. However, Maples's explanation of policy went further, and did have some credence: 'The fact that our name being thereon must be considered, not in any way as representing that each identical piece of furniture was made by us, but as a guarantee to the public of the durability of the article.'[47]

In his evidence to the Select Committee on the Sweating System, Sir John Blundell Maple gave an insight into the purchasing practices of the firm. Maple told of the case of a cabinet-maker named 'Richards' who produced a set of three bedroom suites as samples for Maples to select from. The chosen model cost £22.15s.0d. Maples then offered to buy more at a repeat price of £19.10s.0d. Roberts rejected this and the original model was used by another manufacturer and produced for Maples at the required sum, no doubt being labelled as manufactured by Maple and Co.[48]

Retail shops and business types

At the beginning of the nineteenth century, the organization of the retail furnishing trade was still influenced by the activities of the previous century. This included the continuing separation of workshops from showrooms,[49] the craftsman-shopkeeper selling from his workshop, the large enterprises selling exclusive furnishings with a very high level of individual attention and service, and the retail-only establishments that were increasingly meeting the demands of the growing middle and artisan classes. However, in the following one hundred years changes would also occur, with the development of the department store, the change of some drapers' businesses into complete house furnishers, the growth of the specialist concept stores, and the slow development of multiple shops.

The antagonism between different parts of the trades that furnished homes was becoming evident in the nineteenth century. The particular clash appears to

---

[46] Maple (1888), *Select Committee on the Sweating System*, p. 629.

[47] Cited in Barty-King, H. (1992), *Maples Fine Furnishers: A Household Name for 150 Years*, p. 39.

[48] Maple (1888), *Select Committee on the Sweating System*, p. 630.

[49] Examples might include:

Business	Showroom	Factory
Jackson and Graham	37–8 Oxford Street	18 Newman Street
Wm. Smee and Son	6 Finsbury Pavement	34 Little Moorefields
Wm. Snell	27 Albemarle Street	1 Belgrave Road Pimlico
Trapnell and Holland	19 Marylebone Street	6 Silver Street
Seddon and Co.	Aldersgate Street	Gray's Inn road

have been between the drapers and upholsterers, who were often dealing in similar product groups. In May 1864 *The Decorator* noted in an 'advertorial' that:

> White cotton diaphance will appeal directly to upholsterers as making a valuable addition to their resources, which if taken in good time, will tend to reclaim the trade of window furnishing from drapers, who have suffered to monopolise at the expense of those to whom such custom is more legitimately due.

More generally, the *Furniture Gazette* could comment in 1875 that:

> It was the drapers who added furnishing goods to their establishments, who just began to make window displays of curtains, carpets and many of the old upholsterers finding the drapers were running away with a great deal of their trade were compelled to adopt the system in self-defence.[50]

The following sections will consider the six major groups of suppliers of house furnishings in the nineteenth century.

Department stores

The department stores have rightly been seen as an important phenomenon of the nineteenth-century retail scene. However, although they had distinctive features they represented an amalgam of a variety of developments that occurred during the nineteenth century. The distinctive features that the department stores brought together under one roof included: a greater level of capitalization, a diversity of merchandise, new methods of buying and selling and store management, a range of services not directly associated with retailing, and a spatial orientation that related on the one hand to the external city itself, and on the other hand to the internal and social requirements of the consumers they served. Importantly, the policy of open entry, the emphasis on marketing and advertising, the depersonalized process of buying and selling, and an emphasis on displays and spectacle ensured that consumers were able to learn both what and how to consume. In this sense, the department store was a diffuser of culture and an originator of lifestyles. This created a paradox, in as much as the culture being sold was one of luxury, indulgence and good taste, yet many of the goods sold were bulk-produced, aggressively priced and widely affordable, even if on credit.

Although the popular image of the department store as a 'universal provider' was a potent one, it was often the case that drapers' establishments developed into department stores. The example of Browns of Chester, who were originally mercers, and later dealt exclusively with clothing, demonstrates this. Expansion began in 1861, when the firm purchased the business of Samuel Gardner, a Chester furnisher of long-established reputation. In 1868 the

---

[50] *Furniture Gazette*, 2 October 1875.

adjoining shop premises were purchased for a 'warehouse for the sale of house and table linen, blankets, curtains, sheeting ...', and in 1869 the premises were enlarged to accommodate furniture showrooms, including goods of their own manufacture.[51] This piecemeal development based on purchase or acquisition of the leases of adjacent premises was a common method of growth for these kinds of stores. In some cases, expansion meant the eventual redevelopment of the site.[52]

Another example is Timothy Eaton's store in Toronto, Canada. This is a case whereby in the early days of its life, the business was based on textiles, each division having its own section. In the 1890s further sections for housewares, drugs, silver and jewellery, china and furniture were added. It is interesting to see how the furniture department established an identity within the store. From the early days of 'house furnishings' that included a small selection of textiles, lines such as floor coverings, beds and bedding merchandise were gradually added. In 1886 folding armchairs were offered, and in 1890 suites of furniture were first sold. By 1892 advertisements described the new furniture department and commented upon its 'most gratifying success'. The location of this new department was in the new extensions to the store that were made at this time. The Fall–Winter catalogue of 1893–4 showed nearly thirty pages of furniture, and the text demonstrated the company's ability to furnish a complete house at a reasonable price. Soon after the successful establishment of the furniture department, the firm was in a position to manufacture upholstery lines as well as bamboo furniture and picture frames in its own workshops.[53]

Miller has suggested that the role of the department store was far-reaching and profound: 'far more than a mirror of bourgeois culture in France, the Bon Marché [department store] gave shape and definition to the very meaning and concept of a bourgeois way of life'.[54] In terms of furniture, this was a gradual process for the Bon Marché. In the 1850s they began to sell beds; by the 1870s they had added chairs and tables, and only in the 1880s did they offer a full selection of furniture and furnishings.[55] In the same way, stores in other countries and serving other clienteles helped to construct their own particular ways of expansion so that this pattern of piecemeal growth and vertical integration was repeated across much of Europe and North America.

It is important not to overestimate the impact of department stores in terms of furniture retailing, but clearly they had an impact not only in terms of merchandising. As shopping continued to develop as a social occasion and a

---

[51] Mass Observation (1946), *Browns of Chester: Portrait of a Shop 1780–1946*.

[52] For example, the premises of Shoolbred, Maples and Heals in Tottenham Court Road were all witness to this process. See also the example of Jackson and Graham below.

[53] This section relies on Santink, J. (1990), *Timothy Eaton and the Rise of His Department Store*.

[54] Miller, M. (1981), *The Bon Marché: Bourgeois Culture and the Department Store*, p. 182.

[55] Ibid.

spectacle, the department store rose to the occasion and developed iconic building types. For example, in 1855 the business of Messrs Wylie and Lochhead had a purpose-built store erected in Buchanan Street, Glasgow. The iron-framed building was some 200 feet in length and 70 feet high. The *Glasgow Herald* reported that:

> The main salon consists of a spacious street floor, and three lofty open galleries, rising one above another, and extending round the whole building in a semi-circular form. A magnificent cupola of ground glass, extending the whole length of the galleries throws down a perfect flood of light, but at the same time so well subdued and tempered as to fall softly all around, and exhibit with the best effect the elaborate decoration of the structure, and the goods of every kind and hue with which it is so abundantly stored.[56]

Its popularity as an attraction was so great that free admission tickets had to be issued on Saturdays to control the crowds of visitors who went to see the premises.

William Whiteley's London store also demonstrated the potential of the department store type. Only seventeen years after it had started as an unpretentious shop with two or three assistants helping the proprietor, Whiteley's was describing itself as a 'universal provider.' Following gradual expansion, Whiteley built a new store in Bayswater Road. The furnishing trade press was most taken with the shop, suggesting that it set new standards of display, pricing and even offered a form of self-selection. Household furniture requisites were displayed in:

> a magnificent room, over 300 feet long and proportionately wide. Up stairs there was a floor of bedroom furniture which was described as 'the finest exhibition of such furniture in the Metropolis [adding] one peculiarity about the setting out of this department is original and remarkably pleasing: it consists in arranging the goods according to quality, and marking every article in plain figures. For instance commencing at the end of this splendid showroom, we find bedroom suites of ten pieces commencing at £5 7s 6d., with bedstead and bedding to match: from the lowest prices they range consecutively round the walls up to 150 guineas … customers can be their own salesmen; they can compare qualities side by side … without being worried into buying things more costly than they desire.[57]

The awareness of the 'just looking' syndrome, where customers could inspect goods in peace as opposed to being met by a sales person upon entering the shop, was one of the big advantages of the department store compared to the specialist shop. This change meant that the process of shopping was beginning to be transformed from active buying to passive purchasing, so that the merchandise had to 'sell itself' through displays, ticketing, price and its

---

[56] Cited in Moss and Turton (1989), *A Legend of Retailing: House of Fraser*, p. 19.
[57] *Cabinet Maker*, November 1880.

particular 'symbols' or 'commodity signs' which the customers could 'read' and then decide if they represented what they wanted.[58]

Specialist furnishers

The distinctions between the various specialized furniture retail outlets established by the *Furniture Gazette* in 1875 (see above) in terms of window display are also useful as a basis for business categorization. The first group was identified as the 'very superior', and included such luminaries of the trade as Gillow, Morant, Hampton and Sons, Holland and Sons, and Thomas Dowbiggin. The status that these sorts of enterprises maintained is comparable to:

> The quiet house of the honourable tailor, with the name inscribed on the window blinds or on the brass plate on the door, tells you that the proprietor has no wish to compete with or undersell his neighbour.[59]

At this level, it is not surprising to find that these businesses attended to the furnishing requirements of the Royal Household and wealthy patrons. The role of these important stores as a source of inspiration and knowledge for the consumer was noted. One business, Gillows, was also heralded as being educators of its public:

Figure 5.4 Heelas of Reading showroom

---

[58] See Laermans, R. (1993), 'Learning to Consume: Early department stores and the shaping of the modern consumer culture (1860–1914)', *Theory Culture and Society*, 10(4), pp. 79–102.

[59] Cited in Fraser, W. H. (1981), *The Coming of the Mass Market, 1850–1914*, pp. 175–6.

> It may at first be thought rather curious to say that Gillows showrooms are more instructive to those interested in the decorative arts than the great museums ... but it must be remembered that while the Museums almost entirely satisfy themselves with collecting authentic pieces, Gillows collection has been brought together with the view of representing a complete and comprehensive stock ... illustrating the history of decoration through every period worthy of notice.[60]

It is important to remember that this class of enterprise, as well as numerous smaller concerns, was still in the business of producing much of the furniture they sold right through the century. Although they bought in goods for resale, their reputation was built on the products they made in their workshops, many of which would be displayed at the great exhibitions and fairs of the later nineteenth century.

The second group were identified as artistic furnishers. The development of high-class West End firms, which made furniture on the premises and supplied a wide variety of furnishing needs for clients, had been well established since the eighteenth century. The comprehensive policy of these firms was based on their size, and the range of skills that met all the demands of the newly prosperous middle classes in matters of furnishing, decorating and fitting out their homes. In addition, many of them ran their own factories.[61]

Firms like Jackson and Graham continued and consolidated the trend during the nineteenth century.[62] Thomas Charles Jackson and Peter Graham established the partnership of Jackson and Graham, trading at 37 Oxford Street, London, in 1836.[63] The partnership clearly prospered, for by 1839 it was listed at 37–38 Oxford Street as well as 18 Newman Street;[64] and on its trade card of about that date it was already described as 'Upholsterers, Carpet Manufacturers, Furniture Printers and Interior Decorators'. By 1855 it had added 35 Oxford Street, and by 1866 it occupied 29, 33, 34, 35, 37 and 38 Oxford Street, as well as premises in Perry's Place, Freston Place, and Newman Yard, all adjoining. By this date, the firm designated itself more ambitiously as 'upholsterers, cabinet-makers, carpet manufacturers, interior decorators and importers of French silks, bronzes and ornamental furniture'. The success of the business was reflected in Peter Graham's private address that was located in Kensington Palace Gardens, where he kept a household with five servants and a coachman.[65]

---

[60] Gillow and Co. (1903), *Examples of Furniture and Decoration*, citing *The Ladies' Field*.

[61] Charles Williams, 21 Mortimer Street W1, factory Berners Mews, upholstery undertaken in Mortimer Street premises; Howard and Sons, 25–7 Berners Street, 200-hand factory in Cleveland Street: Johnstone Norman, 37 New Bond Street, 150-hand factory in Clipstone Street, Fitzroy Square; Morant, 91 New Bond Street, works, Woodstock Street.

[62] Edwards, C. (1998), 'The firm of Jackson and Graham', *Furniture History*, 34, pp. 238–65.

[63] *The Times*, 16 May 1882, p. 11.

[64] *Pigot's London Directory*, 1839.

[65] 1871 Census returns.

Although the firm appeared to be well established, it had to respond to the growing threat of competition from non-traditional sources, including the department stores, so in 1872 Jackson and Graham developed a new department concerned with drapery. The trend in poaching business from one sector by another was again commented upon in the trade press:

> It is whispered that Messrs. Jackson and Graham intend, on the completion of the new additions to their premises in Oxford Street, to open them as a drapery department in their already colossal establishment ... In recent times, the draper who has secured for himself a good connection believes he is quite justified in adding a carpet department. From that to furniture, bedding &c., is but a moment's thought; and Messrs. Jackson and Graham at least, can point to instances within a short distance where this course has been followed.[66]

Hungerford Pollen, writing in 1876, commented on the high profits to be made from this kind of enterprise, as well as the commensurate risks: 'It is the variety and comprehensiveness of these operations that is so profitable as a speculation. Such a business requires, as it need hardly be said, a large capital, and must be liable to fluctuations.'[67] By 1872 there were yet further additions to the Jackson and Graham business, but as Hungerford Pollen had warned six years earlier, on 27 June 1882, financial pressures forced Jackson and Graham to cease business temporarily. An unsettled period ensued which was only finally resolved by the take-over of the firm by the rival company Collinson and Lock in 1885.

A similar profile is found in the business of Charles Hindley. The business was established in 1817 when Hindley took over existing premises at 32 Berners Street, London.[68] In the mid-1830s the premises at 31 Berners Street were added for the sale of cabinet and upholstery, and a wholesale facility was developed. During 1844 Hindley purchased the business of Miles and Edwards, including its premises at 134 Oxford Street. The shop was supported by workshops adjacent to the showrooms, and it ran a factory on Red Lion Yard, Cavendish Street and a fringe workshop at 41–2 Bartholomew Close. The firm was very successful, but towards the end of the nineteenth century suffered a gradual decline in its market. Along with similar firms such as Jackson and Graham, Johnstone and Jeanes, and Wright and Mansfield, it succumbed to the pressures of the newer, larger-scale department stores and major furnishers such as Maples and Shoolbred. Hindley's eventually closed in 1892.

---

[66] *House Furnisher and Decorator*, September 1872, p. 97.

[67] Pollen (1876), *British Manufacturing Industries*, p. 155.

[68] Berners Street runs off Oxford Street and is close to Tottenham Court Road, London. It was known at one time as a 'furnishing' street with manufacturers' showrooms and the headquarters of NARF.

Three small but telling points demonstrate the distinctions between these high-class shops and those catering for a larger clientele. The first was that the salesmen in Hindley's were described as 'respected experts' in their own particular line. Secondly, and in direct opposition to the open-door policy of department stores especially, the store entrance was intimidating:

> Within the swing doors was a main entrance hall or lobby … in this hall stood for many years a high enclosed mahogany desk which, with it seated clerk or salesman, seemed to suggest that permission to enter the premises was granted as a favour, or confirmed as an honour bestowed or as a welcome according to the status of the visitor.'[69]

Thirdly and following on from the entrance policy, was their approach to sales promotion. In October 1875, the *Furniture Gazette* noted how 'high class stores had … held aloof from window dressing … looking upon it as excessively vulgar and obtrusive and regarded ticketing as a system which no respectable house would resort to'.[70]

Second-hand and antique dealers

The third group of retailers were the dealers in old furniture, operating curiosity or antique shops. Brokers and dealers had already met a taste for supplying used furniture and furnishings in the eighteenth century. As with other trades, the dealers were often located in particular areas of cities. In the Moorfields area of London, for example, there was a Brokers Row where, in 1775, Samuel Swain, an upholsterer and broker, had insured his house for £800.[71] By 1817 *Johnston's London Directory* listed Brokers Row, Moorfields as having 28 premises housing ten brokers and appraisers, two furniture brokers and six upholders/cabinetmakers. In the south of London in 1838 another Brokers Row, near Redcross Street, Southwark, had nine premises, seven of them occupied by furniture brokers.

A description of such a shop in the 1820s would appear to reflect the second-hand rather than the antique:

> When I remember Moorfields first [it had] a line of shops without fronts, occupied chiefly by dealers in old furniture, to the east and north. Most of these shops were covered in by screens of canvas or rough boards, so as to form an apology for a piazza … a broken down four poster or a rickety tent bed might be secured at almost any price … a tall stiff upright easy chair, without a bottom; a cupboard with one shelf left of three, and with half a door; here a black oak chest groaning to be scraped …[72]

---

[69] V & A Hindley papers, employee's comment cited in Microulis, L. (1988), 'Charles Hindley and Sons, London house furnishers of the nineteenth century: A paradigm of the middle range market', *Studies in the Decorative Arts*, 5, Spring and Summer, pp. 82–3.

[70] *Furniture Gazette*, 2 October, 1875.

[71] Wainwright, C. (1989), *The Romantic Interior*, p. 34.

[72] Aleph, *London Scenes and London People*, (1864), cited in Wainwright (1989), *The Romantic Interior*, p. 34.

There was clearly a distinction between the collectors of 'antiques' and those who simply purchased second-hand goods out of necessity. Antique furniture dealers as such, appear to be first mentioned in directories from 1826.[73] J. C. Loudon wrote in his *Encyclopaedia,* of the dealers who could satisfy the taste for an antique interior:

> The exterior of chests or wardrobes might be rendered curious, and highly interesting, though we do not say in correct or architectural taste, by covering them with the Elizabethan, Dutch, Louis XIV, or Francis 1. Ornaments which are now to be purchases in abundance, either at home or abroad. We have already referred to Nixon and Son [with premises in Great Portland Street], for the two latter kinds of furniture; and we may here observe that Wilkinson of Oxford Street, and Hanson of John Street, have extensive collections of Elizabethan and Dutch furniture and carvings, from which a judicious complier of exteriors might clothe skeleton frames, so as to produce objects of curiosity and interest at a very trifling expense. Kensett of Mortimer Street has also some curious specimens of both Elizabethan and more ancient furniture.[74]

Clive Wainwright has shown how Wardour Street, Soho, developed into a centre of antique shops and traders. In 1817 there were no brokers, but 13 cabinetmakers-upholsterers. By 1838, there were 9 brokers and 12 cabinetmakers-upholsterers. By 1850, this had increased to 23 brokers and 24 cabinetmakers/upholsterers. The reputation of the trade in this quarter was recognized by the term 'Wardour Street English' – defined as a modern article with a sham antique appearance about it.[75]

The call for 'antique furniture' grew to such an extent that the regular furniture retailers also began to sell products under this designation. Articles such as that published in the *Cornhill Magazine*, which in 1875 declared that 'the art of furnishing must for the present moment be closely connected with the judicious buying of old furniture', stimulated this demand.[76] This would appear to relate to the taste for 'picking up' objects that would help to furnish an eclectic or artful interior. However, around 1871 the retailers Oetzmann and Co. warned their customers about the issue of appropriateness of furnishings, particularly concerning the antique:

> Of late years, a taste for antique furniture has developed … This taste may appropriately be displayed in the furnishings of a house, which is architecturally appropriate, but … for modern houses, we should prefer the comfort and elegancy of modern furniture to antique and for drawing rooms, antique furniture is simply inadmissible. [77]

---

[73] Muthesius, S. (1988), 'Why do we buy old furniture? Aspects of the authentic antique in Britain 1870–1910', *Art History*, 11(2), June, p. 243.

[74] Loudon, J. C. (1839), *An Encyclopedia of Cottage, Farm and Villa Architecture and Furniture*, p. 1101.

[75] For more on this material, see Wainwright (1989) *Romantic Interiors*, Chapter 2.

[76] 'The Art of Furnishing' (1875), *Cornhill Magazine*, p. 537, cited in Muthesius, (1988), 'Aspects of the authentic antique in Britain 1870–1910'.

[77] Oetzmann and Co. (*c.* 1871), *Hints on House Furnishing and Decoration*, p. 293.

Figure 5.5 Heal and Sons, Antique Department, 1908

Although Oetzmann eschewed the sale of antique furniture in its business, other stores were not so concerned. Debenham and Freebody, better known for drapery and clothing, started to sell antique rugs and embroidery. In 1897 the company published *The Chippendale Period in English Furniture* by K. W. Clouston, and then soon opened an 'antique furniture' department. In 1905 Harrods store opened a gallery for 'Antique and second-hand modern furniture' and some shops even specialized in appropriate textiles: 'Heal and Son have spent much time in hunting out pieces and patterns of every kind and form, and from this research has resulted a stock of fabrics to go happily with period furniture-cretonnes, chintzes, printed linens.'[78]

Complete house furnishers

The fourth group of store types comprised some of the most successful retailers of the period who catered for the new middle and upper classes, and included what were once 'household names'. The best example from London is the business of Maples. This was a 'classic' development. John Maple, a 26-year-

---

[78] Adburgham, A. (1979), *Shopping in Style*, p. 300. Heals also had an 'antique' department at the time.

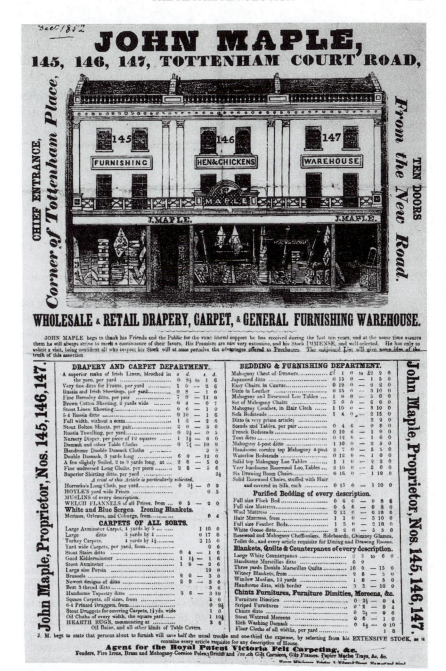

Figure 5.6   Maple and Co. price list, 1850s

old who had had an apprenticeship in shopkeeping, acquired a drapers' shop at 145 Tottenham Court Road. He entered into partnership with James Cook. Eight months later they purchased the shop of an upholsterer next door at number 147. In 1851 the partnership was dissolved and the original site was redeveloped by Maple with a unified frontage. Success bred success and by the late 1850s the firm was doing very good business. In a retrospective commentary on Maples, a correspondent in *The Times* noted:

> [Originally] the shop was not to be distinguished from the ordinary 'goods on the pavement' type which was at that time common in the Tottenham Court Road; and it remained open 'til 9 o'clock, doing much of its business with small people who came to buy household furniture after their own shops were closed. Somehow or other, John Maple the elder gradually came to secure some richer customers, and early in the sixties he has contrived to enlarge his borders to make business well known by advertisement and to take his place as one of the leaders of the new commercial movement-the movement for big shops where the owner of a house, however large or small could come and find all the furniture he wanted on the premises.[79]

The firm went from strength to strength, building its business particularly on contract furnishings for the hotel and club trade. It also opened a store in Paris and extended its manufacturing capabilities. By the 1880s it employed over 2000 staff, including 1295 in the factories, and 365 salesmen and clerks, as well as 391 girls.[80]

Another case of this type of development is that of James Shoolbred.[81] Having established his drapery business at 155 Tottenham Court Road in the 1820s, he soon purchased the adjacent properties, 154 and 156, and built a new shop that was called 'linen and woollen draper, silk, mercers, haberdashers and carpet warehouse'. Further property purchases were made between 1847 and 1861 with the aim of creating an island site. In the 1880s the whole site was rebuilt as a fully developed department store. In 1899 further facilities were added. It was only in 1913 that the business became a limited company, which was probably too late to save it, as in 1931 its demise occurred.[82]

Furniture shops

The fifth group of stores, namely those that 'emphasised price over artistic merit', included London firms such as Tarn, Oetzmann, and William Whiteley. These London stores were often located on the outskirts of the central shopping districts. Oetzmann was on Hampstead Road, beyond Euston Road, Whiteleys was established in Bayswater, and Tarn was trading in Newington Causeway

---

[79] Cited in Barty-King (1992), *Maples Fine Furnishers*, p. 15.

[80] Ibid., pp. 37–8.

[81] De Falbe, S. (1985), 'James Shoolbred and Co.' MA, Royal College of Art.

[82] See *Cabinet Maker*, 7 March 1931, p. 555.

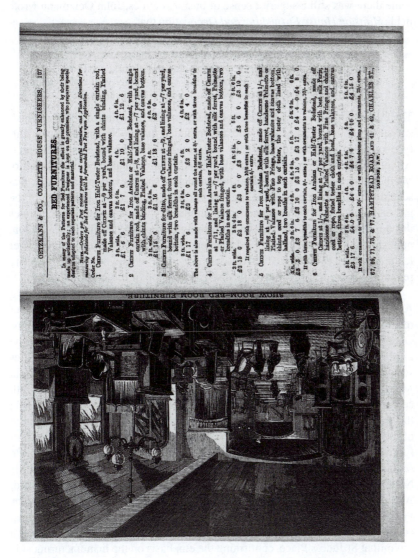

SHOW ROOM—BED ROOM FURNITURE.

BED FURNITURES.

In many of the Patterns for Bed Furniture the effect is greatly enhanced by their being made up artistically; an experienced Designer is kept on the premises, who prepares special designs adapted to each separate pattern and material.

NOTE.—*Orders per Post receive prompt and careful attention, and Plain Directions for measuring Reduced for Bed Furnitures will be forwarded Post Free upon Application.*

Order No.

1 Casement Furniture for Iron Half-Tester Bedstead, with a single curtain rod, made off Cretons at —/9 per yard, bound with chintz binding, Plaited Valance and canvas bottom, and base valance.

3 ft. wide.	3 ft. 6 in.	4 ft.	4 ft. 6 in.
£1 6 6	£1 7 6	£1 10 0	£1 12 6

2 Casement Furniture for Iron Arabian or Half-Tester Bedstead, with a single curtain rod, made of Cretons at —/8, and lining at —/7 per yard, bound with chintz binding, Plaited Valance, base valance, and canvas bottom.

3 ft. wide.	3 ft. 6 in.	4 ft.	4 ft. 6 in.
£1 15 0	£1 16 6	£1 18 6	£2 0 0

3 Casement Furniture for ditto, made off Cretons at —/9, and lining at —/7 per yard, bound with silk ferret, front valance fringed, base valance, and canvas bottom, two breadths in each curtain.

3 ft. wide.	3 ft. 6 in.	4 ft.	4 ft. 6 in.
£1 17 6	£2 0 0	£2 2 0	£2 4 0

The above is also made with valance all round the tester, at 8/- extra, or with three breadths to each curtain, 6/6 extra.

4 Casement Furniture for Iron Arabian or Half-Tester Bedstead, made off Cretons at —/11, and lining at —/7 per yard, bound with silk ferret, Palmeto or Plaited Valance fringed, with base valance and canvas bottom, two breadths in each curtain.

3 ft. wide.	3 ft. 6 in.	4 ft.	4 ft. 6 in.	5 ft.
£2 15 0	£2 18 0	£3 0 0	£3 3 0	£3 6 0	£3 10 0

If required with ornaments to valance, 10/6 extra; or with two breadths in each curtain 6/- extra.

5 Casement Furniture for Iron Arabian Bedstead, made off Cretons at 1/-, and lining at —/6 per yard, bound with silk ferret, handsome Palmeto or Plaited Valance with Fine Fringe, base valance and canvas bottom, chintz cord or rope to top of tester, the tester cloth lined with holland, two breadths in each curtain.

3 ft. wide.	3 ft. 6 in.	4 ft.	4 ft. 6 in.	5 ft.	5 ft. 6 in.	6 ft.
£3 5 0	£3 7 6	£3 10 0	£3 15 0	£3 17 6	£4 4 0	£4 8 0

If with three breadths to each curtain, 9/- extra; or with ornaments to valance, 10/- extra.

6 Casement Furniture for Iron Arabian or Half-Tester Bedstead, made off Cretons at 1/3, and lining at —/7 per yard, bound with best silk Parti, handsome Palmeto or Plaited Valance with Fine Fringe and chintz cord or rope, fluted tester cloth and lead, base valance, and canvas bottom, three breadths in each curtain.

3 ft. 6 in.	4 ft.	4 ft. 6 in.	5 ft.	5 ft. 6 in.
£3 17 6	£4 0 0	£4 10 0	£4 16 0	£4 16 0

If with ornaments to valance, 30/- extra; or with handsome gimp and ornaments, 36/- extra.

67, 69, 71, 73, & 97, HAMPSTEAD ROAD, AND 41 & 42, CHARLES ST., LONDON, N.W.

Figure 5.7 Oetzmann and Co. showrooms and price list, c. 1870

and the New Kent Road. They were generally catering for the lower-middle-class and artisan groups, although Whiteleys drew from a wide-ranging clientele. Even though they were not particularly 'exclusive' in their trade, for some there was still a superior sense of business ethics. John Oetzmann wrote in his *Hints on House Furnishing and Decoration* that:

> [customers should not] allow themselves to be talked into having any articles that their own taste does not approve, by the glib tongue of some so-called clever salesman-a salesman should certainly assist the customer to the best of his ability when requested ... but in any well conducted establishment would not be allowed to obtrude his advice unasked.[83]

The final group, 'who depend solely on ticketing and startling announcements', was at the bottom end of the trade and included the 'goods on the pavement' type of shop mentioned above in connection with the origins of Maples. Although these shops clearly met a need, critics maligned them. Henry Mayhew commented that: 'at the show and slop shops every art and trick that scheming can devise or avarice suggest, is displayed to attract the notice of the passer-by and filch the customer from another'.[84] One example demonstrates this approach. In 1892 the Crown Furnishing Company of Holloway, London, published a flyer that emphasized the deposit and weekly terms, whilst other featured services included 'free delivery' and credit with 'no security required'. There was precious little discussion of the furniture itself.[85]

Away from the capital, the trade was also separated into small producer retailers, larger-scale producer-retailers, and retail-only establishments. Overall, the development of the complete house furnisher was amongst the most interesting. Many of these businesses were already established in cities such as Leeds, York, Edinburgh, Sheffield, Manchester, Bristol and Bath, where an appropriate clientele could support such a venture.[86] In the nineteenth century a new market was also developing in other cities that grew wealthy on the products of the industries they spawned. One example is Bradford, a centre of the woollen textile industry. The instance of Christopher Pratt, a Bradford furnisher, shows how a firm expanded to meet the developing and more sophisticated demands made upon it. In 1830 Pratt was apprenticed to a Mr Nutter, who was in business from *circa* 1820 at 2–4 North Parade, Bradford. After completing his apprenticeship, Pratt went into partnership with Thomas Price, and in 1850 they leased a dwelling, workshop and showrooms, continuing Nutter's business. In 1866 they acquired timber stores and a sawmill at St Jude's Place, confirming the emphasis on the manufacturing side

---

[83] Oetzmann and Co. (*c.* 1871), *Hints on House Furnishing and Decoration*, p. 293.

[84] Cited in Fraser (1981), *The Coming of the Mass Market, 1850–1914*, pp. 175–6.

[85] Crown Furnishing Co. pamphlet, Bodleian Library.

[86] For example, Lamb of Manchester, Robson of Newcastle, Marsh and Jones of Leeds, and Johnson and Appleyard of Sheffield.

Figure 5.8   Wilbee and Co., Herne Bay, *c.* 1870s

of the company. In 1873 a new retail showroom block was built. In 1880, after Price's retirement, the business was renamed Christopher Pratt and Sons, and in 1882 a decorating department was opened. They developed a reputation for artistic furnishings, and from 1890 to 1920, the firm was an agent of Liberty and Co.[87] The success of the firm is shown in the profit figures:

1851	£707
1861	£9864
1871	£20066
1900	£44000

A similar development may be traced in a Sheffield business, Johnson and Appleyard, where in 1879 the company of Appleyard took over the concerns of Johnson and set up a new business called Johnson and Appleyard. This new arrangement was clearly successful, as in 1883 the firm built new showrooms and workshops in the city centre. It is revealing that it maintained the old arrangement of workshop and showroom on the same premises. The new building was impressive, with its 130-foot frontage, eleven show windows, two entrances and other facilities. Internally, the layout of the building was divided betweens showrooms at the front of the floors and workshops at the rear. By

---

[87] For Christopher Pratt, see Gilbert, C. (1969), 'Pratt's of Bradford', Bradford City Art Gallery, November 1969–January 1970. For a similar example see also Banham, J. (2001), 'Johnson and Appleyard Ltd of Sheffield: A Victorian family business', *Regional Furniture*, 15, pp. 43–63.

1892 additions were made to the building, and the workshops were mainly removed to a separate four-storey building a short distance away. This remodelling allowed the incorporation of 'general goods' to the stock, which included glass, china, lighting and so on, as well as the introduction of room settings. In 1891 the business converted to a limited company that was formed to:

> Acquire and take over the … businesses carried on at Sheffield and Rotherham … and in Melbourne in the Colony of Victoria, Australia. To carry on all or any of the businesses of cabinet makers, furniture manufacturers and dealers, upholsterers, ironmongers, drapers, undertakers, carpenters, joiners, decorators, painters, paperhangers, builders, mechanical engineers, contractors and dealers …
> To carry out business as auctioneers and valuers, house and estate agents, and commissioning agents.
> To lay out for building purposes, and to build on, improve, let on building leases, advance money to persons building, or otherwise develop the same …[88]

This extract from the Memorandum of Association demonstrates the very wide range of activities undertaken by complete house furnishers, who were also well equipped to execute commissions for ecclesiastical and business contracts as well.[89]

The third example of a provincial business is instructive, as it demonstrates continuity of practice. W. Purkis of High Street, Portsmouth, ran a business as cabinetmaker, upholsterer, undertaker and auctioneer. In 1812 he advertised in the *Hampshire Telegraph* that he 'has a large assortment of paper hangings, carpeting, cabinet furniture and upholstery *manufactured at his own house* [original emphasis] which he is determined to sell on most reasonable terms'.[90] His emphasis on his own manufacture indicates that retail-only shops had something of a reputation.

However, the working master had not died out. In 1851 Arthur Foley was employed as an apprentice upholsterer. By 1861 he was trading in his own right as a cabinetmaker and upholsterer, and in 1871 he had three premises in Fisherton Street, Salisbury, and employed 12 men and 8 boys, as well as a female assistant in the 'front shop'. In May 1874 the *Salisbury Times and South Wilts Gazette* described his business and emphasized the displays:

> The stock is conveniently arranged, including upward of 50 bedsteads varying in price from 11s to £100 each, all fixed for inspection, with

---

[88] Banham (2001), 'Johnson and Appleyard Ltd of Sheffield', p. 57.

[89] Johnson and Appleyard furnished woodwork and fittings for Rotherham Parish Church and for Sheffield Town Hall. The firm was Gold Medal winner in York, 1879, and Paris, 1900.

[90] Stabler, J. (1991), 'English newspaper advertisements as a source of furniture history', *Regional Furniture*, 5, p. 101.

wardrobe and other articles en suite. Visitors are shown through the spacious showrooms (quite an exhibition of furniture) without the slightest importunity to buy.[91]

It did not stop there. By 1881 Foley was a fully fledged cabinet manufacturer complete with retail showrooms.[92]

A final example demonstrates the continuity of older trading patterns in rural areas. The accounts of Bapchild, a Kentish upholsterer in the late 1830s, shows that he sold chairs, sofas, tables, beds, chests, mirrors, picture frames, mats and carpets, kitchenware, fire tools and ornaments. In addition, he traded in used furniture, and repaired furniture in his workshop. He also rented furniture out, and turned small wooden objects. As an upholsterer, he continued the tradition by carrying out funeral arrangements, including the upholstery of the coffin and the supply of associated textiles.[93]

The variety of retail outlets, services and products demonstrates a response to the growing demand for furniture at all levels of society.

How did people acquire furniture?

As the following chapter shows, the importance attached to home furnishings and the effects they created became of paramount importance for many families throughout the nineteenth century. Although some retailers were simply a source of supply, the role of the better-class retailer became even more that of an arbiter of taste and fashion. At the top end of the trade, in addition to the selection and supply of furniture, there were also advisory schemes and plans that were prepared for execution by the interior decoration and building departments of London firms such as Jackson and Graham, Gillows, and Collinson and Lock, as well as similar enterprises in other major cities.

Even some of the nineteenth century's most famous critics and reformers were themselves not immune to the authority of the fashionable furnisher. John Ruskin's father had set up a home for his son and his new wife whilst they were away in Venice. The fashionable upholsterers Snell and Co. were given *carte blanche* to furnish the home with a budget of £2000. The result was apparently not to Mrs Ruskin's liking, and she complained that it was 'furnished in the worst possible taste and with the most glaring vulgarity ... Mr Snell had naturally done it up as cheaply and vulgarly as he could and put half of the money in his pocket.'[94] Ruskin himself referred to the house as 'inconceivably cockney after Venice', but oddly, he later employed the same firm to furnish

---

[91] Jones, R. (1997), 'Arthur Foley, a nineteenth century furniture manufacturer in Salisbury', *Regional Furniture*, 11, p. 43.

[92] Ibid., p. 44.

[93] Kent County Archives Q/Cl/498 cited in Alexander (1970), *Retailing in England During the Industrial Revolution*, p. 157.

[94] Jervis, S. (1973), 'Ruskin and furniture', *Furniture History*, 9, pp. 97–109.

his Lakeland home, Brantwood. Nevertheless, reformers have echoed Effie Ruskin's comments upon profiteering and bad taste ever since.

Charles Eastlake, who did not succumb to the blandishments of the retailer, vented his spleen on those based in the Tottenham Court Road. He complained of the furniture retail system that existed in the mid-century:

> Anyone can get drawing room chairs designed by an architect and executed by private contract for six guineas a chair. What the public want is a shop where such articles are kept in stock and can be purchased for £2 or £3. Curiously enough, in these days of commercial speculation, there is no such establishment. People of ordinary means are compelled either to adopt the cheap vulgarities of Tottenham Court Road or to incur the ruinous expense of having furniture 'made to order'.[95]

Eastlake revisited the Tottenham Court Road furnishers when he gave a back-handed compliment to them: 'You may buy some [dining chairs] of a really fair design even in Tottenham Court Road, that vanity fair of cheap and flimsy ugliness ...'[96]. At the end of the nineteenth century it was clear that the artistic reformers still despised the commercial furnishers. In 1897 Mrs Marriot Watson was quoted by *The Artist* magazine as saying: 'Some of the most illustrious writers of today inhabit homes and houses that decoratively speaking are a slur upon civilisation.' The magazine continued to explain that the reason for this was to be found 'in the hire purchase system and in Tottenham Court Road ... especially that portion of it which nearly joins hands with the highway to Hampstead'.[97] This was yet another attack on the retail fraternity of the area, and especially the big stores of Maples, Hewetsons, Oetzmanns, and Shoolbreds. Perhaps it is needless to say that the only firm in that street with a tolerable reference was Heals: 'This notorious thoroughfare notwithstanding, we have at last found something which should help to remove the slur upon civilisation. This is a bedroom at Heal and Son, decorated and furnished at moderate cost...'.[98] These attacks on Tottenham Court Road were later echoed in the1920s by the Modernist architect Le Corbusier, who said: 'the existing plan of the dwelling house takes no account of man and is conceived as a furniture store. This scheme of things, favourable enough to the trade of Tottenham Court Road, is of ill omen for society.'[99]

As was shown above, buying furniture meant going shopping. The retailers, in their various ways, set out their stall to attract their clientele through the use of window displays, model rooms, pavement or arcade displays and other demonstrations of the goods on offer. In 1877 the *Furniture Gazette* explored

---

[95] Eastlake (1872), *Hints on Household Taste*, pp. 62–3.

[96] Eastlake, C. (1864), 'The fashion of furniture', *Cornhill Magazine*, July.

[97] Cited in Adburgham, A. (1977), 'Give the customers what they want', *Architectural Review*, May, p. 295.

[98] Ibid.

[99] Le Corbusier (1927), *Towards a New Architecture*, p. 114.

Figure 5.9   Waring and Gillow showroom, Manchester, 1897

in-store displays and concluded that: 'to meander down a corridor of interminable bedroom suites is not only diverting but also necessary as part of [the customers'] education. Their admiration ... and disapproval form the basis of the salesman's judgement as to what will suit them best.'[100] This was exactly the method used by Whiteley's.

Other sales techniques were disguised as assistance with design and planning. For example, Waring and Gillow's customers could see in the store a series of rooms furnished at costs varying from £100 to £750, so that the total impact could be quickly assessed. In addition, customers were offered an empty room space that could be fitted out with their choice of furniture so as to see the full effect of their own selection before purchase.[101]

Apart from window displays, in-store vignettes of rooms and full interior decorating departments, the later nineteenth-century retailer made a point of producing a wide variety of magazine-style catalogues for consumer use.[102] These catalogues often included estimates for furniture that were clearly

---

[100]   *Furniture Gazette*, 6 October 1877, p. 9.

[101]   Shaw Sparrow, W. (1907), *Flats, Urban Houses and Cottage Homes*, Appendix, p. 7.

[102]   An example of the development of these is Shoolbred and Co. which published a 38-page catalogue in 1874, an 84-page catalogue in 1876, and an astonishing 400-page catalogue in 1884.

intended to be a guide to the correct and appropriate furnishing of various rooms based on a scale of prices. Some firms did not attempt to disguise their selling aims, whilst others clothed their estimates in a cloak of respectability by employing fashionable decorators to endorse their products, and in some cases to design settings and recommend furnishings. What is interesting about the various company estimates is that they illustrate a considerable homogeneity of styles across financially varying levels and house sizes that were deemed appropriate for typical lifestyles, thus endorsing the idea of a common understanding of an established taste.

The retailers also worked with magazine editors and style advisers to promote their wares. For example, the fashionable retailers Oetzmann and Co., combined journalism with salesmanship in their massive catalogue issued *circa* 1900. The firm reprinted some illustrated articles first published in *The Lady* that recounted how a young bank manager and his fiancée were able to furnish their rooms for £120. The articles were lightweight, didactic narratives based on the story of a couple setting out to furnish their home with the assistance of a knowledgeable female friend, a theme that was often returned to by such publications. The prose is an odd mixture of fact and fantasy: in one case the helper noted how 'Cherie [had] said she really dreamt several beautiful ideas, though once she was papering the walls with Turkey carpets' and in another instance one of the items in the drawing room was described as 'a bamboo table devoted to the dispensing of the fragrant cup at the mystic hour of 5 p.m.'[103]

Another interesting case is that of William Wallace and Co. of Curtain Road, Shoreditch, incidentally in the heart of the East End furniture manufacturing district. The firm employed author and journalist Mrs Panton to prepare schemes that were 'artistic' but still commercial. She condemned 'the cheap dining room suites: [where] one finds half a dozen sticky chairs covered in American leather and a terrible veneered sarcophagus known to the initiated as a sideboard', and went on to say that 'in our dining room we are frankly all we pretend to be'.[104]

Advice was freely given but was often very partisan, as the link between retailers and home interest magazines was also forged at this time. One example demonstrates this well. *The House* published a series of articles in 1899 by 'Penelope', entitled 'How to furnish for five hundred'.[105] She pointedly emphasized that practical guidance over principles of art was far more useful for those about to furnish. She went on to consider the various rooms in the house, and engaged some of the better-known furnishers to help set them up. Although this was blatant 'advertorial' copy, it was probably quite useful to the readers. The firm, Smee and Cobay of New Bond Street, designed

---

[103] Oetzmann and Co. (*c.* 1896), *Catalogue*, p. 94. Campbell's Romantic Ethic and hedonistic daydreaming appear to be exemplified here.

[104] William Wallace (*c.* 1880), *Catalogue*, p. 132.

[105] *The House* (1899), 5, p. 52–5, 133–5, 182–4, and 213–15; 6, pp. 28–30, 138–40 and 175.

the drawing room, which was considered the principal room. As the 'Georgian style' had been selected for this room, it is not surprising to find mahogany furniture there, but tastefully finished with grey upholstery, combined with yellow draperies and a rose colour scheme. The main bedroom executed by Heal and Son of Tottenham Court Road indicated that 'rigid simplicity is by no means incompatible with a high degree of beauty'. The use of fumed oak accorded with the contemporary taste, but in this case the furniture specified was fitted with hammered steel fittings, fine examples of the influence of the Arts and Crafts Movement. Finally, the spare bedroom has a suite made of bass wood stained watercress-green highlighted by copper fittings supplied by Druce and Company.[106]

The above works were definitely aimed at the middling classes, but many retailers were conscious that the formula could work for other income brackets as well. Most therefore published other estimates for both higher and lower price ranges. The Midland Furnishing Company of Southampton Row, Holborn, for example, offered estimates ranging from £27 for a four-bedroomed house to £655.4s.6d. for an eight-roomed house.[107] At the very top of the scale was Hampton and Sons of Pall Mall and Trafalgar Square, which devised estimates for a twenty-room house to be furnished and equipped for £2000. Even the lower end of the trade used these estimates to sell, although the main point was the credit terms. For example, the Crown Furnishing Company of Seven Sisters Road, London, could furnish one room for £5 by paying 10 shillings deposit and 2 shillings a week thereafter.[108]

In 1891 the trade journal *Furniture Gazette* published a series of generic 'model estimates' listing all the requirements of a six-roomed house to be furnished for £100, the same house for £150, and an eight-roomed house for £200.[109] These were probably useful to retailers who were unable to produce their own catalogues and estimates, and was almost certainly a useful selling aid.

Much of the market of the middle to better ends of the trade was not only selling to domestic customers but also to clients travelling to or coming from overseas. The acquisition of furniture for use abroad in Australia throws some interesting light on the buying process. Not surprisingly, British firms supplied Australian customers – mainly Britons emigrating or undertaking a tour of duty. The Inspector General of Public Works, William Wardell, noted that purchasing furnishings for Australian homes from overseas companies and then importing them was 'the course most private persons take'.[110] As was seen in the examples of American buyers in the eighteenth century, the idea of employing a specialist to select and buy on one's behalf was a possible

---

[106] Ibid., p. 183.

[107] Midland Furnishing Company estimate, National Art Library.

[108] Crown Furnishing Company estimate, National Art Library.

[109] *Furniture Gazette*, September, October and December 1891.

[110] Lane, T. and Searle, J. (1990), *Australians at Home*, p. 30.

approach to the purchase process. For example, in 1877, Edward Knox enlisted the help of an agent in London, one John de Villiers Lamb, to help furnish his Australian house. Knox expressed his wish for the furniture selected to meet the 'need for comfort over appearance', and stated that 'nothing should be large enough to look out of proportion in a small room'.[111] Lamb suggested they avoid 'the crack West End men' and 'the cormorants of the fashion circle' who charge for their name. Instead, he proposed visiting the showrooms of Smee's and Filmer and Sons of Berners Street.[112]

Others shopped in person. Mrs Mackinnon and her daughter Ella visited London in 1886 to select furnishings for their Australian home. The process was planned to take six weeks, and during that time Ella entered details of their progress in her diary. These entries reveal much about the day-to-day sequence of shopping events. On 22 June, the diary recorded: 'Hunting at different furniture places … for dining chairs.' Six days later they spent 'most of the day at Maples'. On 1 July they were 'furniture purchasing for both dining and drawing room', and on 31 July they 'returned to Maples to finish up.'[113]

It was not only Australian relatives who shopped *en famille*. In 1867 Lady Georgina Peel and Archibald Peel, younger brother of Sir Robert Peel, had taken a house in Wales called 'The Gerwyn' and had enlisted the help of the family to set about furnishing it. Georgina records in her *Recollections* that this help came particularly from her husband's aunt, Lady Anne Baird:

> When buying furniture for 'The Gerwyn' she helped me in every way she could, her house in Eaton square was always open to us, and she ordered the carriage every morning, driving me to Maple's or any out of the way place of which I might have heard as having nice things. Many times was I aided by her advice as she had excellent taste.[114]

These references confirm John Maple's successful attempts to attract the carriage trade and the export business.

The acquisition of furniture and furnishings was not only conducted through retail stores but also through mail order, auction sales and second-hand brokers. Incidentally, a retail company might operate some of these methods as subsidiary branches of their main business. The development of mail order specialists in the later nineteenth century was a feature of the whole arena of distribution. Although Mr Godey, of *Godey's Ladies Book* fame, introduced mail order or a buying service in 1852, which shipped goods from New York

---

[111]   Ibid., p. 31.

[112]   Smee was a favourite establishment, but other firms recorded include the London-based Gillows, Sadgrove, William Walker, Maples, Shoolbred, and Henry Cooper of Conduit street, as well as Saul Moss of Manchester and John Taylor of Edinburgh.

[113]   Lane and Searle (1990), *Australians at Home*, pp. 31–2.

[114]   Peel, E. (Ed.) (1920), *Recollections of Lady Georgina Peel*, p. 224, cited in Girling-Budd (1998), 'Holland and Sons of London and Gillows of London and Lancaster: a Comparison of two nineteenth century furnishing firms', MA Royal College of Art, p. 88.

Figure 5.10   Old furniture shop, London, 1877

and Philadelphia to his readers across the USA, it was towards the end of the century that mail order became an important distribution phenomenon. For example, the Sears Roebuck catalogue for Fall 1900 had over eleven hundred pages packed with everything and more that a retail store would stock – all available to buy for cash on delivery and on approval. Its importance in America, where the large distances often precluded customer visits to city centres, ensured its success. In terms of home furnishings, these were organized so that they made evident the categories of consumer culture by offering a range of slightly differentiated models at a range of prices. For example, in the 1900 catalogue there were 12 rattan rocking chair models varying in price from $3.55 to $6.50. Distinctions between worth or value are based on comparison of objects. In this case, it is through catalogue images; in a retail showroom it is done physically. In the British case, the mail order system was run as much by department stores as by specialists.[115] Although less popular for furniture, there was to be considerable growth in this area of furniture retailing during the twentieth century.

The opportunity to buy used, second-hand or antique furniture from auctions or house sales, or sometimes from sales of bankrupt stocks, continued to be a useful outlet for some people. The continued existence of brokers and second-hand dealers demonstrated both a continuing supply and demand for part-used

---

[115] For example, see the extensive catalogues of retailers such as Harrods, Army and Navy Stores and so on.

furniture and furnishings, but according to Stana Nenadic, the customer base had changed:

> By the second decade of the nineteenth century, it was much less likely that middle-rank men and women would own either furniture or clothing that had previously belonged outside their family, and it was much more likely that working people would be able to purchase second hand goods that had once belonged to the relatively wealthy.[116]

It is no surprise to find that the brokers and second-hand dealers were established in the poorer parts of towns and cities.

Since the eighteenth century, auctioneers had also sold new furniture, and it was still annoying retailers in the nineteenth.[117] In the *Hampshire Telegraph* of 10 March 1817, the following advertisement appeared:

> To be sold by Auction by Mr. Garnett at his auction room, Queen Street [Portsea], on Friday 14th March 1817, – About twenty sets of handsome drawing room and other painted chairs, twelve bedsteads, feather beds, tea trays, six copper coal scuttles, twelve sets of fire irons, dining and Pembroke tables, two slipper baths …[118]

Two weeks later, the newspaper included an advertisement for the sale of a cabinetmaker's stock that made the following point:

> When the public are satisfied that the goods are really of the late Mr. Eastman's manufacture, any further comment on them will be unnecessary: and the failure of the several attempts lately made to sell large quantities of cheap London made goods by Auction, in this neighbourhood, leads him to conclude that the attention of the public is not diverted from this opportunity of purchasing as a cheap rate…[119]

The problem was still an issue in 1851. James Hopkinson, a cabinet-maker and shop keeper, purchased what he thought was old furniture at an auction, only to find later that it was 'new slop made and darkened to look like old'.[120]

In relation to the issue of taste transfer and goods acquisition, Katherine Grier has pointed out how public contact with the auctioning of household furniture 'on the premises' of the vendor provided a chance to see the goods *in situ* as well as to have an opportunity to purchase them. She cites a passage from 'A Bargain: Is a Penny saved Twopence Got?', published in 1854 in *Gleason's Pictorial Drawing Room Companion*, which explains how tasteful objects filter down the social scale through the function of the auctioneer and the second-hand market. Commenting on the swarms of viewers:

---

[116] Nenadic (1994), 'Middle rank consumers and domestic culture in Edinburgh and Glasgow 1720–1840', p. 134.

[117] See Chapter 3, 'Other outlets'.

[118] Cited in Stabler (1991), 'English newspaper advertisements as a source of furniture history', p. 101.

[119] Ibid.

[120] Hopkinson, J. (1968), *The Memoirs of a Victorian Cabinet-maker*, pp. 95–6.

That's it, you see. Mr Allen said ... that's the way so many people of moderate means have their house so handsomely furnished. A man of taste like Lyons [the vendor] or yourself, collects books, and pictures and furniture, to be dispersed eventually after this fashion [that is, by auction]. The next owner 'declines housekeeping'[sells] in turn, and things being a little more tarnished by removal and use, are purchased a shade cheaper by a class a grade lower in the scale, and so *decencus averni*.[121]

Of course, traditional retailers were very disparaging of auction sales, as they detracted from the sale of new goods. In a catalogue introduction, the Oetzmann Company re-published an extract from the *London Mirror* of 16 September 1871:

Attend any [furniture] sale you like either at a private dwelling house or an auction mart and you will find yourself out bidden in all directions by a knot of noisy clamorous, unwashed greasy looking individuals who dub themselves 'the trade'. [They outbid you, then proceed to knock it out between themselves] ... Depend upon it, a room – be it a dining room, drawing room or bedroom – furnished out of a saleroom has a saleroom look, which will cling to it as long as the articles hold together ...[122]

Nevertheless, the second-hand market remained important for the social groups who could not afford to buy new.

This chapter has looked at some aspects of how retailing operated and interacted with its customers. The changing circumstances of the nineteenth century meant that at various stages retailing methods and objectives would develop so that the growing and broadening customer base could be dealt with 'suitably'. This issue of appropriateness (whether of the store or the goods) was at the heart of nineteenth-century furnishing, and was clearly understood by both parties – the retailer and the customer – as one of the bases of home creation.

It seems clear that the growth in the consumption of goods was linked to changes in retailing, and the new possibilities they introduced. For the bourgeois culture of the later nineteenth century, it was in the department stores and shops that:

The nineteenth century aesthetic observer discovered the most powerful aesthetic activity and experience of the modern man, and even more important, the modern woman: the attractions of commodity and luxury items and the pleasures of purchasing same; in short, the aesthetics of buying and selling.[123]

---

[121] Grier (1988), *Culture and Comfort*, p. 25.

[122] Oetzmann and Co. (*c.* 1871), *Hints on House Furnishing and Decoration*, p. 294.

[123] Saisselin, R. G. (1985), *Bricabracomania: The Bourgeois and the Bibelot*, p. 19, cited in Dant, T. (1999), *Material Culture in the Social World*, p. 139.

Chapter 6

Consumption, identity and everyday life: nineteenth-century homes and their importance in society

This is the true nature of home-it is the place of Peace, the shelter, not only from all injury, but from all terror, doubt and division …So far as it is a sacred place, a vestal temple, a temple of the hearth watched over by Household Gods…(John Ruskin, *Sesame and Lilies*, 1864)

Status and identity

Although it had its roots even earlier, the development of bourgeois respectability that occurred in the period 1750–1850 meant that, in part at least, the idea of a person's goods being part of the expression of self-identity (as opposed to the earlier eighteenth-century idea of goods as part of 'social performance') was widely accepted. Following on from this, consumer culture moves into two different pathways. The first is the importance of the urban and public scene and its spectacles supplied by shops, galleries, arcades, museums and exhibitions. The second or contrary notion involves the inward-looking private and domestic sphere. What linked these two aspects in the goods that were bought and sold as a part of a material culture was that consumer goods could be seen as (a) signs of status and identity, (b) vehicles of meaning, and (c) bearers of aesthetic values. This chapter will investigate these aspects, and how they connect.

In 1881 the architect Robert Edis wrote that: 'in the houses we live in, it is first of all essential that everything shall be as fitting as possible, and that extravagance of all kinds, or so-called "high art" shall be subservient to comfort, truth of construction, utility and general convenience'.[1] Edis's idea of things being 'fitting' relates well to the concept of appropriateness of one's furnishing to position and status. These ideas are reflected in the manner of description and the matter described by Victorian novelists when they wrote about interiors. Their concerns were also often about making comparisons that reflected differences in status and identity. Comparisons were made between ostentation and modesty; between rooms intended for use or for show; between dirt and mess, and cleanliness and tidiness; between comfort and discomfort,

---

[1] Edis, R. W. (1881), *Decoration and Furniture of Town Houses*, pp. 1–2.

and between conscious and unconscious taste.[2] Each state reflecting the owner's personality.

In addition to these general considerations, the goods that were purchased by people to make their homes, carried meanings that were not necessarily overt, but did reflect ideas about the individual and the culture of the period. These meanings (although not inherent in the merchandise itself) included concerns about social position, identities, lifestyles, gender and nationality, to name a few. In the nineteenth century, this conjunction of goods and ideas reached a wider range of consumers than ever before.

Improvements in manufacturing and supply, as well as in attitudes, were seen as providing a positive improvement in society. The architect and landscape gardener John Claudius Loudon wrote of the working man:

> All the evils which have for so long afflicted him … will be dispelled by the education of the rising generation, and the new order of things which will thenceforth be established …They will obtain those comforts and enjoyments which ought to be in the possession of the industrious labourer, as well as of the wealthy capitalist.[3]

A·Dining·Room·Sideboard   MESSRS JACKSON & GRAHAM

Figure 6.1 Jackson and Graham room setting, 1881

---

[2] See Tristram, P. (1989), *Living Space in Fact and Fiction*, pp. 179–95. See also Dillon, S. (2001), 'Victorian interior', *Modern Language Quarterly*, 62(2), June, pp. 83–115, for a more theoretical discussion.

[3] Loudon, J. C. (1839), *An Encyclopedia of Cottage, Farm and Villa Architecture and Furniture*, p. 353.

Over seventy years later it seemed that although there had been a marked increase in domestic comforts for the working classes that Loudon had foreseen, some did not view this as an improvement. For example, Mrs Loane had difficulty with their attitudes to room use:

> To have a locked parlour full of fine furniture is an aesthetic and moral advance upon squalor and utter indifference to appearance, but as proof of civilisation, it ranks very far behind the tidy, threadbare room, which is used every evening, and where the elder children may occupy themselves on wet days.[4]

This comment about honest but worn interiors reflected the thoughts of the eighteenth century critics and their concerns with the 'vice' of luxury. Commenting on the frugal interior, John Ruskin said: 'I know what it is to live in a cottage with a deal floor and roof, and a hearth of mica slate; and I know it to be in many respects healthier and happier than living between a Turkey carpet and a gilded ceiling, beside a steel grate and polished fender.'[5] Neither of these commentators really knew what it was like to live meagrely.[6]

However, although there were some improvements in working-class housing, the nineteenth-century ideal of home was really an expression of the middle classes, who, to use Mary Douglas's words, were intent on 'making visible and stable the categories of culture'.[7] Putting it another way, Jules Michelet, writing in a French republican context in 1846, explained: 'people had to recognize themselves in one another'.[8] Although he was referring to a hypothetical national taste and identity, the idea transfers to particular classes, social groups and lifestyles. In France, as elsewhere, consumers aspired to various tastes and styles that reflected their self-image, class location or aspiration.

The categories of culture were flexible and relative, but they also were distinctive, distinguishing and remarkable for the variety of nuances in them. Bourdieu's idea of *habitus* (as social position based on consumption choices) and the social differences that are expressed by cultural capital are directly linked to the lifestyles considered here. Rosalind Williams has considered the example of France, but her analysis can be usefully applied to other Western countries.[9] Williams has identified that the bourgeoisie worked with a common

---

[4] Mrs Loane (1910), *Neighbours and Friends*, pp. 152–3, cited in Daunton, M. J. (1983), *House and Home in the Victorian City*, p. 279.

[5] Ruskin, J. (1891), 'The Lamp of Sacrifice', *Seven Lamps of Architecture*, p. 32.

[6] See Hewitt, M. (1999) 'District visiting and the constitution of domestic space in the mid-nineteenth century', in Bryden, I. and Floyd, J., *Domestic Space: Reading the Nineteenth Century Interior*, for a discussion about working-class domestic spaces.

[7] Heap, H. S. and Ross, A. (Eds) (1992), *Understanding the Enterprise Culture: Themes in the Work of Mary Douglas*, p. 21.

[8] See Auslander, L. (1996), *Taste and Power: Furnishing Modern France*, p. 421.

[9] Williams, R. H. (1982), *Dream Worlds: Mass Consumption in Late Nineteenth Century France*.

theme based on the old pre-revolutionary 'courtly models' in their striving for higher status. This model used specific goods, often based on 'patina' and hereditary values, to carry cultural meanings. It was a survivor from the previous centuries but still remained exclusive enough to counter attempts to infiltrate that particular part of culture that itself survived into the nineteenth century. This old order was to be challenged by a new range of lifestyles, all of which could be obtained with the help of the appropriate retailer.[10] Williams goes on to classify these 'distinctive groupings of interdependent lifestyles'.

She first considers the 'elite lifestyles' that were based on apparently superior aesthetic sensibilities and tastes, which took precedence over breeding and nobility. Thus the elite positioned themselves above the banal bourgeoisie by using an invented language of goods as well as an increasing range of objects as part of a process of social creation. The deliberate use of goods to create a lifestyle was built around a new taste-led elite who used stylish objects to invent a self-image that was specific to them. They held no pretensions to using goods to educate or reform others. This attitude was exclusive, being based on an information system that was limited to this group and reinforced by specialist publications and retail outlets. The best example of this in England and America is the Aesthetic movement of the later nineteenth century, which had its own complete lifestyle expressed in housing, fashions and furnishings. The role of retailers such as Arthur Liberty (who also developed a series of dealerships for his own products) in supporting and supplying these customers was crucial.[11] In France (and other parts of Europe), the bourgeoisie wanted to follow the courtly model of consumption and taste to support their need for legitimized social status, rather than a republican taste derived from Rousseau and others.[12] In America, the 'commercial aesthetic' which was based on an eclecticism derived from Renaissance, Baroque, Classical and a eccentric mix of other styles was also not republican in nature, but rather imitative of the same vague patrician tastes that were found in the homes of the European aristocracy.[13]

Secondly, Williams introduces the 'democratic lifestyle', the production of which came out of the decorative arts movement and was based on ideals of modesty and dignity and a simple lifestyle, which could apparently be taught using goods as exemplars. In this case furnishings were used for didactic and instructional purposes to reform social groups other than one's own. The reform movements attempted to 'resocialize' people and their aspirations by changing their ideas about consumption, and to instruct them in the 'proper'

---

[10] Ibid., p. 35. See also Lukacs J. (1970), 'The bourgeois interior', *American Scholar*, 1970, 339(4), pp. 616–30, for a discussion of the notion of the bourgeois.

[11] See Gere, C. and Hoskins, L. (2000), The *House Beautiful: Oscar Wilde and the Aesthetic Interior*.

[12] Williams (1982), *Dream Worlds*, p. 53.

[13] Lynes, R. (1949), *The Tastemakers: The Shaping of American Popular Taste*.

ways. The famous examples of retail businesses such as Heal and Sons and Morris and Co. were clearly part of this group of didactic retailers.

Thirdly, there was the lifestyle of 'mass consumption', which was partly based on the dual planks of growing disposable income for an increasing majority and on retail store development.[14] Here consumers were offered the opportunity to purchase goods that expressed their choices about their status within society. The old ideas of appropriateness and position were being eroded by the new retail opportunities that offered a novel world of consumption to a great many people. The German architect Hermann Muthesius pointed out in his work *The English House* (1904) that: 'England is the one country in which one can nowadays find in furniture shops a selection of furniture that, while it cannot pretend to be great art, yet meets all the requirement of good taste, and at extremely reasonable prices.'[15]

This category is too big to encompass the remaining consumers, and a fourth sub-division should be added here. This derives from the original aristocratic model and supported parts of the middle class who by the latter part of the century still aspired to an aristocratic model of living. Hermann Muthesius observed that:

> Imitation eighteenth century furniture accounts for by far the largest part of present day [1900] demand ... Large factories, each employing hundreds of workers, devote all their efforts to the production of this furniture, furniture shops are full of new copies of Sheraton and Chippendale, for these are the pieces that the English public most desires.[16]

Even a cursory examination of the trade catalogues of the major English retailers will confirm this position.

As these social meanings were being loaded onto commodities in an ever-increasing way, the importance of the correct selection of goods became paramount. In the case of the elite and the middle classes, the values of gentility, propriety, civility and appropriateness were embedded in the goods sold. In the case of the aspirational and the mass consumers, the meanings they wanted were often watered-down versions of these images, but might also be simply different.[17] It was here that the salesperson's experience and knowledge would mix and match to suit the expressed (or hidden) requirements of the customer.

Don Slater has considered the contradictory directions that consumer culture took in the later nineteenth century. He has identified two aspects. On one side

---

[14] The term 'mass consumption' is meant to reflect a wider participation in consumption not as a corollary to the term mass production.

[15] Muthesius, H. (1904), *The English House*, reprint 1979, p. 196.

[16] Ibid., p. 195.

[17] An examination of retailer estimates does indicate that particular timbers, colours and styles were linked to price levels and room types, but they do not necessarily represent a filtering down from the expensive to the cheap.

were the urban experience and the production of public spectacles of display, including shopping itself, and the shops, department stores, exhibitions and museums that were part of this culture. On the other side was a private bourgeois domesticity that made consumption respectable – a middle way that was neither the luxury nor decadence of the aristocracy nor the excesses of the working-class mob.[18] The retail furnishers provided both a public display for 'window shopping' and desiring, and the real possibilities of private acquisition of home-making merchandise compatible with particular lifestyles.

In the previous chapter, the rise of a retail culture in the business of supplying home furnishing has been looked at. The important roles of the department stores and the specialist retailers, amongst other retail outlets, were considered in relation to the creation of homes. It is the purpose of this chapter to examine what this role was, and how consumption practices were related to the home and its furnishing.

For many critics looking at the nineteenth-century home, the starting point is often the novels of the period that delight in exploring the home as both fact and fiction.[19] Although the use of fiction is not strictly a primary resource in one sense, in another it can be seen to reflect the society in which they were produced, and in this way may be useful for providing impressions of ideas and ideals. In fact, many perceptive comments can come from this approach. Philippa Tristram persuasively argues that because ideals such as 'comfort' and 'home' have no connection to aesthetics, a true home, for the Victorian novelist at least, was an honest expression of individuality, its contents not conforming to any particular taste or style but being a reflection of the owner's affections.[20] It is also clear that novels have the power to express a situation through accounts of locations and particularly of interiors. These forms of expression were communicated by descriptions of objects and their placement, but also by consideration of personal items that reflected the character of the family or individual. The idea of furnishing and decorating in one style exclusively, which might reflect conformity and insipidness, was replaced with an eclectic approach so that goods might have some narrative content: a painting, or a family piece of furniture, or a particular textile that softened a roomscape but was not in itself referential. Consideration of the novel and its descriptions leads into a questioning of the actual motives of the purchasing public, particularly in relation to issues of appropriateness and conformity as opposed to individuality.

---

[18] Slater, D. (1997), *Consumer Culture and Modernity*, p. 15.

[19] Examples are myriad, but see, for example, George Eliot, Jane Austen, Emily Brontë, Charles Dickens, Benjamin Disraeli, Mrs Gaskell, Thomas Hardy, Henry James, Walter Scott and Anthony Trollope. See also literature studies such as Cohen, M. (1998), *Professional Domesticity in the Victorian Novel*.

[20] Tristram, P. (1989), *Living Space in Fact and Fiction*, p. 23.

It has always been the case that the purchase and consumption of home furnishings has required various levels of decisionmaking, as against the habitual or intuitive purchase of everyday goods. In the case of home furnishings, the criteria of choice include the technical or performative aspects of functions and convenience, and the obvious considerations of cost and comparative ranking with other goods needed. As well as these, though, two very important factors are the psychological ones relating to self and community, including ideas about conventions, fashion, status and the need to resolve uncertainties due to lack of experience in these sorts of infrequent purchases. The latter factor is directly related to the retailer's role, and therefore includes consideration (by the consumer) of the quality of advice, reputation, guarantees and service.

Above all this, though, is the idea that purchasing furniture and furnishings was about homemaking. Victorian society was undergoing a vast series of substantial and sustained, and in some cases rapid, changes. These changes were unsettling, as Mark Girouard succinctly notes:

> It is so easy to think of the Victorian as a smug and self-confident age, but one has only to make a very superficial dip into Victorian letters and literature to see how far this was from being the case: doubt, despair, fear of revolution, dislike of the way the world was changing round them, mystification and worry as to what science was up to, are all too apparent.[21]

In these circumstances it is easier to understand how, for the middling classes at least, the home ideal became so potent a refuge from the outside world. The home was one of the opposites in a series of culturally separate spheres, which included 'the inside' and 'the outside', respectability and deviance, and industry and home. Even though it might be a representation of respectability and stability in contrast to other spheres, concerns over the home, its possessions and their messages bred their own anxieties for people.

For nineteenth-century homemakers, responses to their 'status anxiety' were often expressed through the furnishings of their home. The concept of respectability, like comfort, needs its opposite to have any real meaning; therefore, there was a conscious effort for most of the time to maintain a veneer of respectability at least to maintain an image.[22] The home was consequently a bulwark against its opposite: the coarseness and impropriety apparent in the world outside. The idea of a bulwark was expressed literally in fiction in the example of Wemmick's *cottage ornée,* complete with drawbridge that was intended to cut off the outside world.[23] The American author Almira Seymour, in her book *Home, the Basis of the State*, expressed the ideas in another way.

---

[21] Girouard, M., 'Introduction', in Lasdun, S. (1981), *Victorians at Home*, p. 20.

[22] Charles Dickens, in *Our Mutual Friend*, introduces the Veneering Family, who were 'bran-new people, in a bran-new house in a bran-new quarter of London'. This applied to all levels of society.

[23] Dickens, *Great Expectations*, Chapter 25.

She argued that domestic reform was the proper ordering of 'the hidden source of all growth and expansion ... the organization of the family, the institution of home'. Home therefore afforded the safeguard against the potential turmoil that rapid changes in industry and society threatened.[24]

Gillian Brown has suggested that 'this construction of a vigilant domesticity that absorbs exterior threats is of course a model of capitalist consumption: the realization and reinforcement of personal life in the acquisition of things believed to be necessary for self-sufficiency'.[25] Brown develops this connection between commerce and self-identity to include the role of shops, and especially department stores that were seen as 'magnified model homes' which 'embodied the unlimited possibilities of domestic space'. Eileen Elias evoked the attraction of the department store and its opportunities for reveries of home. Recalling her mother's shopping in a suburban department store at the end of the nineteenth century, she explained how: 'you got a glimpse into a dream world where a suburban house could be furnished from top to bottom with Turkey carpets and aspidistra-pots and kitchen labour-saving devices; you got a picture of yourself as you would be',[26] and by inference, how you would like others to see you. This was clearly what furniture store managers were aiming for in their displays, windows and publications, most of which emphasized the domestic nature of the settings.

Despite these positive connections between retailing and the home, Grier has pointed to the tensions between symbolic values of furnishing and their commercial origins, which allowed industrially produced goods to enter the sanctity of homes.[27] To deal with this situation, furniture was often deliberately designed to be non-industrial, perhaps being referential to nature, while the women of the household often worked textiles into 'soft designs'. This mediation between the 'hard' outside and 'softer' inside worlds, expressed in part through goods, and especially textiles, was particularly important as it created a real sense of comfort and relaxation, which was reflected in the layering of fabrics at windows, rugs on carpets, over-stuffed upholstery and so on. Another approach, suggested by Lizabeth Cohen, considers that the parlour was a particular point of contact that mediated between the outside world and home, both through the reception of people and the use of technologically produced goods such as fitted carpets, wallpaper, veneered furniture, pressed glass and so on.[28] However, even

---

[24] Grier (1988), *Culture and Comfort*, p. 5.

[25] Brown, G. (1990), *Domestic Individualism: Imagining Self in the Nineteenth Century*, p. 182.

[26] Cited in Hosgood, C. (1999), 'Mrs Pooter's purchase: Lower middle-class consumerism and the sales 1870–1914', in Kidd, A. and Nichols, D. (Eds), *Gender, Civic Culture and Consumerism*, p. 159.

[27] Grier (1988), *Culture and Comfort*, p. 7.

[28] Cohen, L. A. (1984), 'Embellishing a life of labour: An interpretation of the material culture of American working-class homes, 1885–1915', in Schlereth T. J. (Ed.), *Material Culture Studies*, p. 293.

if technology made these sorts of decoration affordable, it seems that these origins were often hidden under a imitative surface or were embellished with handworks.

For other critics, another useful way that can be combined with the literary approach is to consider the motivations, processes and influences that precipitated such a major change in homes and lifestyles during much of the nineteenth century. There was clearly a rapidly growing disposition to buy goods for the home. The path of increasing urban population, the generally rising income levels and a society that valued 'the home' as an institution that required nurturing all led inexorably to the retail house furnishers' doors.

Industrialization and urbanization had created an anonymity that was only countered by representations of the self, both as an individual and as a member of a social group. This could be achieved somewhat by purchasing furnishings, in part pre-selected by the retailer, that appeared to represent the individual's self-image, but also, and probably more importantly, by the display of personal items, crafted objects and accumulations of 'things.' Despite the apparent emphasis on individualizing an interior space, the evidence shows a great homogeneity in the styles offered and purchased. Although it changed over time, the concept was remarkably stable. Here we return to the issue of appropriateness of goods for a particular class, occasion or home. The ideals of respectability and certitude were found in many goods, but particularly in clothing and furnishing.

These ideals were often difficult to sustain. 'Genteel poverty' described many of the lower middle classes who struggled to keep up appearances, often resorting to buying goods on hire purchase and waiting for the semi-annual sales.[29]

To support the retailers in developing their responses to the 'commodity aesthetic' that was developing rapidly in the period, a raft of other consumption apparatus was developed or expanded to help to nurture the demand. These included a plethora of advice books and magazines,[30] as well as catalogues and estimates that acted as 'primers' to show the various classes (mainly middle) how they should furnish appropriately and explain the 'language of the upholsterer' to them. Demand was also stimulated by the development of exhibitions of all kinds that introduced potential consumers to the world of goods, as well as the active involvement in 'reading the customer' or marketing developed by many progressive manufacturing businesses.[31] Michael Ettema neatly sums up this change, although the process had begun many years before:

> Authority had always accrued to the people who defined the categories by which objects were understood; this fact gave them the greatest individual

---

[29] See Hosgood (1999), 'Mrs Pooter's purchase'.

[30] See *Journal of Design History* (2003), 16(1), Special Issue, 'Domestic Design Advice'.

[31] For an analysis of this process in the glass and china business in America, see Blaszczyk, R. (2000), *Imagining Consumers: Design and Innovation from Wedgwood to Corning*.

control over what made objects desirable. But now [the 1870s onward] the
authorities for consumption also had a direct interest in the production and
sale of those very goods. By virtue of this growing ability to manipulate
the categories of culture, authority was increasingly passed on to capitalist
business organisations.[32]

So far, the homes that have been discussed can be generally categorized as
'middle-class homes'. The definition of home is essentially middle-class.
Nevertheless, the evidence is that, over the century, the poor and working
classes did aspire to improved domestic arrangements, although the meanest
habitations had appalling conditions to live in and hardly ever entered the
chain of purchase and renewal. Even artisans of some standing often possessed
little in the way of furniture. In 1840 Thomas Ashworth explained to the
Health of Towns Committee that workers in regular employment with him
would, after two or three years as tenants in company housing, begin to
think about furnishing their homes, because 'before that they had not
been accustomed to furnishing'.[33] This is not surprising, as many immigrants
from the countryside had precious few possessions to bring with them to the
town.

The reformers and philanthropists documented scenes that were a shocking
contrast to the gentility of the parlour. Mayhew recorded such a 'room' in
London in 1851:

> A few sacks were thrown over an old palliasse, a blanket seemed to be
> used for a quilt; there were no fire irons or fender, no cooking utensils.
> Beside the bed was an old chest, serving for a chair, while a board resting
> on a trestle did duty for a table. The one not very large window was thick
> with dirt and patched all over.[34]

However, the poignant report from the *Daily Telegraph* of 1864, reprinted by
Ruskin in red type in his *Sesame and Lilies*, shows how strong an image of the
idea of home was imprinted on people.

> Deceased died on Saturday morning. The family never had enough to eat.–
> Coroner: 'It seems to me deplorable, that you did not go into the
> workhouse.'–
> Witness: 'We wanted the comforts of our little home.'
> A juror asked what the comforts were, for they only saw a little straw in the
> corner of the room, the windows of which were broken. The witness began
> to cry, and said they had a quilt and some other little things. The deceased
> said he would never go into the workhouse.[35]

---

[32] Ettema, M. J. (1991), 'The fashion system in American furniture', in Pocius, G. (Ed.), *Living in a Material World*.

[33] *Select Committee of the Health of Towns 1840*, cited in Gauldie, E. (1947), *Cruel Habitations*, p. 99.

[34] Mayhew, H. (1851), *Life and Labours of the London Poor*, cited in Quennell, P. (1969), *Mayhew's London*, p. 288.

[35] Cited in Tristram (1989), *Living Space in Fact and Fiction*, p. 93.

Despite these examples of dire poverty, many working-class people were not without the skills to make a 'home', and increasingly had the means to do so. For example, an early-nineteenth-century Lancashire weaver possessed:

> a dozen good rush-bottom chairs, the backs and rails bright with wax and rubbing, a handsome clock in mahogany case, a good chest of oaken drawers, a mahogany snap table, a mahogany corner cupboard, all well polished; besides tables, weather glass, cornish and ornaments, pictures of Joseph and his Brethren.[36]

This description demonstrates the move away from simple functional wants to embrace other perceived needs, often based on egotistical notions of self-worth and self-display.

In another example, the evidence of letters written *circa* 1850 to *The Morning Chronicle* from correspondents in the manufacturing and mining districts as well as rural and urban areas demonstrates a varied picture in terms of working-class interiors. An extract from the example cited of a cottage at the iron works in Merthyr Tydfil shows a great sense of pride and value in the home surroundings:

> In the parlour there was a good four-post bedstead, a French-polished chest of drawers, covered with a profusion of glass and other articles … In a corner was a glass fronted cupboard, filled with china and glass and displaying ostentatiously silver sugar tongs and set of spoons. There was also a mahogany table with a bright copper tea-kettle reposing on it …[37]

The description of a cottage in a pit village in Northumberland gives a similar picture:

> As a general rule the furniture is decidedly good; some articles even costly. The visitor's attention will be especially drawn to the bed and the chest of drawers. In a great proportion of cases, neither of these would be out of place in a house of some pretensions …[38]

It goes on to explain the mechanics of the purchase:

> The women are the great agents in getting the houses so well furnished as they are. They strive to outdo each other in matters of beds and chests of drawers, the two great features of their rooms. When a young couple get married, they generally go to a furniture broker in Newcastle or Sunderland with perhaps £10 of ready money, obtaining a considerable part of their 'plenishing' upon credit, and paying for it by instalments.[39]

In these, as in many others case, at all levels of society, comfort, utility and convenience were often subservient to extravagance and display in defiance of Edis's plea mentioned at the beginning of this chapter.

---

[36] Cited in Chapman, S. D. (1971), *History of Working Class Housing*, p. 262.

[37] Ginswick, J. (Ed.), *Labour and the Poor in England and Wales 1849–1852*, 3, p. 53.

[38] Ibid., p. 39.

[39] Ginswick (1983), *Labour and the Poor in England and Wales 1849–1852*, 2, p. 40.

Function and display

The second category is objects as vehicles of meaning, in which there is a basic utility in goods that is then overlaid with meanings that locate the object in terms of a culture's particular sets of values. To paraphrase Baudrillard, furniture *serves* as equipment and *acts* as an element of prestige, comfort and so on.

Mike Hepworth reminds us that 'it is important to recognise that the Victorian home was not simply a place for a relaxed presentation of a "real" self, away from the prying eyes of the world, but a complex arrangement of spaces for the presentation of a miniaturised array of variable domestic selves'.[40] The control of this conduct was partly by way of the cultural authorities, who, having established the rules of behaviour, asserted a strong influence over the purchase of goods to meet the requirements. Ruskin made the distinction between goods purchased for display as opposed to function:

> I would fain introduce into it [home] all magnificence, care and beauty where they are possible: but I would not have that useless expense in unnoticed fineries or formalities; cornicing of ceilings and graining of doors, and fringing of curtains, and thousands such ... things on whose common appliance hang whole trades, to which there never yet belonged the blessing of giving one ray of pleasure or becoming of the remotest or most contemptible use ... I speak from experience: I know what it is to live in a cottage with a deal floor and roof, and a hearth of mica slate; and I know it to be in many respects healthier and happier than living between a Turkey carpet and a gilded ceiling, beside a steel grate and polished fender.[41]

For much of the nineteenth century, furniture was purchased and used to serve two purposes: as either a physical function or a ritual or symbolic function (or both). Ettema has described this as a didactic role, saying that 'the purpose of furniture was to serve as a guide to the appropriate behaviour in each room'.[42] This connects well with my emphasis on the appropriateness of furniture to the room. In other words, one prompted the other. Furniture and furnishings intended for display, such as sideboards and hallstands, were often used in public spaces where formal behaviour and ceremony reigned. On the other hand, in less formal and private spaces the emphasis was on comfort and a lack of ceremony, illustrated by, for example, the use of rocking or reclining chairs. The rationale behind the selection of furniture served as a guide to appropriate behaviour, and vice versa.

This approach often resulted in the purchase of goods that looked appropriate but were not up to the job. In an American publication of 1856, pretensions to refinement were gently burst:

---

[40] Hepworth, M. (1999), 'Privacy, security and respectability', in Chapman, T. and Hockey, J. (Eds), *Ideal Homes?*, p. 19.

[41] Ruskin (1891), 'The Lamp of Sacrifice', p. 32.

[42] Ettema (1991), 'The fashion system in American furniture', p. 194.

Even the hardest and homeliest bench that was ever made of oak plank, is a more comfortable and more respectable article of furniture than many of the spring-seat and hair-cloth sofa and rocking chairs, which we have met with, soft, plump and elastic to all appearance, but which when we, in good faith, accept their invitations, let us down with a sudden jerk and make us painfully acquainted with their internal mechanism.[43]

If display, based on etiquette and formality, was the key issue for middle-class homes in the middle of the century, by the latter part the function of display had changed to being more of an expression of self. This meant that an aesthetic demonstration of taste superseded the ceremonial role of goods as style overtook function. As styles could be chosen 'off the shelf' in a retail store, and crucially did not require intimate knowledge of rules of behaviour or etiquette, they became more under the control of retailers and manufacturers.

A brief excursion into two of the main rooms will elucidate these ideas as practised. In the nineteenth century, room types were established with a grammar of signs and signifiers based on notional ideal examples. In this way it was possible to create rooms that emulated the ideal but were not competitive; rather, they were demonstrative – a paraphrase of the ideal.

The dining room

The dining room is a useful focus for understanding some of the changes in the nineteenth century home, as it encapsulates the way middle-class society operated and adapted to change. Rachel Rich has suggested that analysis of these rooms can be made according to three considerations: the architectural, the decorative and the organizational.[44] The architectural aim refers to the separation and isolation of the dining room; the decorative was for personal pleasure and to impress visitors, and the organizational she represents as a partial feminization of the room through table settings and layouts. However, the dining room was often represented as a male space.

At the beginning of the century, Thomas Sheraton wrote: 'The furniture of the dining room ought to be bold, substantial, and magnificent, in proportion to its dimensions.' Furthermore, 'the dining parlour must be furnished with nothing trifling, or which may seem unnecessary'. For Sheraton, the necessary furniture comprised a 'large sideboard, included or surrounded with Ionic pillars: the handsome and extensive dining table; the large face glass; the family portraits; the marble fireplaces; and the Wilton carpet'.[45] It must not be forgotten that Sheraton was writing for the benefit of furniture retailers.

---

[43] Cleaveland, H. W. et al. (1856), *Village and Farm Cottage: The Requirements of American Village Homes Considered and Suggested*, p. 133, cited in Grier, K. C. (1988), *Culture and Comfort: People, Parlors and Uholstery, 1850–1930*, p. 100.

[44] Rich, R. (2003), 'Advice on dining and décor in London and Paris 1860–1914', *Journal of Design History*, 16(1), pp. 49–59.

[45] Sheraton, T. (1803), *The Cabinet Dictionary*, pp. 194 and 218.

As Juliet Kinchin has shown, variations on this sort of scheme remained well into the twentieth century.[46] As an example of gendering, it clearly links masculinity with dining and the dining room. This trend is also reflected in the iconography of sideboards and pictures used in dining rooms, which often showed scenes of hunting and the results thereof.[47] Ames notes that this iconography changes in the latter part of the century, and he considers that this reflects the trend towards making a home more of a place of retreat and seclusion from the outside world. By implication, the imagery, applied to sideboards or painted on canvas, that depicts acts of violence between man and nature was disruptive to the comforting process. Although critics such as Harriet Spofford and the Garret sisters decried this form of ornament, the retailers were aware of the desires of their customers. The retailer John Oetzmann wrote in his company's catalogue that the various items of furniture for the dining room 'should be of a solid massive character, either mahogany or oak and may be either plain or carved as preferred'.[48]

Nevertheless, there was a change in dining room use, and the retailer was quick to spot it. The catalogue of Holland and Sons, a London furniture business, noted the change of use from simply dining to a use that included utilizing the room as a second sitting room:

> This room is so arranged as to be suitable as dining or sitting room, and can be furnished completely for £100.00. The articles included are enumerated below: A sideboard bookcase, a dining table, 6 dining chairs, a writing table, 2 easy chairs, a corner cabinet, a pair of tapestry curtains, a Brussels carpet.[49]

This was in line with other advice, which recognized that not all could maintain a dining room for a single purpose. Mrs Loftie wrote: 'It thus arises that the eating room, perhaps the best in the house, must in large families often serve as parlour, study, or schoolroom.' Nevertheless, she still warned that: 'This entails a considerable amount of inconvenience, to be avoided if possible.'[50]

In the case of the dining rooms of the working class, the degree of change in use is fully reflected in the example of a native-born American worker's home in 1910:

> In five-room houses we find an anomaly known as the dining room. Though a full set of dining room furniture ... are usually found in evidence, they are rarely used at meals. The family sewing is frequently done there, the machine standing in the corner of the window; and sometimes too, the ironing ... but rarely is the room used for breakfast, dinner or supper.[51]

[46] Kinchin, J. (1996), 'Interiors: nineteenth century essays on the masculine and the feminine room', in Kirkham, P. (Ed.), *The Gendered Object*, pp. 12–29.

[47] See Ames, K. (1992), *Death in the Dining Room and Other Tales of Victorian Culture*.

[48] Oetzmann and Co. (n.d.), *Catalogue*, p. 300.

[49] Cited in Symonds, R. and Whineray, B. (1962), *Victorian Furniture*, p. 104.

[50] Loftie, Mrs W. J. (1876), *The Dining Room: Art at Home*, p. 3.

[51] Byingon, M. (1910), *Homestead: The Households of a Mill Town*, cited in Cohen (1984), 'Embellishing a life of labour', p. 301.

Even if the furnishings on offer changed to suit new ideas about the decoration and furnishings of rooms, other influences far beyond the control of the retailer and tastemaker occurred in room use. These influences included the personal taste or circumstances of individuals and the messages they read into the furnishings. One fictional example will stand for many. Trollope, in his *Barchester Towers*, describes Archdeacon Grantly's distaste for round dining tables. Grantly thought there was something 'democratic and parvenue in a round table', and fancied that 'dissenters and calico-printers chiefly used them'.[52]

The parlour

The main characteristic of a refined house was a parlour that represented the front space of their lives. The room was the gateway to a home, in which the right furniture correctly arranged was part of the stage management. The parlour was furnished and decorated in a manner that appeared to deny the world of business or production. Yet the way to achieve this state of affairs was to spend large sums of money with shopkeepers and artisans who provided manufactured products to make this room into a ritual space. Richard Bushman perceptively discusses the contradictions in the nineteenth-century home, in which there is a clear disjuncture between the economically useless, decorative parlour, which itself is a product of much activity in the market, and the factory that produced it. Bushman recognizes that this disjuncture is based upon the idea that parlours are conceptually borrowed from the aristocratic culture. They were not natural developments growing from everyday experience.[53] Therefore, the real comfort was often found in other spaces in the home away from the applied decorum of the parlour.

The parlour was originally a smaller room set apart from the medieval great hall, designated as a space for private conversation and display of property. Its particular reinvention for most levels of society in the nineteenth century was crucial to the culture of domesticity. As early as 1825 William Cobbett had raised complaints against the new furniture and fashions that had displaced the old. He wrote of a Wealden farmhouse that: 'every thing about this farm-house was formerly the scene of plain manners and plentiful living'.[54] It was once all furnished with oak pieces, some of which had the advantage of being many hundreds of years old but were all now in a state of decay and disuse. Cobbett particularly complained of the creation of the 'parlour'. He grumbled that: 'one end of this once plain and substantial house had been moulded into a *parlour*: and there was the mahogany table, and the

[52]   Cited in Burton, (1972), *The Early Victorians at Home*, p. 85.

[53]   Bushman, R. L. (1992), *The Refinement of America: Persons, Houses, Cities*, pp. 262–5.

[54]   Cobbett, W. (1830), *Rural Rides* (1967), p. 226, entry for 20 October 1825; also see Gilbert, C. (1991), *English Vernacular Furniture 1750–1900*, p. 43.

fine chairs, and the fine glass, and all as bare-faced [an] upstart as any stock-jobber in the kingdom can boast of'.[55]

At the other end of the century a commentator wrote about the British parlour: 'It is shut up for six days of the week, and is only kept for brag: ostentatious superfluity in the idea of the artisan's wife is, as with those in higher grades of society, a sign of superiority.'[56] Both these comments reflect the fact that the function of the parlour was for display rather than use. It was often the case that these rooms were decorated to create a sense of gentility that would then highlight the difference between those with the room and those without.[57] Whatever the reason, Grier persuasively argues, images of the parlour were available in everyday life, offering examples of luxury furnishings for consumers to interpret in their own homes.[58]

One of the main ways of simply achieving these effects was to purchase a 'suite'. The connotations of the courtly style established in the eighteenth century in particular transferred themselves to the idea of the suite of matching furniture. The image of completeness and the cohesiveness of the suite gave the impression of not only the ability to make a single purchase of matching goods but also of social standing. Retailers played upon this snobbery. John Oetzmann reminded the readers of his catalogue that: 'a room furnished out of … [an auction] saleroom has a saleroom look which will cling to it so long as the articles hang together'.[59] The inference was that mismatched furniture would reflect badly on the occupants.

In homes that were either too small or were not able to afford the furnishings of a parlour, the ideal of appropriateness was demonstrated through paraphrase, in the use of multi-purpose convertible furniture. An example of a respectable working-class home describes both the attempt at parlour-making and the necessity of convertible furniture:

> The 'parlor' is usually gaudy with plush furniture (sometime covered with washable covers) carpet on the floor, cheap lace-curtains at the windows, crayon portraits of the family on the walls … sometimes a couch, and the ubiquitous folding bed.[60]

The 'ubiquitous folding bed' may have been disguised as a cabinet, chest or even a piano, all of which could be converted to a bed in private but were ideal for working-class parlours in which illusion blended into reality.

---

[55] Cobbett (1830), *Rural Rides*, p. 226.

[56] Clarke, A. (1899), *The Effect of the Factory System*, cited in Barrett, H. and Philips, J. (1987), *Suburban Style*, p. 58.

[57] The terminology of the parlour is examined briefly in Grier (1988), *Culture and Comfort*, p. 64.

[58] Grier considers the examples of hotels, steamboats and railroad cars, amongst others, in Chapter One of *Culture and Comfort*.

[59] Oetzmann Catalogue.

[60] More, L. B. (1907), *Wage Earners' Budgets*, cited in Grier (1988), *Culture and Comfort*, p. 315.

Comfort

As a specific vehicle of meaning, comfort is at the heart of the Victorian home. It not only serves a practical purpose, but it also acts as an element in the creation of meaning in the interior.

The home as an ideal is therefore inextricably tied to the notion of comfort. It was in the eighteenth century that the concept of comfort was fully established, albeit being mainly reserved for those who could afford it. During the nineteenth century the obsession with domesticity, respectability and comfort reached its zenith. Richard Bushman points to the dual nature of physical comfort, which was easy to overdo at any level of society: 'comfort defined both the merits and the limits of vernacular gentility'.[61] Appropriateness in furnishing and behaviour was the key, whether it was for the aristocracy or the working class. In terms of furnishing practice, gentility was particularly reflected in the emphasis on matching suites and unified interior decoration schemes.

Robert Southey, writing in 1807 in the guise of a fictional Spanish visitor, neatly expressed a view of comfort that has become specifically associated with the nineteenth century: 'There are two words in their language on which these people [the English] pride themselves, and which they say cannot be translated. Home is the one by which an Englishman means his house ... The other word is comfort; it means all the enjoyments and privileges of home ...'.[62] The terms 'home' and 'comfort' were finely drawn and hid many subtle variations in meaning. For example, comfort and neatness were still seen as representative of morality as well as of bodily ease, but on the other hand too much physical comfort implied luxury and extravagance, and by extension, a lack of moral fibre. This dilemma was explored in much nineteenth-century literature, where the interior and its 'comforts' could put people at ease, or conversely, create a feeling of being ill at ease: where interiors represented the moral self, or where interiors reflected inappropriate luxury.[63] This 'comfort' of ease was described by Maria Edgeworth in a letter dated 5 December 1821:

> This antient house with modern furniture and arrangement of luxuries and comfortable luxuries is delightful ... I am now writing in a delightful armchair – high backed antiquity – modern cushions with moveable side cushions with cushion elbows lying on the lowest low arms, so that there is just comfortable room to sit down in a place between the cushions in which on niches snugly – so snugly that when Harriet sat down she thought she was so happy she would never get up again. Think what a luxurious chair that must be which so affected her Stoic philosophy. God help me I have wasted ten lines upon a chair![64]

---

[61] Bushman (1992), *The Refinement of America*, p. 269.

[62] Cited by Crowley, J. E. (2000), *The Invention of Comfort*, p. 170.

[63] See, for example, Tristram (1989), *Living Space in Fact and Fiction*.

[64] Edgeworth (1812), *The Absentee*, p. 385.

By the mid-nineteenth century, the changes in home comforts for the middle classes were very noticeable, especially in comparison to the situation in the latter part of the eighteenth century. The comments below emphasize the distinction between a state of comfortlessness and the new-found luxury that had become commonplace. Writing in 1846 one commentator thought:

> As one instance, it is not necessary to go back much beyond half a century [1795] to arrive at the time when prosperous shopkeepers in the leading thoroughfares of London were without that now necessary article of furniture, a carpet, in their ordinary sitting rooms: luxury in this particular, seldom went further with them than well scoured floors strewn with sand, and the furniture of the apartments was by no means inconsistent with the primitive, and as we should say, comfortless state of things. In the same houses we now see, not carpets merely, but many articles of furniture which were formerly in use only among the nobility and gentry.[65]

Thirty years later, in 1876, the American Henry Ward Beecher noted the improvements in home comforts for the working class, and commented admiringly of the achievements possible:

> The average American household is wiser, there is more material for thought, for comfort, for home love, today, in the ordinary workman's house, than there was a hundred years ago in one of a hundred rich men's mansions…The labourer ought to be ashamed of himself … who in 20 years does not own the ground on which his house stands, and that too an unmortgaged house; who has not in that house provided carpets for the rooms, who has not his China plates, who has not his chromos, who has not some picture or portrait hanging upon the walls, who has not some books nestling on the shelf, who has not there a household he can call his home, the sweetest place upon the earth. This is not a picture of some future time, but the picture of today, a picture of the homes of the working men of America.[66]

Beyond the physical examples that represented a rise in the standards of living as well as people's expectations, the ideal of home for the Victorians was equated with respectability, contentment and security. John Ruskin's well-known portrayal of 'the true nature of home – it is the place of peace: the shelter, not only from all injury, but also from all terror, doubt and division' reflects this thought precisely.[67] This idea had been expressed earlier in 1853, when a 'happy home', or rather a moral home, was defined in the *Family Friend* as:

> A dwelling comfortable furnished, clean, bright, salubrious and sweet … a small collection of books on the shelves – a few blossoming plants in the window – some well selected engravings on the walls … these are

---

[65] Porter, G. R. (1847), *The Progress of the Nation*, p. 532.

[66] Cited in Orvell, M. (1989), *The Real Thing: Imitation and Authenticity in American Culture 1880–1940*, pp. 46–7.

[67] Ruskin, J. (1864), *Sesame and Lilies*, p. 108.

conditions of existence within the reach if everyone who will seek them – resources of the purest happiness, lost to thousands, because a wrong direction is given to their tastes and energies, and they roam abroad in pursuit of interest and enjoyment which they might create in abundance at home.[68]

The idea of incorrect 'tastes and energies' missing out on the benefits of home was an essentially middle-class idea which hinted at the need for education, self-help and commitment to the idea of 'home sweet home'.

Much has been made of the rise of the middle class and their concepts of home comforts and cosiness. According to the contemporary architect Robert Kerr, it was a very particular form of comfort:

What we call in England a comfortable house is a thing so intimately identified with English customs as to make us apt to say that in no other country but our own is this element of comfort fully understood; or at all events that the comfort of any other nation is not the comfort of this.[69]

This probably had a grain of truth, as English ideas of comfort, as well as the goods that supported them, were exported worldwide.[70] Certainly, for the latter half of the century this comfort was generally associated with the old, the traditional and the natural as opposed to the modern or urban. The use of textiles to soften interiors, the 'working' of objects as crafts, the employment of models from past styles and a continuing interest in antique furniture or reproduction all demonstrate this. Balancing these ideas with the appropriate furnishing style and correct behaviour was the strategy best employed by people so that they might be at ease.

John Crowley uses two contrasting nineteenth-century American authors, Andrew Jackson Downing and Catherine E. Beecher, to demonstrate the differences of opinion over the issue of comfort in American society. Downing represents the 'male' view that appearance and taste was part of the ideal, whereas Beecher maintained that comfort should be more real than apparent. In Downing's case, these ideas were published in architectural treatises and in the case of Beecher, in housekeeping manuals. The distinction between male and female publishing genres is obvious, but Crowley also points out that these two authors transposed traditional gender roles into another sphere. Downing was more interested in the 'sentimentalization of domestic relations',[71] whilst Beecher became more involved with the creation of comfort using technology in the home.

---

[68]   Cited in Forty, A. (1986), *Objects of Desire: Design and Society 1750–1980*, p. 108.

[69]   Kerr, R. (1871), *The Gentleman's House*, p. 69.

[70]   Not only did this occur through exports and emigration, from magazines and books on furnishing, but also from the establishment of overseas branches of furnishing stores. Maples' business in Paris and Buenos Aires is one example.

[71]   Crowley (2000), *The Invention of Comfort*, p. 288.

As Crowley has shown, comfort is best described and analysed in relation to both the physical objects that it manifests and the cultures that created it. The more that comfort is considered in terms of a construct between necessity and luxury, the more it seems to be a middle way. From whichever end you look, comfort appears to be a very middle-class invention.

Gender

Objects as vehicles of meaning also define and are defined by gender roles. John Tosh has pointed out that: 'the nineteenth century home was widely held to be a man's place, not only in the sense of being his possession or fiefdom, but also as the place where his deepest needs were met'.[72] There was a move towards making men more interested in the home: 'If the crusade against the upholsterer has given a new attraction to the home and added more to the narrow list of interests which lie beyond the range of business life, it is a further and appreciable advantage.'[73] Despite this sort of initiative, for much of the nineteenth century the onus was on women to meet these needs and to manage the 'cult of domesticity', which necessitated a shared process of transforming ideas about home into objects and rooms. Auslander suggests that it was also the role of nineteenth-century women to 'make' the family, and by extension, the bourgeois class, through consumption. In France, they then had the added task of representing the nation, and then finally the representation of self. These were cumulative roles.[74] Less dramatic and more recognizable were the comments of Francis Power Cobbe. Writing in 1881, she considered the powerful role of home-making for women:

> The making of a true home is really our peculiar and inalienable right –a right, which no man can take from us; for a man can no more, make a home than a drone can make a hive … It is a woman, and only a woman – and a woman all by herself, if she likes, and without any man to help her – who can turn a house into a home.[75]

It was the establishment and upkeep of the domestic façade that was primarily the role of women, and mainly of the middle class. This role was ambiguous, as it was intended to insulate and separate women from commerce, but was in fact intimately tied to it via goods and services that were required to make and run a home. The intervention of taste professionals in this process, whether retailers or writers, was an important link which connected the home to the outside world.

---

[72] Tosh, J. (1999), *A Man's Place: Masculinity and the Middle Class Home in Victorian England*, p. 1.

[73] 'The Art of Furnishing', *Cornhill Magazine* (January–June 1875), p. 536. See Tosh (1999), *A Man's Place*, especially pp. 27–53.

[74] Auslander (1996), *Taste and Power*, p. 278.

[75] Cobbe, F. P. (1881), *The Duties of a Woman*, p. 139.

However, control over the choice, arrangement and purchase of goods indicates a potentially important role for women. Although Eastlake was vociferous in his comments: 'the faculty of distinguishing good from bad design in the familiar objects of domestic life is a faculty which most educated people- and women especially-conceive they possess'.[76] He goes on to suggest that: 'It is scarcely too much to say that ninety-nine out of every hundred English gentlewomen who have the credit of dressing well depend entirely upon their milliners for advice as to what they may, or may not, wear.'[77] This argument might also be applied to the retailers of home furnishings, although one at least was not going to admit superiority in matters of taste. John Oetzmann said in his *Hints on House Furnishing and Decoration* that: 'in our remarks upon furnishing and decoration, our aim will be to give a general idea of what should be the governing principle … The selection of most of the items requiring special good taste may be safely left to the ladies.'[78]

Within the home, gendered divisions of styles were based on concepts of femininity or masculinity, and were usually associated with particular styles and room use. Underneath all these ideas were the stereotypes of gender that were clearly acknowledged and understood by manufacturers, retailers, consumers and commentators. One example will suffice. In *The Gentleman's House*, Robert Kerr wrote that 'the dining room should have an air of 'masculine importance' and the drawing room should be 'entirely ladylike'.[79] Chase and Levenson point out that in Kerr's ideal: 'The gentleman's well-dressed house fuses with his well-adorned wife. They even share manner. "Elegence, therefore, unassuming and unelborated, touching in no way the essentials of home comfort, never suggesting affectation and pride, moderated by unimpassioned refinement, and subdued even to modesty, will invariably be accepted in England."'[80]

The choosing of colour schemes and domestic furnishings was beginning to be seen as particularly suitable for women at home, especially if they were decorating rooms that were intended for their own use. This was also connected to a gradual change in room use that meant that libraries, for example, were becoming less of a male preserve and more of a family room.[81] Disraeli declared that: 'Woman alone can organize a drawing room; man succeeds sometimes in a library.'[82]

---

[76] Eastlake, C. (1872), *Hints on Household Taste*, p. 8.

[77] Ibid.

[78] Oetzmann and Co. (*c.* 1871), *Hints on House Furnishing and Decoration*, p. 294.

[79] Kerr (1865), *The Gentleman's House*, p. 107. For more, see Auslander (1996), *Taste and Power*, pp. 279–84 and Kinchin, J. (1996), 'Interiors', pp. 12–29.

[80] Chase, K. and Levenson, M. (2000), *The Spectacle of Intimacy: A Public Life for the Victorian Family*, p. 162.

[81] Thornton, P. (1984), *Authentic Decor*, p. 150. See also p. 98 above.

[82] Disraeli, B. (1844), *Coninsby*, Book III, Cp. 2, cited in Tristram (1989), *Living Space in Fact and Fiction*, p. 59.

This role of homemaker meant that women became more involved not only in the management of the home but also in the practicalities of domestic crafts that were often intended for utilization within the home. Typical advice for young women went as follows:

> Girls who are clever with their fingers can do very much towards making the home beautiful, not only by needlework painting and drawing, and the various kinds of fancy work, but by the practice of amateur upholstery.[83]

The development of home crafts could indicate the application of female talents and industry, or alternatively it could represent the borders of angst and misery. Logan proposes that: 'the sheer number of useless decorative objects produced by women might be better viewed as a manifestation of anxiety, boredom, and depression rather than a satisfying and healthy engagement with art'.[84] This position was recognized by contemporary writers. *The Habits of Good Society*, published in 1859, explained that: 'all accomplishments have the one great merit of giving a lady something to do: something to preserve her from ennui: to console her seclusion: to arouse her in grief: to compose her to occupation in joy'.[85] By the end of the century, women were still defined by their ability to create crafts for the home. In 1893 Helen Mather was described as 'a great needlewoman, not only are the long satin curtains by her own hand, but the pillow, cushions and dainty lampshade'.[86] As Daniel Miller has suggested, this re-working of goods:

> May be defined as that which translates the object from an alienable to an inalienable condition: that is, from being a symbol of estrangement and price value to being an artefact invested with particular inseparable connotations.[87]

In other words, the commercial origins of goods were disguised by symbolic additions applied by the homemaker.

The application of craftwork to home furnishings could also refer to practical matters as well as saving money and being careful with budgets. For example, Catherine Beecher wrote in 1869, in *American Woman's Home*, that prudence with fabric would allow the covering of ottoman frames which 'your men folk knock up for you, out of rough, unplanned boards, and to cover any broken down armchairs reposing in the oblivion of the garret'.[88] This may reflect more of a democratic approach to homemaking than Mrs Delaney's comments of *circa* 1856, when shell working was recommended as 'an elegant

---

[83] *Young Ladies Treasure Book* (1881–2), p. 161.

[84] Logan, T. (1995), 'Decorating domestic space, Middle-class women and Victorian interiors', in Dickerson, V., *Keeping the Victorian House*, p. 213.

[85] Nunn, P. (1987), *Victorian Women Artists*, p. 8.

[86] Ibid., p. 7.

[87] Miller, D. (1987), *Material Culture and Mass Consumption*, p. 190. See also Cohen, (1982), 'Embellishing a life of labour'.

[88] Beecher, C. (1869), *American Woman's Home*, p. 87.

drawing room occupation, as well as one calculated to call forth the artistic taste and inventive powers of the worker'.[89]

By the second half of the nineteenth century, middle-class women were even more involved in the consumption of goods for the home and the maintenance and arrangement of their interiors. If anything, there were increasing pressures on women to apply their artistic endeavours to decorate and enhance the home for the family, as they became consumers and managers rather than producers. This was not, however, without its problems. Auslander suggests that there was a major conflict between fashioning the nation, the class and the self through consumption: 'Women were essential to the new [French] republic in their role as producers of the domestic symbolic nation. But women were also important to the economy as consumers, and the tasks-consuming and nation making-were not always easy to combine.'[90] It was the role of the taste professionals (and the distributors of goods) to come together to sort out the situation through instruction. As the home was the centre of social order, this was not only economically but also politically sensible.

Objects as bearers of aesthetic values

It has already been suggested that a change occurred during the mid-nineteenth century from rooms being used as signs or indicators of status and gentility to being representations of self, through styles. To meet the demand for furnishing and setting up these homes, changes had to occur, not only in the distribution system but also in the provision of information and direction in matters of setting up and running a home. As the subtle graduations of goods developed ever more, the meanings they held, which were designed to deal with the non-verbal communications relating to the home, became more complex. The viewer needed to become ever more resourceful to read and recognize the signs. A knowledge and understanding of the narrative nature of selected objects intended to reinforce respectability was increasingly important.

Furnishings became more domesticated and homely; they initially related morals to comfort, and not directly to show. Indeed, one of the functions of 'good taste' was to establish oneself as 'middle-class' so as to allow furnishings to be a reflection of position. This was achieved in great measure by the common use of a language of display that was both shared and individual, which was both purchased from a retailer and constructed at home. In a French example from 1825, Mme Pariset, writing a furnishing manual, gave full details of the 'correct' methods of home furnishing with a particular grasp on the idea of comfort. She explained that 'real good taste involves buying useful,

---

[89] *Elegant Arts for Ladies* (1856), p. 16.
[90] Auslander (1996), *Taste and Power*, p. 383.

practical, durable goods that should, above all, go together. I think that this harmony is the essential aspect of what the English express in the word *comfortable*.[91] Importantly, she recommended her readers not to attempt any choices themselves, but to rely on a decorator to make purchases on her behalf.[92]

Thus we see the development of ground rules that controlled behaviour and established the correct style of furnishings, and ensured that these were seen to be carried out. As a family status changed, so did the appropriate possessions, and anxiety ensued if these changes were not correctly organized. Again, the role of the retailer was to ensure the suitability of any goods chosen. Another French example is instructive of the whole idea:

> Here is … the horoscope of Parisian furniture. For the worker, the artist, the lawyer, the doctor, the scientist, the man of letters, oak – the strong robust wood-and solid walnut, or their analogues. For wealthy households, sculpted furniture in the dining room, the living room and the study; veneered furniture from Boutung or Godin [fashionable and expensive stores] in the bedroom. For chateaux and palaces, elaborate furniture: mantelpieces, canopy beds, book cases, filing cabinets, wardrobes … for the dubious professions, for shady opulence, for boudoirs that are really salesrooms, junk. Birds of a feather should flock together.[93]

Mary Douglas's comments, noted above, about 'making visible and stable the categories of culture' are fully exemplified in this passage.

However, whether as signs of gentility or symbols of self, for those who needed help it was often the upholsterer who was instrumental in setting the scene. The apparently happy result of their endeavours can be found in Maria Edgeworth's *The Absentee*, when Lady Clonberry had just finished refurnishing her rooms under the advice and guidance of Mr Soho the upholsterer. The result was just what she wanted, and her delight in showing it off was evident:

> With well practiced dignity, and half subdued self-complacency of aspect, her ladyship went gliding about – most importantly busy, introducing my lady this to the sphinx candelabra, and my lady that to the Trebisond trellice; placing some [guests] delightfully for the perspective of the Alhambra; establishing others quite to her satisfaction on seraglio ottomans; and honouring others with a seat under the Statira canopy. Receiving and answering compliments from successive crowds of select friends, imagining herself the mirror of fashion, and the admiration of the whole world.[94]

---

[91] Mme Pariset (1825), *Manual de la maîtressse de la maison* … cited in Auslander (1996), *Taste and Power*, p. 223.

[92] See Auslander (1996), *Taste and Power*, pp. 223–4.

[93] Luchet, A. (1868), *L'art industriel à l'exposition universelle de 1867*, p. 134, cited in Auslander (1996), *Taste and Power*, p. 218.

[94] Edgeworth (1812), *The Absentee*, p. 27.

The pleasure to be found in 'showing-off' one's new home should not be underestimated.

For the Victorian consumer, the correctness of furnishing decisions was highly important and significant. Grier suggests that prior to the 1850s, room designs had a tendency to be based on a planned and unified décor, having little individuality. From 1850 to 1880 more comfort was encouraged, and room uses developed particular functions, and required appropriate furnishings. From the 1880s, an interest in comfort, accessorization and individual expression grew apace.[95] The impact of these changes on retailing is evident in the changing demand for particular goods (and their subsequent disposal and renewal), as well as in an expectation of an ability to guide the consumer as to a fitting choice.

Victorian taste is complex but can be simplistically reduced to four essentials: elitist, arriviste, reform and mass consumption. The *elitist* consumption was clearly based on using the power of objects and their symbols to maintain self-centred social strata that used goods to retain the acquired status.

For the *arrivistes* it was essential to distance oneself from the common culture but to be seen to 'fit in'.[96] Alice Neal's short story *Furnishing or two ways of commencing life*, published in *Godey's Ladies Book* in 1850, tells of two girls, one who marries well and the other not so well. The discussion about carpet purchase is revealing not only of taste, but also of the problems associated with it:

> 'And what sort of parlor carpet did you get chérie?'
> 'A beautiful three ply, wool coloured and green. I thought it would be cheaper on the whole than an ingrain.'
> 'Dear me! Mamma chose a velvet at Orne's, and I have a Brussels in my own room and the third story. I hate tapestry, they are so common.'
> 'I think those in the parlour are beautiful.'
> 'So I thought: but that was when they first came out. Now they are so cheap that everyone can afford them. A three-ply! Why, what sort of chairs and tables are to go with such a carpet?'[97]

The *reform* movement carried forward the idea that goods had pedagogical natures and they could change and re-socialize people in a democratic way, as opposed to the self-centred way of the elites. Gervase Wheeler, in his *Rural Homes*, published in 1855, made a less superior approach, but one that acknowledged the beneficial impact of changes on local surroundings:

> The teaching influence soon shows its effects. The furniture, the internal plenishing and details take a tone from the dwelling. Articles in improved taste are demanded from the country store, or perhaps sent for from the

---

[95] Grier (1988), *Culture and Comfort*, p. 82.

[96] This attitude was fertile ground for satirists and cartoonists of the time. See *Punch* magazine for examples.

[97] *Godey's Ladies Book* (November 1850), cited in Winkler, G. and Moss, R. (1986), *Victorian Interior Decoration,* p. 38.

distant city. There are some inquired for by others, and the building of one moderately good house (good in the artistic sense) will often occasion the introduction of a thousand commodities of a better taste into the rural community.[98]

The *mass consumers* took their cues from each other, but most particularly from the retailer and the professional tastemakers. The popularity of suites of furniture for bedrooms, lounges and so on as symbols of respectability and unity as opposed to the bohemian fragmentation and individuality of the reformers grew. The image of fragmented pieces of 'art' furniture and accessories espoused by artists and critics and the stores that supplied this taste (for example, Liberty and Co.) was utterly contrary to the symbols (and safety) of completeness offered by suites.

For all these consumption groups, one of the main problems was that choices had to be made which appeared to put identity creation directly onto the shoulders of the individual. In reality, this often meant that another party was called upon for assistance. Although these influences obviously varied, it was often not so much which taste or style one selected but which retailer one chose to rely on. The issue of education and knowledge of products and styles and their relation to purchasing was taken up by McClaugherty, who has suggested that the late nineteenth-century 'Household Art' movement 'sought to educate homeowners, who were quickly becoming consumers of the plethora of ready-made items rather than patrons of local community cabinet-makers and upholsterers'.[99] Mrs Haweis recognized the 'problem' of consumers not thinking for themselves. In her *Art of Decoration* she wrote that: 'just now every shop bristles with the ready means: books, drawings, and *objets de vertu* from all countries are within everybody's reach, and all that is lacking is the power of choice'.[100] At the very least this support from the retailers meant that the issue of social demarcation lines was confirmed through their comments and suggestions as to the appropriateness of goods for a particular social situation.

A useful example of a similar process is found in the 1855 Paris exhibition, where the intention of the *Galerie de l'économie domestique* was to include 'a successive progression of specimens of the domestic home at each step of the social scale, from poverty to affluence'.[101] Bourgeois interiors were seen as highly differentiated (in terms of status, location, gender, age, religion), and working-class homes were seen as undifferentiated.[102] However,

---

[98] Wheeler, G. (1855), *Rural Homes*, p. 276.

[99] McClaugherty (1983), 'Household art: Creating the artistic home, 1868–1893', *Winterthur Portfolio*, 18(1), p. 1.

[100] Mrs Haweis (1881), *The Art of Decoration*, p. 42.

[101] Auslander (1996), *Taste and Power*, p. 214. A more complete exercise on this idea was the Salon des Arts Ménagers in the twentieth century; see Segalen, M. (1994), 'The Salon des Arts Ménagers, 1923–1983: A French effort to instil the virtues and the norms of good taste', *Journal of Design History*, 7(4), pp. 267–76.

[102] Auslander (1996), *Taste and Power*, p. 214.

differentiation was itself based on a 'grammar' of appropriateness. The intention of the organizers of the 1855 exhibition was clear – the avoidance of what they considered 'fraudulent' or 'illusory' furniture that carried the signs of high design – but was in fact impractical and false in design and aesthetics. In other words, as Auslander explains: 'for everyday people (workers) to own luxurious objects or luxurious seeing objects, was – implicitly – inappropriate'.[103] The decisions about the appropriateness or not of any merchandise were left to the judgement of the taste professionals and the retailers.

One example of this coded status was found in the retail mail order catalogues, which codified distinctions by setting out the book in price and quality order, thus making visible the categories of society that were representative of the process that was occurring in a more fragmented way in the high street. As the stores often displayed goods in a hierarchy of style and price, so the planned mail order catalogues 'served as a surrogate for the three-dimensional display, offering the advantage, besides, of being amenable to solitary contemplation and unencumbered dreaming'.[104] This again seems to reflect the idea of consumption as being partly about hedonistic 'day-dreaming'.[105] The idea of classification and coding is interesting, not only as examples of the whole business of organization and arrangement that were so dear to the Victorians, but also as establishing the principles that goods had their qualities and classes, as did people. Although these ideas penetrated all aspects of society and culture, perhaps it was within the home they were expressed most clearly.

Within the rules of interior design, there was some scope for self-expression and individuality as long as one used the 'grammar' that had to be learned. Bourdieu's idea that income was not as relevant as education when it came to distinctions based on codes used to identify a position in society can explain this situation. The author and decorator Mrs Haweis considered that taste and room arrangement expressed individual personality, which should be based on free expression, and not on an established orthodoxy of taste: originality, not rules. For an accomplished woman it was an opportunity for a display of her aesthetic qualities and abilities. However, there was a paradox of being encouraged to believe that they lived in a world of unfettered personal expression but actually having to live in a rule-governed society, no less in interiors and homemaking than in any other area. The connections between needlework and other homemaking accomplishments mentioned above, and the idea of collecting to make transformations in interiors are becoming evident in this mix of individualism and conformity. Tim Dant, following de Certeau, considers that:

---

[103] Ibid., p. 215.

[104] Orvell (1989), *The Real Thing*, p. 43.

[105] See Oetzmann catalogue example on page 137.

The arts of 'making-do' or *bricolage* are combined with ritual practices, habits and routines out of which the shape of everyday life emerges. These actions of people are not reducible to individual choice, but neither are they wholly determined by learned patterns of action. Rituals may be followed knowingly because it suits the purposes at hand but these purposes might lead to a modification of the ritual, of material objects or of skills to meet varying situations or event to bring about variations in action, experience or environment. This is why the practices of every day life are treated as 'arts'; the agent uses a skill of making, or making do, not to create from nothing, but to creatively adapt both ways of doing things, and material things themselves.[106]

The idea of furnishing to a prepared design was important, as much to create a 'proper scheme' as it was to avoid going wrong. Mary Haweis explained that:

> To make a beautiful and artistic room it is not sufficient to collect a mass of good materials and mix them together. You may spend a fortune at a fashionable decorator's and make out home look like an upholsterer's showroom; or you may fill your house with antiquities of rare merit and calibre, and make it look like an old curiosity shop; but it may be most unpleasing all the same. The furnishing ought to be carried out on some sort of system ...[107]

She made an interesting point about furnishing in an antique style that would clearly have hit home in the 1880s: 'The distinction between an eclectic room furnished upon some reasonable system, and a room furnished after a given period must here be noted. The one is really a medley, directed with taste: the other reproduces a scene that a contemporary might have viewed, and must have *no anachronisms.*'[108]

Associated with this advice was the joy of 'picking up' or collecting so encouraged by writers such as Clarence Cook, Edith Wharton and Elsie De Wolfe. There were dangers to this collecting for some contemporary critics. Herman Muthesius considered the British drawing room. He wrote:

> It suffers in general from having too many odds and ends packed into it and the deliberate informality all to often degenerates into confusion. Actually the province of the lady of the house, it bears the marks of her preferences; lightness, mobility and elegance but usually combined with caprice and that love of frippery and knick-knacks by the thousand that characterises the modern English society woman.[109]

The taste for knick-knacks reflected in part the dilemma for the Victorian (female) homemaker, who was on the one hand encouraged to represent herself and her family, and on the other, to follow formulae established by tastemakers for particular rooms. Janna Jones puts it thus:

---

[106] Dant (1999), *Material Culture in the Social World*, p. 72.

[107] Haweis (1881), *The Art of Decoration*, p. 201.

[108] Ibid., p. 207.

[109] Muthesius (1904), *The English House*, p. 210.

> Both popular advertisers and design manual writers laid claim to authority by promising women answers to the dilemma of modern life ... While advertisers created desire by helping consumers see their way to a point of purchase amidst plentiful product choices, the writers of these design manuals instructed readers that what was worth having was nearly impossible to attain.[110]

It seems that the roles of the retailer as an arbiter between these two positions was probably welcome, as they could direct customers to the products available and interpret the advice manuals. However, shopping was becoming more than just the passive reception of advice and products. Household manuals began to advocate that women should learn to shop, thus sowing some seeds that would grow in the twentieth century: 'Well and properly carried out it [shopping] becomes almost a science.'[111]

---

[110] Jones, J. (1997), 'The distance from home: The domestication of desire in interior design manuals', *Journal of Social History*, 51(2), Winter, p. 323.

[111] Praga, Mrs A. (1899), *Starting Housekeeping*, cited in Hosgood, C. (1999), 'Mrs Pooter's purchase', p. 156.

Chapter 7

Twentieth-century retail responses: from mass to niche marketing

Theodore Dreiser praised the American 'five and ten cent' store as a 'truly beautiful, artistic, humanitarian thing bringing the "stock of overproduction" within "the range of the poor" and thereby democratising the fulfilment of desire'.[1] Although it is probably too much to equate the development of furniture shops with the 'five and ten', it is the case that the furniture retailer has acted as a conduit for the growth of demand for home furnishings that started in the nineteenth century and continues into the twenty-first century. The retail industry that was well established by the end of the nineteenth century was in a good position to respond to the new and greater demands of the twentieth.[2]

Role of retailer

Although the infrastructure of the retail furnishing trade had changed substantially during the nineteenth century, and was set to change even more during the twentieth, the role of the retailer had not substantially changed. As a supplier of goods and services as well as advice, the retailer continued to have an important part to play in the furnishing of homes. In a 1924 editorial, the trade journal *The Cabinet Maker* explained that the furniture retailer's role was more than just selling goods; it was intimately linked to the creation of homes:

> The word 'home' is the key that unlocks many doors: its proper use and the proper backing for that use will arrest more attention, claim more interest than any amount of comment concerning quality … the overstressing of this point [quality] may be fruitless … whereas the emphasis on use, the final effect of the furniture, a hint of the ultimate value of its character in the home will prove more effective salesmanship because it creates an intimate atmosphere it suggests in a subtle way a desire to assist the home maker and thereby implies good service.[3]

Seventeen years later the trade press returned to the theme it had raised in 1924, and suggested that the retailer should ask himself what his role was:

---

[1] Dreiser, T. (1911), cited in Orvell, M. (1989), *The Real Thing: Imitation and Authenticity in American Culture 1880–1940*, p. 47.

[2] For a personal view of the early years of the twentieth century as a furniture salesperson, see the autobiography of Jobson, A. (1977), *The Creeping Hours of Time*, especially Chapter 10.

[3] *Cabinet Maker*, 1 January 1924.

> Am I making more homes for the people or am I producing a greater
> number of furnished houses, which bring more profit but detract from my
> reputation as a man of taste? Am I creating the impression of a specialist in
> designing and carrying out furnishing schemes as distinct from the mere
> selling of furniture?[4]

These considerations reflected the tendency of some retailers to abrogate their
responsibilities (and skills) to others, including manufacturers (particularly
through brand advertising), critics and advisers, who made an industry out of
providing furnishing and decorating advice.

As has been shown in previous chapters, the retail furniture trade has long
suffered from a bad press from many quarters. Some manufacturers have
thought that the retailers have had too much power in the pivotal position of
intermediary between the maker and the consumer.[5] The consumer has often
considered the retailer as a profiteer with no interest other than to sell a product
for an inflated price, whilst the design reformers and critics have seen the
retailer as a brake on the diffusion of better design.[6]

The old chestnut of the retailers only supplying what customers want was
always countered by the idea that customers can only select from what is
stocked. In the nineteenth century, Charles Eastlake had asked his readers not
to rely on the taste of furniture salesmen. In the early part of the twentieth
century, the reformer's passion was still burning. Shaw Sparrow said: 'do not
allow yourself to be talked over by any salesman. His duty is to sell what his
employer has purchased or manufactured and to do that he has to contradict
many principles of decorative art.'[7] Oddly, though, Sparrow was contradicting
a previous consideration he had made that: 'if the public want Art which is not
Art, and cry out for cheapness which is so dear at any price, what are tradesmen
to do? When the public dictate, the manufacturers must obey.'[8]

This brought into sharp focus the main arguments of the role of the furniture
retailer in the twentieth century. Disparaging remarks like those of the critic J.
Elder Duncan had a derogatory effect on customers' perceptions of retailers
and their stocks. For example, he made comments such as: 'Drawing room
suites are undesirable, especially the cheap and spidery Louis Quinze
concoctions, comprising a couch, two arm and six ordinary chairs, which are so
much to the fore in the credit furnishers.'[9] He added: 'the plush saddle-bag
suites, a prominent exhibit at the cheap and nasty shops, are quite hideous, and

---

[4] *Cabinet Maker* (1937).

[5] The 1985 GLEB report *Turning the Tables: Towards a Strategy for the London Furniture Industry* suggested that obstacles to change included the power of the retailer due to concentration of ownership, often combined with a buying strategy using exclusive retailer–manufacturer relations.

[6] See below in this section, and Chapter 5.

[7] Shaw Sparrow, W. (1909), *Hints on House Furnishings*, p. 172.

[8] Ibid., p. 19.

[9] Elder-Duncan, J. (1907), *The House Beautiful*, p. 135.

no amount of trouble will ever eliminate their evil influence'.[10] In 1919 Sir Leo Chiozza-Money, a labour economist, considered that: 'the average furniture shop in poor districts is full of stuff only fit for a bonfire, and it is palmed off on the hire purchase system at extravagant prices to poor people who have no chance of getting anything better'.[11] These criticisms seem to be as hostile to credit and hire purchase as they were to design matters. In 1924 *The Cabinet Maker* commented on another problem, that of the lack of product knowledge:

> At one time, a retailer's job was simply that of a purveyor and his salesman were there to sell. Technical knowledge of the goods was considered immaterial … But time has changed all this. The public itself is pretty well instructed and the salesman who can rely on an ingratiating manner and a persuasive tongue to hold his job finds the sales he could formerly count with certainty were far less secure. The fact is that he is not technically efficient, however detailed and complete his knowledge of salesmanship as an art in itself.[12]

Although some retailers would ignore these jibes and continue to sell cheap merchandise on expensive credit and not show any interest in the goods sold, other parts of the trade were more aware of the retailer's responsibilities. According to C. A. Richter of the manufacturing company Bath Cabinet Makers, the retail furnisher:

> should be the furnishing artist par excellence. Unless he makes some attempt to be this, he does not justify his existence. He should do something more than rent a few thousand square feet of showroom space and fill it with a miscellaneous assortment of articles culled from manufacturers, leaving his salesmen to sell what is easiest to sell, or to his customers to select what their uninstructed fancies suggest. Like the taylor, the confectioner and the *maitre d'hôtel*, he must sell something more than goods. He must make himself known as an artist whose rare natural endowments and long years of careful training have fitted him for exceptional service: whose taste, judgment and experience are worth paying for.[13]

Despite this type of supportive comment, critics have been continuing their attacks in various forms ever since. In 1934 the critic John Gloag, quoted from a radio programme of the late twenties in which an anonymous commentator had suggested that: 'somebody ought to write a guide called "How to buy furniture in spite of the salesman" '.[14] This jibe was mild compared to Gloag's own remarks, in which he castigated the retail furnisher for his lack of

---

[10] Ibid., p. 137.

[11] *Cabinet Maker* 25 January 1919.

[12] *Cabinet Maker,* 19 January 1924.

[13] Richter, C. A., *Cabinet Maker*, July 1927.

[14] Gloag, J. (1934a), *English Furniture*, p. 166. In another publication of the same year, *Industrial Art Explained*, Gloag called retail buyers 'arrogant obstructionists' (p. 112).

knowledge of design: '[he] is not even passively ignorant of design; he is aggressively ignorant'.[15] Three years later, Nikolaus Pevsner, in his investigation into *Industrial Art in England*, found that:

> In a high-class store at Birmingham ... the proprietors refused to take any interest in my research, saying that if I succeeded in improving the taste, cheaper shops everywhere would take up lines similar to the ones, which so far they alone displayed, and this would be detrimental to their business.[16]

Pevsner should not have been surprised at this reaction. The hierarchy of business types had been long established, and was not going to be upset by attempts to democratize design by a handful of reformers.

Nevertheless, these reformers continued their dispute with the retailer. In 1955 Michael Farr wrote that: 'if there were no retailer, no middlemen between the manufacturer and the public, the design standards of industrial products would undoubtedly improve'.[17] Farr justifies this remark by contrasting the retail furniture trade to the architect-led contract furnishing industry, where the customer deals directly with the manufacturer.[18] To support his argument further, Farr reported that when manufacturers were discussing design standards with him, they complained that: 'We are entirely in the hands of the retail buyer, [who] constantly demands variety.'[19]

To balance this destructive argument, Farr noted the reasons why 'post-war' retailers embraced 'pre-war' designs. Firstly, it appeared to the retailers that the public did not want modern furniture; the example of Utility had shown that. Secondly, there were financial risks involved in introducing products and designs that were unproven, especially in an extremely difficult economic climate. Thirdly, a rate of stock turn of at least four to five per annum was required to run profitably, therefore proven selling lines were in the main required.[20] In addition to these factors, it seems obvious that the retailers, through long experience, had a better idea of their customers' needs and wants than the commentators did.

Two conflicting views of the trade, one from outside, and one from inside, show how wide was the gap that existed. Whilst Nikolaus Pevsner indicated that 'many of the shopkeepers realize the bad taste of their cheap goods'[21] but, by inference, were happy to go on selling them, the furniture designer and businessman, Gordon Russell suggested that the retailer's responsibility as far

---

[15] Ibid., p. 156.

[16] Pevsner, N. (1937), *An Enquiry into Industrial Art in England*, p. 39.

[17] Farr, M. (1955), *Design in British Industry*, p. 151.

[18] Ibid., p. 152.

[19] Ibid., p. 11.

[20] Ibid., p. 153.

[21] Pevsner (1937), *An Enquiry into Industrial Art*, p. 38. More recently, in the 1990s, the managing director of a jewelry business referred to the products he successfully sold as 'crap'.

as design was concerned was to introduce new ideas to the public. This was not to be at the expense of profitable 'bread and butter' lines, but with an enthusiasm for feeding the constantly changing public taste. In addition, Russell considered that the retailer was required to employ buyers who were aware and enthusiastic for contemporary lines, that the goods should be displayed in their context, and that the sales staff needed the education to enthuse.[22] These would in the main, appear to be sensible retailing practices. Other critics implied that change be imposed from outside the retail trade:

> Something was badly needed to jolt people out of the acceptance of the dreary furnishing conventions that have gripped the public for so many years. Once people find out, and see for themselves, different ways of composing their home surroundings, the trade will no longer be able to impose its slovenly standards on them.[23]

In 1952 John Gloag wrote in support of this idea. In this case, Gloag thought that the Government-sponsored wartime Utility Scheme had played a significant part in customer education at the expense of the retail buyer and his judgement:

> It is the responsibility of the intelligent public to improve the character and stimulate the enterprise of the retail furnisher. In normal times when austerity in design is not imposed by the state and the virtues of competition keep all traders in a condition of alert efficiency for the benefit of their customers, people with independent minds and educated judgement could insist on getting what they wanted and on seeing the sort of furniture progressive designers made. That anonymous arbiter of taste, the retail buyer, could no doubt continue to offer to everybody the rubbish that is acceptable to the undiscriminating, but taste has progressively improved even since this book was first published, fourteen years ago [1938]. The 'utility' period of the nineteen forties may have lasting effects, and as a purge for extravagance and folly in design it may be comparable to the puritan regime which England endured three centuries ago.[24]

In fact, the Utility scheme was soon broadened with the 'freedom of design', and although some products were to be derived from the scheme, for many retailers the new circumstances signalled a return to styles that sold. The ideal of standardization of design promoted by reformers was anathema to retailers in principle.[25]

The trade was also quick to discuss the problem of the furniture retailer's role. In 1948 the trade magazine *Furnishing* hosted a lively debate in its letter columns.[26] The first point was the difficult role of the buyer, who had to satisfy two masters: the profit-related employer and the apparently design-conscious

---

[22] Sheridan, M. (Ed.) (1955), *The Furnisher's Encyclopedia*, pp. 209–21.

[23] Tomrley, C. G. (1940), *Furnishing Your Home: A Practical Guide to Inexpensive Furnishing and Decorating*, p. 198.

[24] Gloag, J. (1934a), *English Furniture* [4th edn, 1952], p. 168, cited in Attfield, J. (1996), 'Give 'em something dark and heavy', *Journal of Design History*, 9(3), 1996.

[25] See Attfield, J., 'Freedom of design' in Attfield (1999b), *Utility Reassessed*, pp. 203–21.

[26] *Furnishing Magazine* (1948), 4(56), p. 235.

customer; secondly, it was argued that it was the responsibility of the customer to be selective, and this would only be learnt through education; thirdly, why should there be a dictation of design by a few pundits who were not in touch with the grass roots of public taste?[27]

It seems clear that the retailer knows his trade best. In 1949 Sir Ralph Perring, chairman of a small multiple group, made a valid point when he said that: 'the furniture trade is one of the few retail trades in which there is no counter'.[28] Although this definition may now be less valid, the sentiment behind it still seems applicable. Perring meant that the true furniture seller takes on the role of adviser rather than an order-taker, and it is this distinction that still separates the home furnishings expert from the furniture trader.[29] The furnishing retailer D. A. Catesby, who commented on the crucial role of the salesperson in the business, made a similar point: 'for any merchandise which depends not entirely on the cheapness of its price but the appreciation of its qualities, both manufacturer and retailer are entirely dependant on the ability of the sales force'.[30] This acknowledgement of the importance of the salesman from within the trade was not always supported from without.

The example of Richard Hoggart's 1957 description of the duping of working-class consumers (particularly in areas where they have little or no experience) through the skills of an assistant in a furniture shop who approached in a friendly and homely manner is worth quoting in full. It not only illustrates the physical details of some post-war stores, but also comments on the psychological problems sometimes associated with furniture buying:

> The louder furniture stores are of unusual interest, especially because of an apparent paradox. At first glance, these are surely the most hideously tasteless of all modern shops. Every known value in decoration has been discarded: there is no evident design or pattern; the colours fight with one another; anything new is thrown in simply because it is new. There is strip-lighting together with imitation chandelier lighting; plastics, wood, and glass are all glued and stuck and blown together; notice after notice winks, glows or blushes luminously. Hardly a homely setting. Nor do the superficially elegant men who stand inside the doorway, and alternately tuck their hankies up their cuffs or adjust their ties, appear to belong to 'us'. They are not meant to. With their neat clothing, shiny though cheap, shoes, well creamed hair and ready smiles they are meant (like the equally harassed but flashier motor-salesmen) to represent an ethos. One buys the suggestion of education and elegance with the furniture.[31]

---

[27] The case for considering differing tastes from a marketing point of view as being quite distinct from each other is well argued in Blaszczyk, R. (2000), *Imaging Consumers: Design and Innovation from Wedgwood to Corning*, pp. 138–41. She uses the case study of the supply of goods to the mass ceramic market, which sold its products through 'five and ten cent' stores.

[28] Perring, R. (1949), 'Retail distribution - popular', *Conference on Design*, p. 147.

[29] In some retail outlets, staff are known as furnishing advisers rather than salespeople.

[30] *Cabinet Maker*, 24 June 1939.

[31] Hoggart, R. (1957), *The Uses of Literacy*, p. 90.

Hoggart's perceptive comments about the suited salesmen acknowledge that furniture purchasing is about much more than need. The buying of 'the suggestion of education and elegance' was the psychological crux of the matter. It was this idea that the successful salesman sold best.

Another aspect of the equation was that in many cases, customers' decisions about what to buy were based on an item 'taking the fancy' immediately it was seen, rather than through any process of careful comparative shopping.[32] When the customer was ignorant of what choices were available, this was often the easiest decision. In addition, the store with the most advantageous credit terms would often receive the order. The *Financial Times* (1954) appears to have recognized this when it suggested that: 'It can now almost be said that in furniture retailing a good hire-purchase organization is as, or more important than, a wide range of designs.'[33]

Hoggart's descriptions above continued to reflect a pervasive suspicion of the trade, its products, and its methods. The reputation of the trade was clearly in jeopardy during the post-war period, so it is no surprise that the retail furnishers' trade association published its own guidelines for its members. The retail trade association,[34] supported by many of the well-known retail businesses, both multiple and independent, encouraged high standards of shopkeeping, customer service, manufacturer relations, staff training and education. With an emphasis on education of salespeople, the association introduced the National Furnishing Diploma, which was awarded to students who had successfully completed a rigorous full- or part-time training scheme in all aspects of home furnishings and their retailing. An indication of how they considered their role as furniture retailers is clear from the following statement made in 1965, which reflects the concerns expressed thirty years earlier:

> The retailers' function therefore includes guiding public demand and this is a privilege, which he should jealously guard. As soon as he delegates to others –whether to journalists or to national advertisers of branded products – the task of determining what is to be bought, he has handed over one of his most creative and rewarding functions.[35]

These initiatives were clearly an attempt to try to reclaim the high ground in quality furnishing for the trade association members.

Many retailers had, in fact, understood these issues for years. The establishment of room settings in showrooms in the later nineteenth century, the need for salesmen to have 'product knowledge', and the wide range of merchandise offered all indicated that retailers were linking together the provision of advice and the business of selling. Some retailers developed ideas

---

[32] Associated Rediffusion (1962/3), *London Profiles No. 14: Women and Furniture*, p. 16.

[33] *Financial Times*, 31 December 1954.

[34] National Association of Retail Furnishers.

[35] National Association of Retail Furnishers, (c. 1966) Report of NARF Sub-committee on '*Better Retailing': A Guide for Furnishers*.

of continuity and stability in merchandise ranges that were to be found in 'co-related groups [that are] the antithesis of irresponsibly created obsolescence'.[36] The fact that they tied the customer to a particular range, which could be added to as required, was simply good business practice. More importantly, they went on to say that: 'we have never considered ourselves in the furniture business because what we sell is environment, not furniture'.[37] Although these comments related to an American business, the positive attitude it expressed was also reflected in Europe. Tony Fry, one-time central furniture buyer for the department store group John Lewis Partnership, remarked that: 'Once we have really grasped the idea that we are selling home atmosphere – not factory processed lumps of wood or plastic – our share of the total consumer market will begin to get larger.' He emphasized the need to 'sell the sizzle even more than the steak', and suggested that a combination of quality displays and 'stockiness' would assist in this development.[38] For successful furniture retailers, the concern with home environment and atmosphere were essential ingredients in their business. The successes of specialist stores that have developed a 'lifestyle' approach to selling are witness to this (see further below).

More recently, there has been a move by house-builders to sell new houses, complete with ready decorated and furnished interiors, landscaped gardens – in fact a complete way of life and its environment. In 1995 the sales brochure of the British house-building firm Wimpey explained:

> to help you choose carpets, curtains and blinds we have commissioned interior designers to pre-select a top quality range … if you choose from our range we are able to supply matching accessories such as bedspreads, valances and lampshades … the cost of these goods can be added to the basic price of your new home and may be included in your mortgage.[39]

Thus, this completely removed the retailer's function!

Those businesses that ignored the increasing emphasis on domestic surroundings and their ambience suffered. The lack of attention that some furniture retailers paid to the basic precepts of retail practice resulted in the decline of once well-established stores, as they ceased to function as true house furnishers by allowing an erosion of their traditional markets to other sources of supply. In 1964 a respected financial report found that 'retailers tend to regard themselves as sellers of furniture and seem little concerned with the efficient, economic, and profitable retailing of consumer goods'.[40] More

---

[36] Ethan Allen line by the Baumritter Corp. (1967), 'The Furniture Industry in Transition', *Industrial Design*, May, p. 32. British examples could be G-Plan, Ercol, and so on.

[37] Ibid.

[38] Fry, T. (1971), *Selling Modern Furniture*.

[39] Chapman, T. (1999), 'Stage sets for ideal lives', in Chapman, T. and Hockey, J. (Eds), *Ideal Homes,* p. 54.

[40] Economist Intelligence Unit (1964), *Retail Business*, 81, November, p. 17.

Figure 7.1   Furniture department, John Lewis store, Oxford Street, London,
1950s

specifically, they were criticized for tending to keep too narrow a range, for a
lack of merchandising, for cramming all available space with unattractive
displays, and for offering long delivery dates.[41] Most importantly, 'they fell
down on the job of watching a changing population and economy'.[42] This was
crystallized in 1967 by Leslie Julius, director of furniture makers Hille and Co.
who had this to say about the great majority of furniture retailers:

> [Their] opposition to change would be understandable at any other period
> in history, but today we live by change and should welcome it as a
> stimulus and challenge as well as a way of opening up new markets as new
> wants and needs arise. I still maintain that retailers, with great, notable and
> noble exceptions have failed the public and the industry miserably. [43]

More recent reports have criticized retailers for selling goods in 'an uninteresting
way',[44] and that the 'product on offer is frequently unadventurous in design, and
of poor quality'.[45]

Despite these stinging criticisms, by the 1980s the polarity between the
design establishment and the trade had not moved much and it seemed as if

---

[41] Ibid.

[42] Slom, S. H. (1967), *Profitable Furniture Retailing*, p. 19.

[43] Julius, L. (1967), 'The furniture industry', *Royal Society of Arts Journal*, May, p. 443.

[44] Kelehar, R. (1988), 'Furniture starts to polish up its act', *Marketing Week*, 19 August, p. 38.

[45] Design Council (*c.* 1990), *Key Themes in the UK Furniture Industry*.

little had been learned on either side. A report prepared by the Design Council in 1983 concluded that:

> In spite of the shrinking numbers, there has been a rapid increase in the strength and power of the retailers as arbiters of public taste during the last few years, with more and more of them initiating products themselves. This together with their advertising muscle could allow them a substantial influence in terms of design and quality. What seems to be happening however, and particularly at the lower end of the market, is that the initiation takes the form of global sourcing of cheap copies of existing products.[46]

For reformers and critics, the obsession with the issue of the role of the retailer as an arbiter of design took priority over an understanding of commercial realities. At the shop front, it was quite different. Even style leader and founder of Habitat Terence Conran was clear as to the retailer's role. In the early 1980s, he pointed out that:

> As retailers we are not educators, it is not our responsibility to increase design awareness or put on design exhibitions. There would be more successful modern design if there was a greater demand from the buying public and that would happen with better education.[47]

The critics continue to have a problem with this issue. In 1989 it was said that: 'British furniture and product designers are unanimous that the problem with British furniture begins with myopic reactionary retailers.'[48] Nothing much had changed one hundred years after Eastlake's similar comments.

The role of the retailer has always been to meet a demand, but for much of the twentieth century the retail furnisher was seen as a reactionary who was spoiling the chances of the gospel of the Modernist's 'good design' ideas being disseminated to the population at large. More recently, and reflecting what retailers have always known, Post-Modernists have acknowledged that consumers are widely varied in tastes, finances and self-images, therefore the retail marketplace should reflect this, so that particular shop types will meet the needs of particular customers. Nevertheless, a survey undertaken in 1994 showed what consumers appeared to want from the 'ideal' furniture retailer. These included value for money, a quality product, quality service, easy assembly of KD furniture, stock availability, durability of goods, good product design, car-parking facilities, product knowledge, a delivery service and lifestyle compatibility.[49] If these general requirements can be matched with products offering both use-value and identity-value, the retailer's role will be both profitable and significant.

---

[46] *Report to the Design Council on the Design of British Consumer Goods* (1983), p. 29.

[47] Phillips, B. (1984), *Conran and the Habitat Story*, p. 144.

[48] *Blueprint*, May 1989, p. 46.

[49] Davies, G. (1994), 'Repositioning MFI', in McGoldrick, P. (Eds), *Cases in Retail Management*, p. 52. In fact, most of these features should be being addressed by competent retailers.

Marketing and display

To meet consumer desires, retailers have first to understand what they are, and then go on to target their products appropriately, so that individual consumers can relate (or not) to what is on display. Although in some stores merchandise would be crammed in, even hung from rafters, during the twentieth century it was becoming increasingly commonplace for room settings of one sort or another to be employed in-store. The nineteenth-century idea of fully furnished room settings had continued in some specialist furnishing stores, but it was reintroduced with considerable vigour by department stores in the post-war era. Other shops also adopted this idea, and many followed suit and created individual room settings appropriate to their business. Even if there was not much floorspace, small groups of related merchandise might be set up in 'vignettes' separated by dividers or curtains to demonstrate a style or grouping that was appropriate. The sales logic was clear. Eaton's store in Toronto, Canada, laid out home furnishing stocks within room settings. The manager explained the advantage of this: '[The display] will often cause a person to buy more than they originally intended to. They are looking probably at a living room suite, but the other decorations and goods are shown up so well that they think they would like to have them also.'[50] The schemes could be quite sophisticated. In 1921 Oetzmann promoted a room creation scheme that consisted of an empty 'room-shaped' space in which selected furniture and furnishings could be gathered and laid out as they might be in a customer's house. The salesman would then alter, move and change the display until the required combination was arrived at.[51]

In marketing terms, the roles of exhibitions external to the retail store have also been of some importance in the twentieth century as a focus for products and services. In England these have centred on the annual Ideal Home Exhibitions and the more sporadic 'Furniture Shows' that have been mainly manufacturers' displays. The Ideal Home Exhibition, first opened for business in 1908, has always had a dual identity.[52] On the one hand it had a didactic role with displays and showhouses intended to bring information and new technologies to the consumer, and on the other it was overtly commercial. The retailers who took space and stands expected to sell goods and services in large quantities, so the exhibition often took on the guise of a marketplace.

The prospectus issued to the trade for the 1933 exhibition summed up the successful features of the previous year's show:

> From the rustic charm of a Tudor village set around an old-time village green to the latest expression of modernist art in lighting and display, the

---

[50] *Furniture World,* 7 February 1917.

[51] *Furniture Trades Organiser* (1921).

[52] See Ryan, D. (1997), *The Ideal Home Through the Twentieth Century.*

1932 Ideal Home Exhibition touched every facet of home-life with new light, and resulted in a brilliant stimulus to buying which was powerfully reflected in the order books of exhibitors.[53]

Not surprisingly, it was often the multiple-branch businesses that featured in the Ideal Home Exhibitions, as they could service the orders placed by visitors from all parts of the country.

The trade-oriented furniture shows had an ambiguous relationship with the public because the retailers resented the public attendance at what was essentially an industry exhibition. Nevertheless, some retailers took advantage of the opportunity. In the 1934 Furniture and Allied Trades Exhibition, the Times Furnishing company had a stand with sectional displays based on 'furniture for flats', 'modern furniture', 'period furniture for small houses' and 'period furniture for large houses'.[54]

Apart from these external exhibitions, some firms, particularly the department stores, did produce particular and possibly didactic in-store promotions of modern furnishing design. For example, in 1932 Lewis's of Liverpool introduced a 'Design for Living' Department, which was later extended to their stores in Manchester and Birmingham. The displays consisted of room sets in 'contemporary taste'. In 1938 the Birmingham store displayed room ideas for a 'four-roomed house furnished for £65.00 for a family with an income of £3.00 per week and a five-roomed house furnished for £165.00 for a family with an income of £5.00 per week'.[55] The impact of these displays was considerable. In a letter to the *Cabinet Maker* in March 1950, John Gloag wrote:

One of the most financially successful examples of partnership between furniture manufacturers and a retail house was inaugurated by the great store Lewis's Ltd. in Liverpool, when they opened their 'Design for Living' department in 1932. It was so successful that the department was extended to their Manchester and Birmingham branches and extensions were being considered to Leeds and Glasgow when the war intervened.[56]

In 1938 the department store Heelas of Reading had displays of stainless steel kitchens and a modern birch dining room. In 1939 it had on display a labour-saving kitchen, a chintz room and a setting called 'The Pig and Whistle', apparently 'no less suitable for the lounge bar of a private house than for a public one'.[57]

These pre-war attempts appear to be exceptions, since, as in 1955, Michael Farr could only find one store in a large city selling modern designs. He compared it favourably with the apparently standard furniture displays:

---

[53] *Daily Mail* (1933), *Ideal Home Exhibition Prospectus.*

[54] 1934 exhibition catalogue.

[55] See Jeremiah, D. (2000), *Architecture and Design for the Family in Britain, 1900–1970*, p. 9.

[56] *Cabinet Maker*, 18 March 1950, p. 1026.

[57] See Jeremiah, D. (2000), *Architecture and Design for the Family in Britain, 1900–1970*, p. 95.

> Instead of the tedious badly lit rows of wardrobes, dressing tables sideboards etc., to be seen in most furniture emporia, I found suggestive schemes showing how designs of furniture, upholstery, carpets and light fittings could be arranged together ... instead of limiting them to the shop window spaces, these schemes were used over most of the floor area.[58]

Display was also related to the store architecture. In the same way as other multiple operations, multiple furniture retailers had a house style. This was reflected in the store signage, window displays and the whole corporate identity.

The Gothic script of The Times Furnishing Company, which seemed to reflect the famous newspaper masthead, was one such example. It tied in rather incongruously with the flagship store in Birmingham, which in 1929 was designed on very similar lines to a contemporary film theatre. Post-war redevelopment in city centres and the establishment of new towns with purpose-built retail shops meant that multiple furnishing retailers especially could lay out their store in a more attractive manner than some of the older family-run businesses that simply grew organically on one site. For example, a 1934 description of the store of Druce and Company in Baker Street, London, mentioned 'showrooms quaint and rambling, the old houses in which they are contained having been acquired one by one and not rebuilt but merely adopted to their needs'.[59]

One particular feature of many post-war furniture shops was the use of an 'arcade', whereby the display windows were set on either side of a deep-set entranceway. This served as a display space for odd items during the day and allowed window shoppers to see the illuminated goods by night.

Promotional gimmicks seem to have been popular for many stores, with marketing ideas brought from America in particular. In 1925 The Cabinet Maker commented that: 'ten years ago only potential customers were welcome into furniture shops' – now American 'open door' policies were operated and customers were attracted in to the stores by extraneous methods such as 'silhouette artists, portrait photographers, palmists, phrenologists and so forth'.[60]

The loosening-up of the intimidating image of a specialist furniture shop was partly in response to the openness of the department store and partly as an acknowledgement of a growing and widening customer base. The aracde is interesting in respect of this, as it invites customers into the store space.

An example of the retailers' acknowledgement of the social changes was their response to cinema-going. One publication, devoted to window dressing, noted that the filmgoers of 1934:

---

[58] Farr, M. (1955), *Design in British Industry*, p. 155.

[59] Benjamin, T. H. (1934), *London Shops and Shopping*, entry on Druce and Co.

[60] *Cabinet Maker*, 29 August 29 1925.

Figure 7.2   The Times Furnishing shop, Birmingham, 1930s

see fine Tudor dining halls, luxurious bedrooms, handsome bachelor apartments, typical American labour saving kitchens and the newest ideas in flat furnishing … When they return to their own homes, they unconsciously make comparisons. Women in particular have a predilection for this, and very often the comparison throws up the furnishings of their own homes in a very unfavourable light.[61]

The author recommended that the reproduction of selected schemes suitably adapted to shop windows could be beneficial to furniture businesses: 'In this way, the film-goer, when she does her shopping the following day, can be shown how she can furnish her home in the same delightful film-like way, but at a price that can be compassed by her limited means.'[62] Later on, the same idea of promotional tie-ins with television advertising was used, especially by retailers selling branded goods.

Aping women's magazines of the period, some businesses developed the film theme and produced catalogues that presented the 'homes of the stars', with the furniture being part of the photo studio setup. The Times Furnishing Co.'s *Good Furnishings* booklet was set out like a woman's magazine, with Hollywood stars such as Cary Grant, Randolph Scott and Ida Lupino featured in room settings. The magazine/catalogue included a short fiction story, and beauty tips and knitting patterns, which were intermingled with images of Times furniture and interiors, budgets, furnishing tips and plugs for the company's Furnishing Advisory Bureau.[63] One of the biggest marketing initiatives was the use of manufacturers' brand names.

Branding

The old debate about labelling goods that had been the centre of controversy in the 1880s reappeared in the twentieth century, and although the picture was more complex with the growth of manufacturers' branded goods, the retailer was still keen to guard the details of his sources of supply. This was often done by removing manufacturers' labels and placing retail labels on goods. The intention was mainly to avoid price comparison and discounting, but may still reflect a remnant of the old idea that the purchaser was buying from the maker. In 1928 the British trade journal, *The Cabinet Maker* carried the following passage:

> Nine times out of ten, he (the retailer) tries to suggest that he makes all the goods that he sells and announces in some prominent place that he is a Cabinet Maker and Upholsterer, whereas he may merely have a repair

---

[61] Caradoc, R. L. (1934), *Sales Increasing Window Display Schemes*, p. 79.

[62] Ibid.

[63] Veasey, C. (*c.* 1935), *Good Furnishing*.

shop where odds and ends of work can be done. It seems to be a needless
fiction that the retailer makes every article he sells. And yet there is a
widespread tendency to suggest that the retailer is also a manufacturer.[64]

For the trade unions, the use of branding by retailers was to be deprecated. In
1934 the NAFTA London region secretary commented on some retail shops
where:

> Their whole stock is represented as being made in their own workshops,
> yet the great bulk of it, is in fact, purchased from little workshops, chiefly
> in the East End, where the work is produced under appalling conditions
> and the recognised wage standards have never been observed.[65]

It was the case that several retailers were also still manufacturing some of their
goods, and promoted themselves accurately in these circumstances as the bona
fide manufacturers of the goods they sold. For customers, the old cachet of
buying goods direct from 'the maker' still had a certain distinction about it, and
this has remained. The impression given to the customer of apparently buying
from a craftsman-shopkeeper as opposed to a retail-only establishment put that
store into another bracket in terms of expectations from the customer. In 1937
the trade press succinctly noted its implicit rejection of branding by
manufacturers: 'A retail store is emphatically not the agent of the manufacturer
… The retailer is the agent of the public.'[66] In other words, the retailer was not
in business to promote the manufacturers; rather, he was in the business of
meeting the demands of the public.

The Government's own post-war review of the trade referred to branding
explicitly. The 1946 *Working Party Report* urged that: 'furniture should be
clearly marked with the name or trademark of the manufacturer making it'. In
their opinion, this practice would facilitate recognition and enable comparisons
to be made. The trade's response was clear, and reflected its pre-war position:

> Retailers object to branding by manufacturers because it would tend to
> make them mere 'post-offices', whereas at present their reputation with
> the public is based on the quality of individuality that the retailers' skill in
> buying gives them.[67]

Despite opposition, branding became an important feature of the 1950s and
1960s. Initially reintroduced after the War, it was 'the branded product
manufacturers, who, whilst trading freely through the smaller independent
retailer, have concentrated on the multiple and large independent retail outlet'. At
one point (1960), over 60 per cent of the turnover of multiple retailers such as
Times Furnishing was manufacturer branded.[68] In some cases there was

---

[64] Cited in Kirkham, P., Mace, R. and Porter, J. (1987), *Furnishing the World: The East End furniture Trade 1830–1980*, p. 47.

[65] *Cabinet Maker*, 18 August 1934. See also pp. 117–19 above.

[66] *Cabinet Maker*, 5 June 1937.

[67] *Working Party Report* (1946), p. 144.

[68] Economist Intelligence Unit (1964), *Retail Business*, 81, November, p. 14.

comprehensive collaboration between retailers and manufacturers in the promotion of particular ranges. These were often nationally advertised products, so there was some good sense in joining forces. One very successful example was the installation of 'G-Plan centres' in retail showrooms. These were set up as discreet vignettes of bedrooms, dining rooms and living areas, all fully accessorized and fitted up as a permanent and distinctive exhibition within the showroom. They were intended to remain as fixed exhibits from which customers could select their choice, taking priority delivery over non-stockists. Other companies, including Ercol solid-wood furniture, Priory Oak dining rooms and Limelight fitted bedrooms, also developed this strategy. These manufacturers supported this strategy by national advertising and sales promotion.

One attempt to rise above the power of the manufacturers and the branding issue was through the development from the 1950s of buying groups of independent retailers, small chains, or department store groups and 'own labels'.[69] One example was the Floreat buying group who acted on behalf of a group of independent retailers. The group originated in the co-operation of some NARF members, who negotiated bulk-purchase terms with manufacturers to provide a range of Floreat own-label goods and to supply promotional merchandise.[70] Another similar group was the Green Group, established in the early 1960s especially as importers of Scandinavian furniture. The benefits of bulk purchase and cost savings were a clear advantage, but buying groups can also offer other advantages including central invoice clearing, training, comparative statistical surveys and the like.

In terms of branding, the more recent situation has changed. The department stores still offer branded merchandise to a degree, as do independent stores, but they often sell their 'own label' as well. However, the revival of retail brands associated directly with the store is of increasing importance, with IKEA currently being the most powerful name.

Pricing and credit selling

Linked to the issue of branding and display is the crucial matter of pricing. The links between branded goods and resale price maintenance are well known; in

---

[69] The Good Furnishing Group, established in 1953, included Dunn & Sons Ltd, David Elder Ltd, Findlater Smith Ltd, P. E. Gane Ltd, Hemmings Bros (Nottingham) Ltd, Holmes The Furnishers Ltd, Lee Longland & Co. Ltd, and York Tenn: see Farr (1955), *Design in British Industry*, p. 307.

[70] In 1987 Floreat, merged with AIS. The Associated Independent Stores (AIS) was formed over twenty-five years ago in 1976 by the merger of two separate buying groups, ADS (Associated Department Stores) and ISA (Independent Stores Association). In 2003 it is the largest independent, voluntary, non-food buying group of its kind in the UK, with a combined membership turnover of *circa* £1.6 billion. The group embodies 275 independent department store and specialist retailers, representing 602 outlets across the UK, Ireland and Cyprus.

the case of twentieth-century furniture retailing, price maintenance, even if not strictly enforced, supported the margins of both the full service retailers and those with hire purchase business. The 1946 *Working Party Report* noted that:

> some manufacturers ... printed three separate editions of their catalogues, with prices marked up 50 per cent, 75 per cent, and 100 per cent respectively and found a demand for all editions. This suggests that competition was far from complete amongst retailers, and widely differing margins in fact prevailed on the same article of furniture.[71]

From 1964, when resale price maintenance was abolished, prices were eased, competition from other outlets grew, and credit became a promotional tool and a bargaining chip. This opened the gates for a new type of retailer who discounted prices, offered far less in service, charged for delivery, or even had customers collect their own goods (see 'Superstores' below), encouraging some retailers to follow suit, others to trade up in quality, and yet others to amalgamate or close down.

Much of the success of the twentieth-century house furnishing multiples has been based on their promotion and use of credit selling, which they made respectable. The euphemism 'furnishing out of income' was no doubt intended to appeal to the sensibilities of the middle classes, but much of the credit business was conducted in the lower class brackets.

The intense competition between retailers in this sector and the way some businesses sought trade 'by advertising that they do not seek references, [or] that no deposit is required and even that no payment need be made until thirty days have elapsed' caused some consternation. The fear was expressed that: 'it may lead to furnishing by improvident people, [thus] increase the bad debts on the part of the firms concerned, and consequent prejudice to the genuine buyer of furniture'.[72]

Early in the century, the use of credit to finance home furnishings was seen by one writer as becoming the custom for segments of the population. Louise Boland More, writing in 1907, commented that the 'instalment system' was 'almost universal among the working class' for the purchase of pianos, sewing machines and parlour furniture 'which is far out of keeping with the family income'.[73] Two years later, this demonstration of indulgence was seen as having potentially disastrous consequences. Shaw Sparrow considered that: 'Thrift was looked upon as a foe to business: and we are now beginning to see that an over-stimulated demand in trade weakens the national character and begets an unrest of mind without will-power.'[74] If 'happy and healthy homes' are the backbone of a successful nation, Sparrow was surely out of touch with reality. Sparrow was particularly opposed to the credit or 'hire purchase'

---

[71] *Working Party Report* (1946), p. 33.

[72] London School of Economics (1931), *The New Survey of London Life and Labour*, II, p. 216.

[73] Cited by Grier (1988), *Culture and Comfort*, p. 206.

[74] Shaw Sparrow (1909), *Hints on House Furnishing*, p. 30.

system. His readers were urged to buy only that which could be afforded outright, as well as to furnish according to their needs, not wants. For Shaw Sparrow, the reasons were as much ethical as commercial: not only was it foolish to pay extra for the privilege of spreading payments, but he thought that 'purchase without payment dulls self-respect'.[75] Accordingly, the author suggested the apparently more satisfactory 'stock system', whereby customers were exhorted to visit a reputable firm, to choose wisely, and to ask for a discount for cash. Yet again, the warnings were to be wary of buying too much under persuasion. Sparrow was clearly writing for a middle-class audience, but for the growing working-class demands, forms of credit were to be essential.

Flora Thompson reflected this reality simply when she recalled how a furniture shop used credit facilities to increase its business:

> A man who kept a small furniture shop came round selling his wares on the instalment plan. On his first visit … he got no order at all; but on his second one of the women, more daring than the rest, ordered a small wooden washstand and a zinc bath for washing day. Immediately washstands and zinc baths became the rage. None of the women could think how they had managed to exist without a washstand in their bedroom.[76]

B. L. Coombes noted another example of how credit not only helped furnish homes but also gave a sense of pride to the new owners. When he and his wife moved into two rented rooms in a South Wales mining village during World War One, he recalled: 'how proud I felt when I saw them furnished for the first time, and realised that all that shining new furniture was ours – even if most of it still had to be paid for'.[77]

To overcome the stigma of credit purchasing that clearly existed, especially for the lower middle classes, stores went to some lengths to legitimize the process.[78] For example, the middle-range company, Drages Ltd, used a testimonial by the Countess of Oxford and Asquith to praise the use of hire purchase. In a 1932 advertisement she was apparently 'amazed to think that a man of moderate means can furnish for £100.00 on a payment of only £2.00'.[79]

It was clear that credit availability encouraged purchases, and with the retail trade offering terms over three to four years, and often with no deposit, it meant that the vast majority had access to some new furnishings. In 1924 the *Furnishing Trades Organiser* reported that: 'The amazing capital computed to

---

[75] Ibid.

[76] Thompson, F. (1948), *Lark Rise to Candleford*, reprint 1973, p. 125.

[77] Coombs, B. L. (1939), *These Poor Hands: Autobiography of a Miner*, p. 91, cited in Benson, J. (1994), *The Rise of Consumer Society in Britain 1880–1980*, p. 77.

[78] The stigma is nicely recorded in Roberts, R. (1971), *The Classic Slum*, where a young married woman bought some carpet on hire purchase 'feeling like a criminal', and proceeded only after the family had 'sworn to keep the deed from her parents who would have been horrified to hear of it' (pp. 17–18).

[79] *Good Housekeeping* (1932), cited in Anon. (1986), *Ragtime to Wartime: The Best of Good Housekeeping, 1922–1939*, p. 136.

be directly employed in hire purchase, amounting to not less that £4 million, upwards of two million hire purchase agreements being signed annually.'[80]

Although Sparrow was overdramatic about the iniquitous role of credit, it was argued that some firms had relinquished the responsibility for selling furniture in a proper manner, as they became more interested in usury. The deposit and the weekly payment became more important than the goods, and this approach to retailing certainly encouraged the concentration on price that still persists in some parts of the trade.

The chairman of the retailers Shoolbred added his criticism of disreputable ways of doing business, particularly despising pointless promotions and irresponsible credit. In his foreword to Horace Vachell's book *The Homely Art*, he said that it is: 'an effort to combat the increasing temptations to buy fine phrases and free gifts instead of good furniture'. A little later in the same passage he noted that 'every responsible furniture merchant will be grateful to Mr. Vachell for vigorously condemning the tendency to exploit furniture and the love of home for money-lending purposes'.[81]

The criticisms of parts of the trade were not without foundation, and some practices associated with credit selling certainly increased the low public opinion of parts of the retail trade. Indeed, at various times during the century legislation had to be introduced to curb dubious practices such as the 'snatch back' of goods if payments were not kept up. The iniquities were highlighted at the time. One example will suffice. On 5 December 1928:

> A working class woman bought £62.15s worth of furniture from a Tottenham firm on hire-purchase terms. Through illness she got into arrears after £53.2s had been paid ... In her absence the hire purchase firm (Messrs Webb's of High Road Tottenham) caused her house to be stripped-save for an overlay and two pillows – sought to recover removal charges of £1.11s and offered their client an option to pay £3.11s to collect the repossessed goods at her own expense and to pay 15s a week until the debt was discharged, as a condition of re-letting them.[82]

The trade press was aware of the problems of credit, especially when it was used as a weapon of business. *The Cabinet Maker* commented that: 'Owing to the increasing competition the ''spread-over''period has been extended in many cases to four years, initial deposits have been reduced and goods unsuitable for long term credit have been included.'[83]

As with many distressing situations, they could be challenged by attacking with humour. The amusing song below indicates a popular take on some of the matters associated with the provision of credit from Drages, an Oxford Street furnishing store of the 1920s–30s, well known for its credit provision:

---

[80] *Furniture Trades Organiser*, December 1924.
[81] Vachell, H. A. (1928), *The Homely Art*, Foreword.
[82] Vallance, A. (1939), *Hire Purchase*, p. 62.
[83] *Cabinet Maker*, 11 March 1933.

I've only just got married and I'm on the rocks and broke,
He said 'don't let that worry you, why money is a joke!
Why, we only run our business to oblige you sort of folk,
And we always lay your lino on the floor!'

'But Mr. Drage' my Missus said 'our neighbours know we're new,
And when they see your van, they're bound to say a thing or two.'
He said 'they won't: we send it round in vans as plain as you.
And we always lay your lino on the floor!'

So five hundred pounds in furniture, she spent did my Old Dutch;
'What deposit Mr Drage' said I 'would you require for such?'
He simply smiled and said 'would two and sixpence be too much?
And we always lay your lino on the floor!'

I said 'That's very generous, but no reference I've got'
He said 'we do not want them they're a lot of Tommy-rot.
Why you needn't even give your name, if you would rather not
And we always lay your lino on the floor!

'Well thank you Mr Drage' I said 'you've really been most kind,
But what about the payments?' He said 'that as you're inclined.
Pay half a crown a week, and if you can't well never mind –
For we always lay your lino on the floor!'

(*Drage Way* by Norman Long, *c*. 1930)[84]

Apparently, even legislation such as the 1939 Hire Purchase Act did not cover such unsavoury activities as the substitution or switching of goods seen by the customer in the showroom for inferior ones from a back stock. In addition to this, retailers were castigated for varying the mark-up on credit sales according to the customer, as well as putting on a mark-up far in excess of the normal profit margin.[85]

Some businesses avoided these pitfalls. The Co-operative Societies had a more ethical policy towards credit, but they also embraced it in one form or another. A 1930s training manual for furnishing salesmen noted that 'we know some societies refuse to adopt the system (HP) owing to the disinclination of the committee or members to admit legalised credit'.[86] Instead, they offered a club system that members paid into and then drew on when sufficient funds became available.

Despite all the criticisms, many multiple businesses ran satisfactory credit schemes, and it was through the benefits of hire purchase financing that growth really came. The public confidence in hire purchase was clearly a great incentive

---

[84] Lancaster, B. (1995), *The Department Store: A Social History*, p. 100. Thanks to Bill Lancaster for information regarding this song.

[85] Tomrley (1940), *Furnishing Your Home*, p. 203.

[86] Haigh, A. (1925), *Furnishing and Hardware: A Textbook for Co-operative Society Salesmen*, p. 189.

for other retail sectors to introduce it with vigour (for example, electrical and radio, auto), and in the post-war era hire purchase was part of most furniture retailers' sales repertoire. The days when hire purchase was looked down upon and 'delivery in a plain van' was necessary rapidly passed after the war.

Notwithstanding the acceptance by the public, the effects of hire purchase were still of concern to some critics. Indeed the 1946 *Working Party Report* showed a partial and seemingly deprecating attitude to hire purchase:

> As regards hire purchase, we have been impressed by the unanimity with which *manufacturers* [my italics] have attributed to this section of the retail trade the main responsibility for many of the evils, which prevailed before the war. In particular, we have been told that it was the price pressure on manufacturers practised by some hire purchase specialists which led to the competitive depreciation of quality.[87]

The Report also returned to the earlier criticism of the trade as being more interested in money lending than in furnishing:

> The cost of hire-purchase facilities bears little relation to the value of the article: in fact it is probably true to say that the cheaper the goods, the heavier is the expense involved in the service because of the more frequent collection of the payments and the longer term of credit given in the case of people with small incomes. Although this aspect of the matter has sometimes led to unjustified complaints about the charges made by the hire-purchase firms, it has been an evil of the hire-purchase trade that some firms have tended to use the sale of furniture as a means of conducting a money-lending business and have been more interested in selling terms than furniture. There was also a good deal of public complaint before the war about the bullying methods adopted by some firms and the operation of the 'snatch back' (i.e. the recovery of furniture in cases where the consumer had difficulty in completing the payments).[88]

They conceded that hire purchase had been a useful tool generally to help people on small incomes to reach higher standards of living. Nevertheless, the criticism did not go away. In 1957 the National Council for Social Service reported on the inability of households to balance budgets and the iniquities of high-pressure salesmanship, which increased the debt burden.[89] In the same year, in an effort to provide a more equitable credit system, the Christian Economic and Social Research Foundation suggested that the Government provide credit facilities through Post Offices, especially for young couples setting up home 'instead of occasioning those who supply the service to charge more for it'.[90] This suggestion was not taken up.

In other circumstances the benefits of hire purchase were sometimes checked by factors beyond the influence of the trade or its critics. In the 1960s the

---

[87] *Working Party Report*, (1946), p. 145.

[88] Ibid.

[89] *Furnishing the World* (1987), p. 58.

[90] Ibid., p. 60.

government used credit controls as a crude lever for the management of consumer spending which particularly affected furniture purchases (see Table 7.1) In 1964 an *Economist* report considered that consumer-spending motives on furniture were prompted (or not) by the credit arrangements available:

> The importance of credit trading, together with the fact that furniture purchases tend to be of a capital nature, have made this a trade vulnerable to government credit policy and to the general economic outlook. Perhaps the most important factor that triggers off the consumer purchasing decision is the amount of cash deposit, and the monthly repayments required on furniture.[91]

Table 7.1   Effect of economic measures on demand for furniture, 1958–1968

September 1958	HP restrictions on furniture entirely removed.
April 1959	Purchase tax rate reduced on cars from 60% to 50%, and on appliances from 30% to 25%. No change on furniture.
April 1960	HP restrictions reimposed. Furniture 10% deposit, 2 years to pay. Cars and domestic appliances 20%, 2 years.
January 1961	HP restrictions eased. 3 years to pay on all these products.
July 1961	10% regulator on Purchase Tax – furniture up from 5% to 5.5%, domestic appliances from 25% to 27% and cars 50% to 55%.
April 1962	Purchase Tax on furniture increased from 5.5% to 10% but the rate on cars reduced from 55% to 45%, and on domestic appliances from 27.5% to 25%.
June 1962	HP restrictions eased on domestic appliances. 20% deposit reduced to 10%. No change for furniture or cars.
November 1962	Purchase Tax on cars reduced from 45% to 25%.
January 1963	Purchase Tax on radio and TV sets reduced from 45% to 25%.
March 1963	Add-to facility on hire purchase introduced for furniture.

continued

June/July 1965	HP restrictions tightened on cars and domestic appliances, but not on furniture.
February 1966	HP restrictions tightened again – furniture up to 15% deposit, 30 months' repayments, as well as domestic appliances and cars.
July 1966	Freeze and squeeze budget, including further tightening of HP restrictions on all products. Furniture up to 20%, with 24 months' repayments. Purchase Tax regulator increases furniture Purchase Tax to 11%, cars and domestic appliances from 25% to 27.5%.
June/August 1967	HP restrictions eased on all products. Furniture now 15% with 30 months to repay.
November 1967	Devaluation, inception of pre-budget consumer boom. Tougher HP controls on cars, but not on furniture and appliances.
March 1968	Sharp deflationary budget. Purchase Tax increased on furniture from 11% to 12.5%, and on cars and domestic appliances from 27.5% to 33.3%.
November 1968	Autumn budget to stem resurgent consumer spending. HP restrictions tighten on all products on furniture 20% deposit, 24 months to pay.

Source: M. R. V .Goodman, *Review of the Domestic Furniture Industry 1960/69*, FIRA.

Although these direct controls have been removed, the growing cost of operating and financing a hire purchase trade has led many retailers to contract out their credit business, and the proportion of hire purchase trade financed by the stores has declined. Finance comes from other sources, often in the form of a personal loan via a finance house, credit cards and or in-house financial services.[92]

Retail shops and business types

Writing in 1909, Shaw Sparrow discussed the various 'furnishing systems' and concluded that there were then basically five methods of buying furnishings: hire purchase, the stock system (buying with cash and obtaining a discount),

---

[91] Economist Intelligence Unit (1964b), *Retail Business*, p. 18.

[92] In a hire purchase transaction, the title to the goods remains the property of the seller until they are paid for. In a credit sale, the ownership passes immediately to the buyer.

collecting antiques, buying from artist-craftsmen and having reproductions made to order.[93] Whilst the last three are clearly not standard, they do recognize the diversity of demand types, often based on class or income. The fact that these methods of purchase could be related to social class and to the type of retail outlet was clear. Writing nearly fifty years after Sparrow, J. G. Morrell considered 'furniture for the masses':

> Retailing follows a class pattern for the reason that the customers set themselves into a class pattern. I soon discovered that many working-class customers would not risk the possible embarrassment of making an appearance in the salubrious surroundings of a West End or middle class store. This was despite the fact that it was possible to buy comparable furniture on hire purchase at a total cost slightly below the cash price charged by the [working-class] store to its customers.[94]

This quote recognizes that the diversity of store types is related to the segmented nature of the market. One interesting analysis of store types made at the same time as Morrell demonstrates this. In his 1955 analysis of purchasing for the home, Dennis Chapman pointed out that generally, the exclusive stores catered for the upper middle class and offered no hire purchase, whilst displaying mostly reproduction designs with no contemporary furnishings. Secondly, he identified the specialist store type supplying 'interior design services, Persian carpets and contemporary design' to the middle and upper classes. Here again the payment was nearly all cash. It was in these sorts of stores that parents, apparently continuing a nineteenth-century tradition, often bought all the furnishings for their newlywed offspring. He next listed the department store, with its middle-class trade and credit accounts. According to Chapman, the department stores claimed that their customers preferred flashy, brightly polished furniture and anything with a novel design. The final group he identified was the multiple-store businesses having a mix of clientele, but with nearly all the transactions being financed by hire purchase.[95]

It should be no surprise to find that these outlet types reflected social groups of purchasers. The historian Penny Sparke has said that: 'class differences are the basis of the marketing decisions which determine the nature of the furniture that retailers supply'.[96] After all, it would seem obvious that a store established in a working-class district will supply goods that are immediately identifiable and acceptable to those customers in that area. However, what has become evident in the last few decades is the fact that the most successful retailer of home furnishings in the last quarter of the century, IKEA, has had a marketing approach that is categorically democratic. By providing well-designed

---

[93] Shaw Sparrow (1909), *Hints on House Furnishing*, p. 30.

[94] Morrell, J. G. (1956), 'Furniture for the masses', *Journal of Industrial Economics*, November, pp. 24–9. My thanks to Judith Attfield for this reference.

[95] Chapman, D. (1955), *The Family, the Home and Social Status*, pp. 44–5.

[96] Sparke, P. (1982), *Did Britain Make It? British Design in Context 1946–1986*, p. 141.

furniture at low prices, often with immediate availability (and discreet credit terms) it has become the biggest furniture retailer in the world.[97]

To prepare a satisfactory analysis of the infrastructure of furniture retailing, it has been necessary to divide this explanation of the trade into store types.

Department stores

The department store has always been associated with one-stop town centre shopping built around the twin merchandising themes of fashion and the home. The early involvement in furnishings can be seen in the catalogues of the later nineteenth-century stores, and since then the department stores have maintained a serious interest in maintaining furniture and furnishing sections. In many cases the drapery origins of these store types accounts for the move into furniture sales. As Jeffreys rightly pointed out, the success of these businesses in supplying middle-class homes with furnishings was due not only to a wide selection of goods sold by experienced staff, complete with full service, but also to the other amenities offered all under one roof.[98]

The early structure of department stores shows a reliance on full customer service and, in the case of home furnishing departments, the development of their own manufacturing capacity. The example of Cockayne's of Sheffield, *circa* 1913, shows a heavy involvement in this side of the furnishing aspects of the trade. The high numbers staffing the workrooms included a manufacturing capability as well as supplying services, again continuing a tradition of vertical integration (see Table 7.2).[99]

Table 7.2   Cockayne's of Sheffield: Staff list relating to house furnishing departments, *c.* 1913

	managers/sales	workroom
Carpets and floor coverings	5	24
Soft furnishings	5	12
Making up bedstead bedding	2	4
Selling, polishing, upholstering and		
fixing of cabinet furniture	5	54
Removal and storage	1	12
Decorating and painting	1 (30 storekeepers)	5
Manufacture of cabinet work	1	31
Preparation and machinery of		
timber for above	—	3

Source: Extracted from Benson and Shaw (1992), Table 8.4.

---

[97] This refers to the IKEA Company. See further below.

[98] Jeffreys, J. B. (1954), *Retail Trading in Britain 1850–1950*.

[99] Business records cited in Table 8.4 in Benson, J. and Shaw, G. (1992), *The Evolution of Retail Systems 1800–1914*, p. 150.

Large-scale complete house furnishers such as Maples, and Waring and Gillow were not department stores in the true sense, but their size and trading volume puts them into a similar category, since they had a wide range of specialist departments in some cases including a fashion department.

In 1906 Waring and Gillow opened a new store on Oxford Street, with 40 000 square feet of selling space. This included 100 galleries, 150 specimen rooms, a rotunda and arcaded passages. On display were model houses, including a £100 country cottage, and then £200, £300 and £500 versions. Supplementary specimen rooms to mix and match were on show. For example, there were dining rooms in the following styles: Elizabethan, Jacobean, Sheraton, Chippendale, Colonial, Tyrolean and Modern. There was even a replica of the Long Gallery at Knole. Until 1949 the company still occupied the whole building. Then the fashion department closed, six floors were let, and the furnishing showrooms were only to be found in the basement and on the ground and first floors. In 1973 the business closed in Oxford Street and moved to smaller premises in Regent Street.[100]

In the USA the emphasis was slightly different. There, 'the department store was able to move in on the lower-end furniture business by offering and increasing the amount of credit at rates which were more favourable to the consumer than those offered by the furniture stores and also by offering greater selection'. Their wider selection also poached business from some of the medium and higher-priced outlets.[101]

The British department store's emphasis has often been on selling branded goods at the middle to upper price ranges, but in more recent years own brands have become more important. The various store groups such as the House of Fraser, John Lewis Partnership, Sears and others now wield considerable buying power through central buying organizations, bulk buying and global sourcing.

It is likely that the department stores will carry on their leadership of the branded end of the furniture market, but will find it increasingly difficult to compete on price and choice with the large out-of-town retail stores. More directed niche marketing, such as the 'Allders at Home', which is an example of a specialized spin-off from the main department store group, would point to some future for these store types.

Specialist furnishing retailers

It is important to remember that the Census of Distribution of 1950 recorded that over 70 per cent of retail businesses operated from a single site, and a further 11 per cent were run by businesses with four or less outlets.[102] In terms

---

[100] *Souvenir of the Opening of the New Waring and Gillow Store,* 1973.

[101] Slom, S. (1967), *Profitable Furniture Retailing,* p. 25.

[102] Jeffreys, J. B. (1954), *Retail Trading in Britain,* p. 471.

of furniture and furnishings, this demonstrated a continuity of the tradition of personal relations with customers in a particular location.

In the twentieth century these specialist retailers were amongst the leaders of the trade. In an editorial description of the business of A. Watts and Son published on 18 May 1907, the *Northampton Independent* described the shop in detail:

> In the basement of the building are to be found a magnificent variety of cork lino and inlaid lino including a lot of very exclusive designs. Ascending to the second floor there is to be found an admirable assortment of bedroom and dining room suites including two special lines in satin walnut bedroom suites, well worth inspecting. On this floor also are a fine assortment of bedsteads, and everything necessary for healthy sleep including a fine stock of Northampton-made 'Comfy' bedding. You then turn into the carpet room on the same floor, and find a rare assortment of fine designs in Axminster, Brussels, Tapestry Carpets as well as some fine designs for stairs. There are also to be noticed some tasty designs in Sheraton and Chippendale work, together with some very fine hand carved solid oak dining room furniture. In the upper storey are the showrooms devoted to the lighter class of goods, such as bamboo and wickerwork, and the smaller article for the home.[103]

These stores were community based and offered services that were required by the local clientele. These included salesmen's canvassing with catalogues as well as collecting payment instalments such as Flora Thompson noted (see above). The example of Morley's of Leicester show how once a year the store sent a salesman, along with a range of stock, to a particular village on an appointed day and sales would be made to these outlying customers. Alternatively, a local carrier would bring in a group of villagers to the store who would be treated specially as club members.[104]

Under this heading of specialist retailers can also be found businesses that made their own furniture, offered a full service of furnishings and repairs, as well as being able to meet all the demands of a customer's home furnishing requirements. Often, despite the fact that these stores had only one branch, they were nevertheless known throughout the design world. London examples included Dunn's of Bromley, Heals of Tottenham Court Road and Bowman's of Camden Town. Most major towns have had a similar store. Often these stores have been in the vanguard of the promotion of 'good design' so the impact of their influence has often been wider than their size would indicate. Importantly, these businesses have often been run by later generations of the founding family, so there was a sense of service to the community as well as a pleasure in the business. Interestingly, many of these particular stores have promoted European and American-designed products and have remained elitist to a degree. The fate of these stores has been variable. Due to the high costs of

---

[103] *Northampton Independent*, 18 May 1907.

[104] Morley and Co., Leicester Record Office.

supplying the services that are associated with this kind of business, many have been forced to close; some have been through changes of ownership, whilst others remain as family-run businesses. Their survival has often been based on moves to up-market trading that often combine interior decoration and contract work. They maintain exclusivity and interest by careful merchandise selection and co-ordination, but above all, they continue to offer a personal service.[105]

Not all independents were at the forefront of their trade. An interesting example of entrepreneurship was the case of a Mr Sagalov. Born in 1910, he left school and was employed as a cabinet-maker for eleven years. His 'spare-time earnings' allowed him to save £500 to set up his own business as a furnisher. In 1935 he opened a shop, but closed it after a year. He opened another straight away, and another a year later. It was a cash trade to begin with, but he progressed to offering hire purchase. At some point a finance company covered three-quarters of his total debt. In 1938 he opened a branch in Oxford Street, but in 1939 the business folded and he was bankrupt.[106] This case is probably representative of many.

In contrast to the specialist furnisher, there have also been independent generalist shops that sold a range of products, including particular types of furnishings. Jeffreys noted that there were, for example, drapers who handled furnishing fabrics, floor covering and bedding, and hardware dealers who sold linoleum and various metal and kitchen furniture.[107] The practice has been substantially extended with the rise of the DIY superstores.

Co-operative stores

The development of the Co-operative store system during the period 1880–1920 was phenomenal. In 1881 there were 971 societies, and by 1903 this number had risen to 1455. Membership rose from 350 000 in 1873 to 2 878 000 in 1913. Furniture ranges were gradually added to the selection of retail society's stocks from the late nineteenth century. In the late 1880s the Co-operative Wholesale Society began to manufacture furniture, and by 1920 there were up to five factories exclusively supplying the retail societies. In the 1920s the furniture departments operated in liaison with the Wholesale showrooms in Manchester, London, Birmingham, Newcastle, Bristol, Cardiff and Nottingham, where customers could view the full range of products and then buy them, to be delivered via the local store. After 1930 the Co-ops started selling furniture seriously. Prior to this there had been reluctance to stock full ranges, and displays were often poor. After 1930 there was a concerted effort to establish furniture departments in newly built stores, rather than having them squeezed

---

[105] See Joscelyne, H. (1980), 'Has the retailer's job really changed?', *Cabinet Maker*, 19 September.

[106] PRO BT 226/5054 and B9/1327.

[107] Jeffreys (1954), *Retail Trading in Britain*, p. 422.

into existing stores. The vertical integration and the new approach gave them a competitive edge, and during the 1930s furniture sales improved. New factories were built at Enfield, London and Radcliffe, Manchester, in the 1930s, and made the CWS furniture operation one of the largest in the country.[108] Although in 1964 some 380 stores produced a £17 million turnover in furniture, over recent years the importance of the Co-operative Society has waned.[109] Nevertheless, the concept of manufacturing (originally to overcome sweated labour competition) and then retailing the products continued the long-standing vertical integration that was a feature of the furniture industry for many years.

Concept stores

It has already been pointed out that the role of the furniture retailer has as much to do with a concern for the home environment and its atmosphere as it does with business practice. The combination of these two parts has led to many successful enterprises. When this is taken a stage further and a business concentrates on one particular lifestyle or image, this is often called a concept store. Under this heading can be found businesses such as Habitat, Next Interiors and Laura Ashley, or in the United States Ralph Lauren, Pier One or the Ethan Allen chain. Although they are usually a multiple-outlet operation, they are distinctive in their portrayal of a particular and identifiable house style. These businesses ideally operate in a niche market that they have established for themselves.[110] The following American example of the Ethan Allen chain demonstrates well the development of a store group.

In 1932 the Baumritter Corporation, which ran a successful hardware business, considered expanding into furniture and furnishings. In 1936 it started to manufacture colonial furniture, and by 1939 it had set up a limited number of dealerships selling its merchandise. By 1943 it had eleven manufacturing plants and three saw mills. By the 1960s the concept idea developed strongly with the establishment of 'gallery stores', complete with fully accessorized room settings. The firm also published a catalogue-book – the *Ethan Allen Treasury of Home Interiors*. By 1968 it operated one hundred dealer-run showcase galleries in the USA, which had grown to two hundred by 1982. By 1996 it was considered the second largest furnishing retailer in the USA.[111]

---

[108] Redfern, P. (1938), *The New History of the CWS*.

[109] This accounted for approximately 6 per cent of total furniture sales. Since 1961 the percentage of the total market share has fallen from 9 per cent to 4 per cent. See Economist Intelligence Unit (1964b) *Retail Business*, p. 16, and Office of Fair Trading (1978a), *Furniture and Carpets: A Report*.

[110] Walters, D. and Hanrahan, J. (2000), *Retail Strategy: Planning and Control*, pp. 373–91. See case study of Freedom Furniture Co. of Australia.

[111] In 2003 it operated 310 stores, both company-owned and retailer-operated, in North and South America, the Middle East and Asia.

The concept stores usually operate within a narrow band of customer profiles and limit their appeal to this particular sector. However, the notion of being the right business, providing the right goods, for the right time is clearly part of their success. By selling a 'package' and offering a wide choice of services, they have become a success story. The sustaining of this achievement has been more problematic. Habitat, for example, was acknowledged as a master in creating an in-store atmosphere that appealed to middle-class younger customers of the 1970s who were able to purchase a form of instant 'good taste'. Although Habitat did not create the idea of co-ordinated setting displays, they developed it successfully and in conjunction with a 'market atmosphere' selling items to take away in other parts of the shop. They also sourced goods from a wide range of locations and specified designs, thus creating their own brand image. All this led to the successful retail brand identity that consumers could relate to.

Founded in 1964 in London by Terence Conran and his partners, partly in response to the lack of interest from retail buyers for his designs, Habitat hit the market at exactly the right moment, and grew so that by 1972 there were twelve shops in the organization. The development of a catalogue and a mail order system linked to the stores' selection was popular. By 1981 it had 47 stores and the company was floated on the London stock market. At its height the chain had over fifty branches. However, following a series of take-overs of other retail businesses, it was clear that by the late 1980s the company's appeal was waning and Habitat was being challenged on many sides by newer concepts. In 1992 an erstwhile rival, IKEA, purchased the company.[112]

The case of a more recent example, Next Interiors, is interesting. The company, an offshoot of the successful clothing business, opened for business in 1985 with a nationwide chain of 35 shops. The 'new idea' was to treat furnishings as fashion items. The designer Tricia Guild was employed to create a series of specially planned ranges that would appeal to the target market. The stores were deliberately aspirational: they had no specific mission to preach any 'good design' message, but managed to catch the mood of the time.[113] A similar example of the concept store idea would be Laura Ashley. It started business as a clothes retailer, but later introduced lifestyle ranges of home furnishings as part of the product mix. Like the other concept stores, it produced lavish catalogues and supplied goods by mail. All the concept stores have a clear corporate identity that is recognizable as a house style. In the case of Laura Ashley, for example, the ingredients tend to reflect the image to be promoted: green boxed window dressing, tile or wood floors, wooden shop fittings, and green paint. In many ways, concept stores are, of course, similar to other multiple-store operations.

---

[112] Brown, M. (1994), 'Sell me a sofa not a lifestyle', *The Independent*, 14 October.

[113] Palmer, C. (1985), 'Next on the agenda: Home furnishings and a nationwide chain of fashion', *Design*, p.13. In 1995 they were relaunched as 'Next for the Home'. For a jaundiced view of concept stores, see Brown, M. (1994), 'Sell me a sofa not a lifestyle'.

Multiples

At the turn of the century and until World War One, the retail furniture trade was firmly in the hands of the small-scale or independent retailer. Whilst the department stores in the large towns and the Co-operative retail societies sold some furniture, the independent trader undertook nine-tenths of the total sales. The only multiple organizations of any significance were Jackson's Stores Ltd (32–40 branches before World War One), the Warwickshire Furniture Co. Ltd, and Smart Brothers. By 1914 the total was only nine companies, with some 150 branches in all.[114]

It was during the years between the wars that the rapid development of multiple-shop trading occurred. The estimated increase was from under two hundred branches in 1920 to around eight hundred in 1939, a fourfold increase. The value of sales by the multiples in the total furniture and furnishings market also rose more than fourfold, from about 4 per cent in 1920 to about 18–20 per cent in 1939. This pattern reflected the growing purchasing power of a new group of consumers, especially from the working class.

One of the key players in multiple retailing was the Great Universal Stores group (GUS). The business was founded in 1917 as Universal Stores (Manchester) Limited. Initially, it was mainly a catalogue-based selling operation. It was so successful that by 1934 it claimed to be the biggest in Europe. In that year the company took over the Midland and Hackney furniture chains with £100 000 worth of HP debt, and became Great Universal Stores. In 1943 the multiple furnishing groups, Jays and Campbell's (200 stores) were bought for £1.2 million from the owner, Sir Julien Cahn, who had to sell after he ran into trouble with wartime price controls legislation.[115] The expansion of GUS into the furniture retail trade continued when in 1945 the British and Colonial Furniture Company sold a controlling interest to GUS for *circa* £1 million, along with company names such as Cavendish and Woodhouse. The successful activities of GUS were also based on the foresight to see that a boom in housing and credit would follow the war, and that the pre-war property valuations in balance sheets were completely out of date. In 1948 the chairman, Sir Isaac Wolfson, bought the furnishing store group Smart Brothers for £1 million. In this case the property values were the key, with the unwanted shops being sold off at a profit of £130 000.[116] One interesting aspect of the GUS group's development was noticed by the *Working Party Report* published in 1946, which expressed concerns over GUS's growing influence on the trade:

---

[114] Jeffreys (1954), *Retail Trading in Britain 1850–1950*, p. 424.

[115] Aris, S. (1970), *The Jews in Business*, p. 123. Between April and November 1943 sales in second-hand furniture were being made with excess profit margins above the 42.86 per cent established by the Goods and Services Price Control Act.

[116] Ibid., p. 142.

> A large group has recently acquired control of several well-known multiple house-furnishing businesses and now owns 480 retail shops throughout the country. In addition it has still more recently obtained control of several large manufacturing units and one plywood plant ....
> [so] it is clear ... this organisation will be in a position to exercise very considerable influence on the trade.[117]

The field of popular retailing in the twentieth century, boosted as it was by the ever-growing need to furnish urban homes, meant that there were opportunities for rapid growth. An example was The Times Furniture Company.[118] Founded by John Jacobs in the last quarter of the nineteenth century (*circa* 1894), it was one of the first specialist multiple furnishing businesses. The company were also one of the first to promote instalment payments as a natural way to buy furniture. In the 1920s it published a guide for potential customers, which now offers a fascinating insight into its trading methods. The inducements used to promote the company's service over other retailers were very varied. Some are recognizable today, whilst others have been long forgotten. For example, customers were strongly advised not to be guided by credit terms alone, but rather to study them in relation to the quality of the furniture being supplied. However, incentives were connected to the credit terms. These included schemes such as free insurance to cover eventualities such as death, fire and misfortune. Other 'free' services were the storage of purchased goods until required, and the fitting of carpets and linoleum if bought with furniture. Customers from out of town were even reimbursed with rail fares if they spent over £20 on goods from the store. But perhaps the most significant of all was the Times policy of a guarantee for all goods purchased. The 'Green Disc' guarantee was against 'fault in material or workmanship for all time'.[119] This was an impressive marketing tool, especially when the quality of much furniture at the time was so maligned.

The post-war period, once the immediate shortages were past, had been a period of boom for all types of retailers in the trade. There is some evidence to suggest that the multiples further increased their share of the trade; in 1954 they undertook some 26–28 per cent, while department stores were responsible for about 16 per cent, and the Co-operative Societies for 7–8 per cent, leaving the independent retailer with about 50 per cent of the trade. The importance of chain store furniture retailing was recognized when in 1944 the Multiple House Furnishers' Association was formed with not less than 500 shops represented.[120] By 1950 there were an estimated 22 firms controlling 839

---

[117] *Working Party Report* (1946), pp. 142–8.

[118] In 1948 it became a public company, and in 1968 it was taken over by GUS.

[119] Times Furnishing Company sales brochure (n.d., *c*.1935).

[120] *Furnishing World*, February 1944, pp. 112–13.

branches, with GUS amongst the largest, controlling over two-thirds of all the multiple shop branches in the furniture trade.[121]

The advantage of size in multiple trading in the furniture business was mainly due to strong hire purchase financing, the economics of administration from a central head office, and influential purchasing power with manufacturers. In the case of privately run multiple groups, such as Cantors, Times or Perrings, the power of individual family directors was also often a potent driving force.[122] Part of the development of multiples was based on the retention of family influence in companies, and by an ethos of business leadership as public service. For example, Sir Ralph Perring, chairman of the company John Perring, was Lord Mayor of London, and many other principals of multiple businesses held office in trade associations, livery companies and elsewhere.

In the 1980s further amalgamations and closures changed the multiples into even larger groups. These included Maple/Waring and Gillow (with a hundred retail outlets in 1987), Harris-Queensway, and MFI.[123] The power of some of these groups can be seen in the following examples. In 1987 MFI was the largest retailer of self-assembly furniture, with 134 stores nationwide with sales of £334 million. Harris-Queensway, which, at the height of the 1980s boom, operated over 750 outlets, controlled an estimated 20 per cent of the domestic carpet market and 7.5 per cent of the domestic furniture market.[124] This company was established as Harris Carpets in a small shop in Peckham in1957. By 1974 there were18 carpet shops operating under the Harris name. In 1974 the Keith Royle carpet retailing chain was taken over, adding another 20 shops. In 1977 Harris purchased the superstore group Queensway for £2 million. Later the multiple furnishers Hardys, Henderson Kenton, Ukay and General George were all added to the stable. In 1990 the business collapsed.

The main reasons for the relative demise of the multiples were, paradoxically, originally their strengths. Most were situated in urban high streets, and as the move to out-of-town sites grew, they lost trade to the newly developing superstores. Other problems included an increasingly fragmented market in which they did not have a true identity, the absence of brands, the

---

[121] In 1955 Great Universal Stores controlled Cavendish, Jay, Campbell, Jacksons, British and Colonial Furniture, Smart Bros, Godfrey, and James Broderick, and also the manufacturers, Universal Furniture Productions, Gill and Reigate, Joseph Johnstone, Northern Bedding, Tyne Furniture and Tyne Plywood.

[122] Multiple groups in the United Kingdom have included Cantors, Cavendish-Woodhouse, Colliers, Courts, Grange, Hardys, Harrison Gibson, Jacksons, Kentons, Maple, New Day, Phillips, Smart Bros, Times, Williams and Perrings.

[123] Barty-King (1992), *Maples Fine Furnishers*. In 1980 Waring and Gillow took over Maples. The Manny Cussins group then comprised Waring and Gillow, Harrison Gibson, Wolfe and Hollander, and John Peters Furnishing Stores, 42 in all. In January 1987 they absorbed Wades, Kingsbury and Homestore to become the fourth largest retailer of furniture with 150 branches. In 1989 the company was divided between Allied Maples and Gillow PLC (Saxon Hawk PLC).

[124] Rawsthorn, A. (1988), 'Awakening may be rude for some', *Financial Times*, 19 April 1988.

wide range of products stocked (often including electrical), large display areas, a slow rate of stock turn, and a slowing customer flow rate, in addition to the increasing need for higher margins to cover operating costs. As customers became more conscious of price and delivery, new business types stepped in. IKEA, for example, shifted cost burdens to the customer by having large shed premises 'out of town' near motorway access points, fewer salespeople, take-away goods to save delivery cost and immediate availability. Added value is available should the customer want it and be prepared to pay for it. The forgoing of many traditional services and the challenge of self-assembly, as well as the savings on price, clearly appeal to many customers.

Other multiple store types have been interested in joining the market, especially in the middle segment. The successful entrance of Marks and Spencer into full furniture retailing is one successful example, whereas catalogue retailers Argos's attempt at an up-market furnishing group – Chesterman – was a failure.[125] Argos's core business of selling brand names through catalogues was partly transferred to the Chesterman idea. Brands give confidence, and even if not widely known, can often be prompted in the memory of well-read consumers. The management considered the importance of information technology and staff training (selling furniture was compared to selling new cars), and in-store consumer education was also important. With a library, coffee lounge and videos of home products, the plan was for the customer to enjoy the purchase process in an unhurried and professional manner. The idea was well-meaning, but the power of cheap prices over relatively expensive service was difficult to break.[126]

Interestingly, Argos has developed its presence in the furniture market in a different way by using its catalogue. The 34 million catalogues printed each year and the fact that there is a store within twenty miles of 90 per cent of the UK population gives great penetration of the market. The catalogue, like similar promotional tools, has attractive room settings, showing an aspirational lifestyle, whilst the practical features of the company policy, including free samples, delivery and a winning idea of 16-day approval for any merchandise, supports the customer demands at other levels. The approval policy gets round the issue of customers being unable to see goods instore. Argos has also embraced e-retailing for furniture, and the full range is available for ordering online, as well as on an interactive shopping service on digital TV.

Superstores

The nature of the trade in the 1960s was delineated by three clear problem factors that were to spawn another retailing style. The first was long delivery

---

[125] *Cabinet Maker*, 28 February 1992 and March 1993.

[126] For an interesting analysis of multiples and price versus service, see Davies, G. and Brooks, J. (1989), *Positioning Strategy in Retailing*.

times for customers. They had to wait due to the high cost of stock holding, the batch production of cabinet furniture and the custom upholstering business. Secondly, floor areas in stores were often generally small, therefore this discouraged room-setting merchandising methods, as well as offering a small selection. Thirdly, there was relatively little price competition, partly due to resale price maintenance.

The out-of-town discount stores which were developed in the 1960s began by offering warehouse prices and limited service.[127] They originally reduced prices by up to 20 per cent but this differential with the high street was gradually narrowed. Their operating expenses were lower, display areas were greater, and car-parking facilities encouraged visits from the public, so they seemed set for success. In addition, some stores were able to offer delivery from stock.

By the early 1970s the idea of furniture superstores was well established in the United States, and it was becoming a force in Britain. The concepts were different in each country.

In the United States the warehouse concept, which in one example boasted 246 showrooms, was able to offer customers instant delivery of anything from a range of 52 000 items. Alternatively, a slightly higher price would buy the same product – delivered, assembled, and fitted into the home.[128] The model was the American furniture business of Levitz, which established this form of trading in the 1960s with showrooms of 100 000–150 000 square feet, displaying up to 750 room sets with an inventory of over $1 million per store.[129]

The British example of Queensway, which started business selling mainly end-of-lines in 1966, is instructive. After the abolition of resale price maintenance, it moved away from selling ends of ranges and miscellaneous items, and began to sell well-known names from stock at reduced prices.[130] It initiated a system of self-selection that used cards on merchandise that customers filled in with their details. These were processed, and the goods delivered at a later date. The problem of waiting for goods was still evident here.

---

[127] See Bates. A. D. (1977), 'Warehouse retailing: A revolutionary force in distribution', *California Management Review,* 20(2) pp. 74–80, and Jones, P. (1984), 'Retail warehouse developments and planning policies in Scotland', *Scottish Geographical Magazine*, 100, April, pp. 12–19.

[128] The example quoted is from United States – Wickes Furniture Warehouse and Showroom, *circa* 1972.

[129] An average high street store might have 10 000–25 000 square feet of display space. By the 1990s this business had foundered, and was relaunched by moving away from the large warehouse idea to more local showrooms. See Michman, R. and Mazze, E. (2001), *Speciality Retailers*, pp. 85–6.

[130] Fulop, C. and March, T. (1979), 'The effects of abolition of R.P.M in two trades', *European Journal of Marketing*, 13(7), p. 235, consider that the abolition of resale price maintenance has resulted in radical changes in the marketing of furniture, the most important being the out-of-town store.

More recently, the MFI flat-pack warehouse-selling method has been very successful.[131] Combined with brand names such as Schreiber and Hygena, it shows massive discounts off the prices of these well-known furniture brands. MFI, which specialized initially in self-assembly furniture, saw phenomenal growth as sales rose between 1977 and 1987 from £15 million to £334 million. With margins rising from 5.5 per cent to 16 per cent, as opposed to a traditional 3–4 per cent, it showed the way. Founded after the World War Two as a mail order business, and later running a group of small shops, the company was floated in 1971. Many problems meant that by 1974/5, the mail order business went bankrupt and the company was reconsidered. Out-of-town premises, often on industrial estates, were developed with the emphasis on immediate delivery and cheap prices, all promoted heavily through advertising. Initially, a 'warehouse' image was promoted, but improvements in display soon occurred. The original attitude of the MFI Company towards design in 1986 was clear in its response to questioning. The company did not have a creative design team; rather it said: 'We want to reach the British buying public. We want to make products at prices they are prepared to pay.'[132] It was successful, as the company grew twentyfold in ten years and revolutionized parts of the furniture trade.

By the mid-1980s the no-frills approach was disappearing into a more sophisticated marketing setup. Following the lead of the American retailers and the more innovative British furnishers, these warehouse operations moved up-market by displaying merchandise in 'vignettes' which allowed them to expand the product range to include soft furnishings and accessories. Although much emphasis remains on price and credit terms, co-ordinated style is now a major ingredient of success.

Furniture supermarkets, where the ethos was to 'pile them high and sell them cheap' were also developed in the 1960s. The idea was to create a high turnover that would allow bulk buying. This in turn would reduce unit costs and allow cheaper retail prices. The level of service would also be reduced. An example of this approach was the Williams Furniture Supermarket Group. This group operated a massive central warehouse that serviced the 27 stores in the South East of England. The furniture was not discounted in the sense of reductions on branded goods with maintained resale prices; rather it was purchased in bulk to gain savings in costs. The emphasis was always on price rather than quality or service, which meant that the 'furniture supermarket' in this form could not survive.

The success of the superstores was bolstered in part by the flat-pack cabinet business, which enables instant gratification for the customer. Flat-pack furniture was often cheap and usually of good value, achieved by placing large orders with companies which specialized in one or two lines. In addition, the

---

[131] Davies, G. (1994), 'Repositioning MFI', in McGoldrick, P. (Ed.), *Cases in Retail Management*.

[132] Brown, R. (1986), 'The furniture oligarchy', *Design*, 449, May, pp. 44–7.

retail buyers were acutely aware of the new generation of customers, who were more fashion-conscious but at the same time wanted to emulate high-style furnishings. This was particularly apparent in upholstery styles and cover designs.

The most successful multiple-superstore operation is perhaps the IKEA company.[133] Originating in Sweden in the 1950s and taking the decision to concentrate on self-assembly furniture, it has grown to become a worldwide retailing force. It sells Scandinavian design, which may be manufactured in Scandinavia, Eastern Europe or elsewhere, through catalogues and showrooms. Indeed, the main promotional tool is the catalogue, of which some 44 million are printed each year, in ten different languages. Working from the premise that the company can make 'a valuable contribution to the democratization process at home and abroad',[134] it aims to offer value for money, on the basis that what is good for the customer is good for the company. In 1993 the company operated 111 stores in 24 countries, of which five were in Britain. With 20 000 employees and worldwide sales of £2.2 billion, IKEA is the world's largest furniture retailer. A long way from the 'pile it high' warehouse concept, IKEA produces classless furnishings that are designed to appeal to all customer profiles. IKEA is clearly more than a furnishings store. The average stay for a customer is one-and-a-half hours, as the 'store' can be experienced as part leisure centre, part restaurant, and part gallery. The selection of furnishings is enormous, ranging from the basic essentials to reasonable copies of fashionable ideas, but this is augmented by the ideas that are sold along with the goods to fulfil them. IKEA calls its customers 'visitors', and although it operates in over 24 countries, the one hundred best-selling lines are approximately the same across the whole business.[135]

The third development in the superstore category has been the expansion of the DIY businesses into furnishings, particularly flooring, kitchens and accessories. The B&Q company is the market leader in the United Kingdom. Originally starting out as comprehensive and accessible builders' merchants and DIY suppliers, it soon moved into self-assembly furniture, kitchens and bathrooms. In general, though, DIY shops have failed to make much impact in the mainstream furniture market.

Whilst some commentators have seen the success of IKEA and the like as the 'triumph of the proles over the middle order',[136] it is clear that traditional

---

[133] The business has generated a large amount of analysis particularly in terms of its business strategies. See, for example, Prime, N. (1999), 'IKEA: International development', in Dupuis and Dawson, *European Cases in Retailing*; Warnaby, G. (1999), 'Strategic consequences of retail acquisition: IKEA and Habitat', *International Marketing Review*, 16, 4/5, 'The wealth of realizing new ideas', *Harvard Business Review*, July–August 1993.

[134] IKEA internal company training manual.

[135] The essence of the merchandise selection in whatever country it is being sold is that it is Swedish.

[136] Pearman, H. (1992), *Sunday Times*, 1 November.

retailers have been able to hold much of their original market. By introducing their own brands or house lines, banding together as buying groups or trading up into merchandise that is more exclusive or offering more services, they seem set to retain their niche.

Mail order

By the early twentieth century, furniture and furnishings were an established part of the repertoire of goods for sale through mail order. The businesses involved ranged from the true mail order companies, with one thousand pages of 'everything for the home', to the specialist dealers selling a few items. Although these avenues have not seriously usurped the more regular retailing processes in furniture, they have become more of a force. The distinction between 'inspection goods' and 'description goods' probably explains why furniture was relatively slow to be sold by mail order.[137] In the former case, goods demanded inspection before purchase – sitting on a chair or laying on a bed – whereas description goods could be bought 'sight unseen', but based on a careful explanation and image. Unlike the American experience, which was based on serving a predominantly rural market with quality merchandise at cut prices, the system of agencies and the granting of credit fuelled the British business of mail order. Indeed, credit was probably the biggest selling point to the predominantly working-class customer base that was established between the wars. Importantly, the credit facility offered by mail order firms was not touched by hire purchase restrictions, as the transaction was essentially a credit sale. In 1986 7 per cent of furniture sales were made by mail order.[138]

In addition to multiple-product mail order, catalogue shopping using the retailers' stock also grew in the second half of the twentieth century. Businesses such as Habitat, Marks and Spencer, Laura Ashley and Next all expanded into this branch of retailing. In the same way that furniture is now being sold via the Internet, the traditional shopping trips to the high street or mall are being challenged, particularly for high-price items. Consumers are reconsidering the amount of time given to purchasing activities as much as they are financing, for example.[139]

Another direct marketing approach to home furnishings has been the specifically targeted brochure/catalogue that identifies with lifestyle aspirations. These offer an image associated with a lifestyle such as 'contemporary', 'conservatory', or one of a range of traditional styles such as

---

[137] See Coopey, R., O'Connell, S. and Porter, D. (1999), 'Mail order in the United Kingdom c. 1880–1960: How mail order competed with other forms of retailing', *International Review of Retail Distribution and Consumer Research*, 9(3), July, pp. 264–72.

[138] Office of Fair Trading (1990), *Furniture and Carpets: A Report*.

[139] Dawson, J. A. (1988), 'Changes in 20th century retailing in the High Street', *Geographical Journal*, 154(1), pp. 1–12.

'Gothic', 'Chippendale' or Victorian. The ordering of goods for direct delivery is also a feature of Web-based purchasing, but as furniture is a substantive purchase, it remains to be seen how this will develop. Conventional mail order companies which sell furniture will continue to serve a small niche market, but will probably struggle in the face of competition from the catalogue showrooms and the big multiples, since any advantage they once offered no longer exists.

Manufacturers' direct sales

A number of other sub-categories of retailer have entered the furniture market at various times during the twentieth century. These have often taken the form of weekly payment clubs, operating either by mail order or by canvassing. In the late 1930s the so-called 'club trade'which dealt especially in fireside and adjustable chairs created another channel of distribution. Middlemen procured orders from catalogues supplied to part-time salesmen employed to run the clubs. The idea was for customers to pay a shilling a week for twenty weeks. On receipt of the first payment, the club notified the contracting chair maker, which then arranged to dispatch the chair. As Mayes points out:

> This trade had an effect on [High] Wycombe's reputation. Out of one pound there had to be found the costs of advertising and commission, the normal overheads and profits of the club firms plus a generous allowance for bad debts, and what was left was available for paying the manufacturer for the chair.[140]

In 1934 a Code of Trading Practice was brought in that 'allowed' retailers to be the only legitimate outlet for manufacturers' products. This was intended to counter the practice of makers selling direct to retail customers.[141] Nevertheless, respectable firms such as Minty (easy chairs and bookcases), Globe-Wernicke (bookcases) and Searle (Berkeley easy chairs) all sold direct to the public. Indeed, some of these firms had their own showrooms. These sorts of direct selling also occurred in less obvious ways. East End of London wholesalers W. E. Hardy of Curtain Road sold direct using an 'easy hire system' and included testimonials from the Marquis of Twedale, the Duchess of Marlborough and the like.[142] Famous manufacturing firms such as Epstein and Hille also sold bespoke work direct to customers who placed orders; others opened showrooms in the East End of London, either as 'display only' or as a source of retail sales – for example, Chippendale Workshops.[143] This system of

---

[140] Mayes, J. (1960), *The History of Chair-making in High Wycombe*.

[141] Judy Attfield discusses an amended code, which changed in 1945 to refer to user-customers, hence allowing manufacturers to deal directly with contract clients. Attfield (1996), 'Give 'em something dark and heavy', p. 189.

[142] Kirkham, Mace and Porter (1987), *Furnishing the World*, p. 45.

[143] Ibid.

buying direct from the manufacturer is still much used for the sale of fitted bedrooms, kitchens and bathrooms, and specialist products.

At the turn of the twenty-first century, furniture retailers are still faced with many of the same problems they have grappled with in the previous one hundred years. There will also be new ones. The market will alter in response to customers developing new or altered lifestyles, as media interest increases and as furniture and furnishings become even more fashion-orientated products. The retailers will have to respond by increasing services, continuing promotional activity, adapting to customer price bartering and demand for interest-free credit, as well as being prepared for developments in Internet shopping. However, customers will still want to see goods in store, so displays, accessories and service will remain important. Therefore, the successful furniture retailers will take up the challenges of professional retailing in the twenty-first century and move away from being simply 'sellers of furniture' to 'efficient and profitable retailers of consumer goods'.

Chapter 8

Changing visions of the ideal and the real: the consumption of home furnishings in the twentieth century

> The Home is the enemy of the woman. Purporting to be her protector it is her oppressor; it is her fortress, but she does not live in the state apartments, she lives in the dungeon (W. L. George (1913), *Women and Tomorrow*, p. 57)

It has been argued that the macro history of the home in the twentieth century has been, at least in part, a stand-off between domesticity and modernism.[1] This has resulted in the home often being a battleground between the forces of modernism and apparent reaction. In terms of home design, this resulted in a variety of attempts to advise consumers to restrict their consumption of reactionary objects and styles, and to encourage the consumption of modern designs appropriate to a new era. This twentieth-century battle of styles has probably been won by the post-modern acceptance of 'difference', which, when applied to the domestic interior, has encouraged consumers' desires for choice and has promoted an ideal of individualism.

For many people during the twentieth century, home has continued as a site of privacy and individuality, a refuge and a comfort from outside life, and a place of mediation between public and private spaces.[2] These features are the continuity of an image of home that was fully established by the end of the nineteenth century. However, this notion has been challenged, refuted and revisited through a number of major developments that have promoted change. These developments include issues associated with matters of choice, gender,[3] lifestyle, aestheticization, identity[4] and

---

[1] See, for example, Reed, C. (1996), *Not at Home: The Suppression of Domesticity in Modern Art and Architecture*.

[2] See, for example, Lawrence, R. J. (1987) 'What makes a house a home', *Environment and Behavior*, 19(2), pp. 154–68, and Sixsmith, J. (1986), 'The meaning of home', *Journal of Environmental Psychology*, 6, 282–98.

[3] See, for example, Hunt, P. (1995), 'Gender and the construction of home life', in Jackson, S. and Moores, S. (Eds.), *Politics of Domestic Consumption*, Gordon, B. (1996), 'Woman's domestic body: The conceptual conflation of women and interiors in the industrial age'. Giles, J. (1993), 'A home of one's own: Women and domesticity in England 1918–1950', in *Women's Studies International Forum*, 16(3), pp. 239–52.

[4] There is an extensive literature on identity but see Lee, M. J. (1993), *Consumer Culture Reborn: The Cultural Politics of Consumption*, and Lunt, P. K. and Livingstone, S. (1992), *Mass Consumption and Personal Identity: Everyday Economic Experience*.

consumption.[5] In addition to these 'social' changes, developments in architecture, design and technology were also to have a considerable influence on the nature of home.

There is no doubt that social issues have greatly affected the twentieth-century interior, both physically and emotionally. An important development through the century was the gradual establishment of decent homes of one sort or another for the vast majority of people.[6] Following on from this was the development of choice, the establishment of lifestyles and identities associated with and promoted to reflect or sell these choices, the increasing awareness of the aestheticization of surroundings, and great technological changes, which all contributed to an increase in consumption of goods and ideas. In addition, the changing role of women in society and the development of feminist histories have gradually changed the way the concept of home is now considered.[7]

A number of other attributes beyond the home were responsible for fuelling changes in consumption during the twentieth century. These include a continuing growth in demand based on increased disposable income, intensified production, revised distribution systems, an increasing social mobility and a growing desire to express individualism, which have all led to consumer acquisitiveness being fuelled by the forces of retailing, fashion and advertising. Glennie identifies this process as a change from people being 'users of things' to 'consumers of commodities'.[8] This process is continual and often difficult to see, but the changes clearly influenced the domestic interior, much as they did other aspects of consumption. It is a reflection of an older idea expressed as the change from 'necessities' to 'decencies'. It is important to remember that consumption practices are based on consumer priorities, home furnishings not often being high on the list. In 1925 the author of *The Modern Priscilla Home Furnishing Book* touched a sensitive point that the furnishing retailers would easily relate to:

> So long as our [the consumer] judgment of others revolves around what
> makes of car they drive, rather than the sorts of homes they live in, good

[5] See, for example, Campbell, C. 'The sociology of consumption', in Miller, D. (Ed.) (1995), *Acknowledging Consumption*; Chapman and Hockey (1999), *Ideal Homes?*; Fraad, H. (1994), *Bringing It All Home;* McCracken, G. (1990), *Culture and Consumption*; Miller (1995), *Acknowledging Consumption*; Putnam, T. (1992), 'Regimes of closure: The representation of cultural process in domestic consumption', in Silverstone, R. and Hirsch, E. (Eds), *Consuming Technologies: Media and Information in Domestic Space*; Reed, C. (1996), *Not at Home: The Suppression of Domesticity in Modern Art and Architecture.*

[6] See, for example, Jeremiah, D. (2000), *Architecture and Design for the Family in Britain, 1900–1970.*

[7] See, for example, Madigan, R., Munro, M. and Smith, S. (1990), 'Gender and the meaning of home', *International Journal of Urban and Regional Research*, 14, pp. 625–47, and André, R. (1981), *Homemakers: The Forgotten Workers.*

[8] Glennie, P. (1995), 'Consumption within historical studies', in Miller, *Acknowledging Consumption.*

furniture will wait until the car in the garage is paid for. And then, likely enough we shall have our eye on a better car and continue to complain because good furniture is not to be had on the bargain counter.[9]

As consumer choices multiply, so the competition for the consumer's purse also grows.

At the stage where consumers are able to exercise choice, it can be seen that individual consumption practices will be informed in part by pre-history, in part by education and social position, and in part by financial considerations: hence the continual dilemmas between continuity and change in the design and use of interiors and their furnishings. In Britain the dilemma of 'the home' can be partly expressed in the conflict between nostalgia for an imagined past[10] (continuity) and the necessity of living in the 'here and now' and attending to future (changing) patterns of life.[11]

In broad terms, two divisions of change can apparently be perceived during the century. Initially, there were the modernizing and infrastructural improvements, led by architects and designers, often with a social agenda: Modernism. The conventions of architectural modernism were established on formal, approved, correct, impersonal, prescribed, universal but often alien ideals, which were received with ambivalence in Britain during the period 1920–1970. Admittedly, stylistic elements were sometimes borrowed and adapted by more popular product ranges, but the principles in general were not. In the more affluent post-war period, certainly, this consensus might mean that consumers had the ability to 'keep up with Joneses'. When individuality becomes more important and consensus breaks down, then, in Don Slater's phrase, it is a matter of 'keeping different from the Joneses'. The second division is said to occur where any consensus appears to break down, where individuality is espoused, and where space is fragmented and personalized in an individual fashion. These distinctions are probably more apparent than real, as a majority of homes were furnished with the fashions available in the stores at the time. Purchasing decisions were being based on the criteria of like/dislike, use/function, availability and cost, rather than principle. Actual practices reflect rejection of the Modernist ideals of hierarchy and symmetry, apparently based on inherent values and truths, and generally advocate eclecticism and value relativity. The furnishings will often be based on an accretion of goods through gift or inheritance, home crafts and retail purchases.

In the second half of the twentieth century the home became an important site of research, which embraced a number of positions that looked at the domestic interior. The 'home' was considered as a site of personal identity, and

---

[9] *The Modern Priscilla Home Furnishing Book* (1925), cited by Grier (1988), *Culture and Comfort*, p. 213.

[10] See, for example, Wright, P. (1985), *On Living in an Old Country: The National Past in Contemporary Britain*.

[11] See Putnam, T. (1999), 'Post modern home life', in Cieraad (1999), *At Home*.

as lifestyle establishment, and a space for consumption practices which reflected social issues such as choice, gender, influence, taste and aestheticization.[12] Many of these issues were contained in the notion of identity, therefore an issue central to the discussion of homes is their role as repositories of ideas and objects – a role that is both physical and emotional, and is inherently linked to the consumers' ideas of themselves.[13]

Identity

The question of identity raises fundamental and contradictory issues in this consideration of the home in the twentieth century. It could be argued that a consumer culture encourages individual freedom of expression and identity, but on the other hand it can appear to construct parameters within which people can consume a ready-made identity. Although identity is often established by a wide range of objects of a more personal nature, in terms of major furnishings the process of development of an identity is often hindered by an individual's lack of control over product choice. Shops established the idea that identity could be learned and purchased, so the market appears to give us tools to create our own identity, but with the retailer often taking the role of taste maker and supplier, this can be a constraining exercise. Combine this powerful aspect with the cluttered, confused and conflicting messages from our personal histories, our location in society, and biological factors, and it will seem like a recipe for confusion. So how is identity created? Firstly, there is the creation of distinction through choice. This is an approach that is intimately linked with financial power, and knowledge of the possibilities available. Secondly, there is the distinction through the individual's idea of home and sense of self, which may be developed by appropriation or DIY or making do. All of these may themselves be influenced by the concept of what is suitable for a particular group.

The idea that the home represented the family, and in particular the female who ran it, was already established in the nineteenth century. The suggestion

---

[12] See, for example, Csikzentmihali, M. and Rochberg-Halton, E. (1981), *The Meaning of Things: Domestic Symbols and the Self*; Dittmar, H. (1992), *The Social Psychology of Material Possessions: To Have is to Be*; Friedman, J. (1994), *Consumption and Identity*; Halttunen, K. (1989), 'From parlour to living room: Domestic space, interior decoration and the cult of personality', in Brunna, S. J., *Consuming Visions*; Lee (1992), *Consumer Culture Reborn*; Madigan, R. and Munro, M. (1996), '"House beautiful": Style and consumption in the home', *Sociology*, 30(1), pp. 41–57. These issues are still current. See Leslie, D. and Reimer, S. (2003), 'Gender, modern design and home consumption', *Environmental Planning, Society and Space*, 21, pp. 293–316.

[13] For work on this theme, see Csikzentmihali and Rochberg-Halton, (1981), *The Meanings of Things*; Koskijoki, M. (1999), 'The home and the treasures of the consumer', in Sarantola-Weiss (Ed.), *Rooms for Everyone*.

that the home represented the particular woman's identity was also part of this thinking.[14] This was taken further during the twentieth century as more people became more aware of and particular about their surroundings, and had the ability to create homes for themselves and families, often for the first time.

Although this idea of home has often been represented as a middle-class phenomenon, the working class were conscious of how a home might represent status and identity. Although the great Booth Survey of working-class expenditure (1889–1902) in London did not mention furniture, there is evidence that home furnishings were becoming important for all sectors of society. A Board of Trade survey conducted in 1889 reported that although the furniture in a working-class home was scanty and lacking in any sort of unity, you might find:

> small ornaments and pictures, a sofa, several chairs, a side table and that
> indispensable necessary of respectable cottage existence – a mahogany
> chest of drawers with an antimacassar of crochet work on its top.[15]

In Walter Besant's description of the East End of London, written in the very early years of the twentieth century, he compared two working-class interiors that explain this process.

One belongs to the house of an 'aristocrat of labour' (a foreman or engineer). In this room: 'you will see a big Bible, here a rosewood desk, here a vase full of artificial flowers, here a bird cage with foreign birds … here something from India carved in fragrant wood …There is always something to show the position and superiority of the tenant.'[16] This is compared to another space, belonging to a 'lower grade of labour', but which reflects the same motives:

> [Here] there is a table, with two chairs; there is a chest of drawers with
> large glass handles. On this chest stands a structure of artificial flowers
> under a glass shade. This is the sacred symbol of respectability. It is for the
> tenement what the Bible or the coral in the window is for the house. So
> long as we have our glass shade with its flowers we are in steady work, and
> beyond the reach of want.[17]

Alfred Simon recognized that even the 'poorest living room has some pretension to taste', and considered that in order to improve standards, it was necessary to educate the taste leaders from whom the majority took their lead.[18]

For many of this new majority, the move from subsistence levels to some degree of comfort was the first opportunity to enter significant homemaking.

---

[14] See Chapter 6 in this work. This also reflects a growing self-consciousness of the domestic environment, which has gone beyond basis needs.

[15] *Family Budgets: Being the Income and Expenses of 28 British Households 1891–1894*, cited in Briggs, A. (1956), *Friends of the People: A Centenary History of Lewis's*, p. 184.

[16] Besant, W. (1901), *East London*, p. 119.

[17] Ibid., p. 120. See also Roberts (1971), *The Classic Slum*, pp. 17–21.

[18] Simon, A. (1918), 'Good and cheap – A reply, *Journal of* DIA, quoted in Benton, T., Benton, C. and Sharp, D. (Eds) (1975), *Form and Function: A Source Book for the History of Architecture and Design 1890–1939*, p. 192.

Consumers were being encouraged to 'be themselves' and to be creative but they were beset with advice from every shade of opinion and interest group. This advice was particularly directed at women. For example, Mary Barkdull commented in *Good Housekeeping* (US) in September 1910 that: 'curtains, table covers and portières when worked out by ... [the housewife] for her own particular rooms, radiate an individuality absolutely impossible to counterfeit with factory productions'.[19] On the other hand, W. L.George considered that the problem lay in established tastes:

> Home labour costs most [women] their individuality, largely because there are home conventions. They are subtle, soul destroying things these conventions that halls should be red or blue, drawing rooms pink or white and gold; and when they changed, as they did when fumed oak came, and Morris chintz and Jacobean furniture, they are as levelling as destructive.[20]

The retailers were aware of these changes in the home. They knew that a home portrayed a lot about the occupier (again considered to be a woman) and they exploited the anxieties and concerns this raised. A turn-of-the-century catalogue from the French Trois Quartiers department store explained:

> The wife's task is to create an agreeable interior; there her personality can express itself in all of the details that make up the home. Her tastes and character will be so clearly reflected there, that without even knowing her, a visitor with some skills at observation could represent to himself the mistress of the house as she really is, 'careful and flirtatious, attentive and artistic', all of these qualities will emerge in the furniture and things ... Of course, all the faults of laziness, of lack of taste, of inattention will also leave their mark.[21]

This idea had been expressed by John Ruskin some fifty years earlier, and was still considered thirty years later, albeit without the intimidating overtones. In 1930 Emily Post wrote a rather whimsical recommendation with regard to the decorating of the house:

> Its personality should express your personality, just as every gesture you make – or fail to make – expresses your gay animation or your restraint, your old-fashioned conventions, your perplexing mystery, or your emancipated modernism – whichever characteristics are typically yours.[22]

This idea of the home having a personality of its own was noted in 1927 by Edward Gregory:

---

[19] Barkdull, M. (1910), 'Curtains, portières and cushions', *Good Housekeeping*, 51, September, pp. 324–7, cited in Gordon, J. and McArthur, J. (1959), 'Popular culture, magazines and American domestic interiors, 1898–1940', *Journal of Popular Culture*, 22(4), p. 45.

[20] George, W. L. (1913), *Women and Tomorrow*, p. 75.

[21] Cited in Auslander, L. (1996), The gendering of consumer practices', in De Grazia, V. (Ed.), *The Sex of Things: Gender and Consumption*, p. 96.

[22] Post, E. (1930), *The Personality of a House: The Blue Book of House Design and Decorations*, p. 3.

Have you ever reflected that the furnishing of your drawing room
will have its effect upon the conversation of your guests? It certainly
will. Put some people in a room of the commonplace kind, and they
inevitably become commonplace in their conversation. Meet them
somewhere else where by accident or design a few odds and ends of some
individual character have crept into the room, and they positively
sparkle.[23]

Whilst these authors were trying to instil some particular ideas of gentility and
self-esteem into the minds of their readers, at the same time the Modernist
architect Mart Stam was clear about the real agenda that consumers were
following. In 1928 he wrote:

Just as the workers and the petty officials long for their own house and
garden ... so they desire to see expressed in their furniture this small ideal
of prosperity. The result is the appearance of furniture which, although
manufactured on a mass scale is intended to create a false impression of
prosperity.[24]

In the same article he crushingly denounced the things that many people would
consider gave them their identity. In their place he extolled the virtues of the
'minimal dwelling', a place where 'people will not cling onto everything:
neither Grandma's furniture nor mementoes of their youth. And wives will not
collect incomplete dinner sets or outdated clothes'.[25]

The issue of identity was often not far from conformity. The advice given in
Woman's Journal of May 1935, to make furnishing easier and to ensure your
identity 'fitted in' was clear about this:

It is so much easier to make out a list of furniture, say, for the dining room,
copied from the dining rooms of one's friends, which included the usual
table, chairs and sideboard – far more easy than to plan an individual
room, using new materials and incorporating new ideas.[26]

Stability was also a component of identity that might be achieved through the
imagery of the goods selected for the home. The continuity of familiar and
durable objects is often compared favourably to the transience of life. The
concept of 'timeless design' avoids the tag of 'old-fashioned' when referring to
stylish furniture apparently past its 'sell by' date. This stability was promoted
by the projected image of the goods themselves and by advice through books,
magazines and shops that were delivering a style appropriate to a particular
group.

In 1904, the German author Hermann Muthesius wrote:

[23] Gregory, E. W. (1925), *The Art and Craft of Home Making*, p. 43.

[24] Stam, M. (1927), 'Away with the furniture artists', *Innenraume*, cited in Benton, T., Benton,
C. and Sharp, D. (Eds) (1975), *Form and Function: A Source Book for the History of Architecture
and Design 1890–1939*, p. 227.

[25] Stam (1927), 'Away with the furniture artists'.

[26] *Woman's Journal*, May 1935, p. 8.

> When an Englishman lives in a house, he expects to find peace there. He looks for neatness, homeliness and all comforts. He seeks a minimum of forms with a maximum of restful relaxed and yet fresh atmosphere. His unalterable preference is for the rural and the unsophisticated. He regards every reminiscence of these qualities as a bond with his beloved Mother Nature, to whom, for all their advanced culture, the English people have remained truer than any other race.[27]

Although these descriptions are rather quaint to modern eyes, nevertheless for a large number of British homemakers they can be easily recognized as images of an ideal that has continued in various manifestations throughout the twentieth century.

The first quarter of the twentieth century saw the beginnings of choice for sections of the population that had previously been unable to engage significantly with interests in homemaking beyond necessity. These changes were brought about by (a) more buyers who were able to afford new furniture (or use credit facilities); (b) planned housing programmes which encouraged new furnishing purchases, and (c) a rise in disposable income – all of which led to a desire for both design differentiation and emulation, which in turn led to greater expectations and a demand for choice.

However, these choices were still controlled by an idea of decorum, based on established taste and knowledge that continued recognized ideals of cultural consumption. This is a pattern of social distinction that legitimizes forms of power and control based on economic situations.[28] Bourdieu considers that taste is therefore ideological, being based on class as quality and as category.[29] Baudrillard identifies consumption as a class institution with an unconscious logic that uses consumption as a coded language to encourage differentiation. This can work in two opposing ways. The dual nature of goods therefore bears commercial values as well as enabling a relatively autonomous form of cultural expression to be made by individuals.[30] The examples of the principle of unity, where some homes have matching sets of dining chairs, three-piece suites, crockery sets and so on whilst others have an ensemble derived from the owners' individual experiences, demonstrate this duality.[31]

Dennis Chapman's *Home and Social Status* (1955) commented on the 'immense variety and complexity of our common domestic material culture'. Chapman declared that:

> There has been an important change towards lighter, brighter and simpler furnishing, which is in part a reaction from the styles of a previous generation. Interest in performance is however, little developed, as is

---

[27] Muthesius, H. (1904), *The English House*, reprinted 1979, p. 63.

[28] For an early exploration of this phenomenon, see Lynes, R. (1955), *The Tastemakers: The Shaping of American Popular Taste.*

[29] Bourdieu, P. (1984), *Distinction: a Social Critique of the Judgement of Taste.*

[30] Lee (1993), *Consumer Culture Reborn*, p. 39.

[31] Corrigan, P. (1997), *The Sociology of Consumption*, p. 105.

shown by the small proportion of the total resources spent on equipping the kitchen.[32]

Chapman's data suggested that furniture was not bought with specific function in mind, but selected in terms of style. He thought that this suggested that performance in a mechanical sense was less important than the social and emotional function of furniture,[33] something that retailers had been intuitively aware of for many years. Chapman reflected:

> Perhaps it may be said that the main achievement of the contemporary movement in design is that it has separated the elements of fantasy and performance so that the conflict between them, evident in the work of even the greatest Victorian designers, is resolved.[34]

Although true for the designs of committed functionalists, much of the furniture of the period displays a degree of whimsy, along with underlying performance capability that links fantasy and performance, which is clearly what consumers really want.

Other social science research of the period analysed the processes adopted by consumers in the furnishing of their homes. Lippit's *Determinants of Demand for House Furnishings and Equipment* was an attempt to analyse the structure and nature of furnishing purchasing decisions.[35] Although these appear to be commonsense categories, they are useful as evaluation tools. The major determinant is clearly income and assets. Secondly, the family type and the stage in the cycle of family life will have a great bearing on buying attitudes. Thirdly, the place of residence, nature of the home tenure and the interval since a house move are important variables. The social group associated with the purchasers will affect their aspirations, as will their existing stock of durables. In the latter case, there is a saturation point. These analyses began to assist the process of manufacturing and distributing furniture, something more than making decisions by presumption or, at best, based simply on previous performance. Unfortunately, it seems that they were ignored by much of the trade.

It is clear that at various times during the twentieth century the furniture industry has had to fight for attention in an increasingly competitive market, and other needs have continually taken precedence in the priorities of consumers. The 1983 Design Council Report found that:

> Most people nurture some conception of the 'ideal home' interior, but are prepared to let furniture give way to more immediate needs such as white goods or high performance products like hi-fi or motor cars, and make do with what furniture they already have. For many households, paying for

---

[32] Chapman (1955), The Family, the *Home and Social Status*, p. 91.

[33] Ibid., p. 41.

[34] ibid., p. 93.

[35] Lippit, V. G. (1959), *Determinants of Demand for House Furnishings and Equipment*.

furniture can be difficult, as borrowing money for durables other than furniture is seen to be less self-indulgent.[36]

The average householder often has a greater understanding of technical matters than aesthetic ones; therefore, money will be spent on those areas where results and performance are obvious. The 1983 report again reiterated that the purchasing of furniture tends to become an emotional rather than a rational process.[37]

This comparison between the technical knowledge of customers and their ignorance of aesthetics was demonstrated some years earlier in the advice given to the fictional couple Bill and Betty in 1952. Making the point that consumers must know what they want, it was suggested that Bill would not: 'dream of buying a motorcar which had bad workmanship disguised by window boxes, a half timbered chassis and chromium knobs all over it, but [he] jolly nearly bought a bedroom suite which was just as dishonest in exactly that way'.[38]

Whatever the type of home tenure (rented or bought), the distinction between spaces and their use tells a lot about how perceptions are made about the home, its visitors and family. The continuity of room types (even if their use changed) showed how set in the collective psyche they were. The concepts of privacy, common rooms and specialized rooms develop these distinctions. Whatever the case, residents nearly always appropriated the space, whether in owner-occupied or rented accommodation, to their own ends. The examples of how modern housing estates have been personalized in differing ways[39] and the importance of differentiation in personalizing homes are well known. In 1952 the architect and designer R. D. Russell brought a rare sense of understanding to the question of the public's attitude to design:

> The development of a contemporary vernacular depends first upon finding out what people want and like in the broadest sense. I think they like warm colour and a certain solidity, and although Jacobean reproductions give them these there must be dozens of alternatives, for it is not really Jacobean furniture that people want but furniture that is warm and cosy.[40]

Manufacturers and retailers had always been aware of this. Judy Attfield has commented upon the role of the manufacturer (using the case study of the High Wycombe-based Clarke business) whereby a diverse range of products

---

[36] Design Council (1983), *Report to the Design Council on the Design of British Consumer Goods*, p. 31. See also note 9 above.

[37] Ibid.

[38] Whitechapel Art Gallery (1952), 'Setting up Home for Bill and Betty'.

[39] Pessac and Le Corbusier are well documented. See Boudon, P. (1972), *Live-in Architecture: Le Corbusier's Pessac Revisited*.

[40] Russell, R. D. (1952), 'People want furniture that is warm and cosy', *Design*, 42, June, p. 21. See also Russell, R. D. (1951), 'Furniture today: Tuppence plain: penny coloured'.

becomes an example of the survival of individuality within a modernist attempt to unify style, taste, and design.[41]

The change from a Modernist agenda based on the simple need for shelter to a more complex set of interiors which reflects the identity of the user was 'officially' noticed in the 1961 Parker Morris Report, which considered that:

> There was a time when for the great majority of the population the major significance of the structure in which they made their home was to provide shelter and a roof over their head. This is no longer so. An increasing proportion of people are coming to expect their home to do more than fulfil the basic requirements. It must be something of which they can be proud; and in which they must be able to express the fullness of their lives.[42]

This tends to show the reality of homes and interiors while exposing the indifference to the rational design approach of the Modernists[43] in favour of an emotionally led one which itself is reflected in later post-modern considerations of choice, personality and individuality. This development of the personalization of interiors was fuelled by further changes in how people related to their homes to overcome the alienation that much modern life provided. These changes included the rise of DIY, which equated with a greater degree of control and personal achievement over one's interior, and perhaps reflects an expression of the sense of self-identity.

The role of DIY raises a number of issues in the context of identity and consumption. Identification for self has been mentioned, but issues relating to conjugality by joint involvement in projects, appropriation of territory and its manipulation amount to a range of interesting aspects. This could extend from panelling staircases and doors, running up new curtains to making furniture and built-in fittings.[44] However, it must be said that interiors with an eclectic collection of objects, picked up and selected over a period of time, as a reflection of personal taste, travel and aesthetic judgement are still one of the best ways to represent oneself and one's identity. It is intriguing that retailers have recognized this and offer such objects in-store.

Nevertheless, this appropriation and control of one's own environment and the achievement and expression of self are not only satisfying in their own right but indicate a degree of resistance and opposition to ready-made concepts of the 'ideal.' This does, however, raise an ambiguity.

---

[41] Attfield (1996), 'Give 'em something dark and heavy', pp. 185–201.

[42] *Homes for Today and Tomorrow*, HMSO, 1961, p. 3.

[43] These imposed solutions are well illustrated by the model rooms for workers' housing set up in exhibitions.

[44] Browne, J. (2000), 'Decisions in DIY. Home improvements and advertising in post-war Britain', in Andrews, M. and Talbot, M. (Eds), *All the World and Her Husband*. For an American perspective see Goldstein, C. (1998), *Do It Yourself Home Improvements in 20th Century America*. See also Clarke, A. (2001), in Miller, d. (Ed.) (2001), 'The aesthetics of social aspiration', in *Home Possessions*.

The dilemma between real self-expression and the dictatorship of style and fashion that is posed as an ideal results in conflict. It is much easier to follow the dictates of fashion than to be truly yourself in creating a home. Hence, we see the spectacular success of ready-made and co-ordinated furnishing schemes of varying degrees of sophistication and the equally successful magazines and television programmes that provide 'ideas'. These represent the continuity of reliance upon advice or pre-selection, but the difference now is that they are often used in conjunction with attempts to personalize one's own space.[45]

The dilemma of the continuity of taste and image was noticed in 1983 when the British Design Council commissioned a report on the 'problem' of the state of design in consumer goods. The roots of the difficulty lay in the attitudes of the past:

> A contemporary interior has never been seen in this country [Britain] as a status symbol worth having – unlike Italy, Scandinavia, Germany or US – and this historical fact still holds true. However vehemently denied, the class structure is still influential and most people given a choice would buy 'antique' rather than 'contemporary' – arguing that it would be a safer investment, but in fact acknowledging that we still look to our peers for guidance.[46]

The issues of taste, style and image that reflect personal identity were the subject of much advice throughout the twentieth century.

Furnishing advice

The twentieth century saw the full flowering of home furnishings as a mass business but also as a source of conflict and confusion. Consumers were being exhorted to make interiors that represented themselves individually, whilst at the same time following advice (often very specific) as to how to achieve this desired state of affairs. The plethora of advice and 'how-to' books, and latterly television programmes, demonstrates this.

Consumer advice had been a feature of the nineteenth century, but during the twentieth century the concerted efforts of organized interest groups to spread a particular type or style of furnishing were far more pernicious than the lady-like publications produced for middle-class Victorian homes. The difficulty for many of the advisers and critics of the first half of the twentieth century was that they did not understand the needs of the latest generation of homemakers. The expectations of many consumers did not coincide with the notions of fitness of purpose, truth to materials, simple elegance and plain order that many

---

[45] Chapman (1955), *The Family, the Home and Social Status*, p. 91.

[46] Design Council (1983), *Report to the Design Council on the Design of British Consumer Goods*, p. 30.

advisers suggested.[47] In contrast to this establishment position, often based on tradition, nationalism and continuity of ideals, was the development of Modernist rationalism that turned its back on history. One idea particularly germane to interiors was the planned imposition of order onto apparent chaos or confusion.[48] This 'call to order' was based on the idea that 'less is more', whether in architecture or interior design. The Modernist ideal was one of unity and clarity in architecture and interiors, which made the home a place for contemplation and freedom from distraction. In a lecture delivered in 1931, Marcel Breuer stated implicitly that the architect was in charge of the interior as much as the exterior (and by implication knew best what the consumer needed, but not necessarily, what they wanted):

> In the ideal (or more properly stated the correct) situation, the interior is no longer an independent unit set in the house, but is constructively tied to the building itself – properly speaking it begins with the floor plan rather than after the completion of the building. Only the ideal situation allows for this organic unity that is the completely furnished new construction.[49]

This Modernist theme of standardization and an apparent lack of personal identity was not popular, although initially, any changes in terms of satisfying real and basic needs were considered useful.[50]

For much of the twentieth century the issue of taste was responsible for the confusion. Home furnishings and decoration are bound by many conventions in the design of the home that are more or less *formal* – approved, correct, impersonal, prescribed, rigid, which is of course, regulated taste. Tastemakers and the so-called rules of taste represented these. However, many householders strive to make their spaces *homely* – comfortable, congenial, cosy, familiar, intimate, modest, plain, relaxed, snug, unpretentious or informal.

The value of this furnishing advice was sometimes doubted. In 1899 it was commented that:

> It is true that there is plenty of idealism and scores of pretty furnishing platitudes to be had for a shilling or two, in various art-at-home manuals, but I doubt whether the economical seeker after tasteful furniture is much informed after perusing scores of dreary sentences as to what should constitute the 'House Beautiful'.[51]

However, it seems that the readers of such magazines did not doubt their efficacy, and the illustrated journal and book continued in importance as a home furnishing guide.

---

[47] See, for example, the writings of John Gloag.

[48] Le Corbusier (1925), *The Decorative Arts of Today*, trans. Dunnett, J., 1987.

[49] Lecture published in *Bauwelt*, 7 May 1931, cited in Wilk, C. (1981), *Marcel Breuer: Furniture and Interiors*, p. 184.

[50] This had a greater impact in the 1950s, when the Modernist architectural principles were employed in slum clearance and redevelopment.

[51] *The House* (1899), 5, p. 52.

In addition to journalists, retailers often published illustrated catalogues and estimates for a variety of room types and costings that were aimed at assisting the would-be furniture buyer to select the 'proper' items for the various rooms in the home.

The popularity of estimates prepared by retailers as guidelines for their customers was an important feature of the retail trade during the first third of the twentieth century. An analysis of these estimates shows how there was a consistency of styles that were deemed appropriate to the various rooms within the house across the social scale. They have also shown how the supply of furniture to meet these demands was often based on a selection of high-style objects that were progressively simplified as they descended the scale, so that the image of the style remained identifiable, even if only symbolically. In this way, the consumer's tasteful furnishing would be recognized.[52] The dining room was invariably recommended as furnished with oak, whilst the main bedroom and the hall also had oak as a preferred furniture finish. It was only in the living or drawing room that the choice was between mahogany (the most favoured) and walnut.[53] These estimates and recommendations were used from the late nineteenth century until well into the 1950s, with essentially the same preferences expressed.

The range of critics who continued the nineteenth-century habit of advising 'how to furnish your home' demonstrates this externalizing of the consumption of interiors. To ensure compliance, commentators and reformers usually peppered their advice with imperatives like 'should, ought' and so on, often with the intention, which was not always explicit, of demonstrating that the home was the most important social institution, so any deviation from the norm could be construed as anti-social, or indeed sinful.

Education played a role in this process of establishing norms. The ideas that started at home were often reinforced at school, particularly for girls, with 'model rooms' and domestic science lessons. The great number of journals and books published to help the homeowner 'get it right' also appear to have had a continuing and wide-ranging impact on home design. Consumers welcomed publications that explained how schemes worked and described new materials and techniques of furnishing, and were glad of advvice as to the smooth running of a household. Apart from books and journals, other external factors are at work to try to influence (and therefore change) consumer habits. Advertising, retail stores, exhibitions[54] and similar sites of persuasion ensured that the influences on consumer homemakers maintained ideas and ideals, and told people what was

---

[52] Edwards, C. (1991), 'Furnishing a home at the turn of the century: The use of furnishing estimates from 1875 to 1910', *Journal of Design History*, 4(4), pp. 233–9.

[53] *Woman's Journal Book of Furnishing and Decorating* (1935), May, Waring and Gillow estimates.

[54] For the Ideal Home Exhibition, see Ryan, D. (2000), '"All the world and her husband": The Daily Mail Ideal Home Exhibition 1908–39', in Andrews, M. and Talbot, M. (Eds), *All the World*

new and what they wanted. This was the basis of the cycle of consumption. For a later generation of advisors in the concluding part of the century, the Pandora's Box of freedom of choice was opened wide. For some, tradition and variants upon it ruled. For others, a purist approach was offered. But for most, an eclectic choice was considered – you could be whoever you wanted to be.

Consumption

In the early part of the twentieth century there were many examples of first-time furniture-buyers entering the market, who were benefiting from improved housing and a better economic situation. These people required furniture as a basic proposition. By the mid-century, second and third generations were furnishing homes, and they demanded more than just the essentials – indeed, they actively wanted an improvement on their pasts. Furnishings were now selected not simply for utilitarian purposes but also as symbols of home, and often as a rejection of parental values. Even these consumers had difficulties with choice, as many people were still inexperienced in the purchase of a major product.

Furniture, over and above the strictly utilitarian, has always been a mark of one's position in a social hierarchy. It was no different for the social groups of the twentieth century. Therefore, it is not surprising to find that there was a demand for furniture that emulated past styles, and by inference, conferred some identity of 'respectability' on the owners. However, there was a gradual move away from the historical bias, and this became apparent during the late 1950s and early 1960s. A number of variables came together to encourage an enlargement of the pluralist approach to furniture that allowed for a growing range of tastes that retailers recognized as market niches. These factors included the marriage bulge of a post-war generation, an increase in more housing completions of modern design, the growth of conspicuous spending, and a rise in replacement demand. In conjunction with these consumption factors were better marketing, a wider range of designs, and the introduction of new types of furniture.

These changes promoted segmentation of the marketplace, and further encouraged homeowners to choose furniture that demonstrated their ideas of status and lifestyle. Whilst this choice included reproductions (which have continued in popularity), there were other possibilities. The so-called Contemporary furniture of the 1950s met the demands of a younger furnishing generation, who constituted a growing band of purchasers. In a more limited segment, developments including 'pop furniture' had a passing effect on

---

and Her Husband. Also see Chapman, T. (1999), 'The Ideal Home Exhibition: An analysis of constraints and conventions in consumer choices in British homes', in Hearn, J. and Roseneil, S. (Eds), *Consuming Culture: Power and Resistance,* pp. 69–90.

modern post-war furniture design and consumption, but whilst much of the buying public indulged in design fads for some furniture types, other types remained fairly constant.[55]

The social changes that have occurred in the past century have been immense, and whilst the interest in the home and interiors has grown just as rapidly, the furniture industry has often been criticized for not engaging with these changes. As recently as 1989 it was said that: 'behind the dilatory nature of British furniture retailing, however, lies the unwillingness of manufacturers to capitalise on the social dynamics of the British interior'.[56] These forces are in part the history of changing attitudes to homes and their furnishing.

In conjunction with these factors, there was also growth in the scope and influence of the media that encouraged an interest in all aspects of the home. The impact of these changes on the industry was noted by *The Times* in 1920:

> Without doubt, the greatly increased spending power of the industrial classes has had a direct effect on the furniture trade. The newspapers have played an important part in educating the people in domestic art, and even the lower middle-classes today furnish with intelligence and good taste. All this is good for the trade, because it encourages the designer and craftsman. Future prospects in the furniture trade are good. The volume of trade is assured, and there are grounds for believing that increased attention will be devoted to the study of domestic art. It may be said without fear of contradiction that beautiful homes make for a contented people.[57]

The comments on the role of the media in educating the public (as well as earning advertising revenue), and thereby encouraging purchases, and the last phrase of the passage reflect the foresight of Lord Northcliffe and the *Daily Mail*. His instigation of the Ideal Home Exhibition sponsored by the *Daily Mail* was clever, since it not only produced a display case for consumers to inspect and a market place for the nation's furnishers but it also provided advertising revenue for the newspaper and publicly associated the paper with an important part of the nation's psyche.[58] The slogan chosen for the Ideal Home Exhibition, made the same point as *The Times*'s idea that 'beautiful home makes for a contended people'. It was a quotation from a speech given in 1910 by King George V, who said: 'The foundations of the national glory are set in the homes of the people.' The political-educational agenda, which encouraged people to become homemakers and to spend and invest in the homemaking process, was partly aimed at providing a bulwark against the social unrest that was evident in much of post-World War One Europe.

---

[55] Random examples of fashion in furniture might include vinyl upholstery, fur fabric corner groups, and chrome tube and glass, whilst teak-finish cabinets and white-painted bedroom furniture have remained fairly constantly available over a long period.

[56] *Blueprint*, May 1989, p. 46.

[57] *The Times*, Trade Supplement, 28 February 1920.

[58] Ryan, D. (1997), *The Ideal Home Exhibitions Through the Twentieth Century*.

The political message of the sanctity of home was clear, and could appear to pre-empt Le Corbusier's famous phrase 'Architecture or Revolution'.[59] The importance of the home in society was reiterated in the 1930s, this time by the *Daily Express*: 'for the average British man or women each day begins and ends in the family centre. The influence of a happy harmonious home is therefore a national asset.'[60] In this context of the political emphasis on quality homes, the debate concerning the furnishings of the working-class home was considered in earnest. Immediately after World War One, the *Design and Industries Association's Journal* aired a number of views about the need to supply 'good and cheap' furniture. Interestingly, compared to some European designers the correspondents were aware of the importance of avoiding standardization, to maintain some idea of freedom of choice for the consumer, whilst at the same time providing good -value in furnishings for small homes. In any event, the role of the retailer remained crucial.

The architect Baillie Scott agreed with the sentiments, but he considered that the answer to providing good and cheap furniture was firstly not to produce the 'gaudy and tasteless' items that were generally available. Scott suggested that: 'as long as people can get cheap and flashy smart-looking things to put in their houses they will choose such things'. The consequence was that whilst the 'commercial system of labour and capital pulling in opposite directions persists, so long will it be impossible to produce good work'.[61] His second point was that the organization of the industry should be based on some Utopian guild system that was free of the profit motive.[62] According to Scott, this would then naturally encourage good work. These ideals, rooted as they were in the Arts and Crafts Movement, were a long way from the realities of providing furniture for working-class homes. The retailers were fully aware that the 'gaudy and tasteless' items criticized by Baillie Scott sold well. In September 1913, *The Cabinet Maker* could say:

> Many of our readers in the North cater to a very large extent for the needs of the working classes, the hundreds of thousands who, in spite of what demagogues may tell us to the contrary, are at present more prosperous that ever before. They have money to spend, and a fair proportion of it is spent on the furnishings of their homes. They make no great demands for things aesthetic, but are anxious to buy something showy at prices suited to their purses.[63]

The priorities of other retailers were nicely expressed in 1911 when the middle-class *The House* magazine described a shop that claimed to pay 'special

---

[59] Le Corbusier (1927), *Towards a New Architecture*, p. 13.

[60] *Daily Express* (1935), *The Home of Today*.

[61] Baillie Scott (1918), 'Good and Cheap', *Journal of the Design and Industries Association*, reprinted in Benton, Benton and Sharp (Eds) (1975), *Form and Function*, p. 25.

[62] See also Chapter 5, note 10.

[63] *Cabinet Maker*, 20 September 1913.

attention to the requirements of the gentleman, and especially of the lady, who desired a home pervaded by comfort and refinement'. It asserted that: 'in producing its new styles it did not seek to overload with ornament, but first to be novel, second to be practical and third to be comfortable.'[64] The sales pitch firstly stressed newness, secondly, use and thirdly, bodily comforts. Each new style was offering particular features, advantages and benefits.

How the furniture was used in the home was another matter. In 1910 Mrs M. E. Loane noticed how working-class families were tempted to buy:

> Furniture, which they can afford to pay for, but certainly cannot afford to use. The blinds must not be drawn up because the carpet will fade; the gas must not be lighted because it will blacken the ceiling; the window must not be opened because the air may tarnish the frame of the looking glass; the chimney must be blocked up lest the rain should fall and rust the fender. Finally, the door must be locked on the outside.[65]

For these consumers World War One was a watershed in many ways. The *Annual Report of the Liverpool Settlement* for 1917 noted how many Liverpool housewives had:

> tasted the joys of home making for the first time during the war. They have become possessed of furniture beyond the bare limits of necessity. Some have even committed the extravagance of buying a piano and in the process severely shocked a number of people ... who have never been without one.[66]

The purchase of a piano appeared to denote respectability and advancement, even if it was purchased on credit, and the pleasures the working classes appeared to derive from this spending, and the apparent confidence this gave, clearly appeared to upset the status quo. In 1924 the *Cabinet Maker* noted that:

> A large number of people have discovered the joys of personal furnishing and most of the educational propaganda affecting the general public has encouraged the idea of self-expression in the choice and arrangement of furniture.[67]

Despite the remarks about self-expression, the furnishings still reflected old habits. A guide written in 1925 for Co-operative Society salesmen made some suggestions about furnishing the kitchen:

> We should also have a couch in the kitchen, which may be of birch, and upholstered and covered in carriage repp ... A pair of small size easy chairs,

---

[64] Cited in Briggs (1956), *Friends of the People*, p. 182.

[65] Mrs Loane (1910), *Neighbours and Friends*, pp. 152–3, cited in Daunton, M. J. (1983), *House and Home in the Victorian City*.

[66] Briggs (1956), *Friends of the People*, p. 136. It has been suggested that the working-class piano purchasing power approximately doubled between 1850 and 1914 due, in part, to hire purchase systems; Ehrlich, C. (1976), *The Piano: A History*, cited in Daunton (1983), *House and Home in the Victorian City*.

[67] *Cabinet Maker*, 12 January 1924.

covered to match the couch or a gents steady armchair and a ladies rocking chair similarly covered would make up a very suitable kitchen suite.[68]

For particular social groups who were purchasing furniture, there was a need to acquire brand new items, especially a three-piece suite, these being seen as the marker of the setting up of a new home.[69] The three-piece suite, which had originated in the nineteenth century, symbolizes unity, taste and order compared to the fragmented furnishings, which may suggest temporary situations, waiting and so on, and a sense of being incomplete. Furniture such as unit and add-on systems was not as successful as suites, as these were often seen as 'ambiguous pieces, of changeable function and therefore of uncertain identity'.[70] The retailers encouraged the purchase of suites, which was deprecated by Modernist critics: 'Dealers will always sell their furniture in suites or "rooms" with selected pieces sold altogether. The crucial factor for every range is a common style. Naturally, this leads the furniture industry astray into crass formalism, as in every industry relying on "ranges".'[71]

Interestingly, the advice to salesmen in Co-operative stores in 1925 followed a more adventurous path (in contrast to the advice about kitchen furnishings above):

> The tendency today is to furnish the drawing room not with a set suite, but with various oddments that will blend and not look out of place ... we can get a nice combination of dainty comfort without the feeling of stiffness, which so often pertains to a drawing room.[72]

Nevertheless, the three-piece suite continued to be the butt of many commentators. In 1935 L. Yakobson wrote: 'Mental laziness, the lack of independent judgement, these it is that lead to the purchase of complete suites of furniture, and the quasi-individualism of the petit bourgeois triumphs.'[73] Despite these criticisms, for a generation that had often only known the second-hand and the homespun, the three-piece suite represented the height of respectability and social prestige.

The continual rise of a suburban culture, influenced in its furnishing tastes in part by the upper class, meant that the demand for reproduction antique furniture was always high.[74] The evidence of furnishing estimates clearly

---

[68] Haigh (1925), *Furniture and Hardware*, p. 120.

[69] The market research of Odhams in the 1960s showed that socio-economic groups C1, C2 and D were purchasing three-piece suites in greater quantity, whilst groups AB purchased many more single easy chairs. Odhams Press, *Woman and the National Market: Furniture and Furnishings*, p. 10.

[70] Putnam, T. and Newton, C. (Eds) (1990), *Household Choices*, p. 92.

[71] Lotz, W. (1927), 'Suites of Furniture', *Die Form*, II, cited in Benton, Benton and Sharp, *Form and Function,* p. 229.

[72] Haigh (1925), *Furniture and Hardware*, p. 118.

[73] Yacobson, L. (1935), 'Standard furniture', *Design for Today*.

[74] See Attfield, J. (2000), 'Continuity: Authenticity and the paradoxical nature of reproduction', in *Wild Things: The Material Culture of Everyday Life*.

shows what retailers thought people expected particular rooms to look like. It really should be no surprise to find that any design changes that occurred in high-style furniture during this period, should remain at best a source to be plundered, rather than a new direction. Whether it was 'Modern', 'Traditional', 'Art Deco' and so on, they could all be bastardized to suit a price bracket or style change for a particular retailer or manufacturer's range.

This choice was seen by some commentators as one that would be gradually eroded to a standardized format. Aldous Huxley, writing some 'Notes on Decoration' (1930), concluded that when furnishing, 'people of moderate means' have to choose between 'affectedly refined cottage decoration' or 'the sort of decoration they can buy at the big shops – some of it fairly good (and dear), but most of it either dear and bad, or cheap and bad'. Huxley then cites the example of a third alternative that was available to German homemakers. This was the modern, standardized, utilitarian furniture, mainly in metal, which seemed destined to become the 'domestic bliss of all but a very few rich people in the future. The time I am sure is not far off when we shall go for our furniture to the nearest Ford or Morris agent.'[75] In fact, standardized utilitarian furniture was just what the majority wanted to avoid, as many found that the 'refined cottage decoration' went very well with their ideas of 'good furnishings' and their self-image.

Whilst it found some approval at an institutional level, the ideal of machine-made 'democratic' furniture was in direct conflict with the cultural values that were being adopted by the British working classes. The attacks on Victorian reproduction design and interiors effectively attacked the working-class structure. Whilst good modern design could be economic, stylish and functional, and therefore considered suitable for the working class by reformers, it ignored the issue of identity and differentiation within class sub-groups that remained the mainstay of working-class design choices for many years.

Whilst standardized ranges were clearly perceived as being the most useful for the lowest income groups, the design of recommended products in this class was questioned. In 1937 an exhibition was held by the British Council for Art and Industry, entitled 'Home: Its Furniture and Equipment'. The objects on display included stove-enamelled metal bedsteads, a suite comprising a sideboard, a chest of drawers and a table made from oak-veneered plywood, and dining chairs of polished oak wood. Other chairs included unpolished Windsor wheel-back or stick-back chairs and rush-seated chairs. The upholstery was recommended to be small-scale and wooden-framed rather than fully upholstered. Apart from normal sofas and chairs, bed-settees were shown along with reclining chairs and extending bed-chairs. These well-meaning products did not stand comparison with their more expensive companions:

---

[75] Huxley, A. (1930), 'Notes on Decoration', *The Studio*, October.

Assuming that the exhibition accurately reflects what is to be had at the moment in this, the cheapest end of the mass-production market, it is remarkable what a difference there is between the minimum suite (i.e. affordable by families with an income of £3.00 per week) and the other rooms on exhibition furnished up to the (£5 a week income) maximum standard.[76]

It was clear that the cheapest end of the market was least well served, and the report recognized this by saying that: 'the planning of mass-produced furniture seems to call for fresh study'. Fresh study did not really interest the industry, as it seemed that the furniture trade's existing products were able to meet a wide variety of demands that covered the whole spectrum of taste.

The political interest in homes and their furnishings, already alluded to, particularly for the less well-off, was reflected in a small way by the involvement of local councils in supplying furniture. One of the results of slum clearance was that families would often not have enough furniture to utilize in the new property. In the 1930s the trade press was aware of the plight of council house tenants: 'it is not an exaggeration to say … that at least 25% of these houses have little or no furniture in their front room … The occupants commence housekeeping with the barest necessities; later they may acquire a sideboard, a little later perhaps a three-piece suite.'[77] Under the Housing (Scotland) Act of 1925, local authorities had powers to supply furniture to tenants who had difficulty providing for themselves. Prior to 1940 about 10 per cent of Scottish local authorities provided some moveable furniture, mostly under hire purchase arrangements, although some authorities supplied it free of charge, 'chiefly in cases where the tenant's own furniture or bedding had to be destroyed because it was verminous'.[78]

The Scottish local authorities recommended essential furniture as follows in order of priority: beds and bedding; tables, chairs, chests, floor coverings. In addition, essential built-in storage was listed. Non-essential items included suites of moveable furniture, rugs, heaters, and electrical appliances. The Scottish Housing Advisory Committee, in their report published in 1944, noted that:

Provision of such items [standard equipment] will not, however, of itself suffice to make the house a home and for this purpose what we call non-standard equipment i.e. moveable furniture and furnishings will, of course, also be required and we have to consider how best local authorities can utilise their powers under the Act of 1925 for this purpose.[79]

This cold official acknowledgment of what might make 'the house a home' is revealing.

---

[76] Minimum Standard (1937), *Art and Industry*, 23, p. 66.

[77] *Cabinet Maker*, 23 August 1930.

[78] Elsas, M. J. (1947), *Housing and the Family*, p. 105.

[79] Scottish Housing Advisory Committee on the Design and Planning and Furnishing of New Homes (1944), *Planning our New Homes*, p. 72.

The 1936 Housing Act, Section 72(2), authorized English local authorities to supply new furniture to tenants on hire purchase terms. Not only did this usually ensure a reasonable supply of furniture, it also avoided excessive hire purchase interest charges. For example, St Helens allowed up to £11, Chesterfield, £12 and Blackburn up to £18, although in the latter case the furniture remained the property of the Council.[80]

These concerns continued after World War Two. In 1945 the Board of Trade Social Survey recommended a minimum standard of furniture. This was based on one bed per person, one straight chair per person, half an easy chair per person, one-third of a wardrobe per person, half a dressing table or chest of drawer, one table used for eating per family, and one kitchen cabinet per family.[81] Whether this minimum standard was enough to counteract any revolutionary tendencies of the tenants, it was clear that similar considerations were still in mind in 1951 when Mayor Darst of St Louis, USA, wrote to his city's aldermen saying that if everyone had good housing: 'no one in the United States would need to worry today about the threat of communism in this country. Communists love American slums. Our clearance of these slums and erection of adequate housing is one of the most effective answers we can give communism locally.'[82]

This American dream of home ownership was not only about consuming practice but also about being seen to consume. In 1940 the editor of the *Ladies Home Journal* reported upon the average-income 'Gillespie family' of West Virginia, who still had an unused best room: '… no matter how bad [times may become], the plush upholstery in the front room will be taboo, so it won't wear shabby, and the huge Masonic emblem on the mantle will get dusted and the flowery rug … [will be] duly swept'.[83]

In England the same attitudes existed, although they were restrained to some extent by the political and financial checks that were placed upon homemaking in the period up to the 1950s. During World War Two and its aftermath, the Utility scheme was introduced into the United Kingdom.[84]

Hailed by some as the great opportunity finally to change the course of furniture design, but by others as bureaucratic interference in an industry quite capable of looking after itself, it was received with ambivalence by the customers it was designed for. It is little wonder that it did not survive much beyond the emergency period. The furniture produced under the scheme was ultimately the response to a peculiar situation, and could not be expected to act

---

[80] Jeremiah (2000), *Architecture and Design for the Family*, p. 120, note 45.

[81] Board of Trade (1945), *Social Survey*.

[82] Mayor Darst Papers cited in Glickman, L. B. (1999), 'The commodity gap: Consumerism and the modern home', in *Consumer Society in American History: A Reader,* p. 300.

[83] *Ladies Home Journal* (1940), August, pp. 68–70, cited in Gordon, J. and McArthur, J. (1959), 'Popular culture, magazines and American domestic interiors, 1898–1940', *Journal of Popular Culture*, 22(4), p. 52.

[84] For the Utility Scheme, see Geffrye Museum (1974), *CC41 Utility Furniture and Fashion*, and Attfield, J. (Ed.) (1999b), *Utility Reassessed: The Role of Ethics in the Practice of Design*.

as a catalyst for major changes in attitudes to furnishing. The problem for Utility was clearly expressed in a contemporary article. In the *Architectural Review* (January 1943), a comparison between Utility furniture and council housing was interestingly made. It was pointed out that even if the council houses were well made and equipped, well above 'jerry-built' standards, the perceived stigma adhering to a council house remained. The article suggests that it is the bare institutional look of the houses that 'spoiled its chances'. They feared the same for furniture, recognizing that all objects are culturally meaningful. Developing the idea further, the article went on to acknowledge the reasons why people rejected ideas of 'good design'. The author noted that: 'the public at large has never accepted this tenet [honesty in design], and so long as furniture looks austere and institutional as the Board of Trade's [Utility], the majority of the forced purchasers will, at their very first opportunity, return to the wildly-grained H.P. walnut suite with stuck-on moulded ornaments'.[85] Richard Hoggart identified the same idea retrospectively when he said: 'it was not difficult to guess that working-class people would go back, as soon as they no longer had to buy Utility furniture, to the highly polished and elaborate stuff the neon-strip stores sell'.[86]

Social scientists and other commentators saw that improvements in home furnishings were only part of a wider programme of change that was rooted in educational improvements. The education of consumers was part of this agenda. Of course, for many years domestic science classes had trained girls in the basics of housewifery, but by the post-war period they were offering additional considerations. For example, Chapman (1949) urged that education for family living should include the aesthetic and functional elements of domestic life to overcome the 'intuition and a debased tradition' that formed judgements about the home.[87] In practical terms, Jack Pritchard floated the idea of a pool of furniture that could be renewed every six months, which would be offered to about 350 schools equipped with 'model flats'. These flats would have sitting rooms that students could furnish as they chose, selecting from the pool. The Furniture Development Council accepted the idea but it was opposed by educationalists as it gave a free choice rather than offering just the expertly chosen designs![88] Yet again, the commercial and the didactic were in opposite camps. The world of working-class aspirations registered the notion of respectability as an important issue, and notions of good and bad design rarely entered the discussion. The role of 'proper' furniture was indicative of appropriateness, with a specific function, or at least a dual and often disguised secondary function, such as a bed settee.

---

[85] *Architectural Review* (1943), 43, January, p. 4.

[86] Hoggart, R. (1957), *The Uses of Literacy*, p. 144.

[87] Ibid., p. 34.

[88] Pritchard, J. C. (1984), *View From a Long Chair*, p. 149. See also Pritchard, J. C. (1953–4), 'Raising the standard', *Decorative Arts*, 53, pp. 7–13.

This did not mean that interest in improving the design of furniture for consumers had been exhausted. The Board of Trade report of 1946 commented quite sincerely that:

> We accept the view that a very large proportion of the furniture made in this country before the war was of poor design and we cannot say too strongly that we feel that the inhabitants of our industrial towns should not be fobbed off with ugly things because they live in squalid surroundings, and because for the moment many will accept such things as natural.[89]

Interest also took the form of market research and analysis to discover why 'ugly things' were considered natural and why certain styles were popular. In 1945 the Social Survey conducted an investigation on behalf of the Council of Industrial Design to gauge public taste. This was a crude experiment using four photographs of a plain, fairly modern wardrobe, an old-fashioned model and two ultra-modern items to offer a choice. They found that the old-fashioned model was liked by 45 per cent of the sample because it 'looked strong' and was an 'attractive colour – dark oak'.[90] They also suggested that the generation up to age 34, as well as higher wage earners, preferred modern Utility-like designs. Any retailer worth his salt could have said that.

The *Working Party Report* (1946) tried to analyse the consumer's requirements in a slightly more rigorous way. Based on a very small sample, it found that criticism of pre-war furniture was not surprisingly related to (a) design, (b) quality, (c) size and weight (d) function and (e) the use of built-in furniture. In the case of design, over a third of those questioned (116 returns out of 350) criticized pre-war furniture for having 'too many frilly bits, too much carving, too much fancy work, too ornate, over-embellished, too many twists, showy meaningless decoration'.[91] Whereas quality was not generally criticized, except in the case of 'cheap furniture', the bulky nature of many pre-war items was critically received. The Report perceptively saw that there was to be 'considerable scope for the introduction of lighter furniture'. Clearly, then, the trade had been advised that there was to be a probable demand for lighter, more modern furniture once some normality had returned to the situation.

Whilst there was an obvious liking for suites as symbols, their use also revealed a desire for harmony in furnishing schemes, which was perhaps difficult to achieve with no prior knowledge of composition using colour and pattern. Again, the report suggested that the development of unit furniture might enable a harmonious look to be achieved without necessarily buying a suite. Indeed, this must have been the case when individual upholstery and cabinet pieces could be harmonized, often from the same supplier.

---

[89] *Working Party Report* (1946), p. 111.

[90] Social Survey (1945), *Furniture: An Enquiry Made by the Board of Trade*, May, p. 20.

[91] *Working Party Report* (1946), p. 199.

For the retailer and consumer alike, the constraints of the Utility scheme were shed gladly when the scheme was dismantled, but this did not mean a golden age for home furnishings. During the post-war revival there was an explosive growth in the range of consumer goods that competed directly with furniture. Between 1948 and 1964 the proportion of total consumer spending, taken up by all consumer durable goods – including furniture, motorcars, radios and electrical goods – *nearly doubled, but the proportion spent on furniture and floor coverings remained static.*[92]

In 1949 newlyweds' priorities were to furnish the bedroom (a third to half of resources), followed by the dining room (less than one third), followed, if affordable, by the lounge.[93] Consumers, despite all the advice, reflect the piecemeal establishment of the home in the lack of any serious planning of interiors. In some cases purchases were spontaneous. It was reported in one research programme that seven out of ten of those purchasers interviewed had 'taken a fancy to an item', rather than coming to like it after having seen it a few times.[94]

By the early 1950s Contemporary or Modern styles were to be seen in many stores, and the success of unitized ranges such as G-Plan and Meredew illustrate how the idea of 'growing' a room by adding components as they became affordable was a useful sales technique as well as a consumer advantage. An advertisement from 1956 for G-Plan explains: 'When you furnish the G-Plan way, you are free from the tyranny of the clumsy old-fashioned three-piece suite; you assemble your own individual room arrangements … combine them as you please to make your own attractive groups.'[95]

Despite the commonsense approach of the Modernist commentators, there were design pundits who considered that the 'general public think that an article with a lot of carving and elaborate work on it must be more valuable than something that is plainer and simpler'. R. D. Russell was one designer who brought a rare sense of understanding to the question of the public's attitude to design:

> The development of a contemporary vernacular depends first upon finding out what people want and like in the broadest sense. I think they like warm colour and a certain solidity, and although Jacobean reproductions give them these there must be dozens of alternatives, for it is not really Jacobean furniture that people want but furniture that is warm and cosy.[96]

---

[92] Consumer Council (1965), *Furniture Trade and the Consumer*, July.

[93] Chapman, D. (1949), *Families: Their Needs and Preferences in the Home*, p. 20.

[94] Associated Rediffusion (1962–3), *London Profiles*, p. 16.

[95] MacDonald, S. and Porter, J. (1990), *Putting on the Style: Setting up Home n the 1950s*, unpaginated, 'Traditional Values' section.

[96] Russell, R. D. (1952), 'People want furniture that is warm and cosy', p. 21. See also Russell (1950), 'Furniture today'.

This notion of the 'warm and cosy', with its overtones of human occupancy over time, was clearly more popular than a rigidly defined and designed look, and indeed remains so for many people.

An interesting example of a kind of market research that reflects Russell's comments was carried out by the DIA. In 1953 it set up two contrasting room sets in an exhibition that was called 'Register Your Choice'. Although both were furnished with current furniture, one was in a conventional style while the other was in a contemporary look. The preferences expressed showed that the 'contemporary' room was considered 'cultured' or 'bohemian', whilst the traditional room was seen as 'suburban' or 'cosy and everyday'. Paul Reilly, commenting on the exhibition, made a number of interesting points that illustrate the distinctions between the cosy and the stylish. He noted how, although both rooms were equipped with furniture and fittings that were available at the same time, the more contemporary look had a 'designed' feel about it, whilst he saw the other room as an 'assemblage'. This does perhaps reflect the distinction between the reality of many homes that are based on accretions of objects, compared to the designerly ideal of new and complete schemes that are furnished in one go. It also reflects the idea that identity is developed, not purchased. A revealing sidelight on the exhibition, and one that Reilly considered significant, was the identification of the National Association of Retail Furnishers with the exhibition.[97] This was an early example of the recognition that public relations efforts were of great importance in giving consumers more confidence in retail furniture shops and stores, whatever designs were required.

Two other examples of furniture promotion at this time are useful, as the distinctions between the two venues reveal something of their agenda. The Whitechapel Art Gallery's 'Setting up Home for Bill and Betty' exhibition of 1952[98] was an example of the didactic Modernist approach to 'good taste and contemporary furnishings'. In that show the organizers used products from high-style makers such as Hille, Finmar, HK, Meredew, and R. S. Stevens. All these suppliers were from a more costly bracket than those selected by the Council of Industrial Design for a show flat at the 1955 Ideal Home Exhibition. The Council used furniture supplied by a high street retailer, chosen by ballot, in this case Williams Furniture Galleries of Kilburn. Not surprisingly, the selection of items, all of restrained contemporary design, included Stag and Loughborough Cabinet Company bedroom furniture, the Jason chair by Kandya, and Goodearl dining chairs, combined with a Reynolds Woodware sideboard and table.[99]

It was thought in the 1950s, that the democratizing role of 'good design' would have a levelling effect on society. One of the most important influences in trying to achieve this was the continuing support of women's magazines.

---

[97] Reilly, P. (1953), 'Same room, same cost', *Design*, April, p. 10.

[98] Whitechapel Art Gallery (1952), 'Setting Up Home for Bill and Betty', exhibition catalogue.

[99] Gundrey, E. and Gundrey, W. (1955), 'Home for Four', *Design*, 75, March, pp. 9–16.

The change from the wartime 'make do and mend' attitudes to an educational role for the new generation of purchasers was provided by magazines in articles and features that discussed the purchase of new furniture on a low budget. In 1949 Chapman noted that salesmen remarked on young couples' tastes, which he thought had come from women's magazines.[100] This is to some extent confirmed by the market research and subsequent editorial material published by women's magazines. McDermott quotes Mary Grieve, editor of *Woman* magazine, who claimed that the public acceptance of a modern look for the home was derived from the initiatives of the home editors of magazines such as her own.[101] The emphasis these magazines placed on ordinary couples helped the buyers to identify themselves and to begin to relate to the experiences described, rather than read the advice of erudite pundits.

The role of the BBC had been important in promoting design matters in the 1930s; it continued to be so in the post-war period. The Corporation supported the CoID index, and often used approved furniture for studio settings. Bearing in mind that 90 per cent of the populace had access to television by 1959, this was a good medium to deliver the message. However, a research survey carried out in 1962 showed that in response to the question 'Have you ever noticed any furniture you liked on television, either in the programme or on the advertising', only 30 per cent said 'Yes'.[102] Wherever ideas were coming from, the retailer remained the main channel, but did not always have an unconstrained influence.

In 1957 Meade wrote a clear attack on unscrupulous salesmen and high-pressure methods of selling furniture to families that could not afford it and for whom it is usually unsuitable. The case of a family persuaded to buy a cocktail cabinet (with an automatic light in the lid, although the house had no electricity) that then kept bread in the cabinet is admittedly extreme, but it helped to prove Meade's point.[103] Rather more naively, she deplored the fact that furniture was 'mass-produced' especially for this market and was designed for show: 'ostentatious, ornate and polished to a mirror finish'.[104] The problem was that homemaking advisers often never understood that the images of modern interiors put forward as exemplars often seemed like improvisation to many families. The furniture made like orange boxes, the hessian fabric on the walls, the scrubbed plain wood floors, all seemed temporary and makeshift compared to real 'proper' furniture.[105] This attitude was clearly understood by

---

[100] Chapman, D. (1949) 'Families: their needs and preferences in the home'.

[101] MacDermott, C. (1982), 'Popular taste and contemporary design', in Sparke, P., *Did Britain Make It?*, p. 21.

[102] Ibid. See also Jones, M. (2003), 'Design and the domestic persuader: Television and the British Broadcasting Corporation's promotion of post-war "good design"', *Journal of Design History*, 16(4), pp. 307–18.

[103] Meade, D. (1957), 'Furnishing by hire purchase', *Design*, 104, August.

[104] Ibid.

[105] See Morley, C. (1990), 'Homemakers and design advice in the postwar period', in Putnam, T. and Newton, C., *Household Choices*, p. 92.

Richard Hoggart. His perception of the working-class taste of the mid-1950s showed how:

> They are nearest of all, though, to the prosperous, nineteenth century middle-class style; the richness showing well and undisguisedly in an abundance of odds-and-ends in squiggles and carvings in bold patterns, a mélange whose unifying principle is the sense of an elaborate and colourful sufficiency.[106]

However, the mass market had definite ideas of its own as to how to furnish. This was noticed by Richard Hoggart, who declared that: 'chain store modernismus, all bad veneer and spray-on varnish stain is replacing the old mahogany; multi-coloured plastic and chrome biscuit barrels and birdcages have come in. This is more than keeping up with the Joneses; these things subserve the domestic values full and rich.'[107] Hoggart thought that home making was changing for the worse. His melancholy considerations continued: 'in homes, the new things are absorbed into the kind of whole instinctively reached after. The old tradition is being encroached upon here as in many other areas.'[108]

Although the problem of competition with other consumer goods had a regular airing, the fragmented nature of the British trade denied many collective attempts at influencing consumption. By 1956 the chairman of the Furniture Development Council pointed out that: 'the volume of furniture bought measured against size of population, has during the last few years averaged less than 75% of the pre-war (1938) figure'. This attitude to furniture by British consumers can perhaps be most clearly seen in the furniture's life expectancy. In 1964 the average replacement period for a three-piece suite was 19 years, and a bedroom suite an astonishing 37 years.[109] Comparing these with figures from the 1950s in the United States, where purchase rates then were on a 16-year cycle for living room furniture, and an 18-year cycle for bedroom furniture,[110] an assessment of the relative importance to furnishings given by the two markets can be made.

By the early 1960s some critics had caught up with the popular mood and had begun to denounce the 'official' good design attitudes. Reyner Banham, for example, declared that the Council of Industrial Design approved 'rubbish', and Stephen Spender pointed out the impersonal nature of serious, simple, functional design.[111] Although these intellectuals had their own agendas, it is clear that furnishing decisions have to be made by individuals, and the interior

---

[106] Hoggart (1957), *The Uses of Literacy*, p 123.

[107] Ibid., p. 22.

[108] Ibid., p. 26.

[109] Consumer Council (1965), *Furniture Trade and the Consumer*, p. 8.

[110] Skinner, W. and Rogers, D. (1968), *Manufacturing Policy in the Furniture Industry*, Figure 24.

[111] Whiteley, N. (1987), 'Semi-works of Art', *Furniture History*, 23, p. 110.

then becomes a statement of the owner. The successful designers and retailers recognized this. The *Architectural Review* highlighted the problem of the remoteness of designers from everyday life. They insisted that some form of co-operation was the only successful way forward so that retailers and designers would be able to work together to help the consumer. It was hopeless to expect the customer, who had very limited experience, to use skills such as specification, value analysis, visual judgement, wear estimation and ageing characteristics to make accurate decisions.[112] The disjunction between the tastemakers and the public was evident in an earlier passage from the magazine *Design*, the mouthpiece of the Council of Industrial Design:

> Their first [mistake] is that they fight shy of open-plan living. As a nation, we like our privacy, and there is a strong tendency to shelter behind net curtains. Large windows are obscured by elaborate drapes and heavy pelmets, by dressing table mirrors and large settees. Corners are cut off by diagonally placed wardrobes and sideboards. By careful arranging and draping, the open plan houses are being closed up again, light rooms are darkened and a feeling of spaciousness is reduced to cosy clutter ... The pity is, I think, that in preventing others from seeing into their houses, people are preventing themselves from seeing out; in achieving cosiness they are completely at variance with the architects' achievements in giving them light and space.[113]

Figure 8.1   Hatfield New Town show house, 1950s bedroom

---

[112] *Architectural Review*, (1967), 141, February, p. 158.

[113] Meade, D. (1957) 'Furnishing in the new towns' *Design*, 98, February, p. 43. See also Russell (1952), 'People want warm and cosy furniture', p. 21.

Figure 8.2   Hatfield New Town show house, 1950s dining room

Interestingly, the commentator continued by looking to the retailer as a source of advice for the consumer, with the spin-off being more business for the stores involved:

> The local furnishing retailers are letting a golden opportunity slip by. A really go ahead retailer, familiar with the new houses he is helping to furnish, with a wide knowledge of the modern furniture market, and with a real enthusiasm for helping to raise standards would find the field open for a flourishing concern.[114]

The reality was rather different. A furniture salesman working in Sheratons, the first furniture shop to be established in Harlow New Town in the 1950s, reflected that:

> You didn't have to sell furniture; it was just a matter of being able to supply it. We used to do hire purchase and cash but the vast majority of our business was hire purchase ... They bought what was going in the shop at a price they could afford. It's difficult to realise today how hard it was for families then to maintain a front room with a three-piece suite, dining set and television all on hire purchase.[115]

However, some retailers were attempting to rise to the challenge. Sheratons themselves furnished showhouses for the Harlow Development Corporation

---

[114] Meade (1957), 'Furnishing in the new towns', p. 44.

[115] Cited in Attfield, J. (1989), 'Inside Pram Town: A case study of Harlow house interiors', in Attfield, J. and Kirkham P., *A View from the Interior: Women and Design*, p. 223.

that emphasized a light, modern and open approach to furnishings. Another furnishing group, William Perring, also established stores in new towns (as well as operating in traditional high streets) and offered contemporary furnishings. Perrings also developed a set of brochures for homemakers that included catalogues, scaled paper for room planning, complete with scaled furniture cut-outs designed to assist in preparing some ideas before purchasing.

Nevertheless, the problems of furnishing were still very real for many. In a revealing survey of furnishing problems on new housing estates in Manchester undertaken in 1960, it was found that space and incompatible furniture sizes were still a major impediment: 'We found that bedroom suites were frequently split up because the bedrooms were so small, with the bed and dressing table in one room and the wardrobe in another.'[116]

In addition, the implications of 'going into debt' meant that many families chose to put up with what they had rather than buy new. For example, the Manchester survey found that one family had newspaper on the floor in the bathroom, another had 'practically no furniture', whilst another bought second-hand items. For those who did buy new, there were often financial strains. One respondent had a 'sparsely furnished home with nothing in the living room except two armchairs, but they said they would not take on hire purchase because they were afraid of getting into debt. Conversely another family admitted they had "to go into a lot of debt" over furniture and a neighbour reported that although their home was "like a palace" she often "comes begging for a cup of tea".'[117] The importance of status goods, as exemplified by the cocktail cabinet example above, remained: 'One family were buying four beds, two double and two single, on hire purchase, and "a very grand" radiogram and a piano from the same firm, with a weekly payment of £2.10.0. The daughter had then given up piano lessons "so it's no use to any of us" said the mother cheerfully.'[118]

For other socio-economic groups the 1960s were partly based on a 'throwaway culture' and a reversal of traditional attitudes to the home. The rise of a youth market that was anxious for a new and exciting approach to home furnishings was one manifestation of this. It was also a period in which a wide variety of stylistic ranges were offered to the various markets that were identified. To satisfy this new market with its eclectic tastes and heightened design awareness, the rise of Habitat, for example, seems in retrospect an inevitable response to the furnishing needs of the new youth. The combination of pine and tubular steel, bentwood and Victorian revivals, with the rise of bright colour and stain, as well as the more exotic paper and plastic furniture,

---

[116] Manchester and Salford Council of Social Service (1960), *Setting up House: Furnishing Problems on New Housing Estates*, p. 16.

[117] Ibid.

[118] Ibid.

Figure 8.3 John Perring, Home Planner Kit, 1960s

created a style that was clearly of its time. However, the Habitat niche was not everyone's aspiration: in 1970 marketing consultants had estimated that nearly half of the population seemed to have wanted the 'middle-of-the-road' G-Plan in their home.[119]

The 1980s was a period when a wide variety of style ranges were offered to the various disparate markets that had begun to be identified. The idea of a single ruling taste had changed. Even a ruling taste that could be watered down to represent high styles was disintegrating. Taste became a matter of lifestyle, which also reflected age and social class.

Despite these new markets and initiatives, the continuing decline in the real value of spending on furniture can be seen when, between 1980 and 1988, the percentage of consumer durable expenditure on furniture went from 27 per cent to 19 per cent. Expressed as a percentage of total consumer expenditure, furnishings fell from 3.3 per cent to 2.5 per cent in the period.[120]

In 1990 a report by the Director of the Office of Fair Trading again found that there was still much for consumers to find fault with. Interestingly, furniture ranked third in the scale of problems relating to purchase; first came cars, then appliances, followed by furniture.[121] As furniture was not people's first priority, the result was that many people put off the furniture-buying decisions until they were triggered by an event. The Report discussed the quality of advice and information available, order payment and delivery problems, questions of quality, and any redress available for breaches of promise or contract. Unfortunately, half of all purchases made gave rise to some problems for the consumers interviewed.[122]

The customers' understanding of the nature of furniture-buying is clearly shown in the 1990 research. The results should not be surprising. In the case of self-assembly furniture, good value was considered the most important attribute, closely followed by satisfactory strength. In the case of cabinets, appearance was put first, followed by value, and for upholstery, comfort was again followed by value for money. It is clear that the combination of appropriate function was closely followed by price considerations, while design and colour were not considered so important.

The research also found that some 84 per cent of the respondents thought that 'you really get what you pay for', presumably related to the high response (76 per cent) that 'a lot of furniture is very poorly made these days.' The problems of customer education and useful advice were clearly confirmed by a

---

[119] *Management Today*, June 1970, p. 166.

[120] Design Council (1990), *Domestic Furniture,* pamphlet for trade use. The percentage of total consumer spending on furniture and furnishings from 1938 onwards remained between 3 and 4 per cent (EIU).

[121] See also the comment made in 1925 in *The Modern Priscilla Home Furnishing Book*, note 9 above and note 36 above.

[122] Office of Fair Trading (1990), *Furniture and Carpets: A Report.*

figure of 61 per cent who thought that 'people have problems because they choose something unsuitable for their needs'.[123]

The recent past has seen an even greater concentration of attention on domestic furnishings and interiors than before. The awareness occurs in the form of a plethora of magazines, part works, radio and television coverage, the introduction of the phenomenon of feng shui, as well as academic interest in the social, political, economic and technological aspects of homes, their furnishings and design. Ultimately, however, furnishing decisions have to be made by individuals, and the interior always becomes a statement of the owner.

Probably the most important development during the latter part of the twentieth century has been the apparent freeing of individuals from the constraints of regulated taste of any complexion, and the development of post-modern eclecticism, which has allowed people to challenge the hierarchy of cultural values and lets them express themselves as they think fit. On the other hand, the issues of continuity and historic influences on attitudes to the home are still reflected in the selection of home furnishings.

Elizabeth Shove's exploration of consumption practices in York reveals something of the attitudes of consumers in the last decade of the twentieth century.[124] In matters of furnishing choice, the more affluent sector of the group she examined considered matters of personal preference and aesthetic value of interest to both parties in a relationship; the result often being individualized by the incorporation of goods that go together but do not necessarily match and may be a mix of old and new. The idea of creating a specific ambience using individual purchases was found in the more affluent group. The less well-off sample group left the homemaking to the women, believing that 'they know best' about such things and were best left to make the decisions. They 'knew' the conventions of 'what went with what', and imposed their 'taste' on the rest of the family. This group had fixed ideas about what went where and what was considered proper or appropriate. As Shove says: 'their [purchasing] decisions were instead guided by a strong sense of decorative propriety and by an implicitly shared understanding of the ideal home'.[125] The conflict still exists between the idea that goods should be chosen for comfort and use value (people as users of things), versus the desire for 'the new' (people as consumers of things) which results in a continual interaction between continuity and change. The old idea of appropriateness, developed in previous centuries, is often still apparent.

---

[123] Ibid.

[124] Shove, E. (1999), 'Constructing home: A crossroads of choice' in Cieraad, I. (Ed.) (1999), *At Home: Anthropology of Domestic Space*, p. 130.

[125] Ibid., p. 141.

Chapter 9

Conclusion

Having examined the changing nature of the retailing and consumption of house furnishings over a long historical period, and considered their relationships, it seems that the three aspects considered by Roche in my introduction – production and commerce, consumption, and objects and style – can also be linked to three fundamental values which connect them.[1] The first is the economic connection, linked to production and commerce, which orthodox economists would recognize as exchange value. This is the classic 'marketplace' situation, whereby a retailer makes goods available, and a consumer makes a selection (or not). Of course, this purely economic connection has many ramifications, including the provision of credit, quality assurance, fair pricing, selection, and a variety of other services.

The second is use value, which refers to the satisfaction of needs and wants, where furnishings 'serve' the consumer. This is an important part of the process, and recognizes changing needs and functions of goods over time. The essential physical aspects, such as the use of products related to needs associated with decoration, hygiene and cleanliness, comfort and entertainment, are the basis of the value. Whilst the fundamental economic relationship is similar in most exchanges, this use-value demands expertise from the retailer to provide solutions to the needs of the consumer. The more carefully this is done and the more directed the efforts, the more successful retailers will be. The problem for them is the changing circumstances to which they need to adapt. Failure to do so is one of the reasons for business collapse.

The third is identity-value, which is linked to objects and style as part of the process of an individual's attempts at both differentiation and self-definition, where goods act on behalf of the owner. Here the retailer is a facilitator, but also a provider of advice on issues of suitability, taste and style, which have meant a special cultural relationship with consumers that may be quite personal. With the growth in both the desire and the ability to engage in home furnishings, it was clear that consumers were not just passive receivers of advice and merchandise selection, but were often very creative in their own right. Inevitably, the apparently passive role of the consumer in the creation of his or her own identity is revealed to be a far more creative process than was once imagined.

Within this outline, the nature of the relationship between the retailer and the consumer has been one of continuities and changes. The economic continuity

---

[1] See Warde, A. (1992), 'Notes on the relationship between production and consumption', in Burrows, R. and Marsh, C. (Eds), *Consumption and Class: Divisions and Change*.

has been seen in the basic relationship between buyer and seller that has been constant for centuries. Buying and selling as an economic act basically remains the same whether it occurs in the market stall or the department store. Having said that, increasing competition within the sector means that issues of merchandising and marketing for the home sector become increasingly important. The structural changes, including the beginning of the separation between maker and supplier and the decline in importance of producer-retailers, the growth of specialist businesses, and the evolving range of outlets, have increased competition in the sector.

This has meant that since the seventeenth century, retailers have had to become increasingly conscious of the physical layout and location of their stores, the nature and style of their advertising and promotions, and the characteristics of their stocks. For the consumer, the range of outlets and purchasing opportunities has grown which has enabled them to select purchasing sites that have more or less reflected their desires.

In terms of the use of furniture and furnishings, there has been considerable continuity in the demands of consumers in the basic functions of furnishings. However, changes in social manners and attitudes have altered these requirements, substantially in some cases, so those retailers have had to react to these as required. The argument as to whether the retailer instituted these or reacted to them has been a feature of comments since the eighteenth century.

Although use-value has been and remains important as a fundamental basis for the retail trade, identity-value has been the developing agent of change upon which improvements in retailing and consumption have been built. There is no doubt that one of the roles of the home is as a marker of identity and position. The home was seen as a marker of 'civilization' and respectability, so it was an important cohesive force in society. Advances in standards of living from the sixteenth century onward have enabled more and more individuals to express themselves through their homes and furnishings. But one of the major continuities has been the matter of appropriateness. The search continues for appropriate styles for the representation of each generation of self and family. Again, this is often a point of dispute as to who leads the search for identity.

The expansion of the market encouraged a greater differentiation in designs for the home, which was reflected in retail showrooms, their products and locations.

The retail responses to the changes in consumer demands were more and more tailored to an ever-increasing range of stylistic and marketing changes, based on a better understanding of the markets. New business types (for example, home selling, catalogues, out-of-town hypermarkets, and the rise of DIY stores) were developed in reaction to changing markets, both locally and internationally. The wheel of retailing explains how we have arrived where we are now. Whether it is the retailer or the consumer, 'A maker of homes sounds quite a good passport to offer the ferry-man when he at last holds out his hand.'[2] This is actually the joint legacy of both house furnishers and their customers.

---

[2] Warne, A. (1933) in Schonfield, H. (Ed.), *The Book of British Industries*.

Bibliography

Abercrombie, P. (1939), *The Book of the Modern House*, London: Hodder and Stoughton.

Ablett, W. (1876), *Reminiscences of an Old Draper*, London: Sampson Low.

Adam, N. (1974), 'Decline of the great shopping streets', *Illustrated London News*, 262, July, pp. 41–5.

Adams, M. (1926), *My Book of Furniture*, London: Maurice Adams.

Adburgham, A. (1971), *Liberty's: A Biography of a Shop*, London: Allen and Unwin.

—— (1977), 'Give the customers what they want', *Architectural Review*, May, pp. 295–300.

—— (1979), *Shopping in Style*, London: Thames and Hudson.

Agnew J.-C. (1989), 'House of fiction: Domestic interiors and the commodity aesthetic', in Bronner, S. J. (Ed.), *Consuming Visions*, New York: Norton.

Alexander, A. (2002), 'Retailing and consumption: Evidence from war time Britain', *International Review of Retail, Distribution and Consumer Research*, **12**(1), pp. 39–57.

Alexander, D. (1970), *Retailing in England During the Industrial Revolution*, London: Athlone Press.

Alexander, E. (1985), '"And a bed is yon seeming bookcase": An interpretation of deception beds in Victorian homes', *Journal of American Culture*, **8**, Fall, pp. 2–10.

Alexander, Nicholas and Akehurst, Gary (Eds) (1999), *The Emergence of Modern Retailing 1750–1950*, London: Frank Cass.

Allen, G. and Crow, G. (Eds) (1989), *Home and Family: Creating the Domestic Sphere*, London: Macmillan.

Amaturo, E., Costagliola, S. and Ragone, G. (1987), 'Furnishing and status attributes: A sociological study of the living room', *Environment and Behavior*, **19**(2), March, pp. 228–49.

Ames, K. (1978), 'Meaning in artifacts: Hall furnishings in Victorian America', in Schlereth, T. J., *Material Culture Studies in America*, pp. 206–21.

—— (1992), *Death in the Dining Room and Other Tales of Victorian Culture*, Philadelphia, PA: Temple University Press.

Anderson, M. L. (1936), *Everyday Things*, catalogue of the exhibition arranged by RIBA, London.

André, R. (1981), *Homemakers: The Forgotten Workers*, Chicago, IL: University of Chicago Press.

Andrews, M. and Talbot, M. (Eds) (2000), *All the World and Her Husband*, London: Cassell.

Anon. (1747), *A General Description of All Trades*, London: Printed for T. Waller.

—— (1763), *Mortimer's Universal Directory*.

—— (1804), *Book of Trades or Library of Useful Arts*, London: Tabart and Co.

—— (1856), *Elegant Arts for Ladies*, London: Ward Lock.

—— (1881–2), *Young Ladies Treasure Book*.

—— (1947), *Modern Homes Illustrated*, London: Odhams.

—— (1973), '278 Years later: Furnishing showcase of Europe', *Sunday Times Magazine*, September.

—— (1986), *Ragtime to Wartime: The best of Good Housekeeping, 1922–1939*, London: Ebury Press.

—— (1988), 'Furniture starts to polish up its act', *Marketing Week*, 19 August.

—— (1993), 'IKEA: The wealth of realizing new ideas', *Harvard Business Review*, July–August, pp. 66–9.

Appadurai, A. (1986), *The Social Life of Things: Commodities in Cultural Perspective*, Cambridge: Cambridge University Press.

Appleby, J. (1999), 'Consumption in early modern social thought', in Glickman, L. B., *Consumer Society in American History: A Reader*, Ithaca, NY: Cornell University Press.

Aries P. (1991), *A History of Private Life*, Cambridge, MA: Harvard University Press.

Aris, S. (1970), *The Jews in Business*, London: Cape.

Ashton, T. S. (1955) 'Changes in standards of comfort in eighteenth century England', *Proceedings of the British Academy*, **41**, pp. 171–87.

Associated Rediffusion (1962/3), *London Profiles, No. 14: Women and Furniture*, London.

Attfield, J. (1995), 'Inside Pram Town: A case study of Harlow house interiors, 1951–61', in Attfield, J. and Kirkham, P., *A View from the Interior: Women and Design*, pp. 215–38.

—— (1996), ' "Give 'em something dark and heavy": The role of design in the material culture of popular British furniture 1939–1965', *Journal of Design History*, **9**(3), 185–201.

—— (1997), 'Design as a practice of modernity – a case for the study of the coffee table in the mid-century domestic interior', *Journal of Material Culture*, **2**(3), pp. 267–89.

—— (1999a), 'Bringing Modernity home: Open plan in the British interior', in Cieraad, I., *At Home: An Anthropology of Domestic Space*, Syracuse, NY: Syracuse University Press.

—— (1999b), *Utility Reassessed: The Role of Ethics in the Practice of Design*, Manchester: Manchester University Press.

—— (2000), 'Continuity: Authenticity and the paradoxical nature of reproduction', in *Wild Things: The Material Culture of Everyday Life*, Oxford: Berg.

—— and Kirkham, P. (Eds) (1989/95), *A View from the Interior: Women and Design*, London: Women's Press.

Auslander, L. (1996), *Taste and Power: Furnishing Modern France*, Berkeley, CA: University of California.

Avery, T. (1997), 'The furnishings of Tattershall Castle *c*. 1450–1550: A display of wealth and power', *Apollo*, 145, April, pp. 37–9.

Ayres, J. (1981), *The Shell Book of the Home in Britain*, London: Faber.

Bachelard, G. (1994), *The Poetics of Space*, Boston, MA: Beacon Press.

Baltes, P. B. (Ed.) (1978), *Life Span Development and Behaviour*, New York: Academic Press.

Bamford, F. (1983), *A Dictionary of Edinburgh Wrights and Furniture Makers 1660–1840*, London: Furniture History Society.

Banham, J. (2001), 'Johnson and Appleyard Ltd of Sheffield: A Victorian family business', *Regional Furniture*, **15**, pp. 43–63.

Baren, Maurice (1998), *Victorian Shopping*, London: Michael O'Mara.

Barley, M. (1963), *The House and Home: A Review of 900 Years of House Planning and Furnishing in Britain*, London: Studio Vista.

Barrett, H. and Philips, J. (1987), *Suburban Style*, London: McDonald Orbis.

Bartrip, P. (1994), 'How green was my valance? Environmental arsenic poisoning and the Victorian domestic ideal', *English Historical Review*, September.

Barty-King, H. (1992), *Maples Fine Furnishers: A Household Name for 150 Years*, London: Quiller.

Bates A. D. (1977), 'Warehouse retailing: A revolutionary forces in distribution', *California Management Review*, **20**(2), pp. 74–80.

Bayley, S. (Ed.) (1989), *Commerce and Culture from Pre-industrial Art to Post-industrial Value*, London: Fourth Estate.

Beard, G. (1975), 'William Kent and the cabinet-makers', *Burlington*, 117, December, pp. 867–84.

—— (1977), 'Three eighteenth century cabinet-makers, Moore, Goodison and Vile', *Burlington Magazine*, 119, July, pp. 479–86.

—— (1990), 'Vile and Cobb, eighteenth century London furniture makers', *Antiques*, 137, June, p. 1394.

—— (1997), *Upholsterers and Interior Furnishing in England, 1550–1840*, London: Yale University Press.

—— and Gilbert C. (Eds) (1986), *Dictionary of English Furniture Makers*, London: Furniture History Society.

Beecher, C. (1869), *American Woman's Home*, reprint, Hartford, CT: Stowe-Day Foundation, 1975.

Beeton, Mrs.(1880), *Housewife's Treasury of Domestic Information*, London: Ward Lock.

Bell, C. (1968), *Middle-class Families*, London: Routledge and Kegan Paul.

Benhamou, R. (1991), 'Imitation in the decorative arts of the eighteenth century', *Journal of Design History*, **4**, pp. 1–14.

Benjamin, D. (1995), *The Home: Words, Interpretations, Meanings and Environment*, Aldershot: Avebury.

Benjamin, T. H. (1934), *London Shops and Shopping*, London: Herbert Joseph.

Benson, J. (1984), *The Rise of Consumer Society in Britain 1880–1980*, London: Longman.

—— and Shaw, G. (1992), *The Evolution of Retail Systems, c. 1800–1914*, Leicester: Leicester University Press.

—— (1999), *The Retailing Industry*, 3 volumes, London: I. B. Tauris.

Benson, J. and Ugolini, L. (2003), *A Nation of Shopkeepers: Five Centuries of British Retailing*, London: I. B.Tauris.

Bentley, I., Davis, I. and Oliver, P. (1981), *Dunroamin: The Suburban Semi and Its Enemies*, London: Barrie and Jenkins.

Benton, T. (1978), 'Up and down at Heals 1929–35', *Architectural Review*, 972, February, pp. 109–16.

——, Benton, C. and Sharp, D. (Eds) (1975), *Form and Function: A Source Book for the History of Architecture and Design 1890–1939*, London: Granada.

Beresford, J. (Ed.) (1929), *The Diary of A Country Parson*, Oxford: Oxford University Press.

Berg, A.-J. (1999), 'A gendered socio-technical construction: The smart house' in Mackenzie, D. and Wajcman, J. (Eds), *Social Shaping of Technology*, Oxford: Oxford University Press.

Berg, M. (1996), 'Women's Consumption and the Industrial Classes of Eighteenth century England', *Journal of Social History*, Winter, **30**(2), pp. 415–34.

—— and Clifford, H. (1999), *Consumers and Luxury: Consumer Culture in Europe 1650–1850*, Manchester: Manchester University Press.

Berger, R. (1993), *The Most Necessary Luxuries ...*, University Park, PA: Penn State University Press.

Berger, R. M. (1980) 'The development of retail trade in provincial England ca. 1550–1700', *Journal of Economic History*, **XL**(1), March, pp. 123–8.

Bermingham, A. and Brewer, J. (Eds) (1995), *The Consumption of Culture 1660–1800*, London: Routledge.

Besant, W. (1901), *East London*, London: Chatto and Windus.

Betters, Paul Vernon (1930), *The Bureau of Home Economics: Its History, Activities and Organisation*, reprint, Washington, DC: Brookings Institution.

Bird, J., Curtis, B., Putnam, T., Robertson, G. and Tickner, L. (Eds) (1993), *Mapping the Futures: Local Cultures Global Change*, London: Routledge.

Birmingham Mail/Council of Industrial Design (*c.* 1956-8), *Guide to the Birmingham Mail Showhouses*.

Blaszczyk, R. (2000), *Imagining Consumers: Design and Innovation from Wedgwood to Corning*, Baltimore, MD: Johns Hopkins University Press.

Board of Trade (1946a), *Furniture: An Enquiry Made for the Board of Trade by the Social Survey*, London: HMSO.

Board of Trade (1946b), *Working Party Report on the Furniture Trade*, London: HMSO.

Bolling, Cunliffe Lawrence (1935), *Hire-purchase Trading: A Practical Guide to Hire-purchase, also Instalment Selling*, London: Sir I. Pitman & Sons.

Borsay, P. (1977), 'The English urban Renaissance: The development of provincial urban culture *c*.1680–*c*. 1760', *Social History*, **5**, pp. 581–603.

Bose, C., Bereano, P. and Malloy, M. (1984), 'Household technology and the social construction of housework', *Technology and Culture*, **25**(1), pp. 53–82.

Boudon, P. (1972), *Lived-in Architecture: Le Corbusier's Pessac Revisited*, London: Lund Humphries.

Bourdieu, P. (1984), *Distinction: A Social Critique of the Judgement of Taste*, Cambridge: Harvard University Press.

Bowden, S. and Offer, A. (1996), 'The technological revolution that never was', in De Grazia, V. (Ed.), *The Sex of Things*, London: University of California Press.

Boxshall, J. (1997), *Good Housekeeping: Every Home Should Have One*, London: Ebury Press.

Boynton, L. (1967), 'High Victorian furniture: The example of Marsh and Jones of Leeds', *Furniture History*, **3**, pp. 54–65.

Braudel, F. (1981), *The Structures of Everyday Life*, London: Fontana.

Brawer, N. (2001), *British Campaign Furniture: Elegance under Canvas 1790–1914*, New York: Abrams.

Breen, T. H. (1988), 'Baubles of Britain: The American and consumer revolutions of the eighteenth century', *Past and Present*, 119, May, pp. 73–120.

Brewer, J. and Porter, R. (Eds) (1993), *Consumption and the World of Goods*, London: Routledge.

Briggs, A. (1956), *Friends of the People: A Centenary History of Lewis's*, London: Batsford.

—— (1988), *Victorian Things*, London: Batsford.

Bronner, S. J. (1989), *Consuming Visions: Accumulation and Display in Goods 1880–1920*, New York: Norton.

Brown, A. (1995), 'IKEA case study', in *Organisational Culture*, London: Pitman.

Brown, F. E. (1986), 'Continuity and change in the urban house: Developments in domestic space organisation in seventeenth century London', *Comparative Studies in Society and History*, **28**(3), pp. 558–90.

Brown, G. (1990), *Domestic Individualism: Imagining Self in the Nineteenth Century*, Berkeley, CA: University of California Press.

Brown, R. (1986), 'The furniture oligarchy', *Design*, 449, May, pp. 44–7.

Browne, J. (2000), 'Decisions in DIY: Home improvements and advertising in post-war Britain', in Andrews, M. and Talbot, M. (Eds), *All the World and Her Husband*, London: Cassell.

Bryden, I. and Floyd, J. (Eds) (1999), *Domestic Space Reading the Nineteenth Century Interior*, Manchester: Manchester University Press.

Bucklin, L. P. (1972), 'Metamorphosis in retailing', in Benson, J. and Shaw, G. (1999), *The Retailing Industry*, Vol. 1, London: I. B. Tauris.

Budden, B. (1930), *The Bride and Her Home*, London: Odhams.

Burgess, F. W. (1912), *The Practical Retail Draper*, 5 volumes, London: Virtue and Co.

Burman, W. (1954), *Housecraft*, London: Macmillan.

Burris-Meyer, E. (1947), *Decorating Livable Homes*, New York: Prentice-Hall.

Burrows, R. and Marsh, C. (1992), *Consumption and Class: Divisions and Change*, London: Macmillan.

Burton, (1972), *The Early Victorians at Home, 1837–1861*, London: Longman. *Cabinet Maker* (1955), *Furniture and Furnishings 1880–1950*, Benn.

—— (1980), *Cabinet Maker Celebrates a Century 1880–1980*, Benn.

Bushman, Richard L. (1992), *The Refinement of America: Persons, Houses, Cities*, New York: Alfred Knopf.

Cain, L. and Uselding, P. (Eds) (1973), *Business Enterprise and Economic Change: Essays in Honour of H F Williamson*, Kent State University.

Cairns, J. (*c.*1950), *Home-making*, London: Waverley Books.

Calder, J. (1977), *The Victorian Home*, London: Batsford.

Caldwell, I. (1985), 'Working women in the 18th century', *Antique Collector*, October.

Calloway, S. (1994), *The Victorian Catalogue of Household Furnishings*, Hampton and Sons, 1894, reprint London: Studio Editions.

Campbell, C. (1987), *The Romantic Ethic and the Spirit of Modern Consumerism*, Oxford: Blackwell.

—— (1992), 'The desire for the new', in Silverstone, R. and Hirsch, E. (Eds), *Consuming Technologies: Media and Information in Domestic Spaces*, London: Routledge.

—— (1993) 'Understanding traditional and modern patterns of consumption in eighteenth century England: A character action approach', in Brewer, J. and Porter, R. (Eds), *Consumption and the World of Goods*, London: Routledge.

—— (1995), 'The sociology of consumption', in Miller, D., *Acknowledging Consumption*, London: Routledge.

—— (1999), 'Consuming goods and the goods of consuming', in Glickman, L.B. (Ed.), *Consumer Society in American History*, Ithaca, NY: Cornell.

Campbell, R. (1969) [1747], *The London Tradesmen*, Newton Abbot: David and Charles.

Candee, H. C. (1906), *Decorative Styles, and Periods in the Home*, New York: F. A. Stokes.

Caradoc, R. L. (1934), *Sales Increasing Window Display Schemes for Furnishers*, London: Furnishing World.

Carrier, J. G. (1994), 'Alienating objects: The emergence of alienation in retail trade, *Journal of the Royal Anthropological Institute*, **29**, pp. 359–80.

Carrington, N. (1933), *Design in the Home*, London: Country Life.

Carson, C., Hoffman, R. and Albert, P. (Eds) (1994), *Of Consuming Interests: The Style of Life in the Eighteenth Century*, Charlottesville, VA: University Press of Virginia.

Carson, M. (1968), 'Thomas Affleck: A London cabinet maker in colonial Philadelphia', *Connoisseur*, March, pp. 187–91.

Chancellor, Beresford (1930), *London's Old Latin Quarter*, London: Cape.

Chaney, D. (1983), 'The department store as a cultural form', *Theory, Culture and Society*, **1**(3), pp. 22–31.

Chapman, D. (1949), *Families: Their Needs and Preferences in the Home*, Report of a Conference held at RIBA, July.

—— (1955), *The Home and Social Status*, London: Routledge and Kegan Paul.

Chapman, S. D. (1971), *History of Working Class Housing*, Newton Abbott: David and Charles.

Chapman, T. (1999), 'The Ideal Home Exhibition: An analysis of constraints and conventions in consumer choices in British homes', in Hearn, J. and Roseniel, S. (Eds), *Consuming Culture: Power and Resistance*, London: Macmillan.

—— and Hockey J. (Eds) (1999), *Ideal Homes?: Consumption and Everyday Life*, London: Routledge.

Chartres, J. A. (1977), *Internal Trade in England 1500–1700*, London: Macmillan.

Chase, K. and Levenson, M. (2000), *The Spectacle of Intimacy: A Public Life for the Victorian Family*, Printon, NJ: Princeton University Press.

Cieraad, I. (1999), *At Home: Anthropology of Domestic Space*, Syracuse, NY: Syracuse University Press.

Clark, C. (1991) 'House furnishing as cultural evidence', *American Quarterly*, 43, March, pp. 73–81.

Clark Jr, C. E. (1986), *The American Family Home 1800–1960*, Chapel Hill, NC: University of North Carolina Press.

Clark, P. (Ed.) (1984), *The Transformation of English Provincial Towns 1600–1800*, London: Hutchinson.

Cobbe, Francis Power (1881), *The Duties of a Woman*, London and Edinburgh: Williams and Norgate.

Cobbett, W. (1830), *Rural Rides*, reprint 1967, Harmondsworth: Penguin.

Cockburn, C. (1944), *Bringing Technology Home*, Oxford: Oxford University Press.

Cohen, L. A. (1984), 'Embellishing a life of labour: An interpretation of the material culture of American working class homes 1885–1915' in Schlereth, T. J. (Ed.), *Material Culture Studies in America*, Nashville: American Association for State and Local History, pp. 289–305.

Cohen, M. (1998), *Professional Domesticity in the Victorian Novel*, Cambridge: Cambridge University Press.

Collins, D. (1993), 'Primitive or not? Fixed shop retailing before the industrial revolution', *Journal of Regional and Local Studies*, **13**(1), pp. 23–38.

Collyer, J. (1761), *Parents and Guardians Directory and the Youth's Guide in the Choice of a Profession or Trade*.

Consumer Council (1965), *Furniture Trade and the Consumer*, London: HMSO.

Consumers Association (1974), *Which? Report on Furniture Shops*, October.

Cook, M. W. (1881), *A Practical Guide to Economical Furnishing*, London: Routledge.

Cooke, E. S. (Ed.) (1987), *Upholstery in America and Europe from the Seventeenth Century to World War 1*, New York: Norton.

Cooper Bros (1953), *Waring and Gillow: A Report on the Administration and Organisation of the Company*, 30 June, City of Westminster Archives.

Cooper, C. (1974), 'The house as symbol of the self', in Lang, J. et al., *Designing for Human Behaviour: Architecture and the Behavioural Sciences*, Stroudsburg, PA: Dowden, Hutchinson & Ross.

Coopey, R., O'Connell, S. and Porter, D. (1999), 'Mail order in the United Kingdom c. 1880–1990: How mail order competed with other forms of retailing', *The International Review of Retail, Distribution and Consumer Research*, pp. 261–73.

Corbusier, Le (1925), *The Decorative Arts of Today*, trans Dunnett, J. 1987, London: Architectural Press.

—— (1927), *Towards a New Architecture*, trans Etchells, F., London: Architectural Press.

Corporate Intelligence on Retailing (1997), *Furniture Retailing in the UK*, London.

Corrigan, P. (1997), *The Sociology of Consumption*, London: Sage.

Council for Art and Industry (1937), *The Working Class Home: Its Furnishing and Equipment*, London.

Council for the Encouragement of Music and the Arts (1943), *Design in the Home*, exhibition arranged by the Victoria and Albert Museum, London.

Council of Industrial Design (1945), *Social Survey Report: Furniture*, London: HMSO.

—— (1946), *New Home*, London: HMSO.

—— (1947, *Furnishing to Fit the Family*, London: HMSO.

—— (1949), *Four Ways of Living*, London: HMSO.

—— (1950), *Ideas for Your Home*, London: HMSO.

—— (1951), *Reports on Design Courses for Furniture Salesmen,* London: HMSO.

—— (1971), *Selling Modern Furniture,* London: HMSO.

Cowan, R. S. (1976), 'Industrial Revolution in the home', in *Journal of Technology and Culture,* January, **17**(1), pp. 1–24.

Coward, R. (1984), 'Ideal homes', in *Female Desire,* London: Paladin.

Cox, N. (2000), *The Complete Tradesman: A Study of Retailing 1550–1820,* Aldershot: Ashgate.

Craik, J. (1989), 'The making of mother: The role of the kitchen in the home', in Allen, G. and Crow, G. (Eds), *Home and Family: Creating the Domestic Sphere,* London: Macmillan.

Crow, G. (1989), 'The post war development of the modern domestic ideal', in Allen, G. and Crow, G. (Eds), *Home and Family: Creating the Domestic Sphere,* London: Macmillan, pp. 14–32.

Crowley, J. E. (2000), *The Invention of Comfort,* Baltimore, MD, and London: John Hopkins University Press.

Csikszentmihalyi, M. and Rochberg-Halton, E. (1981), *The Meaning of Things: Domestic Symbols and the Self,* New York: Cambridge University Press.

Cummings, A. L. (1964), *Rural Household Inventories, 1675–1775,* Boston, MA: SPNEA.

Daily Express (1935), *The Home of Today: Its Choice, Planning, Equipment and Organisation,* London.

Daily Mail (1920), *Ideal Labour Saving Home,* London.

—— (1944), *Daily Mail Book of Post-war Homes,* London.

—— (1946), *Daily Mail Ideal Home Book,* London.

—— (1965), *Daily Mail Book of Furnishing, Decorating and Kitchen Plans,* London.

Daily Mirror (1913), *The Perfect Home and How to Furnish It,* London.

Dan, H. and Morgan, Wilmott (1907), *English Shop Fronts Old and New,* London: Batsford.

Dant, T. (1999), *Material Culture in the Social World,* Buckingham: Open University Press.

Daunton, M. J. (1983), *House and Home in the Victorian City,* London: Edward Arnold.

Davidoff, L. and Hall, C. (1995), '"My own fireside": The creation of the middle-class home', in Jackson, S. and Moores, S., *Politics of Domestic Consumption,* London: Prentice-Hall.

Davidoff, L. and Hall, C. (1987), *Family Fortunes: Men and Women of the English Middle Class 1780–1850,* London: Hutchinson.

Davidson, Caroline (1982), *A Woman's Work is Never Done: A History of Housework in the British Isles 1650–1950,* London: Chatto & Windus.

Davidson, H. C. (1906), *The Book of the Home,* London: Gresham Publishing.

Davies, G. and Brooks, J. (1989), *Positioning Strategy in Retailing*, London: Paul Chapman Publishing.

Davies G. (1994), 'Repositioning MFI', in McGoldrick, P. (Ed.), *Cases in Retail Management*, London: Pitman.

Davis, D. (1966), *A History of Shopping*, London: Routledge.

Dawson, J. A. (1988), 'Changes in 20th century retailing in the High Street', *Geographical Journal*, **154**(1), pp. 1–12.

De Grazia, V. (1996), 'Establishing the modern consumer household', in De Grazia, V. (Ed.), *The Sex of Things: Gender and Consumption*, Berkeley, CA: University of California Press.

De Plas, S. (1975), *Les Meubles à Transformation et à Secret*, Paris: Le Prat.

Dean, D. (1970), *English Shop Fronts 1792–1840*, London: Tiranti.

Deeks, J. (1976), *The Small Firm Owner-manager*, New York: Praeger.

Defoe, D. (1969) [1727], *The Complete English Tradesman*, New York: Kelley.

Denvir, B. (1988), *From the Middle Ages to the Stuarts: Art, Design and Society*, Harlow: Longman.

Design Council (1983), *Report to the Design Council on the Design of British Consumer Goods*, London: HMSO.

—— (c. 1990), *Key Themes in the UK Furniture Industry*, London: HMSO.

Dickerson, V. (1995), *Keeping the Victorian House: A Collection of Essays*, New York: Garland.

Dillon, S. (2001), 'Victorian interior', *Modern Language Quarterly*, **62**(2), June, pp. 83–115.

Director General of Fair Trading (1990), *Report on Furniture and Carpets*, London: HMSO.

Dittmar, H. (1992), *The Social Psychology of Material Possessions: To Have is to Be*, Hemel Hempstead: Harvester.

Donnison, D. (1985), 'Working at home', *Town and Country Planning*, April, pp. 120–22.

Douglas, M. (1992), 'Why do people want goods?', in Hargreaves Heap, S. and Ross, A. (Eds), *Understanding the Enterprise Culture: Themes in the Work of Mary Douglas*, Edinburgh: Edinburgh University Press.

—— and Isherwood, B. (1979), *The World of Goods: Towards an Anthropology of Consumption*, Harmondsworth: Penguin.

Duncan, J. et al. (1985), 'Decoding a residence: Artifacts, social codes and the construction of self', in *Espaces et Sociétés*, **47**, pp. 29–43.

Duncan, J. S. (1981), *Housing and Identity*, London: Croom Helm.

Dupuis, M. and Dawson, J. (1999), *European Cases in Retailing*, Oxford: Blackwell.

Dyer, Glenda and Reed, Martha (1989), *The Consumer Culture and the American Home*, Beaumont, TA: McFaddin-Ward House.

Dyer, C. (1989), *Standards of Living in the Later Middle Ages*, Cambridge: Cambridge University Press.

Eames, P. (1971), 'Documentary evidence concerning the character and use of domestic furnishings in the fourteenth and fifteenth centuries', *Furniture History*, **7**, pp. 41–60.

Eastlake, C. (1872), *Hints on Household Taste*, Farnborough: Gregg Reprints.

Economist Intelligence Unit (EIU) (1958), *Retail Business: A Study of the Furniture Industry and Trade in the UK*, No. 3.

—— (1959a), *Retail Business*, No. 15, May.

—— (1959b), *Retail Business*, No. 17, July.

—— (1960), *Retail Business*, No. 23, January.

—— (1960), *Retail Business*, No. 26 April.

—— (1960), *Retail Business*, No. 34, December.

—— (1961), *Retail Business*, No. 35, January.

—— (1961), *Retail Business*, No. 39, May.

—— (1961), *Retail Business*, No. 42, August.

—— (1962), *Retail Business*, No. 50, April.

—— (1962), *Retail Business*, No. 52, June.

—— (1962), *Retail Business*, No. 57, November.

—— (1963), *Retail Business*, No. 62, April.

—— (1964), *Retail Business*, No. 74, April.

—— (1964), *Retail Business*, No. 81, November, Special Report, Furniture.

—— (1967), *Retail Business*, No. 110, April.

—— (1968), *Retail Business*, No. 121, March.

—— (1971), *A Study on Retail Distribution in Britain, Vol. 1.*

—— (1972), *The Retail Industry in the UK.*

—— (1992), *Trade Review: Furniture Shops*, '*Retail Business* Retail Trade Reviews', No. 21.

—— (1993), *Trade Review: Furniture Shops*, '*Retail Business* Retail Trade Reviews', No 25.

—— (1994), *Trade Review: Furniture Shops*, '*Retail Business* Retail Trade Reviews', No. 29.

—— (1997), *Retail Business, Furniture Part 1*, November.

Edgeworth, M. (1812), *The Absentee*, 1969 reprint, Hildesheim: Olms.

Edis, R. W. (1881), *Decoration and Furniture of Town Houses*, London: Kegan Paul.

Edwards, A. T. (1933), *The Architecture of Shops*, London: Chapman and Hall.

Edwards, C. (1990), 'Press Beds', *Furniture History*, **26**, pp. 42–8.

—— (1991), 'Furnishing a home at the turn of the century: The use of estimates from 1875 to 1910', *Journal of Design History*, **4**(4), pp. 233–9.

—— (1998), 'The firm of Jackson and Graham', *Furniture History*, **34**, pp. 238–65.

—— (1998–9) 'Reclining chairs surveyed', *Studies in the Decorative Arts*, **6**(1), pp. 32–67.

—— (2001), 'Organisation of the trade of the eighteenth century opholsterer', in Mertens, W. (Ed.), *Interior Textiles in Western Europe 1600–1900*, Antwerp: Hessenhuis, pp. 69–78 and 313–20.

Edwards, R. (1964), *The Shorter Dictionary of English Furniture from the Middle Ages to the Late Georgian Period*, London: Country Life.

—— and Jourdain, M. (1955), *Georgian Cabinet Makers*, London: Country Life.

Ehrenreich, B. and English, D. (1978), *For Her Own Good: 150 years of the Expert's Advice to Women*, New York: Doubleday.

Eland, G. (Ed.) (1931), *Purefoy Letters*, London: Sidgwick and Jackson.

—— (Ed.) (1947), *Shardeloes Papers of the Seventeenth and Eighteenth Century*, Oxford: University Press.

Elder-Duncan, J. (1907), *The House Beautiful*, London: Cassel.

Eldridge, M. (1958), 'The plate-glass shop front', *Architectural Review*, **123**, pp. 192–5.

Elliott, C. and Elliott, S. (1937), *The Modern Retailer*, London: Virtue.

Elsas, M. J. (1947), *Housing and the Family*, London: Meridian.

Ettema, M. J. (1982), 'History, nostalgia and American furniture', *Winterthur Portfolio*, **17**(2–3), pp. 135–44.

—— (1991) 'The fashion system in American furniture', in Pocius, G., *Living in a Material World*, Memorial University of Newfoundland, Social and Economic Papers 19.

Evelyn, J. (1959), *Diaries 1620–1676*, Beer, E. S. (Ed.), Oxford: Oxford University Press.

Falke, O. (1879), *Art in the House*, Boston: Prang.

Farr, M. (1955), *Design in British Industry*, Cambridge: Cambridge University Press.

Featherstone, M. (1991), *Consumer Culture and Postmodernism*, London: Sage.

Fiennes, C. (1698) [1982], *The Illustrated Journeys of Celia Fiennes*, London: Macdonald.

Fine, B. and Leopold, E. (1990), 'Consumerism and the Industrial Revolution', *Social History*, **15**(2), pp. 151–79.

—— (1993), *The World of Consumption*, London: Routledge.

Finsberg, H. (Ed.) (1967), *Agrarian History of England*, Cambridge: Cambridge University Press.

Fisher, F. J. (1948), 'The development of London as a centre of conspicuous consumption in the sixteenth and seventeenth centuries', *Transactions of the Royal Historical Society*, **30**, pp. 197–207.

Fleming, E. (1997), 'Staples for genteel living: The importation of London household furnishings into Charleston during the 1780s', *American Furniture*, pp. 335–58.

Fletcher, S. R. and Godley, A. (1999), *International Retailing in Britain 1850–1994*, Reading: University of Reading.

Forty, A. (1986), *Objects of Desire: Design and Society 1750–1980*, London: Thames and Hudson.

Fowler, C. (1999), 'Changes in provincial retailing during the eighteenth century, with particular reference to central-southern England', in Alexander, N. and Akehurst, G. (Eds), *The Emergence of Modern Retailing, 1750–1950*.

Fowler, J. and Cornforth, J. (1984), *English Decoration in the Eighteenth Century*, London: Barrie and Jenkins.

Fox, R. W. and Lears, T. J. (1983), *The Culture of Consumption: Critical Essays in American History 1880–1980*, New York: Pantheon Books.

Fraad, H. (1994), *Bringing It All Home*, London: Pluto.

Fraser, W. H. (1981), *The Coming of the Mass Market, 1850–1914*, London: Macmillan.

Fredericks, C. (1920), *Household Engineering: Scientific Management in the Home*, Chicago, IL: American School of Home Economics.

Friedan, B. (1963), *Feminine Mystique – The Sexual Sell*, London: Gollanz.

Friedman, J. (1994), *Consumption and Identity*, Chur, Switzerland: Harwood Academic Press.

Fry, A. (1971), *Selling Modern Furniture*, CoID, London: HMSO.

Fulop, C. (1964), *Competition for Consumers: A Study of the Changing Channels of Distribution*, London: Deutsch.

—— and March, T. (1979), 'The effects of abolition of R.P.M. in two trades', *European Journal of Marketing*, **13**(7), pp. 223–36.

Furby, L. (1978), 'Possessions: Towards a theory of their meaning and function throughout the life cycle', in Baltes, P. B. (Ed.), *Life Span Development and Behaviour*, New York: Academic Press.

Furniss, A. D. S. and Phillips, M. (1920), *The Working Woman's House*, London: Swarthmore Press.

Furnishing World (1959), *Retailers Guide to Display*, London.

Furniture Development Council (1965), *Sales Planning Guide for the Furniture Industry*.

Furniture Industries Research Association (FIRA) (1970), *Review of the Furniture Industry*, July, Stevenage.

—— (1978), *A Discussion Document on Consumer Attitudes to Buying Furniture*, Stevenage.

—— (1980), *Buying and Selling Furniture*, Stevenage.

—— (1980), *Consumer Trends*, Stevenage.

—— (1982), *Consumer Buying Patterns 1979–1981*, Stevenage.

—— (1983), *Domestic Furniture Purchasing Habits*, Stevenage.

Furniture Industry Post-War Reconstruction Committee (1943–4), *Interim Report, Second and Third Reports*, London.

Fussell, G. E. (1949), *The English Rural Labourer: His Home, Furniture, Clothing & Food from Tudor to Victorian Times*, London: Batchworth Press.

Gardiner, F. M. (1894), *Furnishing and Fittings for Every Home*, London: Record Press.

Gardner, C. and Shepard, J. (1989), *Consuming Passion: The Rise of Retail Culture*, London: Hyman.

Garrett, E. (1990), 'Furnishing the early American home', *Antiques*, September, pp. 540–55.

Garrett, E. D. (1990), *At Home: The American Family, 1750–1870*, New York: H. N. Abrams.

Garrett, R. and Garrett, A. (1876), *Suggestions for House Redecoration in Painting, Woodwork and Furniture*, London: Macmillan.

Gauldie, E. (1947), *Cruel Habitations*, London: Allen and Unwin.

Geffrye Museum (1974), *CC41 Utility Furniture and Fashion*, London: ILEA.

George, W. L. (1913), *Women and Tomorrow*, London: Herbert Jenkins.

Gere, C. and Hoskins, L. (2000), *The House Beautiful: Oscar Wilde and the Aesthetic Interior*, London: Lund Humphries.

Giddens, A. (1991), *Modernity and Self-identity: Self and Society in the Late Modern Age*, Cambridge: Polity Press.

Gilbert, C. (1970), 'Victorian and Edwardian furniture by Pratt's of Bradford', exhibition catalogue, Bradford City Art Gallery, November 1969–January 1970.

—— (1976), 'Wright and Elwick of Wakefield 1748–1824', *Furniture History*, **12**, pp. 39–50.

—— (1978), *The Life and Work of Thomas Chippendale*, London: Macmillan

—— (1991), *English Vernacular Furniture 1750–1900*, New Haven, CT, and London: Yale University Press.

—— (1996), *Pictorial Dictionary of Marked London Furniture, 1700–1840*, London: Furniture History Society.

—— and Murdoch, T. (1993), *John Channon and Brass Inlaid Furniture 1730–1760*, New Haven, CT, and London: Yale University Press.

—— and Wood, L. (1997), 'Sophie von la Roche at Seddons', *Furniture History*, **33**, pp. 30–35.

Giles, J. (1993), 'A Home of one's own: Women and domesticity in England 1918–1950', *Women's Studies International Forum*, **16**(3), pp. 239–52.

Gilliam, J. K. (1998), 'The evolution of the house in early Virginia', in Thompson, E. (Ed.) (1998), *The American Home*, Wilmington, DE: Winterthur Museum.

Gillow and Co. (1901), *Gillow's: A Record of a Furnishing Firm Through Two Centuries*, London: Harrison and Sons.

—— (1903), *Examples of Furniture and Decoration*, London.

Ginswick, J. (Ed.) (1983), *Labour and the Poor in England and Wales 1849–1852* (letters to the *Morning Chronicle*), London: Frank Cass.

Girouard, M. (1978), *Life in the English Country House*, New Haven, CT: Yale University Press.

Giuliani, M. (1987), 'Naming the rooms, implications of a change in the home model', *Environment and behaviour*, **19**(2), March, pp. 180–203.

Glennie, P. (1995), 'Consumption within historical studies', in Miller, D. (Ed.), *Acknowledging Consumption*, London: Routledge.

—— and Thrift, N. (1996), 'Consumers identities and consumption spaces in early modern England', *Environment and Planning* A, **28**, pp. 25–45.

Glickman, L. B. (1999), *Consumer Society in American History: A Reader*, Ithaca, NY: Cornell University Press.

Gloag, J. (1934a), *English Furniture*, London: A. and C. Black.

—— (1934b) *Industrial Art Explained*, London: Allen and Unwin.

—— (1956) *Georgian Grace*, London: A. and C. Black.

—— (1961), *Victorian Comfort*, London: A. and C. Black.

—— and Mansfield, L. (1923), *The House We Ought to Live In*, London: Duckworth.

Goffman, E. (1959), *The Presentation of Self in Everyday Life*, New York: Doubleday.

Goldstein, C. (1998), *Do It Yourself: Home Improvements in 20th Century America*, New York: Princeton Architectural Press and National Building Museum.

Good Housekeeping Institute (1954), *The Happy Home*, London: Grosvenor Press.

Goodden, S. (1984), *At the Sign of the Four Poster*, London: Heal and Sons.

Gordon, B. (1996), 'Woman's domestic body: The conceptual conflation of women and interiors in the industrial age', *Winterthur Portfolio*, **31**, Winter, pp. 281–301.

Gordon, J. and MacArthur, J. (1989) 'Popular culture magazines and American domestic interiors 1898-1940', *Journal of Popular Culture*, **22**(4), pp. 35–60.

Grant, L. (Ed.) (1984), *Medieval Art, Architecture and Archaeology in London*, British Archaeological Association Conference Transactions, London.

Great Britain Board of Trade (1948), *Bring Comfort to Your Home: Catalogue of Illustrations*, London: George Porter & Co.

Gregory, E. W. (1913), *The Art and Craft of Home Making*, London: Batsford.

Greenhalgh, P. (1990), *Modernism in Design*, London: Reaktion Books.

—— (1993), *Quotations and Sources on Design and Decorative Arts*, Manchester: Manchester University Press.

Greig, A. (1995), 'Home magazines and modernist dreams: Designing the 1950s house', *Urban Research Program Working Paper No. 47*, April, Canberra: Australian National University.

Grier, K. C. (1988), *Culture and Comfort: People, Parlors and Upholstery 1850–1930*, New York: The Strong Museum.

Gries, J. M. and Ford, J. (Eds) (1932), *Homemaking, Home Furnishing and Information Services*, Washington DC, National Capital Press.

Groot, M. (1996), 'Reflections on everyday taste: Furniture shops, department stores and the furnishing of the home, 1895–1940', in Schuurman, A. and Spierenberg, P. (Eds), *Private Domain, Public Inquiry*, Hilversum: Verloren Press.

Gross, K. J. (1993), *Home*, London: Thames and Hudson.

Gullestad, M. (1995), 'Home decoration as popular culture: Constructing homes, genders and classes in Norway', in Jackson, S. and Moores, S. (Eds), *Politics of Domestic Consumption*, London: Prentice-Hall.

Gundrey, W. and Gundrey, E. (1955), 'Home for four', *Design*, **75**, pp. 9–16.

Hackney Furnishing Company (1911), *British Homes: Their Making and Furnishing*.

Haigh, A. (1925), *Furnishing and Hardware: A Textbook for Co-operative Society Salesmen*, Manchester: Central Education Committee, Co-operative Union.

Hall, P. G. (1962), *The Industries of London Since 1861*, London: Hutchinson.

Halttunen, K. (1989), 'From parlour to living room: Domestic space, interior decoration and the cult of personality', in Brunna, S. J. (1989), *Consuming Visions*, New York: Norton.

Hammond, A. (1930), *Multiple Shop Organisation*, London: Pitman.

Hanson, J. (1998), *Decoding Houses and Homes*, Cambridge: Cambridge University Press.

Hareven, T. K. (1991), 'The home and family in historical perspective', *Social Research*, **58**(1), Spring, pp. 253–85.

Harris, Ralph and Seldon, Arthur (1958), *Hire Purchase in a Free Society*, London: Institute of Economic Affairs.

Harrison, S. G. (1997), 'The nineteenth century furniture trade in New Orleans', *Antiques*, 151, May, pp. 748–59.

Harrison, William (1587), *The Description of England*, reprint, 1968, Ithica, NY: Cornell University Press.

Harvey, P. D. A. (1976), *Manorial Records of Cuxham, Oxon 1200–1359*, Oxford Record Office.

Hassall, W. O. (1962), *How They Lived: An Anthology of Original Accounts Written Before 1485*, Oxford: Blackwell.

Havenhand, G. (1970), *Nation of Shopkeepers*, London: Eyre and Spottiswoode.

Haweis, Mrs (1881), *The Art of Decoration*, London: Chatto and Windus.

Hayden, D. (1981), *The Grand Domestic Revolution: A History of Feminist Designs for American Homes, Neighbourhoods and Cities*, Cambridge, MA: MIT Press.

—— (1984), *Redesigning the American Dream: The Future of Housing, Work, and Family Life*, New York: Norton.

Hayden, R. (1980), *Mrs Delaney, Her Life and Flowers*, London: British Museum Press.

Hayward, H. and Kirkham, P. (1980), *William and John Linnell, Eighteenth Century London Furniture Makers*, London: Studio Vista.

Heal, A. (1953), *The London Furniture Makers, from the Restoration to the Victorian Era 1660–1840*, London: Batsford.

Heal, J. (1956), *Planning an Ideal Home*, London: Associated Newspapers.

Heals Ltd (1972), *Catalogues 1853–1934: Middle-class Furnishing*, Newton Abbott: David and Charles.

Heap, S. H. and Ross, A. (Eds) (1992), *Understanding the Enterprise Culture: Themes in the Work of Mary Douglas*, Edinburgh: Edinburgh University Press.

Hearn, J. and Roseneil, S. (Eds) (1999), *Consuming Culture: Power and Resistance*, London: Macmillan.

Hellman, M. (1999), 'Furniture, sociability, and the work of leisure in eighteenth century France', *Eighteenth Century Studies*, **32**(4), pp. 415–45.

Hendrickson, R. (1979), *The Grand Emporiums: The Illustrated History of America's Great Department Stores*, New York: Stein and Day.

Hepworth, M. (1999), 'Privacy, security and respectability', in Chapman, T. and Hockey, J. (Eds), *Ideal Homes?*, London: Routledge.

Hewitt, J. (1987), 'Good design in the marketplace: The rise of Habitat man', *Oxford Art Journal*, **10**(2), pp. 28–43.

Hewitt, M. (1999), 'District visiting and the constitution of domestic space in the mid-nineteenth century', in Bryden, I. and Floyd, J. (Eds), *Domestic Space Reading the Nineteenth Century Interior*, Manchester: Manchester University Press.

Hire System (1878), *The 'New Hire System': A Treatise on House Furnishing*, London.

Hodges, F. (1989), *Period Pastimes*, London: Weidenfeld and Nicolson.

Hoggart, R. (1957), *The Uses of Literacy*, Harmondsworth: Penguin.

Hollander, John (1991), 'It all depends', *Social Research*, **58**(1), Spring, pp. 31–49.

Holme, Randall (1688), *The Academy of Armoury*.

Holmes, H. A. (1946), 'Design and the retailer', *Journal of the Royal Society of Arts*, 25 October.

Hopkinson, J. (1968), *The Memoirs of a Victorian Cabinet-maker*, Goodman, J. B. (Ed.), New York: Augustus Kelley.

Horowitz, D. (1985), *The Morality of Spending: Attitudes Toward the Consumer Society in America 1875–1940*, Baltimore: Johns Hopkins University Press.

Horowitz, R. and Mohun, A. (Eds) (1998), *His and Hers: Gender, Consumption and Technology*, Charlottesville, VA: University Press of Virginia.

Horsfield, M. (1997), *Biting the Dust: The Joys of Housework*, London: Fourth Estate.

Hosgood, C. (1999), 'Mrs Pooter's purchase: Lower middle-class consumerism and the sales 1870–1914', in Kidd, A. and Nichols, D. (Eds), *Gender, Civic Culture and Consumerism*, Manchester: Manchester University Press.

Hoskins, W. G. (1953), 'The rebuilding of rural England, 1570–1640', *Past and Present*, **4**, pp. 44–59.

Houston, J. H. (1993), *Featherbedds and Flockbedds*, Sandy, Beds: Three Tents Press.

Hughes, G. (1957a), 'The origins of house furnishers', *Country Life*, 3 October, pp. 650–52.

—— (1957b), 'George Seddon of London House', *Apollo*, 65, pp. 177–81.

—— (1964), 'Furnishers of Georgian Mayfair', *Country Life*, 19 November, pp. 1328–9.

Hunt, P. (1995), 'Gender and the construction of home life', in Jackson, S. and Moores, S. (Eds), *Politics of Domestic Consumption*, London: Prentice Hall.

Hunter, G. (1913), *Home Furnishing*, New York: John Lane.

Hutchinson, C. (1972), 'Victorian cabinetmakers of Leeds', *Country Life*, pp. 550–51.

—— (1976), 'George Reynoldson, upholsterer of York 1716–1764', *Furniture History*, **12**, pp. 29–33.

Huth, H. (1971), *Lacquer of the West*, Chicago, IL: University of Chicago Press.

—— (1974), *Roentgen Furniture*, London: Sotheby's.

Huxley, A. (1930) 'Notes on decoration', *The Studio*, October.

Huxtable, Sally-Anne (1997), 'Seduction of liberty, a nineteenth century parlour game', *Make*, 73, December 1996–January 1997, pp. 6–9.

Ideal Home (1966), *Householder's Guide to Decorating and Furnishing*, London: Odhams.

Ince and Mayhew (1762), *Universal System of Household Furniture*, London.

Jackson, S. and Moores, S. (Eds) (1995), *Politics of Domestic Consumption*, London: Prentice Hall.

Jeffreys, J. B. (1950), *The Distribution of Consumer Goods*, Cambridge: Cambridge University Press.

—— (1954), *Retail Trading in Britain 1850–1950*, Cambridge: Cambridge University Press.

Jennings, H. J. (1902), *Our Homes and How to Beautify Them*, London: Harrison and Sons.

Jeremiah, D. (2000), *Architecture and Design for the Family in Britain, 1900–1970*, Manchester: Manchester University Press.

Jervis, S. (1973), 'Ruskin and furniture', *Furniture History*, **9**, 97–109.

—— (1974), 'Giles Grendey 1693–1780', *Country Life*, 155, pp. 1418–19.

Jobson, Allan (1977), *The Creeping Hours of Time*, London: Robert Hale.

Joel, B. (1935), 'A house and a home', in Valette, J. (Ed.), *The Conquest of Ugliness*, London: Methuen.

Joel, D. (1969), *Furniture Design Set Free*, London: Dent.

Johnson, G. and Scholes, K. (1993), *Exploring Corporate Strategy*, 3rd edn, New York: Prentice-Hall.

Johnson, L. (1996), 'As housewives we are worms: Women, modernity and the home question', *Cultural Studies*, **10**(3), pp. 449-63.

Jones, D. (1988), 'The press bed in Scotland', *Scottish Society for Art History Yearbook*, pp. 28–35.

Jones, E. C. (1973), 'The fashion manipulators, consumer tastes and British industries 1660–1800', in Cain, L. and Uselding, P. (Eds), *Business Enterprise and Economic Change: Essays in Honour of H F Williamson*, Kent, OH: Kent State University.

Jones, Janna (1997), 'The distance from home: The domestication of desire in interior design manuals', *Journal of Social History*, **51**(2), pp. 307–25.

Jones, P. (1984), 'Retail warehouse development and planning polices in Scotland', *Scottish Geographical Magazine*, 100, April, pp. 12–19.

Jones, R. (1997), 'Arthur Foley, a nineteenth century furniture manufacturer in Salisbury', *Regional Furniture*, **11**, pp. 42–9.

Joscelyne, Hugh (1980), 'Has the retailer's job really changed?', *Cabinet Maker*, 19 September.

Jourdain, M. (1924), *English Decoration and Furniture of the Early Renaissance*, London: Batsford.

Joy, E. (1951), 'Chippendale in trouble at the customs', *Country Life*, 110, 24 August.

Joy, E. T. (1960), 'Furniture shops in Georgian England', *Connoisseur Yearbook*, 18–23, London: The Connoisseur.

—— (1968), *The Connoisseur's Complete Period Guides*, London: The Connoisseur.

—— (1978), *English Furniture 1800–1851*, London: Sotheby Parke-Bernet.

Julius, L. (1967), 'The furniture industry', *Royal Society of Arts Journal*, May, pp. 430—47.

Kaye, A. M. (1940), *A Student's Guide to Housewifery*, London: Dent and Sons.

Keating, P. (1976), *Into Unknown England 1866–1913*, Manchester: Manchester University Press.

Keene, D. (1990), 'Shops and shopping in medieval London'. in Grant, L. (Ed.), *Medieval Art, Architecture and Archaeology in London*, British Archaeological Association Conference Transactions 1984.

Keener, F. and Lorsch, S. (Eds) (1989), *Eighteenth Century Women and the Arts*, New York: Greenwood.

Kelehar, R. (1988), 'Furniture starts to polish up its act', *Marketing Week*, 19 August.

Kennedy, P. A, (1963), *Nottinghamshire Household Inventories*, Thoroton Society, 22.

Kerr, R. (1871), *The Gentleman's House*, London: John Murray.

Kidd, A. and Nichols, D. (Eds) (1999), *Gender, Civic Culture and Consumerism*, Manchester: Manchester University Press.

Kinchin, J. (1979), 'Collinson and Lock', *The Connoisseur*, May, pp. 47–53.

—— (1996), 'Interiors: Nineteenth century essays on the masculine and feminine room', in Kirkham, P. (Ed.), *Gendered Objects*, Manchester: Manchester University Press.

Kirkham, P. (1967), 'The careers of John and William Linnell', *Furniture History*, **3**, pp. 29–41.

—— (1969), 'Samuel Norman: A study of an eighteenth century craftsman', *Burlington*, 111, August, pp. 500–11.

—— (1974), 'The partnership of William Ince and John Mayhew 1759–1804', *Furniture History*, 10, pp. 56–67.

—— (1988), *The London Furniture Trade, 1700–1850*, Furniture History Society.

—— (1996), *Gendered Objects*, Manchester: Manchester University Press.

——, Mace, R. and Porter, J. (1987), *Furnishing the World: the East End Furniture Trade 1830–1980*, London: Journeyman Press.

Knell, D. (1992), *English Country Furniture*, London: Barrie and Jenkins.

Koskijoki, M. (1999), 'The home and the treasures of the consumer', in Sarantola-Weiss, M. (Ed.), *Rooms for Everyone*, Helsinki: Otava Publishing.

Kowaleski-Wallace, E. (1997), *Consuming Subjects: Women Shopping and Business in the Eighteenth Century*, New York: Columbia University Press.

Kross, J. (1999), 'Mansions, men, women, and the creation of multiple publics in eighteenth century British North America', *Journal of Social History*, Winter, **33**(20), pp. 385–402.

Laermans, Rudi (1993), 'Learning to consume: Early department stores and the shaping of the modern consumer culture', *Theory Culture and Society*, **10**(4), pp. 79–102.

Lambert, R. (1938), *The Universal Provider: A Study of William Whitely and Co.*, London: Harrap.

Lancaster, B. (1995), *The Department Store: A Social History*, Leicester: Leicester University Press.

Lane, T. and Searle, J. (1990), *Australians at Home*, Melbourne: Oxford University Press.

Lang, J. et al. (1974), *Designing for Human Behaviour: Architecture and the Behavioural Sciences*, Stroudsburg, PA: Dowden, Hutchinson & Ross.

Langland, E. (1995), *Nobody's Angels: Middle Class Women and Domestic Ideology in Victorian Culture*, Ithaca: Cornell University Press.

Lasdun, S. (1981), *Victorians at Home*, London: Weidenfeld and Nicolson.

Latham, R. and Matthews, W. (1970–83), *The Diary of Samuel Pepys: A New and Complete Transcription*, 11 volumes, London: Bell.

Laumann, E. O. and House, J. S. (1970), 'Living room styles and social attributes: The patterning of material artefacts in a modern urban community', *Sociology and Social Research*, **54**, 3 April, pp. 321–42.

Lawrence, R. J. (1983), 'The comparative analyses of homes: Research method and application', *Social Science Information*, **22**(3), pp. 461–85.

—— (1987), 'What makes a house a home?', *Environment and Behaviour*, **19**(2), March, pp. 154–68.

—— (1987), *Housing, Dwellings and Homes*, New York: Wiley.

Leavitt, S. (2002), *From Catherine Beecher to Martha Stewart*, Chapel Hill, NC: University of North Carolina Press.

Lee, M. J. (1992), *Consumer Culture Reborn: The Cultural Politics of Consumption*, London: Routledge.

Legg, P. (1994), 'The Bastards of Blandford', *Furniture History*, **30**, pp. 15–42.

Leiss, W. (1996), 'Icons of the market place', *Theory Culture and Society*, **1**(3), p. 1983.

Leslie, D. and Keimer, S. (2003), 'Gender, modern design and home consumption', *Environmental Planning: Society and Space*, **21**, pp. 293–316.

Leslie, E. (1996), 'The exotic of the everyday: Critical theory in the parlour', *Things*, pp. 83–101.

Levy, H. (1948), *The Shops of Britain*, London: Routledge and Kegan Paul.

Lewis, R. and Maude, A. (1950), *The English Middle Class*, London: Phoenix House.

Lippitt, V. G. (1959), *Determinants of Consumer Demand for Home Furnishings and Equipment*, Cambridge, MA: Harvard University Press.

Lipson, E. (1948), *Economic History of England*, London: Black.

Lloyd, B. (1981), 'Women, home and status' in Duncan, J. (Ed.), *Housing and Identity: Cross Cultural Perspectives*, London: Croom Helm.

Loftie, Mrs W. J. (1876), *The Dining Room: Art at Home*, London: Macmillan.

Loftie, W. J. R. (1876), *A Plea for Art in the Home*, London: Macmillan.

Logan, T, (1995), 'Decorating domestic space, Middle class women and Victorian interiors', in Dickerson, V. (Ed.), *Keeping the Victorian House*, New York: Garland.

London School of Economics (1931), *The New Survey of London Life and Labour*, Vol. II, London: LSE.

Loudon, J. C. (1839), *An Encyclopedia of Cottage, Farm and Villa Architecture and Furniture*, revised edn, London: Longman.

Lovell, M. (1991), 'Such furniture as will be profitable: The business of cabinet-making in eighteenth century Newport', *Winterthur Portfolio*, **26**(1), pp. 27–62.

Lowe, M. and Wrigley, N. (1999), *Reading Retail: A Geographical Perspective on Retailing and Consumption Spaces*, London: Arnold.

Lubbock, J. (1995), *The Tyranny of Taste*, London: Yale University Press.

Luckacs, J. (1970), 'The bourgeois interior', *American Scholar*, **339**(4), pp. 616–30.

Lunt, P. K. and Livingstone, S. (1992), *Mass Consumption and Personal Identity: Everyday Economic Experience*, Buckingham: Open University Press.

Lury, C. (1996), *Consumer Culture*, London: Polity Press.

Lynes, R. (1980), *The Tastemakers: The Shaping of American Popular Taste*, New York: Dover.

MacDermott, C. (1982), 'Popular taste and contemporary design', in Sparke, P. (Ed.), *Did Britain Make It? British Design in Context 1946–1986*, London: Design Council.

MacDonald, S. and Porter, J. (1990), *Putting on the Style: Setting up Home in the 1950s*, London: Geffrye Museum.

Machin, R. (1977), 'The Great Rebuilding: A reassessment', *Past and Present*, **77**, pp. 33–56.

Mackay, H. (1997), *Consumption and Everyday Life*, London: Sage.

Mackay, S. and Gifford, J. (1995), *Behind the Façade: Four Centuries of Scottish Interiors*, Edinburgh: Royal Commission on the Ancient and Historical Monuments of Scotland.

Mackenzie, D. and Wajcman, J. (1999), *Social Shaping of Technology*, Oxford: Oxford University Press.

Madigan, R. (1999), 'The more we are together: Domestic space gender and privacy', in Chapman, T. and Hockey, J. (Eds) (1999), *Ideal Homes?*, London: Routledge.

—— and Munro, M. (1996), ' "House beautiful": Style and consumption in the home', *Sociology*, **30**(1), pp. 41–57.

——, Munro, M. and Smith, S. (1990), 'Gender and the meaning of home', *International Journal of Urban and Regional Research*, **14**, pp. 625–47.

Mallet, F. (1970), 'Miles and Edwards of London', *Furniture History*, **6**, pp. 73–80.

Manchester and Salford Council of Social Service (1960), *Setting up House: Furnishing Problems on New Housing Estates*, October.

Mandeville, B. (1970), *Fable of the Bees*, Harth, P. (Ed.), Harmondsworth: Penguin.

Marcus, Clare Cooper, (1995), *House as a Mirror of Self: Exploring the Deeper Meaning of Home*, Berkeley, CA: Conari Press.

Margolis, M. (1984), *Mothers and Such*, Berkeley, CA: University of California.

Martin, Ann Smart (1993), 'Makers, buyers, and users: Consumerism as a material culture framework', *Winterthur Portfolio*, **28**(2/3), pp. 141–57.

Martin, B. (1984), 'Mother wouldn't like it: housework as magic', *Theory Culture and Society*, **2**(2), pp. 19–36.

Martin, J. E. (1966), *Greater London: An Industrial Geography*, London: Bell and Son.

Mass Observation (1943), *An Enquiry Into People's Homes*, London: John Murray.

—— (1946), *Browns of Chester: Portrait of a Shop 1780–1946*, London: Lindsay Drummond.

Matrix (1984), *Making Space: Women and the Man-made Environment*, London: Pluto.

Matthews, G. (1987), *Just a Housewife: The Rise and Fall of Domesticity in America*, New York: Oxford University Press.

May, E. T. (1999), 'The commodity gap: Consumerism and the modern home', in Glickman, L. B., *Consumer Society in American History: A Reader*, Ithaca, NY: Cornell University Press.

Mayes, J. (1960), *The History of Chair-making in High Wycombe*, London: Routledge.

McAndrew, F. (1993), *Environmental Psychology*, Pacific Grove, CA: Brooks-Cole.

McClaugherty, M. (1983), 'Household art: creating an artistic home, 1868–1893', *Winterthur Portfolio*, **18**(1), pp. 1–26.

McCracken, G. (1988), *Culture and Consumption*, Bloomington, IN: Indiana University Press.

McGoldrick, P. (1994), *Cases in Retail Management*, London: Pitman.

McKendrick, N. Brewer, J. and Plumb, J. H. (1982), *The Birth of a Consumer Society*, Bloomington, IN: Indiana University Press.

McNeil, P. (1994), 'Designing women: Gender, sexuality and the interior decorator c. 1890–1940', in *Art History*, **17**(4), pp. 631–57.

McQuoid, P. (1905), *Age of Walnut*, London: Lawrence Bullen.

Meade, D. (1951), 'Furnishing by hire purchase', *Design*, 104, August.

—— (1957), 'Furnishing in the new towns', *Design*, 98, February.

—— (1967), 'Perrings at the crossroads', *Design*, p. 227.

Melchionne, K. (1998), 'Living in glasshouses: Domesticity, interior decoration and environmental aesthetics', *Journal of Aesthetics and Art Criticism*, **56**(2), Spring, pp. 191–200.

—— (1999), 'Of bookworms and busybees: Cultural theory in the age of Do-it-yourselfing', *Journal of Aesthetics and Art Criticism*, **57**(2), Spring, pp. 247–55.

Merivale, M. (1943), *Furnishing the Small Home*, London: Studio Publications.

Messer-Davidow, E. (1989), '"For Softness She": Gender ideology and aesthetics in eighteenth century England', in Keener, F. and Lorsch, S. (Eds), *Eighteenth Century Women and the Arts*, New York: Greenwood.

Michman, R. and Mazze, E. (2001), *Speciality Retailers: Marketing Triumphs and Blunders*, West Port, CT: Quorum.

Microulis, L. (1988), 'Charles Hindley and Sons, London house furnishers of the nineteenth century: A paradigm of the middle range market', *Studies in the Decorative Arts*, **5**, Spring and Summer, pp. 69–96.

Middlesex Polytechnic (1983), *The Decoration of the Suburban Villa*.

Miles, S. (1998), *Consumption as a Way of Life*, London: Sage.

Millar, L. (1996), 'The notebook of John Davies cabinetmaker, Carmarthen', *Regional Furniture*, **10**, pp. 66–70.

Miller, D. (1987), *Material Culture and Mass Consumption*, Oxford: Blackwell.

—— (1995), *Acknowledging Consumption*, London: Routledge.

—— (Ed.) (2001), *Home Possessions*, Oxford: Berg.

Miller, M. B. (1981), *The Bon Marché: Bourgeois Culture and the Department Store 1869–1916*, Princeton, NJ: Princeton University Press.

Minimum Standard (1937), 'Minimum standard: Furnishing design and economics for the mass', *Art and Industry*, **23**, pp. 64–7.

Mitchell, I. (1984), 'The development of urban retailing 1700–1815', in Clark, P. (Ed.), *The Transformation of English Provincial Towns 1600–1800*, London: Hutchinson.

Monahon, E. B. (1980), 'The Rawson family of Providence Rhode Island', *Antiques*, July.

Monod, D. (1996), *Store Wars: Shopkeepers and the Culture of Mass Marketing 1890–1939*, Toronto: Toronto University Press.

Monroe, D. (1941), *Family Expenditure for Furnishings and Equipment*, US Department of Agriculture, Misc. Publication No. 436.

Montgomery, C. (1966), *American Furniture: The Federal Period*, New York: Viking.

Morley, C. (1990), 'Homemakers and design advice in the postwar period', in Putnam, T. and Newton, C., *Household Choices*, London: Futures Publications.

Morrell, J. G. (1956), 'Furniture for the masses', *Journal of Industrial Economics*, November, pp. 24–9.

Mort, F. (2000), *Commercial Culture*, London: Berg.

Moss, M. and Turton, A. (1989), *A Legend of Retailing: House of Fraser*, London: Weidenfeld and Nicolson.

Moss, Stephen (2000), 'The gospel according to IKEA', *The Guardian*, 26 June.

Motz, Marilyn Ferris and Browne, Pat (Eds) (1988), *Making the American Home: Middle Class Women and Domestic Material Culture, 1840–1940*, Bowling Green, OH: Bowling Green State University Popular Press.

Mui, H. C. and Mui, L. H. (1989), *Shops and Shopkeeping in Eighteenth Century England*, London: Routledge.

Muir, D. (1927), *The Modern Shop*, London and Leicester: Blackfriars Press.

Muldrew, C. (1993), 'Interpreting the market: The ethics of credit and community relations in early modern England', *Social History*, **18**(2), pp. 163–81.

Muthesius, H. (1904), *The English House*, reprint, 1979, New York: Rizzoli.

Muthesius, S. (1988), 'Why do we buy old furniture? Aspects of the authentic antique in Britain 1870–1910', *Art History*, **11**(2), June, pp. 231–54.

National Association of Retail Furnishers (*c*.1966), *Report of NARF Sub-committee on 'Better Retailing': A Guide for Furnishers*, London.

National Economic Development Council (1987), *Furniture Industry Survey*, London.

Nenadic, S. (1994), 'Middle rank consumers and domestic culture in Edinburgh and Glasgow 1720–1840', *Past and Present*, **145**, pp. 122–56.

New Day Furnishing Stores (1956–), *Oak Leaves* (company magazine).

Newton, D. (1953), 'Dunn and Dunns', *Design*, October, pp. 122–6.

Noble, G. (2002), 'Comfortable and relaxed: Furnishing the home and the nation', *Continuum: Journal of Media and Cultural Studies*, **16**(1), pp. 53–66.

Normann, R. and Ramirey, R. (1993), 'From value chain to value constellation: Designing interactive strategy'; *Harvard Business Review*, July–August, pp. 65–77.

Nunn, P. (1987), *Victorian Women Artists*, London: Women's Press.

Oakley, A. (1974), *The Sociology of Housework*, London: Robertson.

Odhams Press Ltd, Research Division (1964), *Woman and the National Market: Furniture and Furnishings*, London.

Oetzmann and Co. (*c*. 1871), *Hints on House Furnishing and Decoration*, London.

Office of Fair Trading, (1978a), *Furniture and Carpets: A Report,* London.

—— (and trade organisations) (1978b), *Voluntary Code of Practice for Furniture*, London.

Office of Fair Trading, (1990), *Furniture and Carpets: A Report*, London.

Ogburn, William F. and Umkoff, Meyer Francis (1955), *Technology and the Changing Family*, Boston, MA: Houghton Mifflin.

Oliver, J. (1966), *Development and Structure of the Furniture Industry*, Oxford: Pergamon.

Oliver, P., Davis, I. and Bentley, I. (1982), *Dunroamin: The Suburban Semi and Its Enemies*, London: Barrie and Jenkins.

Olson, S. (2000), 'Feathering her nest in nineteenth century Montreal', *Historie Sociale–Social History*, **33**, pp. 1–35.

Opie, J. (1986), 'Geoffrey Dunn of Dunn's of Bromley', *Journal of the Decorative Arts Society*, **10**.

Orvell, M. (1989), *The Real Thing: Imitation, and Authenticity in American Culture 1880–1940*, Chapel Hill, NC: University of North Carolina Press.

Owen D. M. (Ed.) (1984), *The Making of King's Lynn: A Documentary Survey*, Oxford: Oxford University Press.

Palmer, C. (1985), 'Next on the agenda: Home furnishings and a nationwide chain of fashion', *Design*, September, 441, p. 13.

Pardailhé-Galabrun, A. (1991), *The Birth of Intimacy: Privacy, and Domestic Life in Early Modern Paris*, Oxford: Polity Press.

Parker, J. H. and Parker, J. (1861), *Our English Home: Its Early History and Progress, with Notes on the Introduction of Domestic Inventions*, Oxford: Parker and Parker.

Parr, Joy. (1999), *Domestic Goods: The Material, the Moral, and the Economic in the Post-war Years*, Toronto: University of Toronto Press.

Partington, A. (1995), 'The designer housewife in the 1950s', in Attfield, J. and Kirkham, P. (Eds), *A View from the Interior: Women and Design,* London: Women's Press.

Pasdermadjian, H. (1954), *The Department Store: Its Origins, Evolution and Economics*, London: Newman.

Patmore, D. (1934), *Modern Furnishings and Decoration*, London: The Studio.

Pennell, S. (1999), 'Consumption and consumerism in early modern England', *Historical Journal*, **42**(2), pp. 549–64.

Pepys, S. (1970), *The Diary of Samuel Pepys: A New and Complete Transcription*, Latham, Robert and Matthews, William (Eds), London: Bell.

Perring, R. (1949), 'Retail distribution-popular', *Conference on Design*, London: RIBA.

Perrot, M. (1990), *A History of Private Life*, Cambridge, MA: Belknap Press.

Pevsner, N. (1937), *An Enquiry into Industrial Art in England*, Cambridge: Cambridge University Press.

—— (1976), *A History of Building Types* (shops), London: Thames and Hudson.

Phillips, B. (1984), *Conran and the Habitat Story*, London: Weidenfeld and Nicolson.

Phillips, R. R. and Woolrich E. (1921), *Furnishing the House*, London: Country Life.

Pinto, E. H. (1963), 'Georgian library steps', *Antiques*, January, pp. 102-4.

Pocius, G. (1991), *Living in a Material World*, Memorial University of Newfoundland, Social and Economic Papers 19.

Pollen, J. H. (1876), *British Manufacturing Industries*, G. Phillips Bevan (Ed.),London: E. Stanford.

Ponsonby, M. (1994), 'Samuel Peat: Chichester cabinet maker', *Regional Furniture*, **8**, pp. 64–72.

Porter, G. R. (1847), *The Progress of the Nation*, London: John Murray.

Porter, R. (1992), 'Pre-modernism and the art of shopping', *Critical Quarterly*, **34**(4), pp. 3–14.

Post, E. (1930), *The Personality of a House: The Blue Book of Home Design and Decoration*, New York: Funk and Wagnalls.

Pratt, C. (1893), *Hints on Furnishing*, Bradford.

Pratt, G., Priestly, U. and Fenner, A. (1985), *Shops and Shopkeepers in Norwich 1660–1730*, Norwich: University of East Anglia.

Prime, N. (1999), 'IKEA: International development', in Dupuis, M. and Dawson, J., *European Cases in Retailing – IKEA*, Oxford: Blackwell.

Pritchard, J. C. (1953–4), 'Raising the standard of furniture', *Decorative Art*, **53**, pp. 7–13.

—— (1984), *View From a Long Chair*, London: Routledge.

Proshansky, H. et al. (Eds) (1976), *Environmental Psychology: People and Their Physical Settings*, New York: Holt Reinhart and Winston.

Pryke, S. (1989), 'A study of the Edinburgh furnishing trade taken from contemporary press notices 1708–1790', *Regional Furniture*, **3**, pp. 52–67.

Pryke, S. (1992), 'At the sign of the pelican', *Regional Furniture*, **6**, pp. 10–21.

—— (1994), 'Pattern furniture and estate wrights in eighteenth century Scotland', *Furniture History*, **30**, pp. 100–105.

Putnam, T. (1992), 'Regimes of closure: The representation of cultural process in domestic consumption', in Silverstone, R. and Hirsch, E. (Eds), *Consuming Technologies: Media and Information in Domestic Space*, London: Routledge.

—— (1993), 'Beyond the modern home: Shifting the parameters of residence', in Bird, J., Curtis, B., Putnam, T., Robertson, G. and Tickner, L. (Eds), *Mapping the Futures: Local Cultures Global Change*, London: Routledge.

—— (1995), 'Between taste and tradition: Decorative order in the modern home', *Bulletin of the John Rylands Library*, **77**, pp. 91–108.

—— (1999), 'Post modern home life', in Cieraad, I. (1999), *At Home: Anthropology of Domestic Space*, Syracuse, NY: Syracuse University Press.

—— and Newton, C. (1990), *Household Choices*, London: Futures Publications.

Quennell, P. (1969), *Mayhew's London*, London: Spring Books.

Rappaport, E. (1996), '"A husband and his wife's dresses": Consumer credit and the debtor family in England 1864–1914', in De Grazia, V. (Ed.) (1996), *The Sex of Things: Gender and Consumption*, Berkeley, CA: University of California.

—— (2000), *Shopping for Pleasure*, Princeton, NJ: Princeton University Press.

Rau, R. R. and Shaw, W. F. (1941), *Selling Home Furnishing: A Training Program*, Washington, DC: US Office of Education.

Ravetz, A. (1995a), 'Women, class and gender in housing', in Kirkham, P. and Attfield, J. (Eds), *A View from the Interior*, London: Women's Press.

—— (1995), *The Place of Home: English Domestic Environments 1914–2000*, London: Spon.

Rawlings, John (1899), *General House Furnishing ...with a Treatise on the Credit Systems of the Day*.

Redfern, P. (1938), *The New History of the CWS*, London: Dent and CWS.

Reed, C. (1996), *Not at Home: The Suppression of Domesticity in Modern Art and Architecture*, London: Thames and Hudson.

Reilly, P. (1953), 'Same room, same cost', *Design*, April, pp. 8–11.

Retail Home Furnishings Foundation (1991), *Retail Trends Study: Serving the Changing Customer*, High Point, NC.

Reyburn, W. (1938), *Selling Home Furnishings Successfully*, London: Pitman.

Ricardo, H. (1906), 'The interior and its furniture', in Shaw Sparrow, W. (Ed.), *The Modern Home*, London: Hodder and Stoughton.

Rich, R. (2003), 'Advice on dining and décor in London and Paris 1860–1914', *Journal of Design History*, **16**(1), pp. 49-59.

Rieder, W. (1970), 'Furniture smuggling for a Duke', *Apollo*, 92, September, pp. 206–9.

Roberts, M. (1989), 'Designing the home: Domestic architecture and domestic life', in Allen, G. and Crow, G., *Home and Family*, London: Macmillan.

Roberts, R. (1971), *The Classic Slum*, Manchester: Manchester University Press.

Robertson, W. B. (1911), *Encyclopaedia of Retail Trading*, London: Educational Book Co.

Robinson. J. R. (1890), *Rules of the First Robinson-Syme Ballot and Sale Furnishing Company*, London: R. Madley.

Roche, D. (2000), *A History of Everyday Things*, Cambridge: Cambridge University Press.

Rogers, J. C. (1928), 'Modern furniture at Shoolbred's: The enterprise of a furnishing trades organisation', *Architectural Review*, **63**, pp. 116–18.

—— (1932), *Furniture and Furnishing*, Oxford: Oxford University Press.

Rothery, G. C. (1923), *Furnishing a Small House or Flat*, London: Collins.

Royal Society of Arts (1920), Conference on House Furnishings, March, London.

Rullo, G. (1987), 'People and home interiors: A bibliography of recent psychological research', *Environment and Behaviour*, **19**(2), pp. 25-59.

Ruskin, J. (1864, *Sesame and Lilies*, 1899 edn, London: George Allen.

—— (1891), *Seven Lamps of Architecture*, London: George Allen.

Russell, G. (1947), *How to Buy Furniture*, London: Council of Industrial Design.

—— and Jarvis, A. (1953), *How to Furnish Your Home* (with a shopping guide by Veronica Nisbet), London: Newman Neame.

Russell, Gordon (1953/4), 'On buying Furniture', *Ideal Home Yearbook*, London: *Daily Mail*.

Russell, R. D. (1951), 'Furniture today: Tuppence plain, penny coloured', in *The Anatomy of Design: A Series of Inaugural Lectures by Professors of the Royal College of Art*, London: Royal College of Art.

—— (1952), 'People want furniture that is warm and cosy', *Design*, 42, June, pp. 21–2.

Ryan, D. (1997), *The Ideal Home Exhibitions Through the Twentieth Century*, London: Hazar.

Ryan, D. (2000), '"All the world and her husband": The Daily Mail Ideal Home Exhibition 1908–1939', in Andrews, M. and Talbot, M. (Eds), *All the World and Her Husband*, London: Cassell.

Rybczynski, W. (1986), *Home: A Short History of an Idea*, New York: Heinemann.

Sack, R. D. (1992), *Place, Modernity and the Consumers' World*, Baltimore, MD: John Hopkins University Press.

Salzman, L. F. (1967), *Building in England Down to 1540*, Oxford: Clarendon Press.

Santink, J. (1990), *Timothy Eaton and the Rise of His Department Store*, Toronto: University of Toronto Press.

Sarantola-Weiss, M. (Ed.) (1999), *Rooms for Everyone*, Helsinki: Otava Publishing.

Sarti, R. (2002), *Europe at Home: Family and Material Culture 1500–1800*, New Haven, CT and London: Yale.

Sarup, M. (1996), *Identity Culture and the Postmodern World*, Edinburgh: Edinburgh University Press.

Saumarez-Smith, C. (1993), *Eighteenth Century Decoration: Design and the Domestic Interior in England*, London: Weidenfeld and Nicolson.

Saunders, P. and Williams, P. ((1984), 'The constitution of the home: Towards a research agenda', *Housing Studies*, **3**(2), pp. 81–93.

Savitt, R. (1989), 'Looking back to see ahead: writing the history of American retailing', *Journal of Retailing*, **65**(3), pp. 326–55.

Schama, S. (1987), *Embarrassment of Riches*, London: Collins.

Schiffer, M. B. (1978), *Furniture of Chester County*, Exton, PA: Schiffer.

Schiller, R. (1986), 'Retail decentralisation: The coming of the third wave', *Estate Gazette*, 279, pp. 648–65.

Schlereth, T. (1982), *Material Culture Studies in America*, Nashville, TN: American Association for State and Local History.

Schonfield, H. (Ed.) (1933), *The Book of British Industries*, London: D. Archer.

Schuurman, A. and Spierenberg, P. (Eds) (1996), *Private Domain, Public Inquiry*, Hilversum: Verloren Press.

Scott, A. F. (1974), *Every One a Witness: The Stuart Age*, London: White Lion Press.

Scott, P. (1997), 'Large scale retailing in Britain 1850–1914', *Refresh*, Spring, pp. 58.

Scottish Housing Advisory Committee on Design, Planning and Furnishing of New Homes (1944), *Planning Our New Homes*, Edinburgh: HMSO.

Segalen, Martine (1994), 'The Salon des Arts Ménagers 1923–1983: A French effort to instil the virtues and the norms of good taste', *Journal of Design History*, **7**(4), pp. 267–75.

Shammas, C. (1980), 'The domestic environment in early modern England and America', *Journal of Social History*, **14**, pp. 1–24.

—— (1990), *The Pre-industrial Consumer in England and America,* Oxford: Oxford University Press.

Shaw Sparrow, W. (Ed.) (1906), *The Modern Home*, London: Hodder and Stoughton.

—— (1907), *Flats, Urban Houses and Cottage Homes*, London: Hodder and Stoughton.

—— (1909), *Hints on House Furnishings*, London: Nash.

Sheraton, T. (1803), *The Cabinet Dictionary*, London, reprint New York: Prager.

Sheridan, M. (Ed.) (1955), *The Furnishers' Encyclopedia*, London: National Trade Press.

Shields, R. (1992), *Lifestyle Shopping: The Subject of Consumption*, London: Routledge.

Shoolbred and Co. (n.d.), *Practical Methods of House Furnishing*, London.

Shove, E. (1999), 'Constructing home: A crossroads of choices', in Cieraad, I. (Ed.), *At home. Anthropology of Domestic Space*, Syracuse, NY: Syracuse University Press.

Silverstone, R. and Hirsch, E. (Eds) (1992), *Consuming Technologies: Media and Information in Domestic Spaces*, London: Routledge.

Sixsmith, J. (1986), 'The meaning of home', *Journal of Experimental Psychology*, **6**, pp. 281–98.

Sizer, P. W. (1974), *Structure of the British Furniture Industry*, University of Aston Management Centre, Working Papers Series No. 31, November.

Skinner, W. and Rogers, D. (1968), *Manufacturing Policy in the Furniture Industry*, Homewood, IL: Irwin.

Slater, D. (1997), *Consumer Culture and Modernity*, London: Polity Press.

Sleep, J. (1994), 'Consumer behaviour across an urban hierarchy 1650–1725', *Regional Furniture Society Newsletter*, 21, Winter, pp. 12–13.

Slom, S. H. (1967), *Profitable Furniture Retailing*, New York: Fairchild Publications.

Smith, H. (1937), *Retail Distribution: A Critical Analysis*, London: Oxford University Press.

Smith, J. T. (1828), *Nollekens and His Times*, reprint 1949, London: Turnstile Press.

Smith, P. and Hannan, K. (1994), *Worlds of Desire, Realms of Power*, London: Edward Arnold.

Smithells, R. (1948), *Make Yourself at Home: Ways and Means of Furnishing Today*, London: Royle Publications.

—— (1954), *News of the World Better Homes Book*, London: *News of the World*.

—— and Woods, S. J. (1936), *The Modern Home: Its Furnishing and Equipment*, Benfleet: F. Lewis.

Snodin, M. and Styles J. (2001), *Design and the Decorative Arts Britain 1500–1900*, London: V&A Publications.

Social Survey (1945), *Furniture: An Enquiry made by the Board of Trade*, May, London.

Southerton, D. (2001), 'Consuming kitchens: Taste, context and identity formation', *Journal of Consumer Culture*, **1**(2), pp. 179–203.

Sparke, P. (1982), *Did Britain Make it? British Design in Context 1946–1986*, London: Design Council.

Spufford, M. (1984), *The Great Reclothing of Rural England*, London: Hambeldon Press.

St. George, Robert Blair (Ed.) (1988), *Material Life in America 1660–1860*, Boston, MA: North Eastern University Press.

Stabler, J. (1991), 'English newspaper advertisements as a source of furniture history', *Regional Furniture*, **5**, pp. 93–102.

Stage, S. and Vincenti, V. (1997), *Rethinking Home Economics*, Ithaca, NY: Cornell University Press.

Stearns P. N. (1997) 'Stages of consumerism: Recent work on the issues of periodization', *The Journal of Modern History*, **69**, March, pp. 102–17.

Steer F. W, (1958), 'Smaller houses and their furnishings in the seventeenth and eighteenth centuries', *Journal of the British Archaeological Association*, 3rd Series, vols 20–21, pp. 20-21.

—— (1969), *Farm and Cottage Inventories of Mid-Essex, 1635–1749*, 2nd edn, London: Phillimore.

Stobart, J. (1998), 'Shopping streets as social space: Leisure consumerism and improvement in an eighteenth century county town', *Urban History*, **25**(1), pp. 4–21.

Stokes, J. (1829), *The Complete Cabinet Maker and Upholsterers Guide*, London.

Storey, J. (1999), *Cultural Consumption and Everyday Life*, London: Arnold.

Stow (1598), *Survey of London*, Everyman Edition, 1980.

Sweeney, K. M. (1988), 'Furniture and the domestic environment in Wethersfield, Connecticut, 1639–1800', in St George, Robert Blair (Ed.), *Material Life in America 1660–1860*, Boston, MA: North Eastern University Press.

Sydney, W. C. (1891), *England and the English in the Eighteenth Century*, 2 volumes, London: Macmillan.

Symonds, R. W. (1951), 'Domestic comfort in the medieval home: An illusion dispelled', *Connoisseur*, Antique Dealers' Fair number, pp. 40–47.

——. (1955), Furniture-making in 17th and 18th Century England, London: Connoisseur.

Symonds R. and Whineray, B. (1962), *Victorian Furniture*, London: Country Life.

Tallis, John (1839), *London Street Views*, reprint 1969, London Topographical Society.

Thirsk, J. (1978), *Economic Policy and Projects*, Oxford: Clarendon Press.

Thompson, E .(Ed.) (1998), *The American Home*, Wilmington, DE: Winterthur Museum.

Thompson, F. (1948), *Lark Rise to Candleford*, reprint 1973, Harmondsworth: Penguin.

Thornton, P. (1984), *Authentic Decor*, London: Weidenfeld and Nicolson.

Thrift, N. and Williams, P. (1987), *Class and Space: The Making of Urban Society*, London: Routledge.

Tilson, B. (1984), 'Modern art department, Waring and Gillow 1928–31', *Journal of the Decorative Arts Society*, **8**, pp. 40–49.

Times Furnishing Co. (*c.* 1936), *Better Furniture*, London.

—— (n.d.), *The Times Furnishing Company*, London.

Timmers, M. (1978), *The Way We Live Now: Designs for Interiors 1950 to the Present Day*, Victoria & Albert Museum.

Tomrley, C. G. (1940), *Furnishing Your Home: A Practical Guide to Inexpensive Furnishing and Decorating*, London: Allen and Unwin.

Torekull, B. (1998), *Leading by Design: The IKEA Story*, New York: Harper Collins.

Tosh, J. (1999), *A Man's Place: Masculinity and the Middle Class Home in Victorian England*, London and New Haven, CT: Yale University Press.

Treadgold, A. (1991), 'Dixon's and Laura Ashley: Different routes to international growth', *International Journal of Retail and Distribution Management*, **19**(4), pp. 447–51.

Tristram, P. (1989), *Living Space in Fact and Fiction*, London: Routledge.

Tryon, T. (1691), *The Way to Health, Long Life and Happiness*, printed for H. C. by R.Baldwin, London.

Turner, M. (1983), *The Decoration of the Suburban Villa*, exhibition catalogue, Middlesex Polytechnic.

Upton, D. (1991), 'Style, mode, fashion and the artefact', in Pocius, G., *Living in a Material World*, Memorial University of Newfoundland, Social and Economic Papers 19.

Vachell, H. A. (1928), *The Homely Art*, London: Shoolbred and Co.

Vallance, A. (1939), *Hire Purchase*, London: Thomas Nelson.

Veasey, C. (*c.* 1935), *Good Furnishing*, London: Times Furnishing Co.

Veblen, T. (1899), *The Theory of the Leisure Class: An Economic Study in the Evolution of Institutions*, reprint 1970, London: Unwin.

Vickerey, A. (1993), 'Women and the world of goods: A Lancashire consumer and her possessions, 1751–81', in Brewer, J. and Porter. R. (Eds), *Consumption and the World of Goods*, London: Routledge.

Von la Roche, S. (1786), *Sophie in London*, trans Williams, C., London: Cape, 1933.

Wainwright, C. (1989) *The Romantic Interior*, New Haven, CT: Yale University Press.

Walsh, C. (1995), 'Shop design and the display of goods in eighteenth century London', *Journal of Design History*, **8**(3), pp. 157–76.

Walters, D. and Hanrahan, J. (2000), *Retail Strategy: Planning and Control*, Basingstoke: Macmillan.

Walton, K. M. (1976), 'Eighteenth century cabinet-making in Bristol', *Furniture History*, **12**, pp. 59–63.

Ward, L. (1996–7), 'Chintz, swags and bows: The myth of the English country house style', *Things*, **5**, Winter, pp. 7–37.

Warde, A. (1992) 'Notes on the relationship between production and consumption', in Burrows, R. and Marsh, C. (Eds), *Consumption and Class: Divisions and Change*, London: Macmillan.

Warnaby, G. (1999) 'Strategic consequences of retail acquisition, IKEA and Habitat', *International Marketing Review*, **16**(4/5), pp. 406–16.

Ways (1952), *Modern Ways of Increasing Your Sales of Furnishings etc.*, London: Trade Chronicle.

Weatherill, L. (1986), 'A possession of one's own: Women and consumer behaviour in England, 1660–1740', *Journal of British Studies*, April, pp. 131–56.

—— (1988), *Consumer Behaviour and Material Culture in Britain 1660–1760*, London: Routledge.

Weaver, L. (1912), *The House and its Equipment*, London: Country Life.

—— (1928), 'Tradition and modernity in craftsmanship, II: Furnishing and shop keeping', *Architectural Review*, June.

Welch, K. C. (1952), 'Department stores', in Hamlin, T. (Ed.), *Forms and Functions of 20th century Architecture*, Vol 4, New York: Columbia University Press.

Wharton, T. (1748), Poems on Several Occasions.

Wheeler, G. (1855), *Rural Homes*, New York: Alden Beardsley.

White, C. (1970), *Women's Magazines 1693–1968*, London: Michael Joseph.

White, L. (1986), 'Furnishing your house and garden in the 1760s', *Antique Collecting*, 321, 4 September, pp. 51–4.

Whitechapel Art Gallery (1952), *Setting Up Home for Bill and Betty*, exhibition handbook, London.

Whitehead, W. J. (1931), *Within the Private Office of the House Furnishing Trade*, Chatham: W. J. Whitehead.

Whiteley N. (1987), 'Semi works of art', *Furniture History*, **23**, pp. 108–26.

Whittock, N. (1827), *The Decorative Painters' and Glaziers' Guide*, London: Isaac Taylor Hinton Wood.

—— (1840), *On the Construction and Decoration of Shop Fronts of London*, London.

Wilk, C. (1981), *Marcel Breuer: Furniture and Interiors*, New York: Museum of Modern Art.

Wilkins, F. (1975), *The Shopkeepers*, London: Allman.

Willan, T. (1976), *The Inland Trade: Studies in English Internal Trade*, Manchester: Manchester University Press.

Williams, C. (Trans.) (1933), *Sophie in London* [1786], London: Cape.

Williams, P. (1987), 'Constituting class and gender: A social history of the home 1700–1901', in Thrift, N. J. and Glennie, P .D. (Eds), *Class and Space*, London: Routledge.

Williams, R. H. (1982), *Dream Worlds: Mass Consumption in Late Nineteenth Century France*, Berkeley, CA: University of California Press.

Wills, G. (1965), 'Furniture smuggling in eighteenth century London', *Apollo*, 82, pp. 12–17.

—— (1969), *English Furniture 1760–1900*, London: Guinness Superlatives.

—— (1971), *English Furniture 1550–1760*, London: Guinness Superlatives.

Winkler, G. and Moss, R, (1986), *Victorian Interior Decoration*, New York: Henry Holt.

Winstanley, M. (1983), *Shopkeepers World 1830–1914*, Manchester: Manchester University Press.

—— (1994), 'Concentration and competition in the retail sector, c. 1800–1990', in Kirby, M. W. and Rose, M. B. (Eds), *Business Enterprise in Modern Britain*, London: Routledge.

Wood, D. (1994), *Home Rules*, Baltimore. MD: Johns Hopkins University Press.

Woodward, I. (2001), 'Domestic objects and the taste epiphany', *Journal of Material Culture*, **6**(2), pp. 115–36.

Wright, L. (1962), *Warm and Snug*, London: Routledge.

Wright, P. (1985), *On Living in an Old Country: The National Past in Contemporary Britain*, London: Verso.

Wrigley, N. and Lowe, M. (1996), *Retailing Consumption and Capital: Towards the New Retail Geography*, Harlow: Longman.

Yacobson, L. (1935), 'Standard furniture', *Design for Today*, September.

Yerbury, F. R. (Ed.) (1947), *Modern Homes Illustrated*, London: Odhams.

Yorke, F. R. S. (1932), 'An architect visits the Ideal Home Exhibition', *Architectural Review*, 71, pp. 216–18.

Young, D. (1955), *Home Furnishing on a Small Income*, London: Hutchinson.

Yoxall, A. (1965), *Teaching of Domestic Economy*, London: Chivers.

Journals

Business Monitor
Cabinet Maker
Decorative Furnisher, The
Decorator and Furnisher
Design
European Journal of Marketing
Furnisher, The
Furnisher and Decorator
Furnishing
Furnishing World
Furniture and Decoration

Furniture Dealers and Cabinet Makers Guide
Furniture Gazette
Furniture History
Furniture Record
Furniture Retailer and Furniture Age (USA)
Good Furniture Magazine of Furnishing and Decoration
Home, The
Home Furnisher, The
House Furnishers and Decorators, Upholsterers and Cabinet Makers Monthly
   Journal
House Furnishers Journal
Interiors
Journal of Decorative Arts Society
Journal of Design History
Repository of Arts, The
Retail House Furnisher
Scottish Furnishing Trade Journal
Woman's Journal

Unpublished dissertations and theses

Billman, Michael (1985), 'The Cabinet Maker and Complete House Furnisher', MA, Royal College of Art.

Constable, L. (2000) 'An Industry in Transition: The British Domestic Furniture Trade 1914–1939', PhD, Brunel University.

De Falbe, S. (1985), 'James Shoolbred and Co.', MA, Royal College of Art.

Fleming, Elizabeth Anne (1993), 'Staples for Genteel Living: The Exportation of English Household Furnishings to Charleston, South Carolina During the Eighteenth Century', MA, Royal College of Art.

Girling-Budd, A. (1998) 'Holland and Sons of London and Gillows of London and Lancaster: A Comparison of Two Nineteenth Century Furnishing Firms', MA, Royal College of Art.

Mitchell, I. (1974), 'Urban Markets and Retail Distribution 1730–1850 with Particular Reference to Macclesfield, Stockport and Chester', DPhil., Oxford University.

Oram, S. (1994), 'Common Sense Contemporary', MA, Royal College of Art.

Rogers, K. W., (1994), 'Art and Mystery of the Upholsterers', MA, Royal College of Art.

Sizer, P. W. (1966), 'Some Economic Problems with Hire Purchase', MSc, University of London.

Spiers, J. (1996), 'A Tale of Two Houses: The Consumption of Luxury Soft Furnishings 1790–1825', MA, University of Southampton, Winchester.

Storie, W. K. (1977), 'Furniture Retailing Toward the Eighties', MSc, Strathclyde University.

Index